SERA FEATHER

Collision Course

art and story
HIROYUKI UTATANE
and
TOSHIYA TAKEDA

translation
DANA LEWIS and ADAM WARREN

lettering and touch-up
SNO CONE STUDIOS

DARK HORSE MANGA™

publisher
MIKE RICHARDSON

series editor
TIM ERVIN *and* PHILIP SIMON

collection editor
CHRIS WARNER

collection designer
DARIN FABRICK

art director
LIA RIBACCHI

English-language version produced by DARK HORSE MANGA *and* STUDIO PROTEUS.

SERAPHIC FEATHER VOL. VI: COLLISION COURSE

This volume collects Seraphic Feather stories from issues forty-three through fifty-one of the Dark Horse comic-book series Super Manga Blast!

Dark Horse Manga
A division of Dark Horse Comics, Inc.
10956 SE Main Street
Milwaukie, OR 97222

darkhorse.com

To find a comics shop in your area, call the Comic Shop Locator Service toll-free at 1-888-266-4226

First edition: January 2006
ISBN: 1-59307-362-3

1 3 5 7 9 10 8 6 4 2

Printed in U. S. A.

collision course

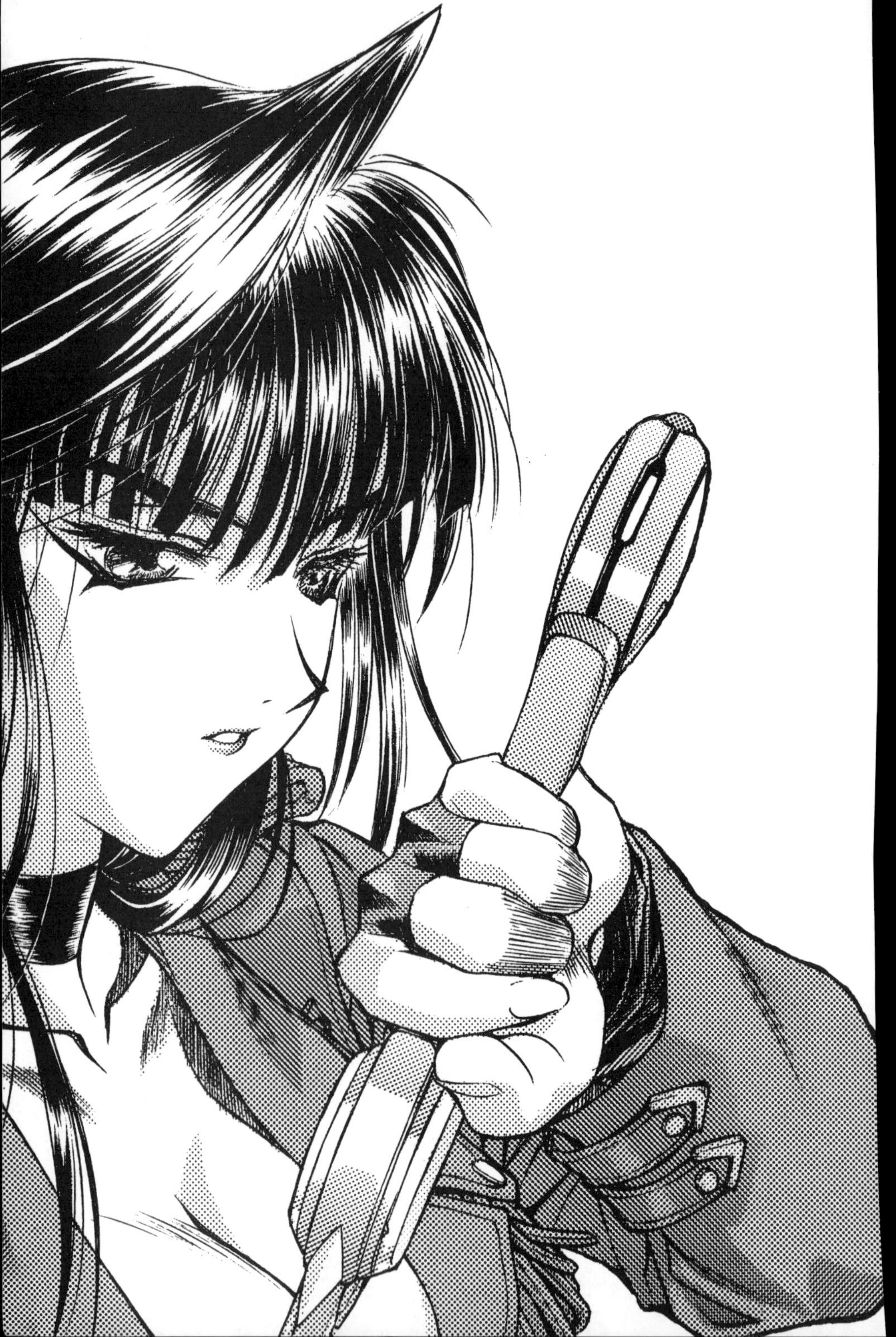

SERAPHIC FEATHER

ACT 57

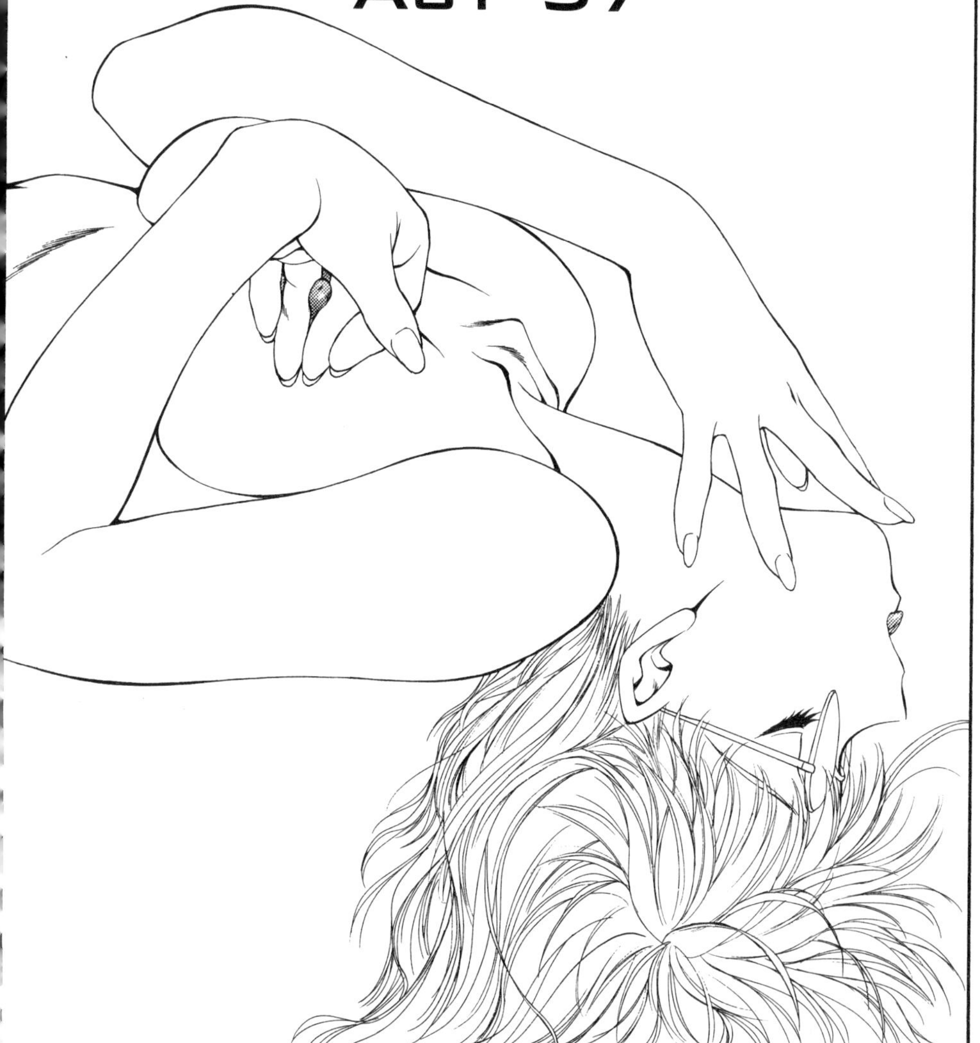

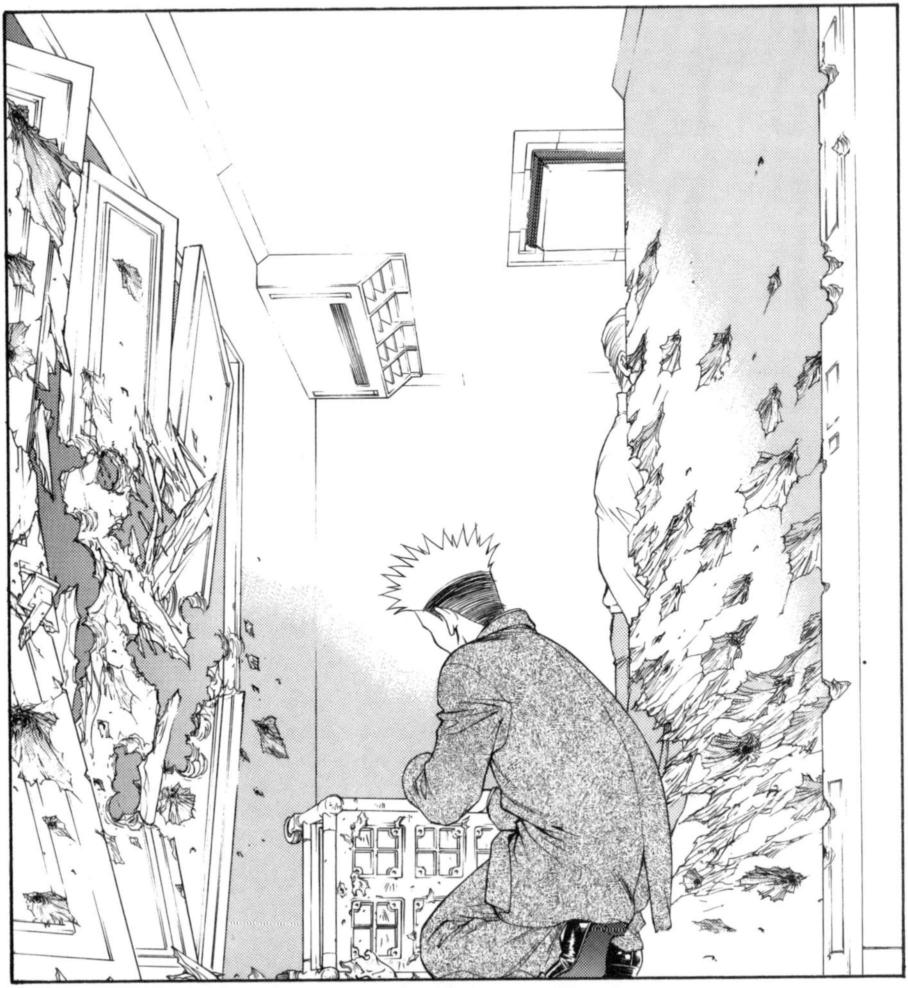

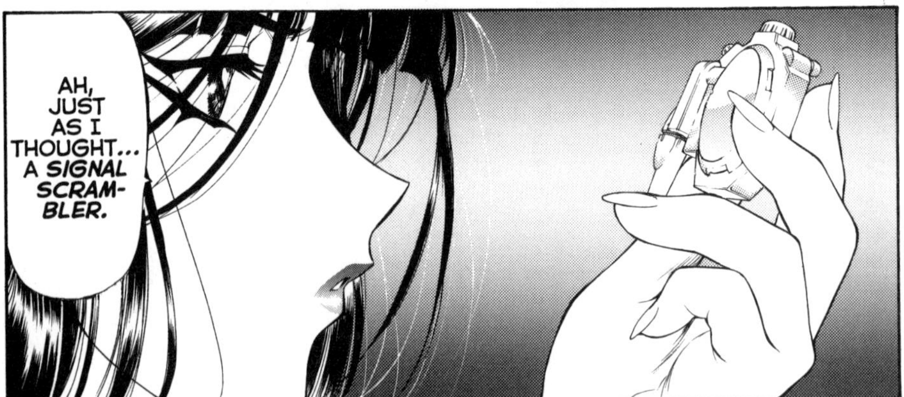
AH, JUST AS I THOUGHT... A SIGNAL SCRAMBLER.

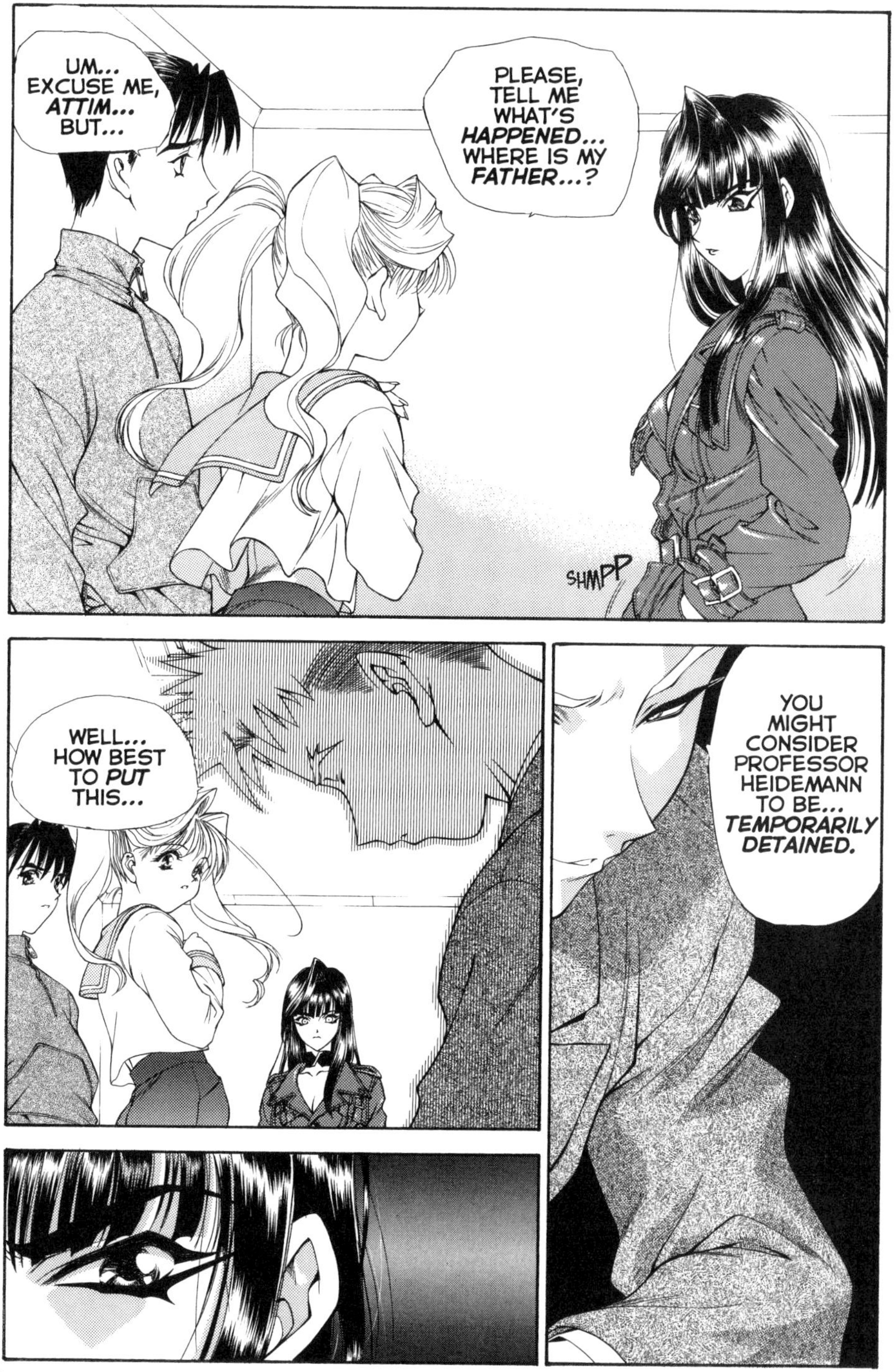
UM... EXCUSE ME, *ATTIM*... BUT...
PLEASE, TELL ME WHAT'S *HAPPENED*... WHERE IS MY *FATHER*...?
SHMPP
WELL... HOW BEST TO *PUT* THIS...
YOU MIGHT CONSIDER PROFESSOR HEIDEMANN TO BE... *TEMPORARILY DETAINED.*

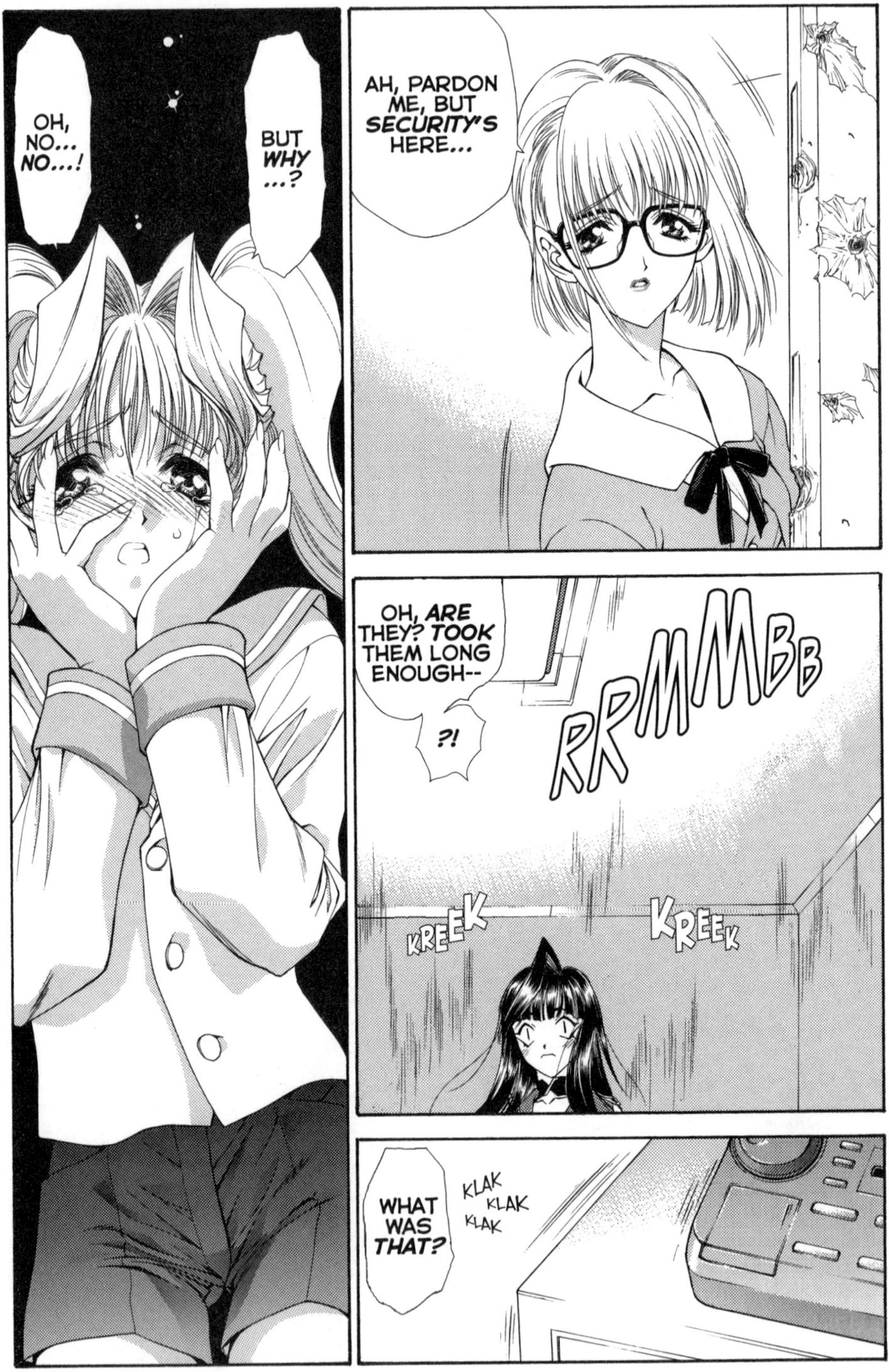
AH, PARDON ME, BUT SECURITY'S HERE...
OH, ARE THEY? TOOK THEM LONG ENOUGH--
?!
RRMMMBB
KREEK
KREEK
WHAT WAS THAT?
KLAK KLAK KLAK
BUT WHY ...?
OH, NO... NO...!

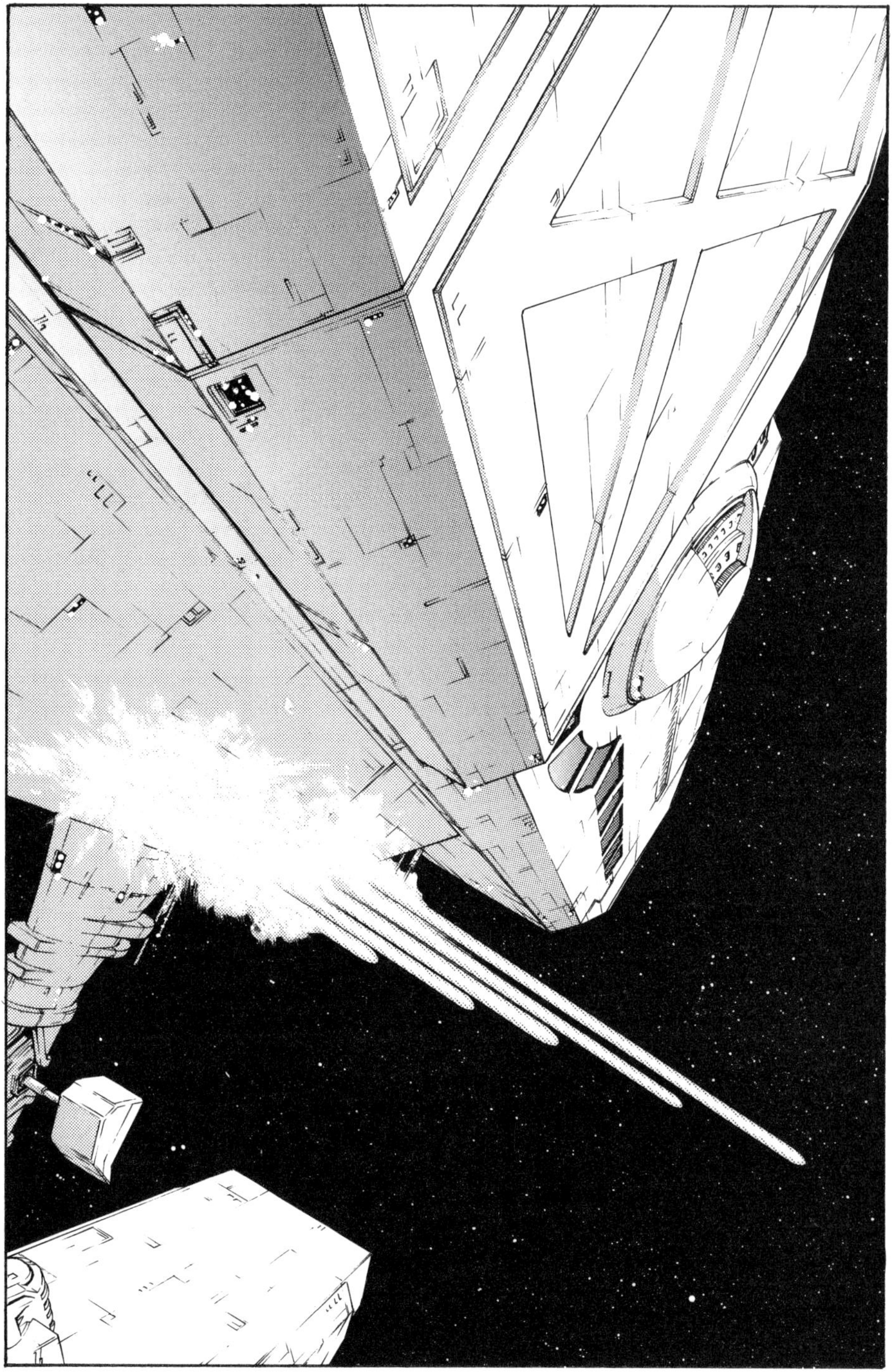

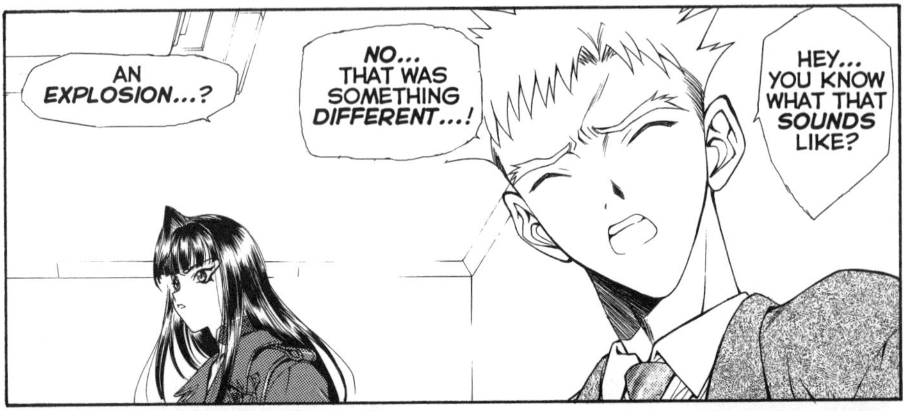
AN EXPLOSION...?
NO... THAT WAS SOMETHING DIFFERENT...!
HEY... YOU KNOW WHAT THAT SOUNDS LIKE?

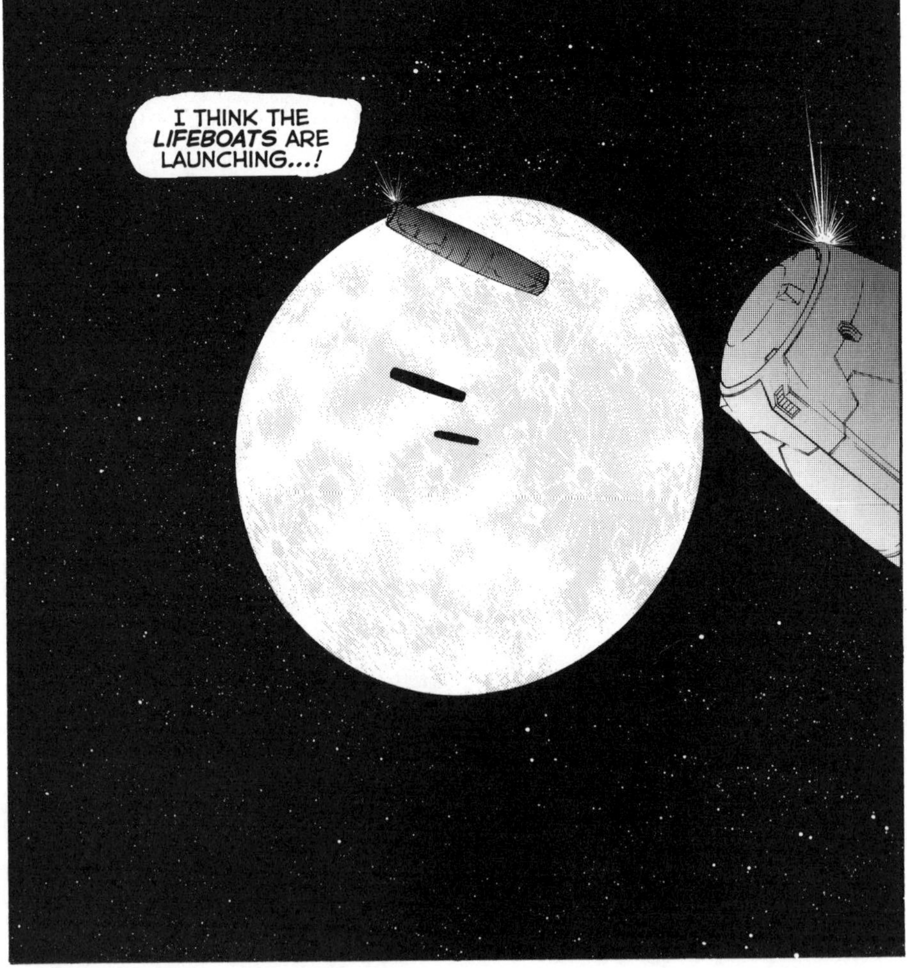
I THINK THE LIFEBOATS ARE LAUNCHING...!

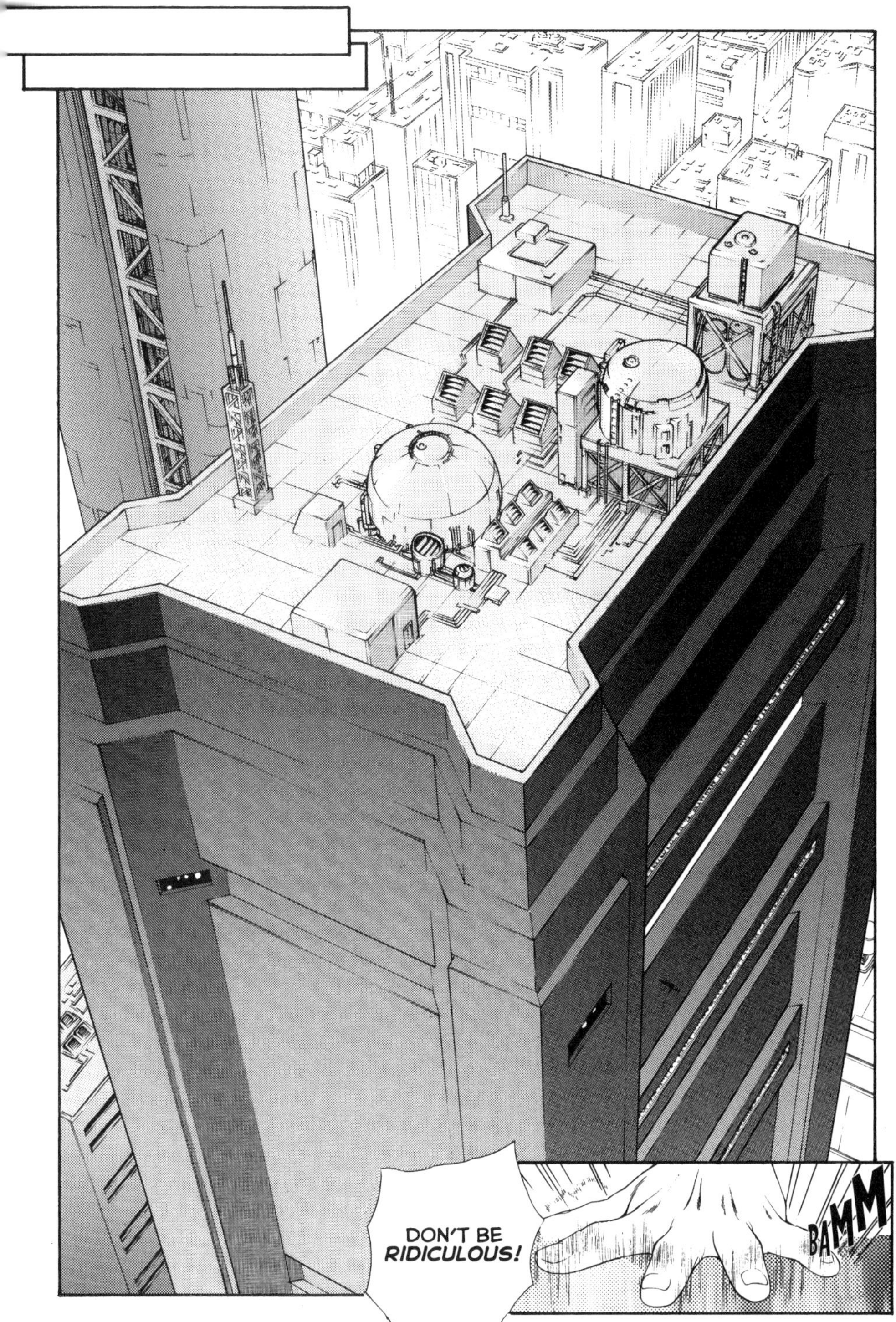
DON'T BE RIDICULOUS!
BAMM

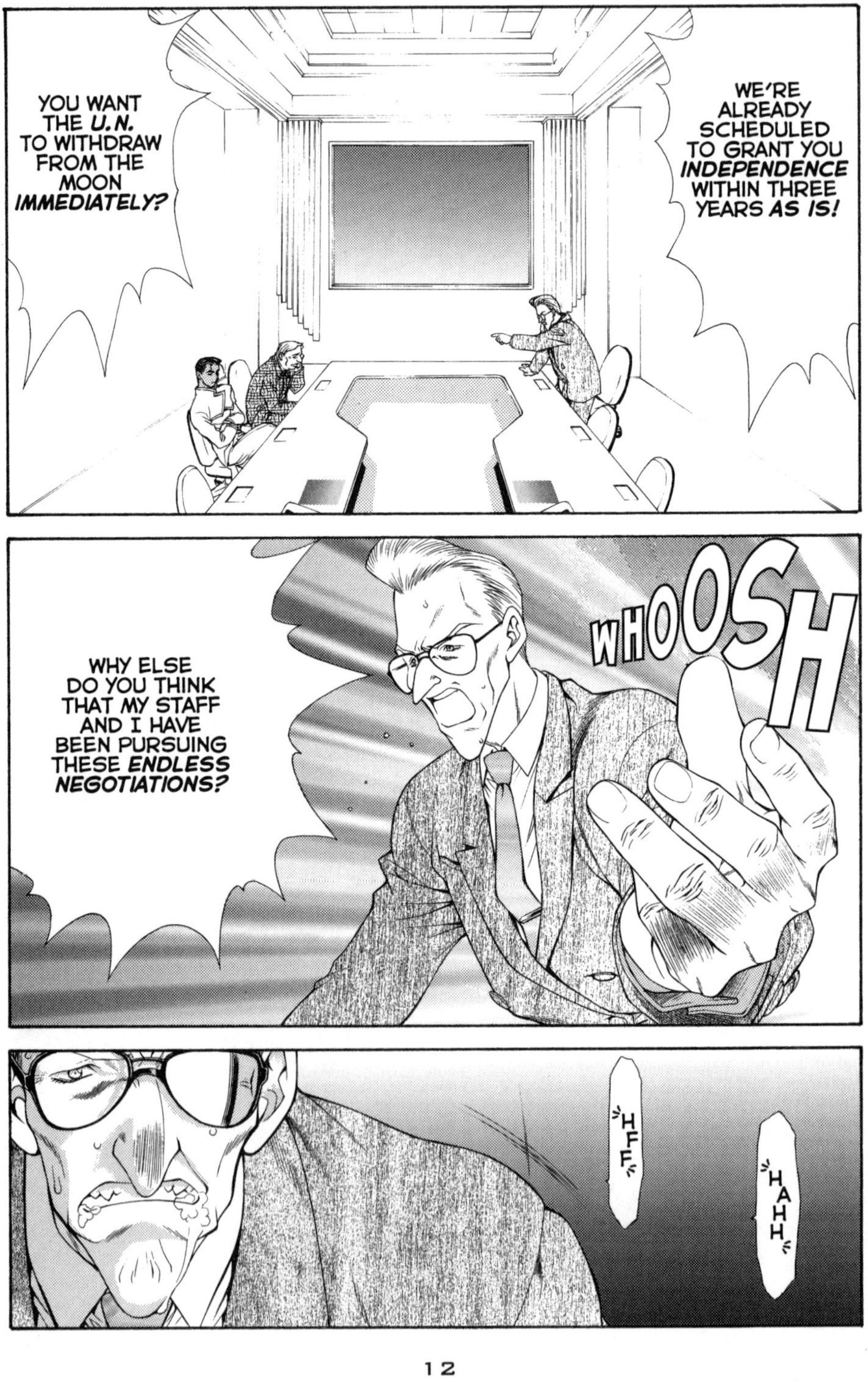
YOU WANT THE *U.N.* TO WITHDRAW FROM THE MOON *IMMEDIATELY?*
WE'RE ALREADY SCHEDULED TO GRANT YOU *INDEPENDENCE* WITHIN THREE YEARS *AS IS!*
WHY ELSE DO YOU THINK THAT MY STAFF AND I HAVE BEEN PURSUING THESE *ENDLESS NEGOTIATIONS?*
WHOOSH
HFF
HAHH

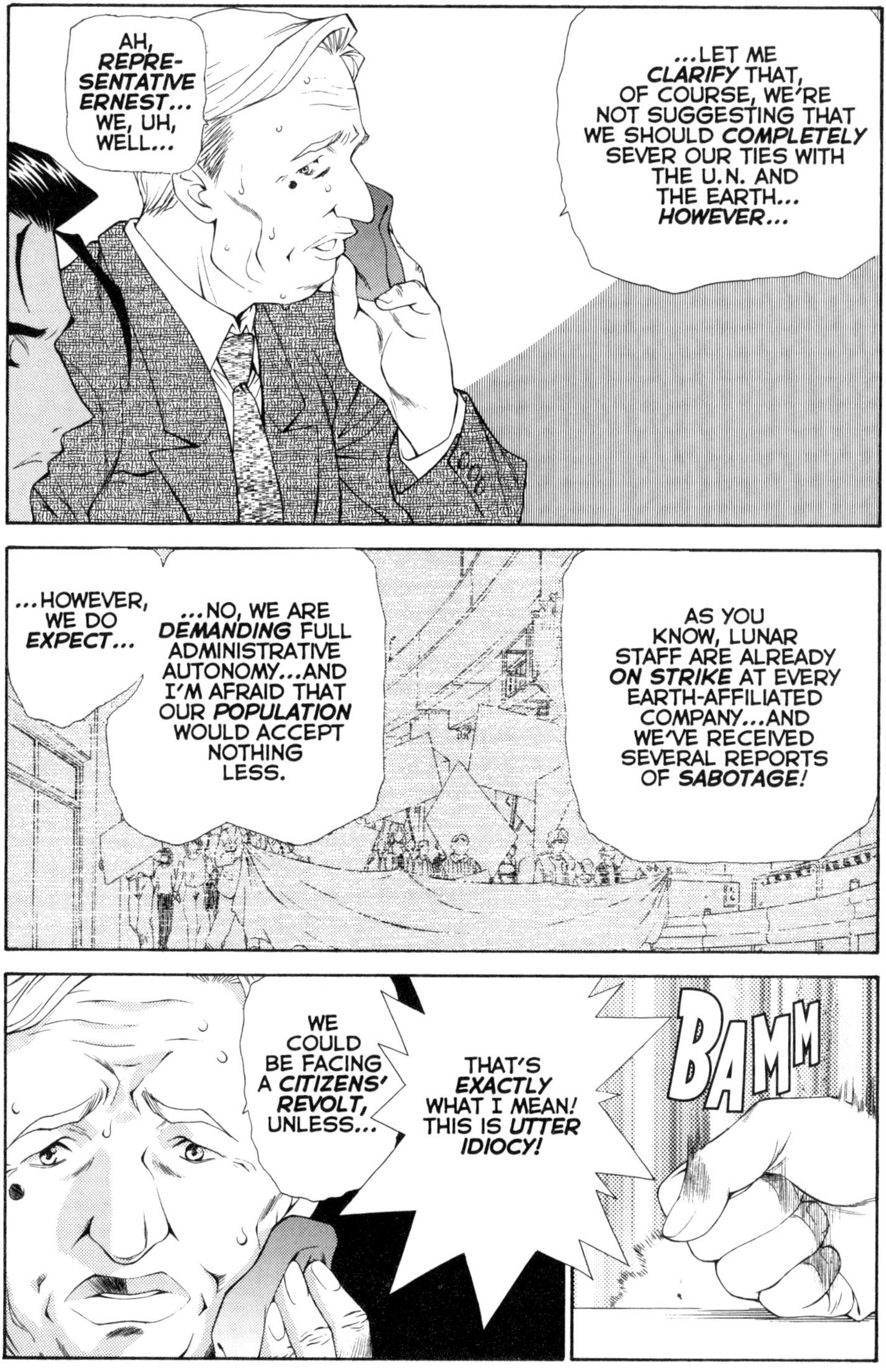

AH, REPRESENTATIVE ERNEST... WE, UH, WELL...
...LET ME CLARIFY THAT, OF COURSE, WE'RE NOT SUGGESTING THAT WE SHOULD COMPLETELY SEVER OUR TIES WITH THE U.N. AND THE EARTH... HOWEVER...
...HOWEVER, WE DO EXPECT...
...NO, WE ARE DEMANDING FULL ADMINISTRATIVE AUTONOMY...AND I'M AFRAID THAT OUR POPULATION WOULD ACCEPT NOTHING LESS.
AS YOU KNOW, LUNAR STAFF ARE ALREADY ON STRIKE AT EVERY EARTH-AFFILIATED COMPANY...AND WE'VE RECEIVED SEVERAL REPORTS OF SABOTAGE!
WE COULD BE FACING A CITIZENS' REVOLT, UNLESS...
THAT'S EXACTLY WHAT I MEAN! THIS IS UTTER IDIOCY!
BAMM

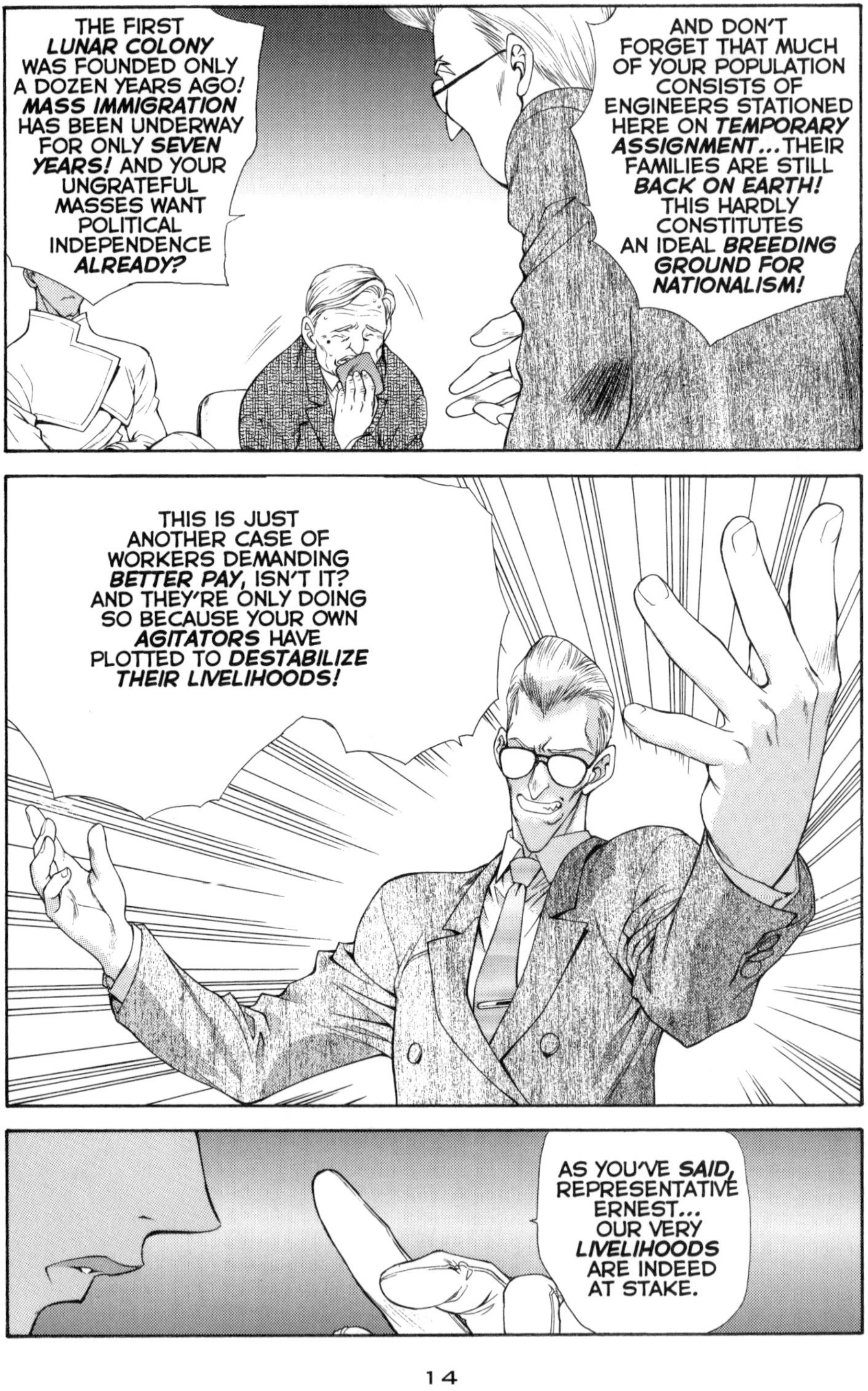
THE FIRST LUNAR COLONY WAS FOUNDED ONLY A DOZEN YEARS AGO! MASS IMMIGRATION HAS BEEN UNDERWAY FOR ONLY SEVEN YEARS! AND YOUR UNGRATEFUL MASSES WANT POLITICAL INDEPENDENCE ALREADY?
AND DON'T FORGET THAT MUCH OF YOUR POPULATION CONSISTS OF ENGINEERS STATIONED HERE ON TEMPORARY ASSIGNMENT... THEIR FAMILIES ARE STILL BACK ON EARTH! THIS HARDLY CONSTITUTES AN IDEAL BREEDING GROUND FOR NATIONALISM!
THIS IS JUST ANOTHER CASE OF WORKERS DEMANDING BETTER PAY, ISN'T IT? AND THEY'RE ONLY DOING SO BECAUSE YOUR OWN AGITATORS HAVE PLOTTED TO DESTABILIZE THEIR LIVELIHOODS!
AS YOU'VE SAID, REPRESENTATIVE ERNEST... OUR VERY LIVELIHOODS ARE INDEED AT STAKE.

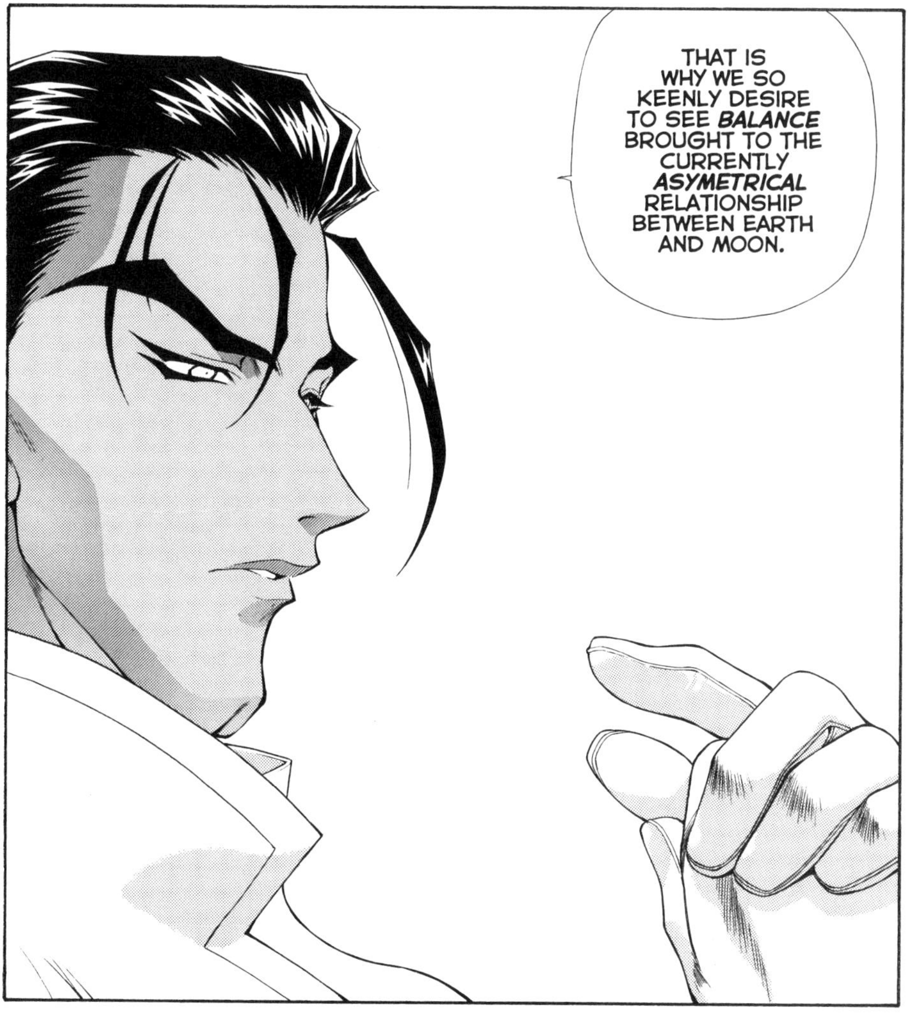
THAT IS WHY WE SO KEENLY DESIRE TO SEE *BALANCE* BROUGHT TO THE CURRENTLY *ASYMETRICAL* RELATIONSHIP BETWEEN EARTH AND MOON.

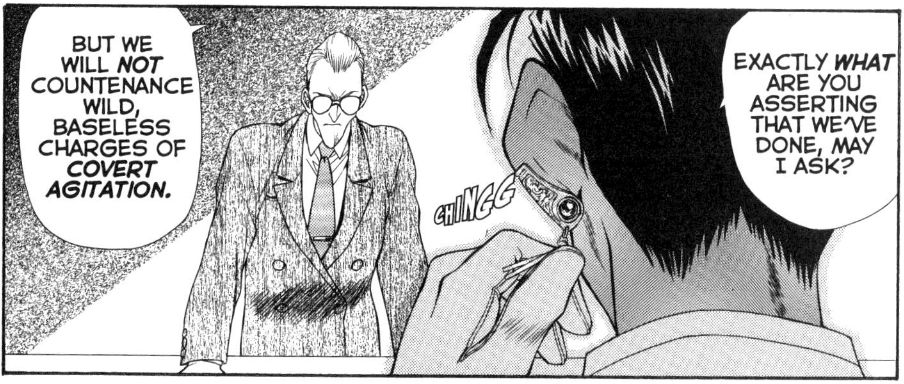
EXACTLY *WHAT* ARE YOU ASSERTING THAT WE'VE DONE, MAY I ASK?
CHINGG
BUT WE WILL *NOT* COUNTENANCE WILD, BASELESS CHARGES OF *COVERT AGITATION.*

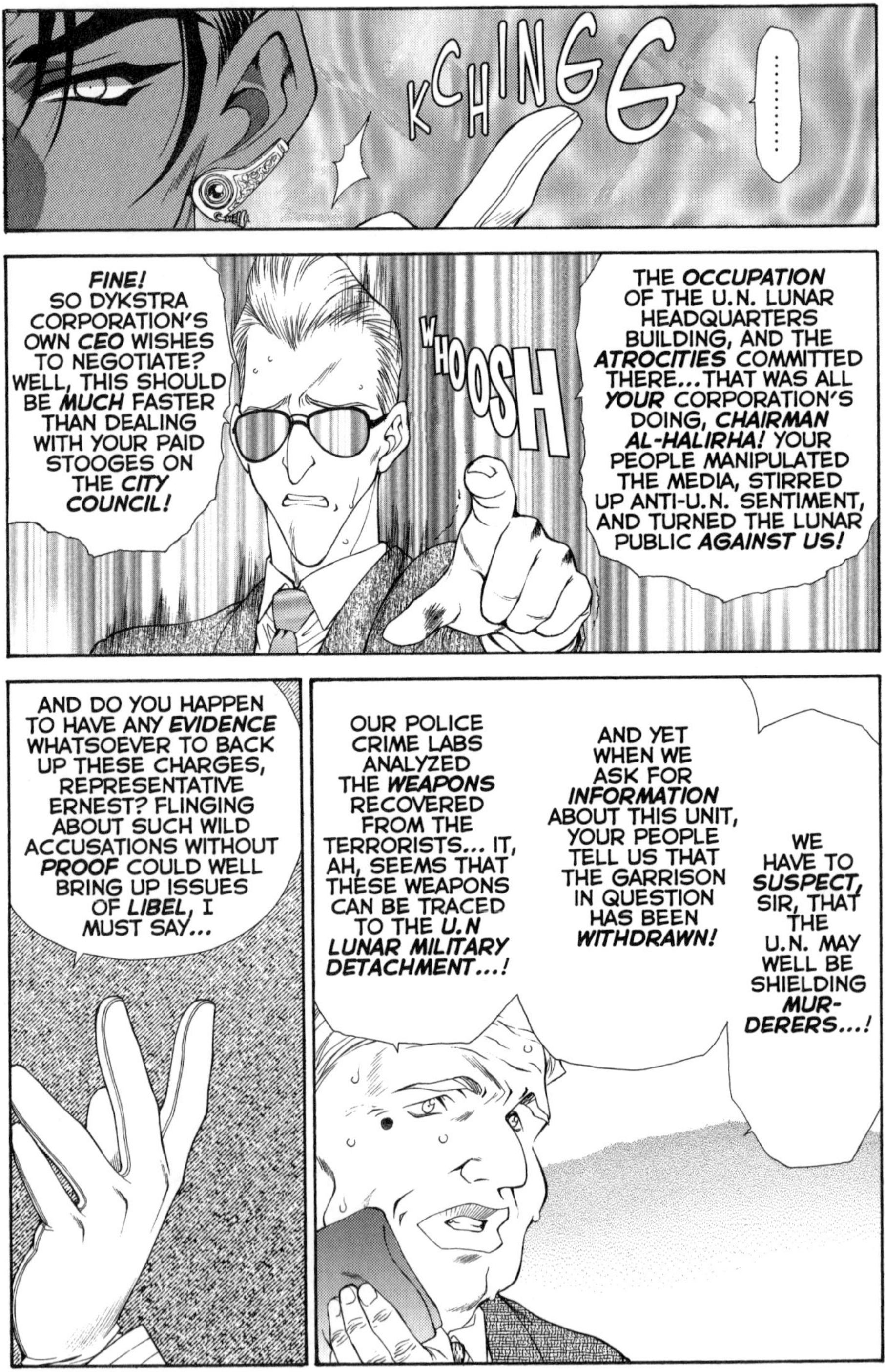
KCHINGG
......
FINE! SO DYKSTRA CORPORATION'S OWN CEO WISHES TO NEGOTIATE? WELL, THIS SHOULD BE MUCH FASTER THAN DEALING WITH YOUR PAID STOOGES ON THE CITY COUNCIL!
WHOOSH
THE OCCUPATION OF THE U.N. LUNAR HEADQUARTERS BUILDING, AND THE ATROCITIES COMMITTED THERE...THAT WAS ALL YOUR CORPORATION'S DOING, CHAIRMAN AL-HALIRHA! YOUR PEOPLE MANIPULATED THE MEDIA, STIRRED UP ANTI-U.N. SENTIMENT, AND TURNED THE LUNAR PUBLIC AGAINST US!
AND DO YOU HAPPEN TO HAVE ANY EVIDENCE WHATSOEVER TO BACK UP THESE CHARGES, REPRESENTATIVE ERNEST? FLINGING ABOUT SUCH WILD ACCUSATIONS WITHOUT PROOF COULD WELL BRING UP ISSUES OF LIBEL, I MUST SAY...
OUR POLICE CRIME LABS ANALYZED THE WEAPONS RECOVERED FROM THE TERRORISTS... IT, AH, SEEMS THAT THESE WEAPONS CAN BE TRACED TO THE U.N LUNAR MILITARY DETACHMENT...!
AND YET WHEN WE ASK FOR INFORMATION ABOUT THIS UNIT, YOUR PEOPLE TELL US THAT THE GARRISON IN QUESTION HAS BEEN WITHDRAWN!
WE HAVE TO SUSPECT, SIR, THAT THE U.N. MAY WELL BE SHIELDING MUR-DERERS...!

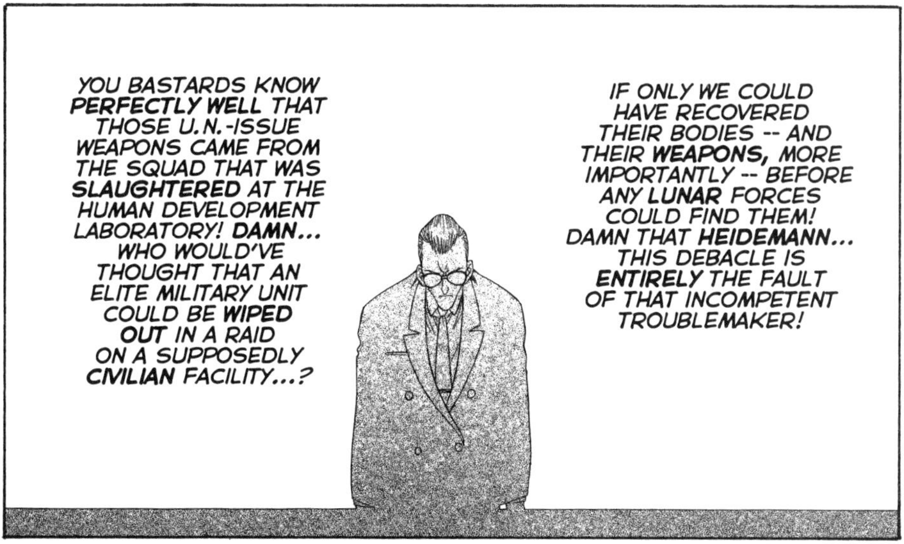
YOU BASTARDS KNOW **PERFECTLY WELL** THAT THOSE U.N.-ISSUE WEAPONS CAME FROM THE SQUAD THAT WAS **SLAUGHTERED** AT THE HUMAN DEVELOPMENT LABORATORY! **DAMN...** WHO WOULD'VE THOUGHT THAT AN ELITE MILITARY UNIT COULD BE **WIPED OUT** IN A RAID ON A SUPPOSEDLY **CIVILIAN** FACILITY...?
IF ONLY WE COULD HAVE RECOVERED THEIR BODIES -- AND THEIR **WEAPONS,** MORE IMPORTANTLY -- BEFORE ANY **LUNAR** FORCES COULD FIND THEM! DAMN THAT **HEIDEMANN...** THIS DEBACLE IS **ENTIRELY** THE FAULT OF THAT INCOMPETENT TROUBLEMAKER!

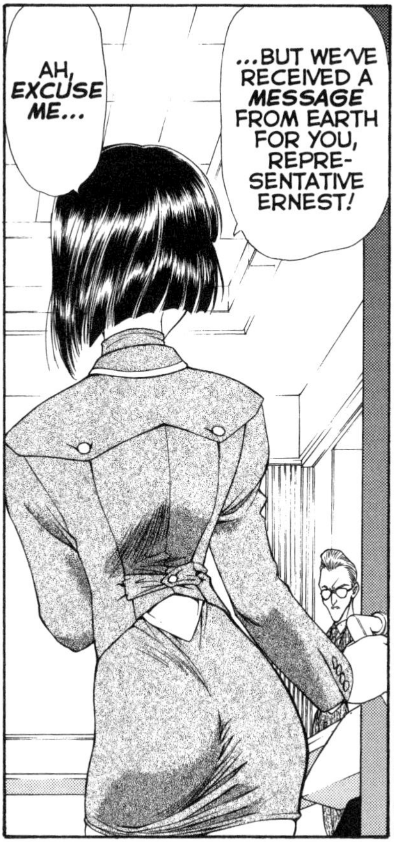
AH, **EXCUSE ME...**
...BUT WE'VE RECEIVED A **MESSAGE** FROM EARTH FOR YOU, REPRE-SENTATIVE ERNEST!

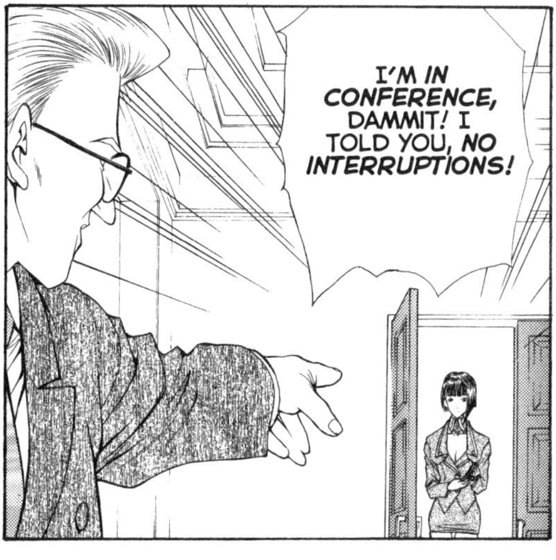
I'M ***IN CONFERENCE,*** DAMMIT! I TOLD YOU, ***NO INTERRUPTIONS!***

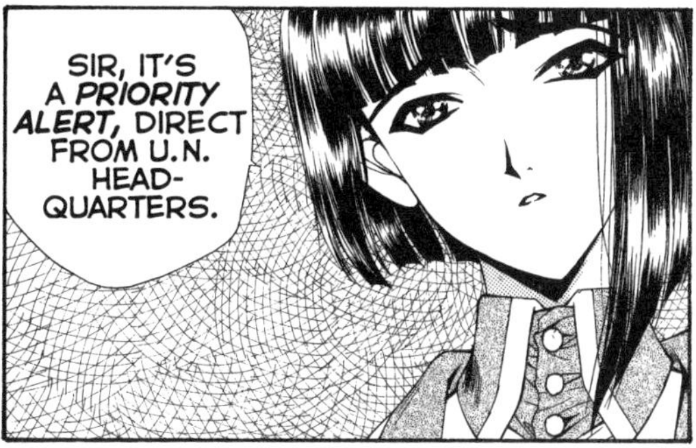
SIR, IT'S A ***PRIORITY ALERT,*** DIRECT FROM U.N. HEAD-QUARTERS.

A *PRIORITY ALERT*...?

WHAT?

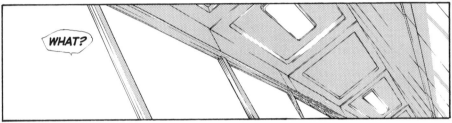

HAS THIS BEEN CONFIRMED? *YES*?

A *CISLUNAR SHUTTLE* HAS BEEN *HIJACKED*?!

Act 58

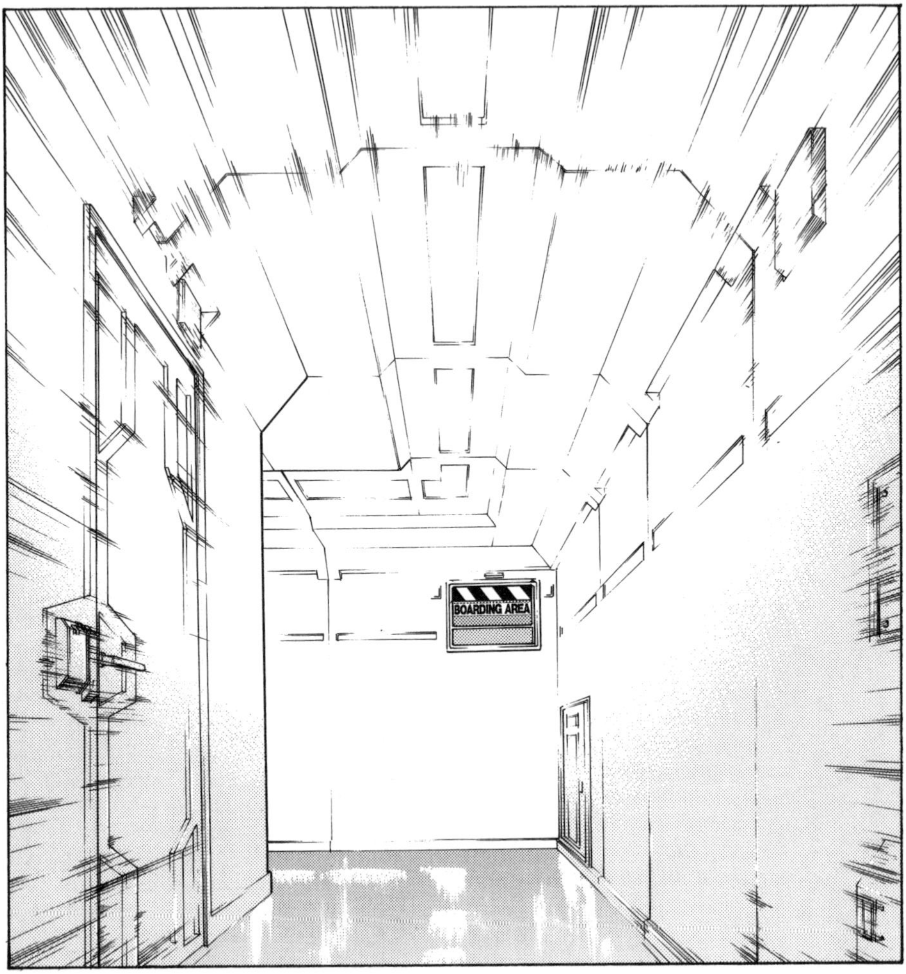
BOARDING AREA

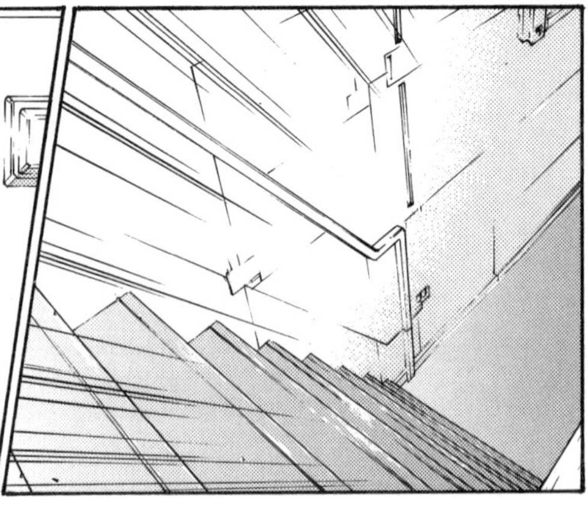

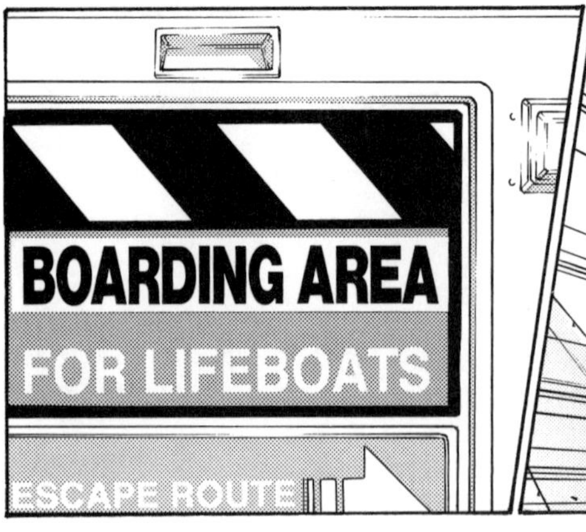
BOARDING AREA
FOR LIFEBOATS
ESCAPE ROUTE

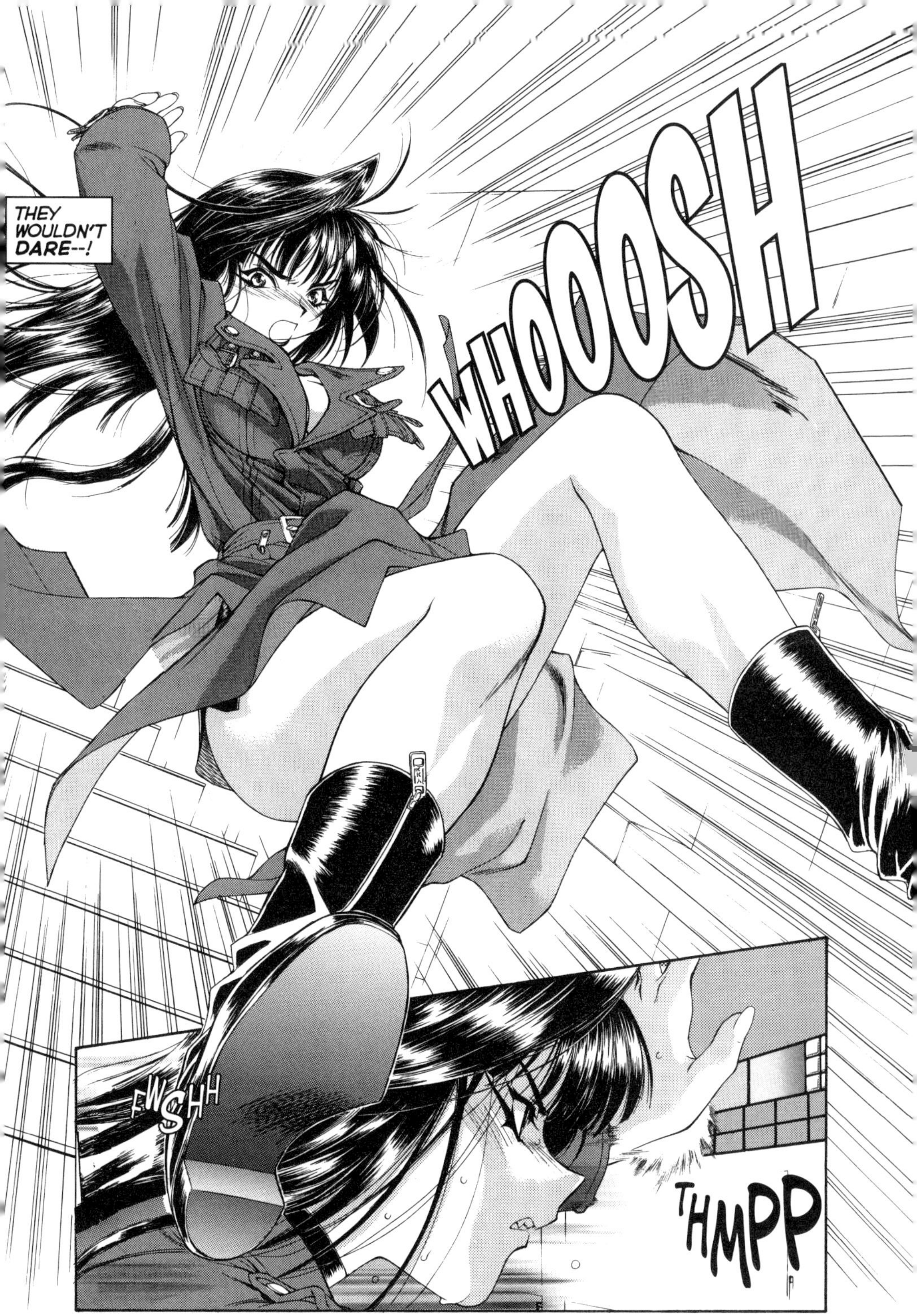
THEY WOULDN'T DARE--!
WHOOOOSH
FWSHH
THMPP

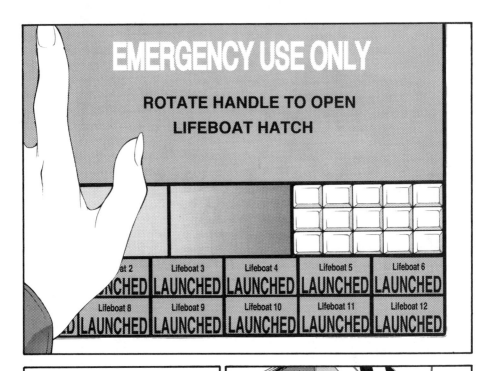

EMERGENCY USE ONLY

ROTATE HANDLE TO OPEN
LIFEBOAT HATCH

Lifeboat 2	Lifeboat 3	Lifeboat 4	Lifeboat 5	Lifeboat 6
LAUNCHED	LAUNCHED	LAUNCHED	LAUNCHED	LAUNCHED
Lifeboat 8	Lifeboat 9	Lifeboat 10	Lifeboat 11	Lifeboat 12
LAUNCHED	LAUNCHED	LAUNCHED	LAUNCHED	LAUNCHED

SO THAT TREMOR WE FELT **WAS** THE MASS LAUNCHING OF **LIFEBOATS,** AFTER ALL... THEY'RE ALL GONE, SAVE ONE...

HRRG

KREEK

BUT WHY ARE THEY DOING THIS ...?

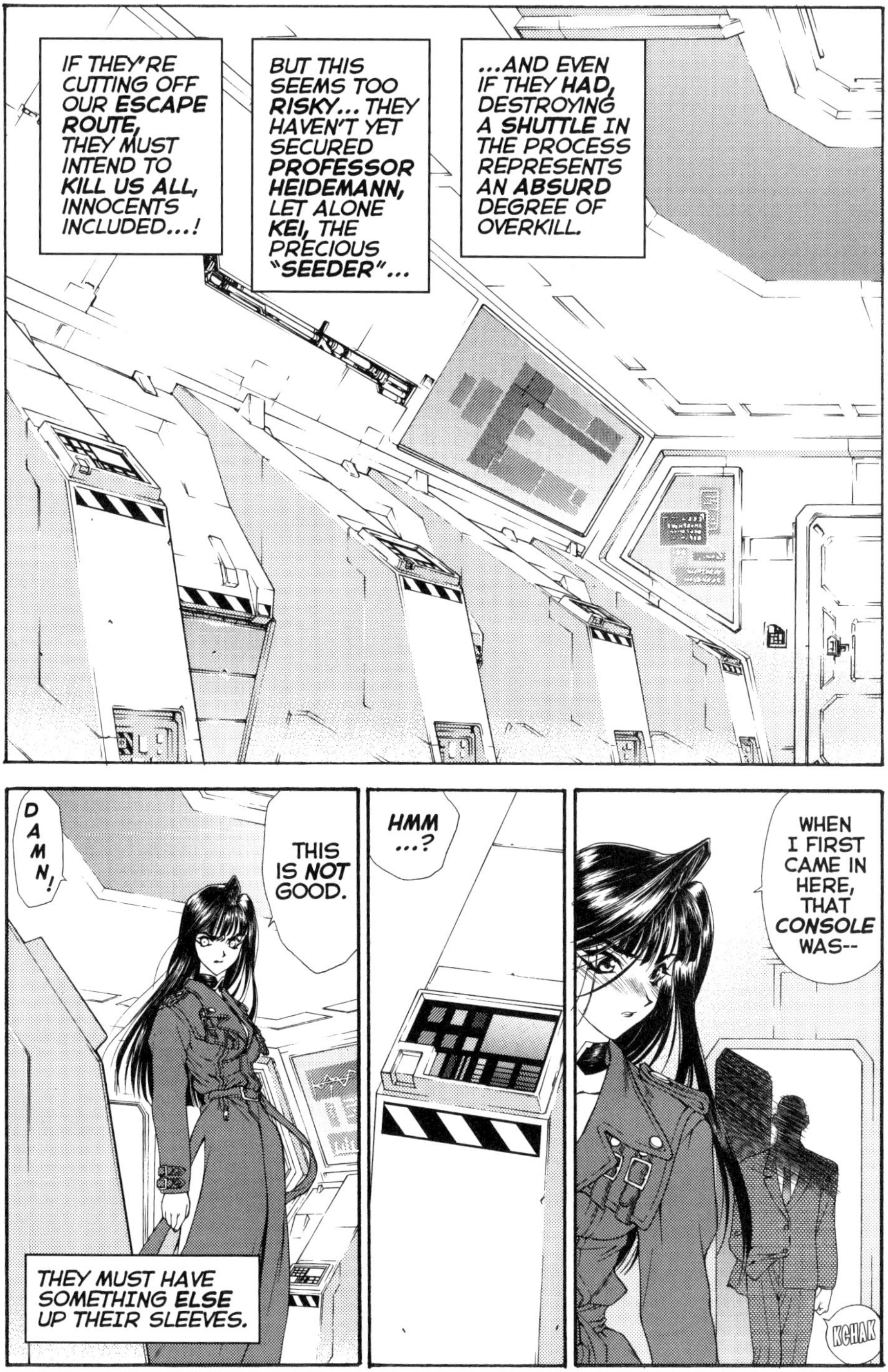

IF THEY'RE CUTTING OFF OUR **ESCAPE ROUTE,** THEY MUST INTEND TO **KILL US ALL,** INNOCENTS INCLUDED...!
BUT THIS SEEMS TOO **RISKY...** THEY HAVEN'T YET SECURED **PROFESSOR HEIDEMANN,** LET ALONE **KEI,** THE PRECIOUS **"SEEDER"...**
...AND EVEN IF THEY **HAD,** DESTROYING A **SHUTTLE** IN THE PROCESS REPRESENTS AN **ABSURD** DEGREE OF **OVERKILL.**
DAMN!
THIS IS **NOT** GOOD.
THEY MUST HAVE SOMETHING **ELSE** UP THEIR SLEEVES.
HMM ...?
WHEN I FIRST CAME IN HERE, THAT **CONSOLE** WAS--
KCHAK

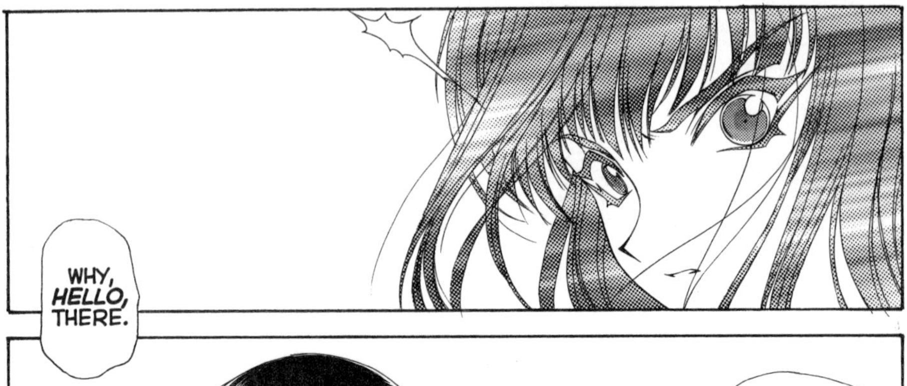
WHY, *HELLO,* THERE.

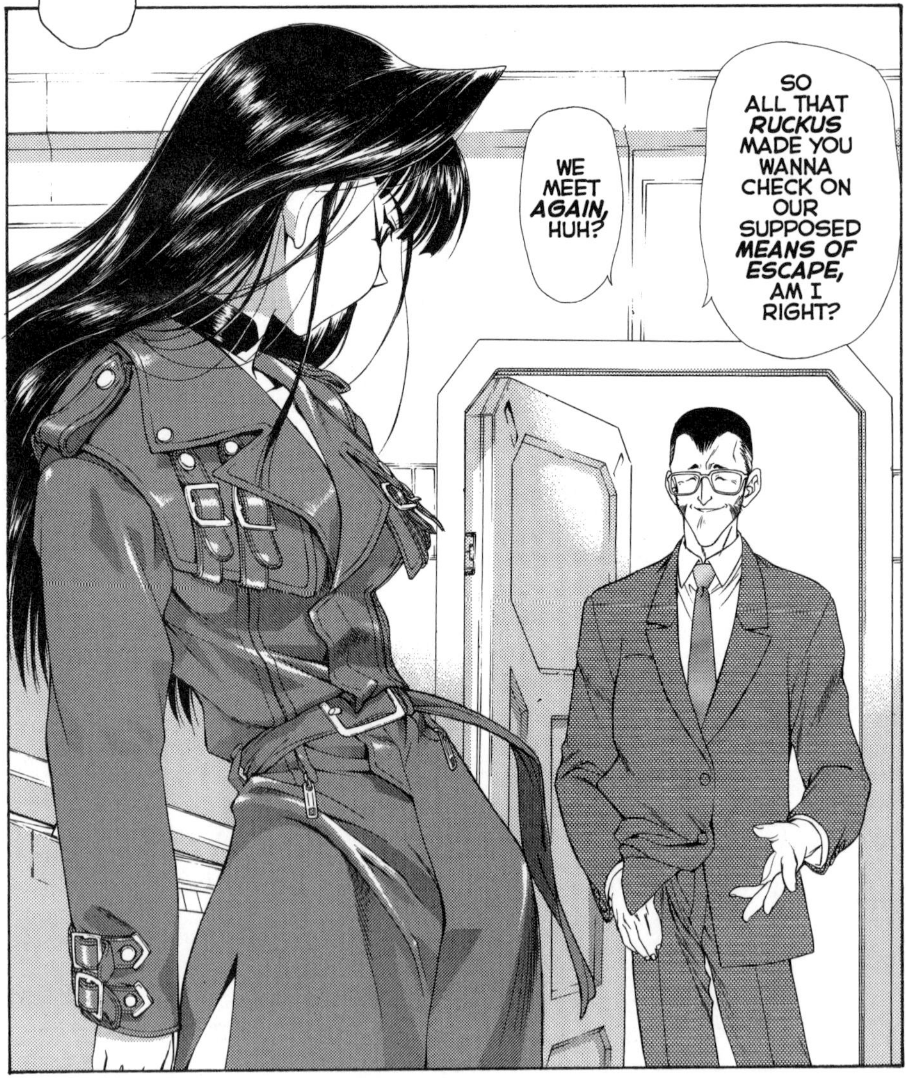
WE MEET *AGAIN,* HUH?
SO ALL THAT *RUCKUS* MADE YOU WANNA CHECK ON OUR SUPPOSED ***MEANS OF ESCAPE,*** AM I RIGHT?

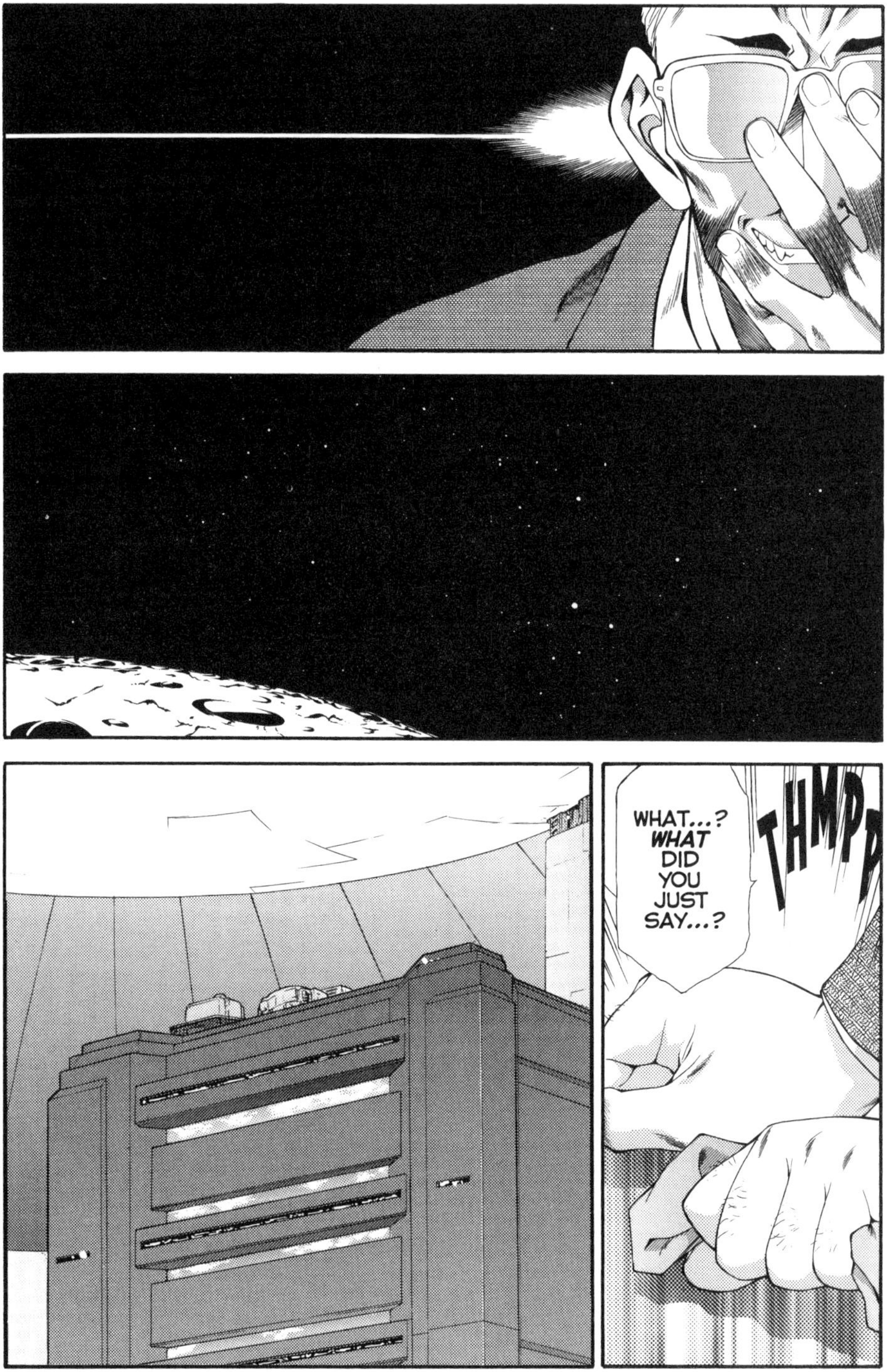
WHAT...? *WHAT* DID YOU JUST SAY...?
THMP

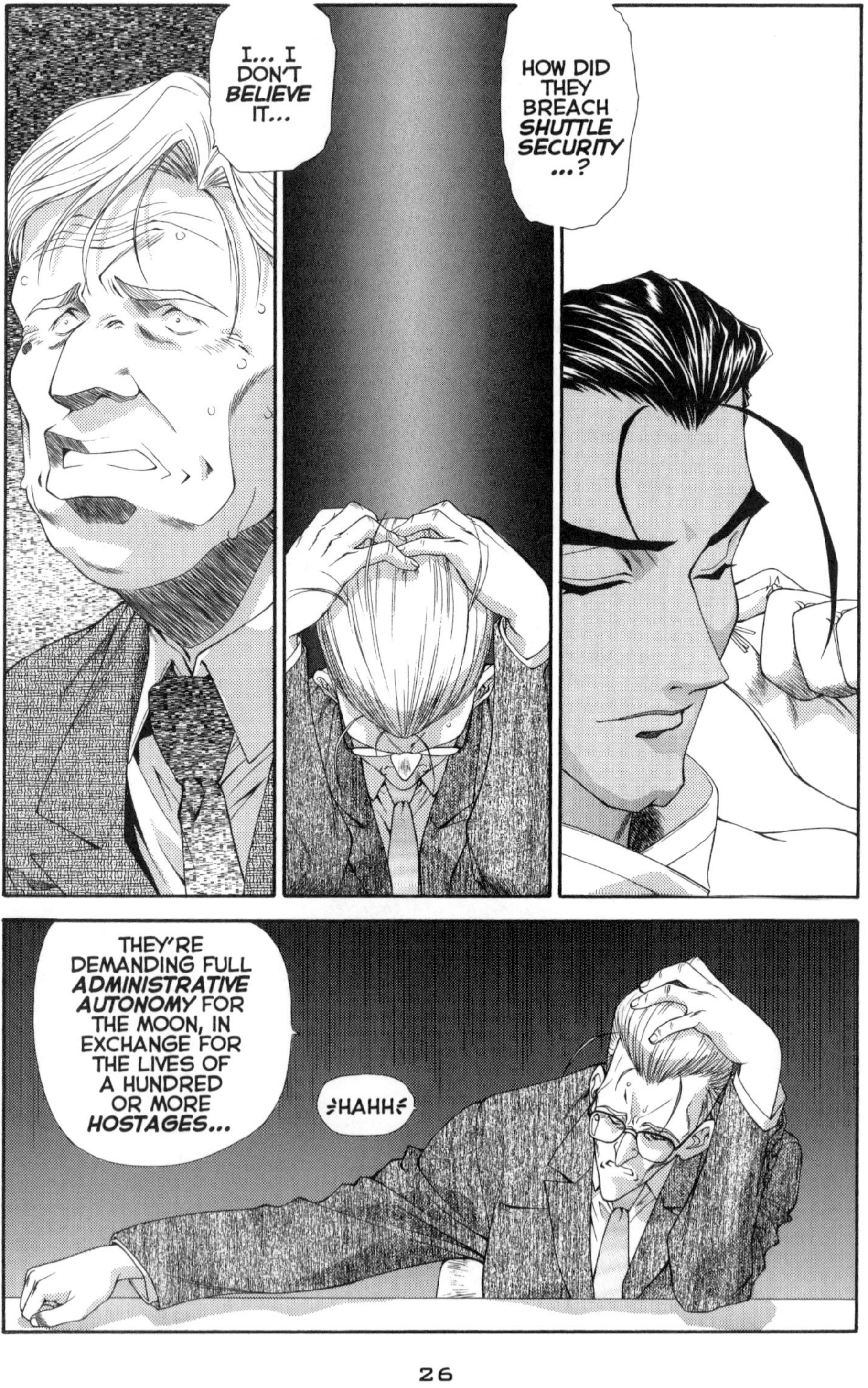
I... I DON'T *BELIEVE* IT...
HOW DID THEY BREACH *SHUTTLE SECURITY* ...?
THEY'RE DEMANDING FULL *ADMINISTRATIVE AUTONOMY* FOR THE MOON, IN EXCHANGE FOR THE LIVES OF A HUNDRED OR MORE *HOSTAGES...*
HAHH

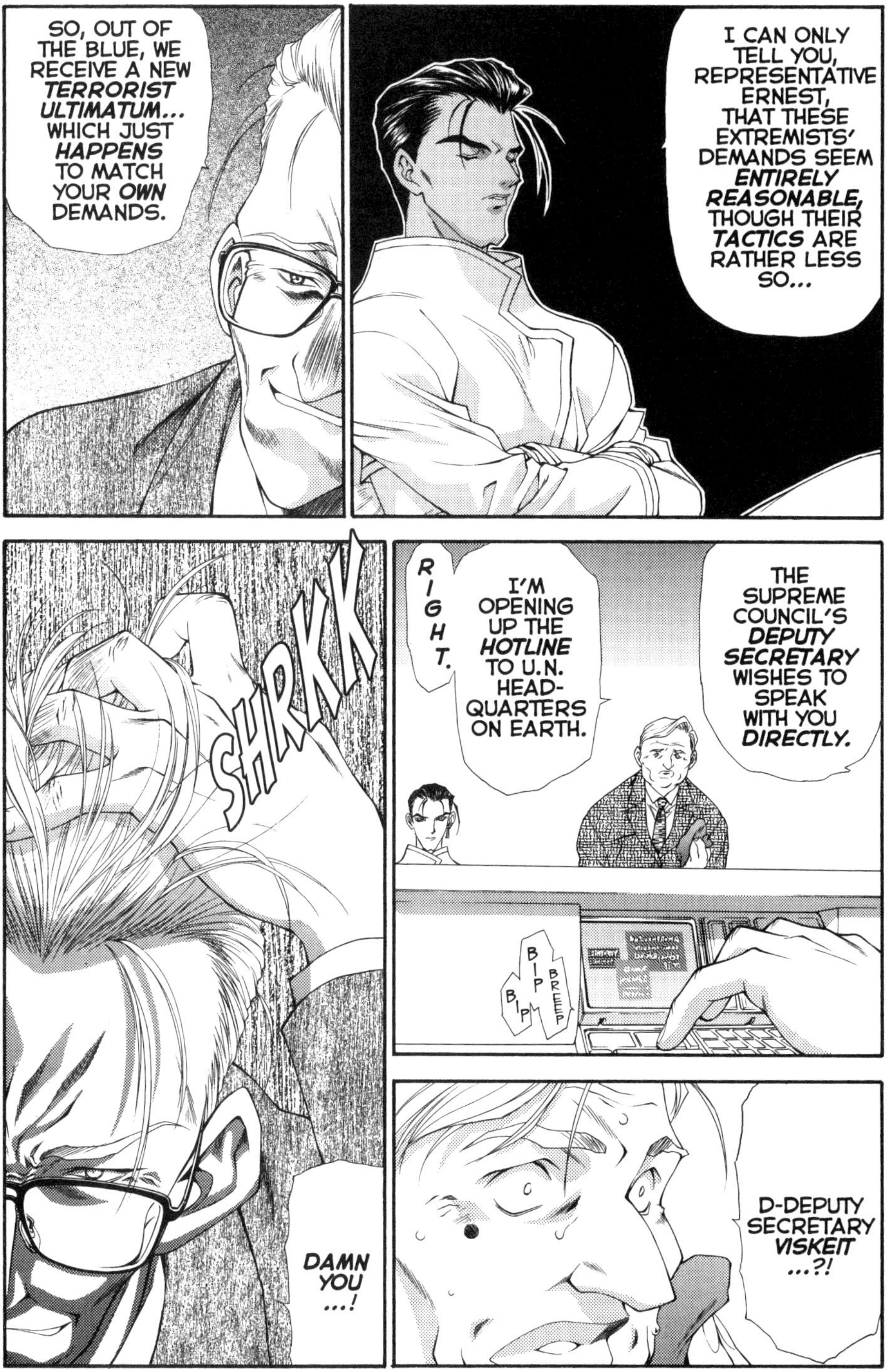
SO, OUT OF THE BLUE, WE RECEIVE A NEW *TERRORIST ULTIMATUM...* WHICH JUST *HAPPENS* TO MATCH YOUR *OWN* DEMANDS.
I CAN ONLY TELL YOU, REPRESENTATIVE ERNEST, THAT THESE EXTREMISTS' DEMANDS SEEM *ENTIRELY REASONABLE,* THOUGH THEIR *TACTICS* ARE RATHER LESS SO...
SHRKK
DAMN YOU ...!
RIGHT.
I'M OPENING UP THE *HOTLINE* TO U.N. HEAD-QUARTERS ON EARTH.
THE SUPREME COUNCIL'S *DEPUTY SECRETARY* WISHES TO SPEAK WITH YOU *DIRECTLY.*
BIP BIP BREEP
D-DEPUTY SECRETARY *VISKEIT* ...?!

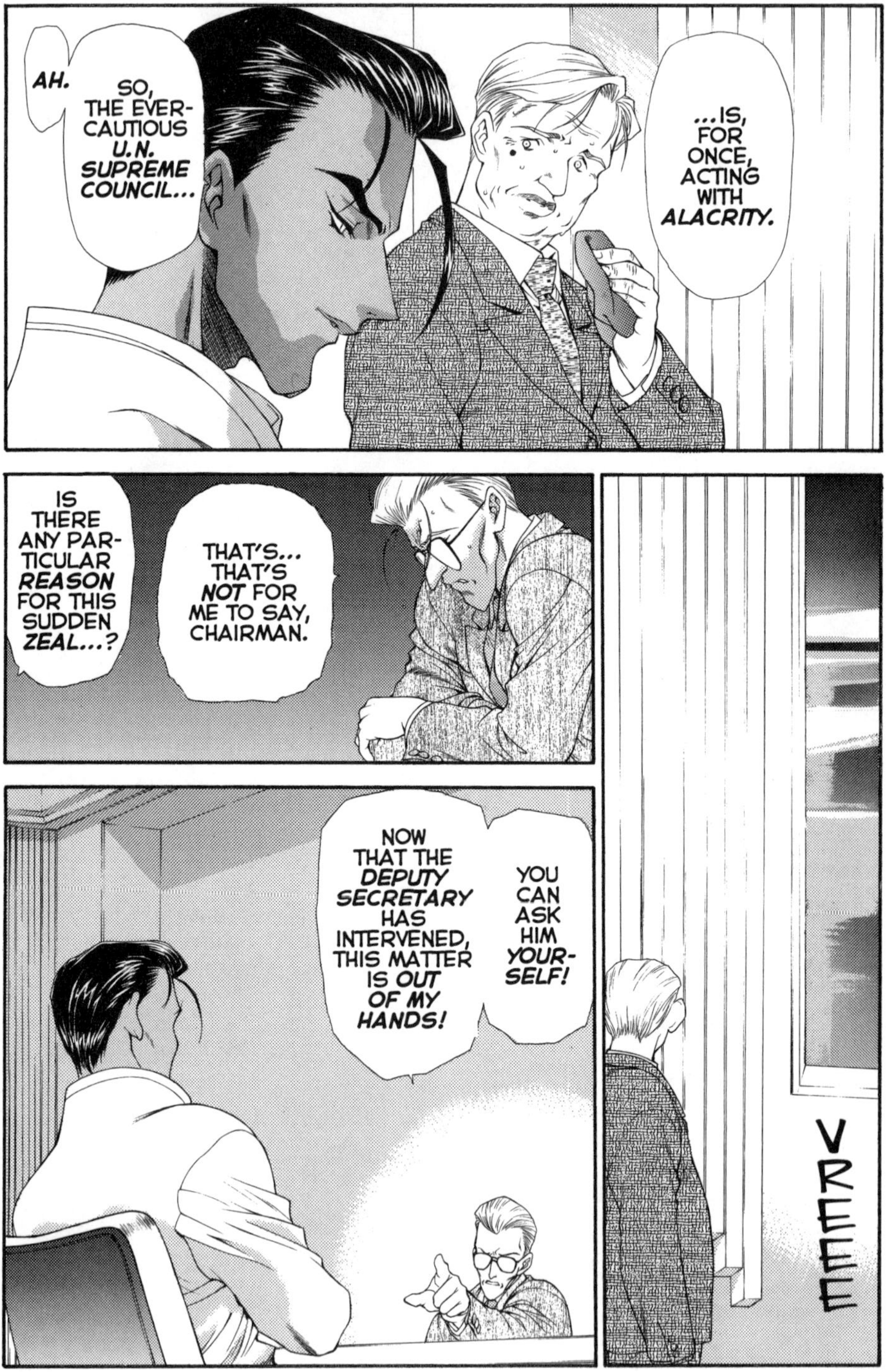
AH.
SO, THE EVER-CAUTIOUS U.N. SUPREME COUNCIL...
...IS, FOR ONCE, ACTING WITH ALACRITY.
IS THERE ANY PARTICULAR REASON FOR THIS SUDDEN ZEAL...?
THAT'S... THAT'S NOT FOR ME TO SAY, CHAIRMAN.
NOW THAT THE DEPUTY SECRETARY HAS INTERVENED, THIS MATTER IS OUT OF MY HANDS!
YOU CAN ASK HIM YOURSELF!
VREEE

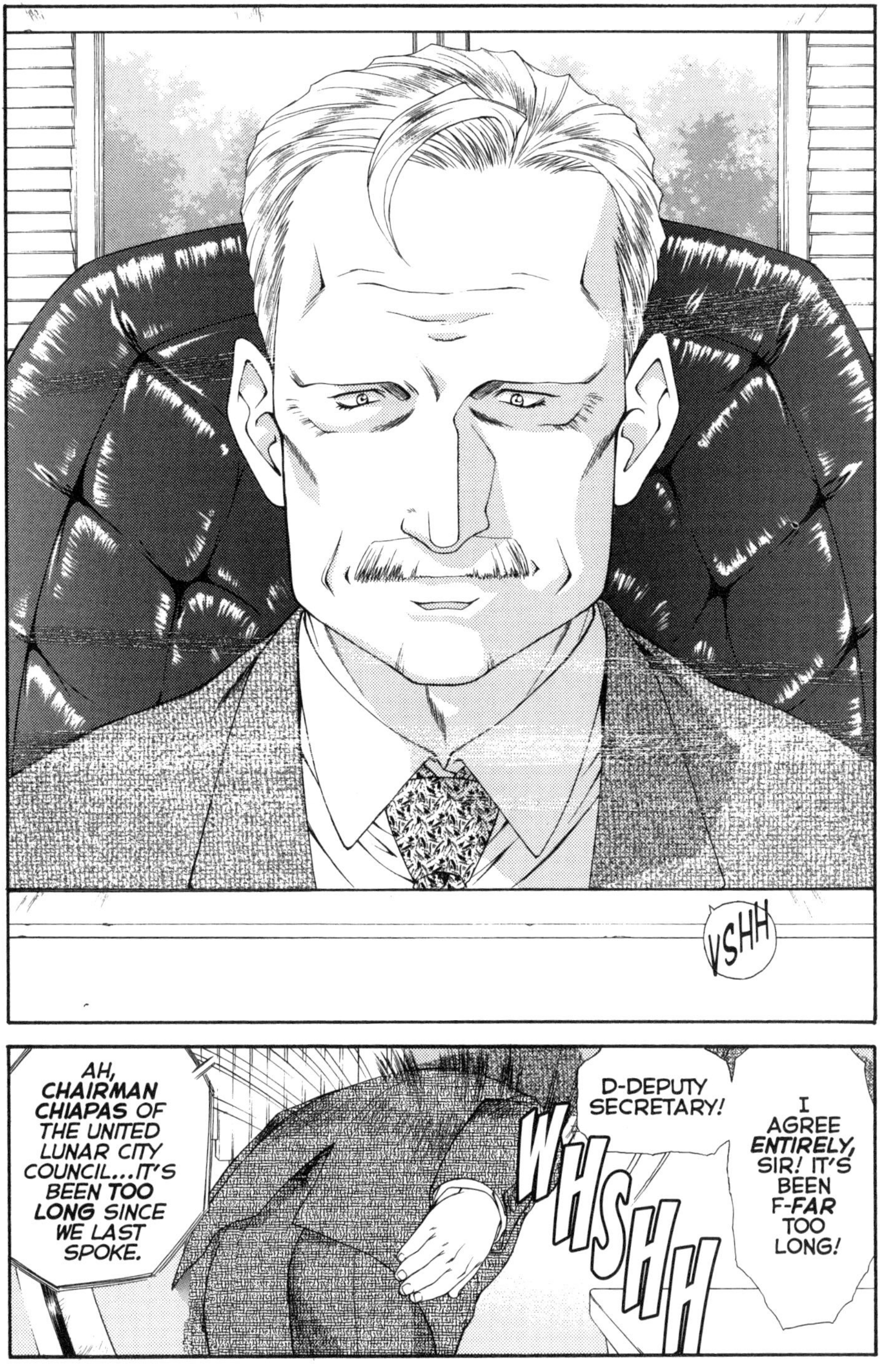
VSHH
AH, CHAIRMAN CHIAPAS OF THE UNITED LUNAR CITY COUNCIL...IT'S BEEN TOO LONG SINCE WE LAST SPOKE.
WHSHH
D-DEPUTY SECRETARY!
I AGREE ENTIRELY, SIR! IT'S BEEN F-FAR TOO LONG!

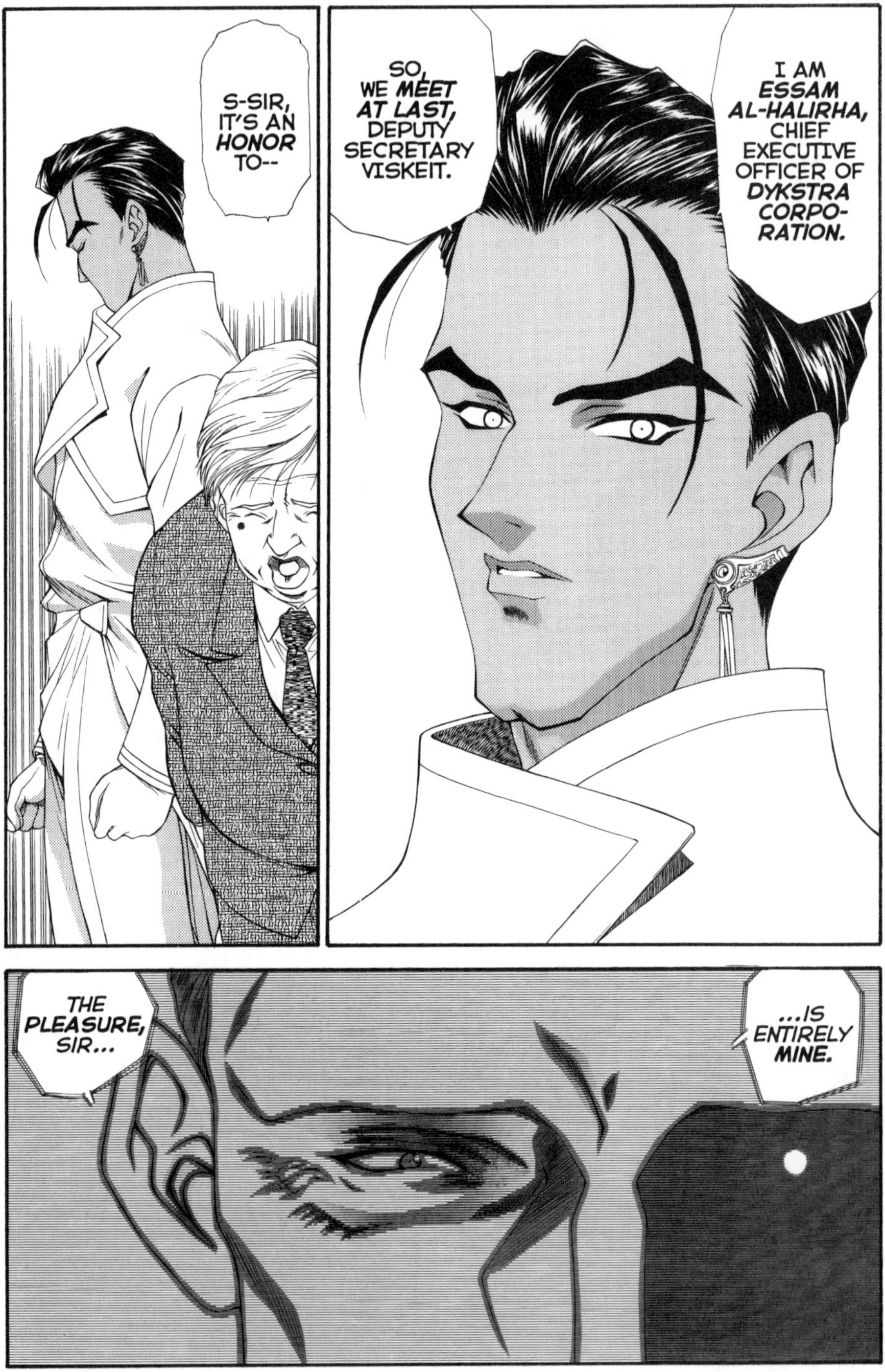
S-SIR, IT'S AN HONOR TO--
SO, WE MEET AT LAST, DEPUTY SECRETARY VISKEIT.
I AM ESSAM AL-HALIRHA, CHIEF EXECUTIVE OFFICER OF DYKSTRA CORPO- RATION.
THE PLEASURE, SIR...
...IS ENTIRELY MINE.

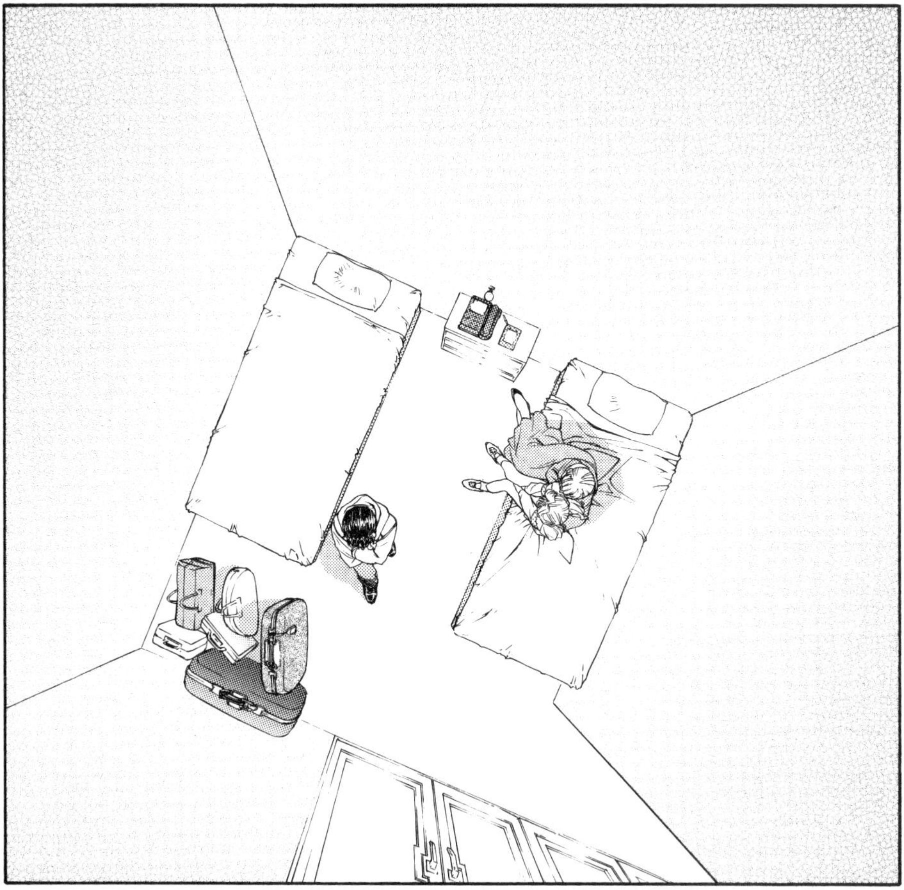

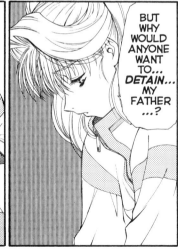

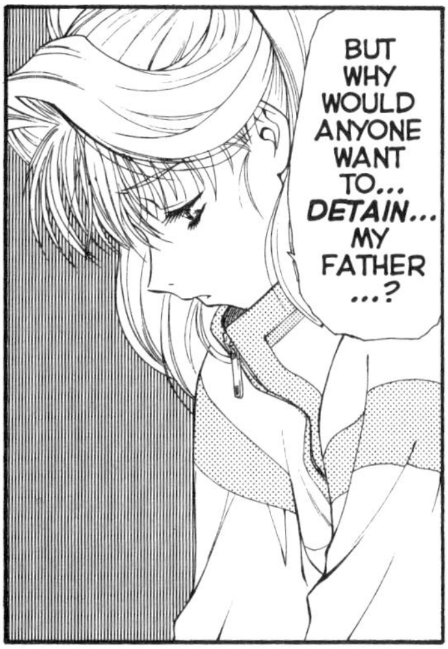
BUT WHY WOULD ANYONE WANT TO... *DETAIN...* MY FATHER ...?

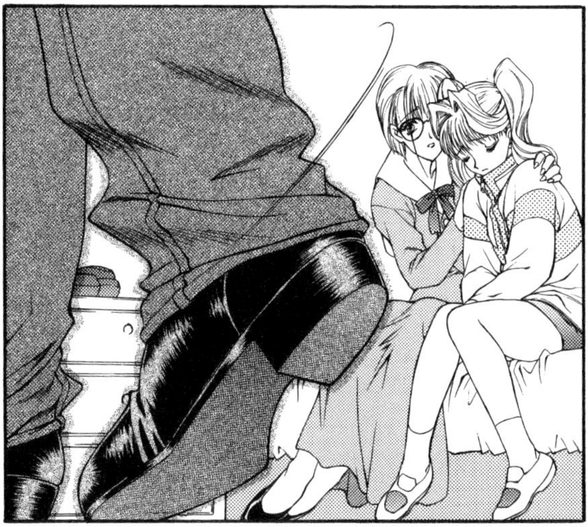

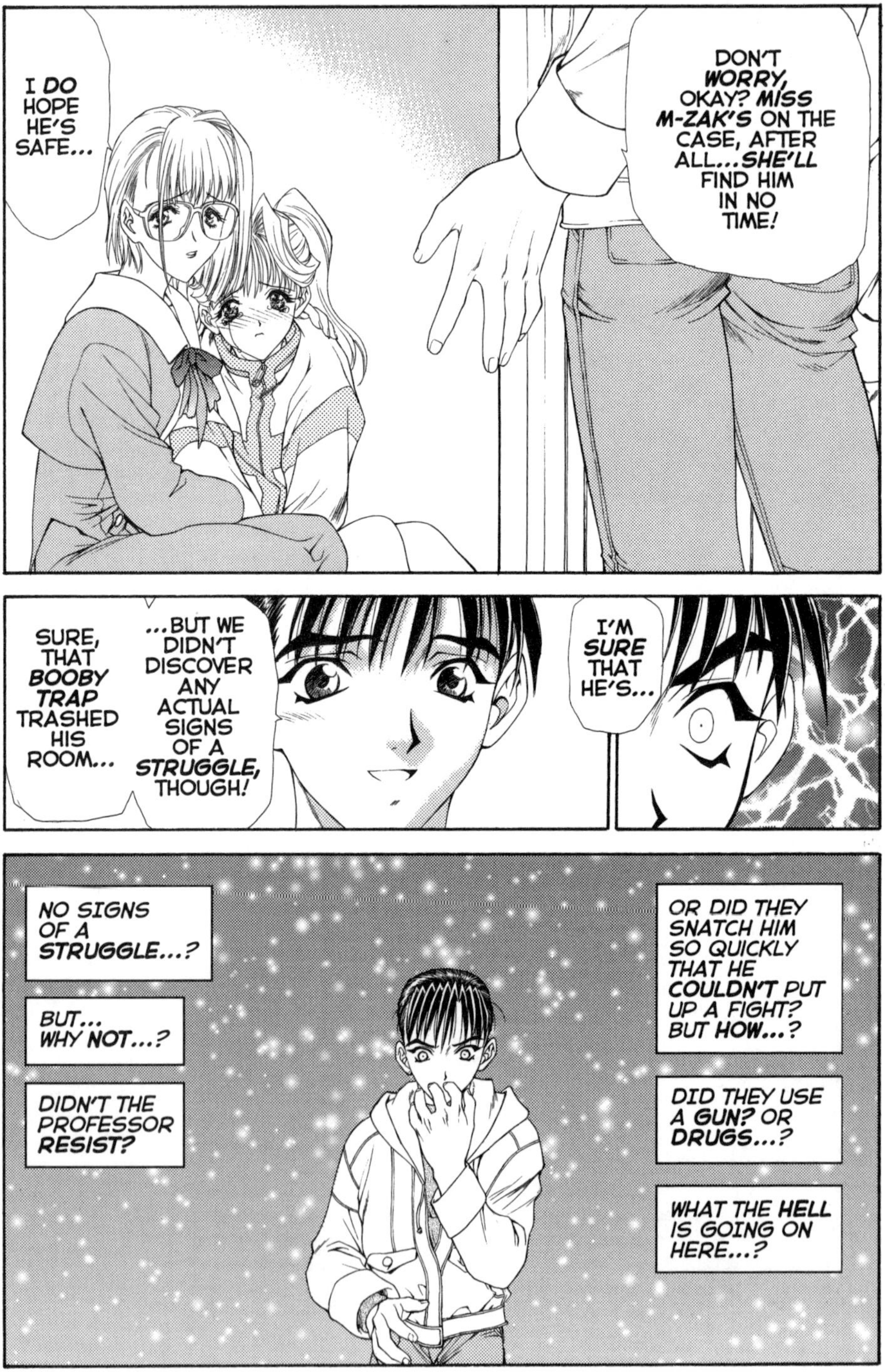
I DO HOPE HE'S SAFE...
DON'T WORRY, OKAY? MISS M-ZAK'S ON THE CASE, AFTER ALL... SHE'LL FIND HIM IN NO TIME!
SURE, THAT BOOBY TRAP TRASHED HIS ROOM...
...BUT WE DIDN'T DISCOVER ANY ACTUAL SIGNS OF A STRUGGLE, THOUGH!
I'M SURE THAT HE'S...
NO SIGNS OF A STRUGGLE...?
BUT... WHY NOT...?
DIDN'T THE PROFESSOR RESIST?
OR DID THEY SNATCH HIM SO QUICKLY THAT HE COULDN'T PUT UP A FIGHT? BUT HOW...?
DID THEY USE A GUN? OR DRUGS...?
WHAT THE HELL IS GOING ON HERE...?

Act 59

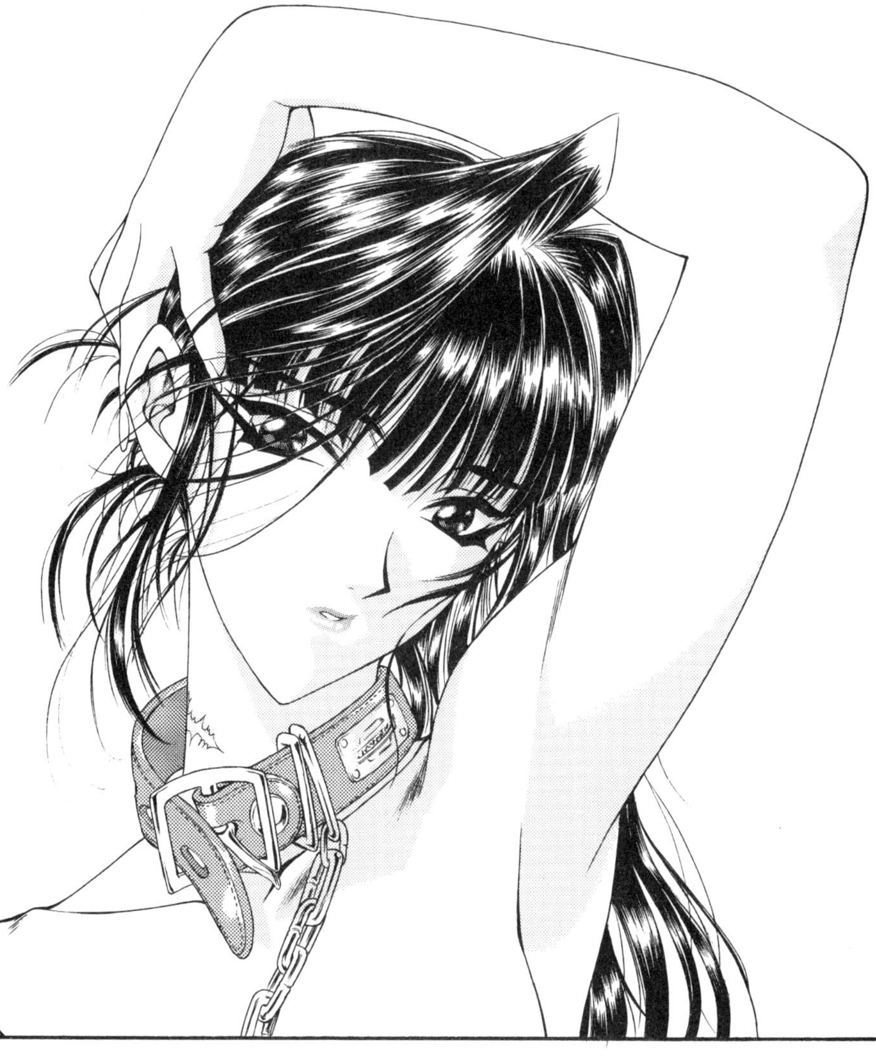

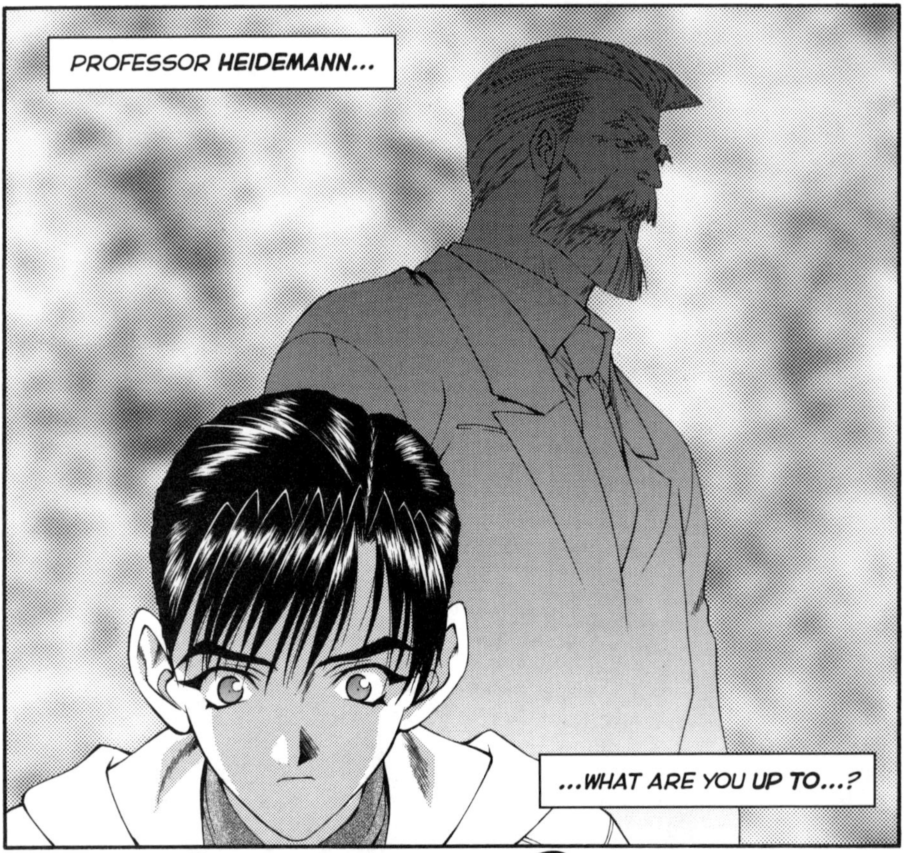
PROFESSOR HEIDEMANN...
...WHAT ARE YOU UP TO...?

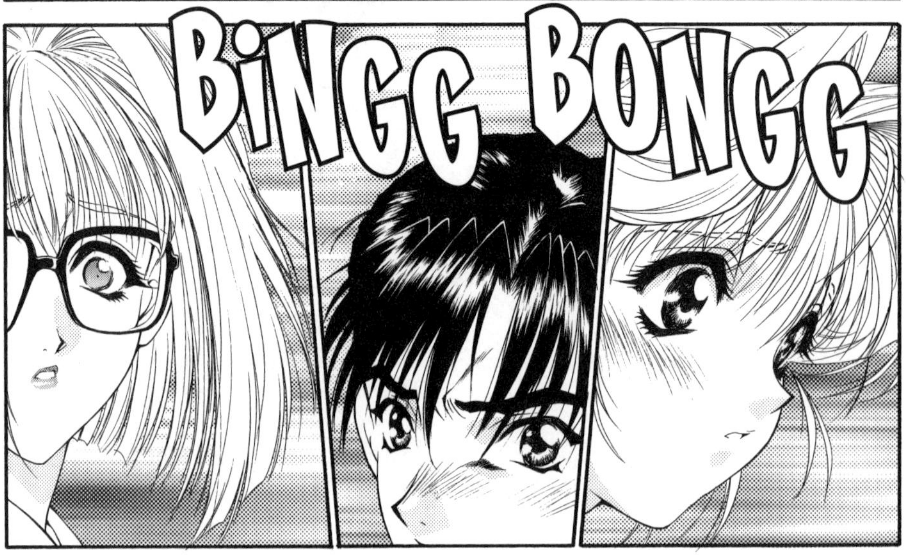
BiNGG BONGG

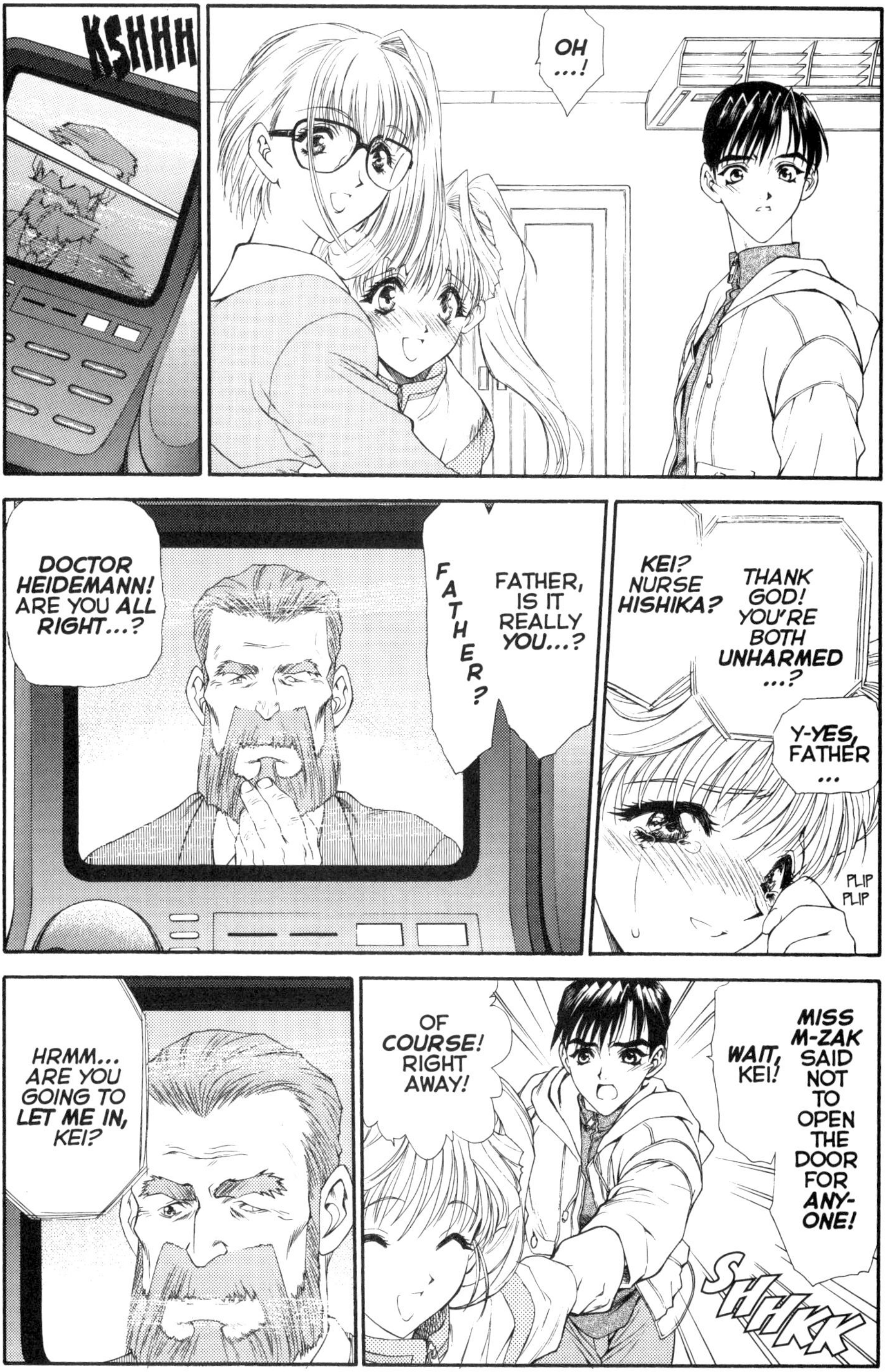
KSHHH
OH ...!
DOCTOR HEIDEMANN! ARE YOU ALL RIGHT...?
FATHER?
FATHER, IS IT REALLY YOU...?
KEI? NURSE HISHIKA?
THANK GOD! YOU'RE BOTH UNHARMED ...?
Y-YES, FATHER ...
PLIP PLIP
HRMM... ARE YOU GOING TO LET ME IN, KEI?
OF COURSE! RIGHT AWAY!
WAIT, KEI!
MISS M-ZAK SAID NOT TO OPEN THE DOOR FOR ANY-ONE!
SHHKK

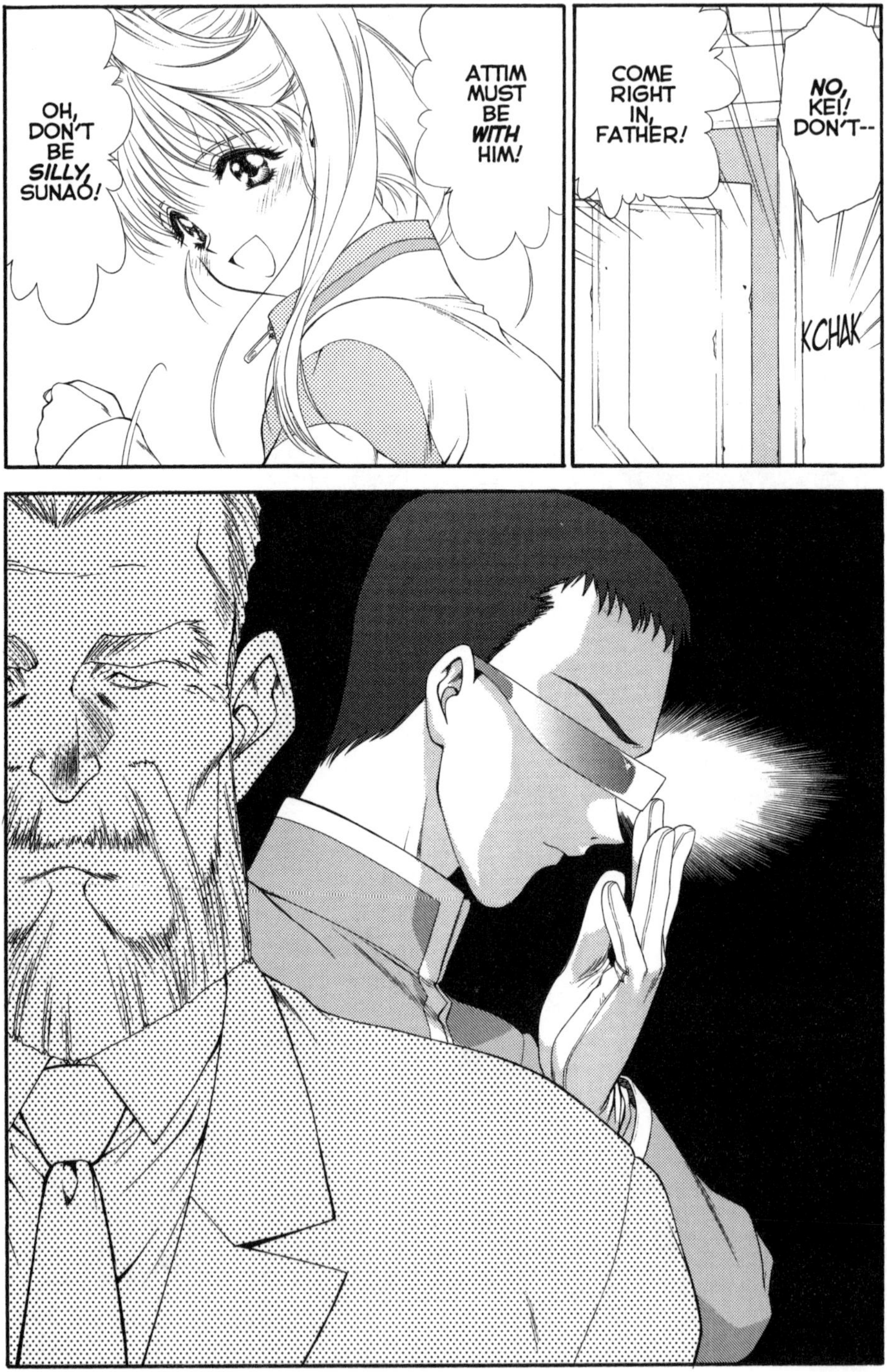
ATTIM MUST BE WITH HIM!
OH, DON'T BE SILLY, SUNAO!
COME RIGHT IN, FATHER!
NO, KEI! DON'T--
KCHAK

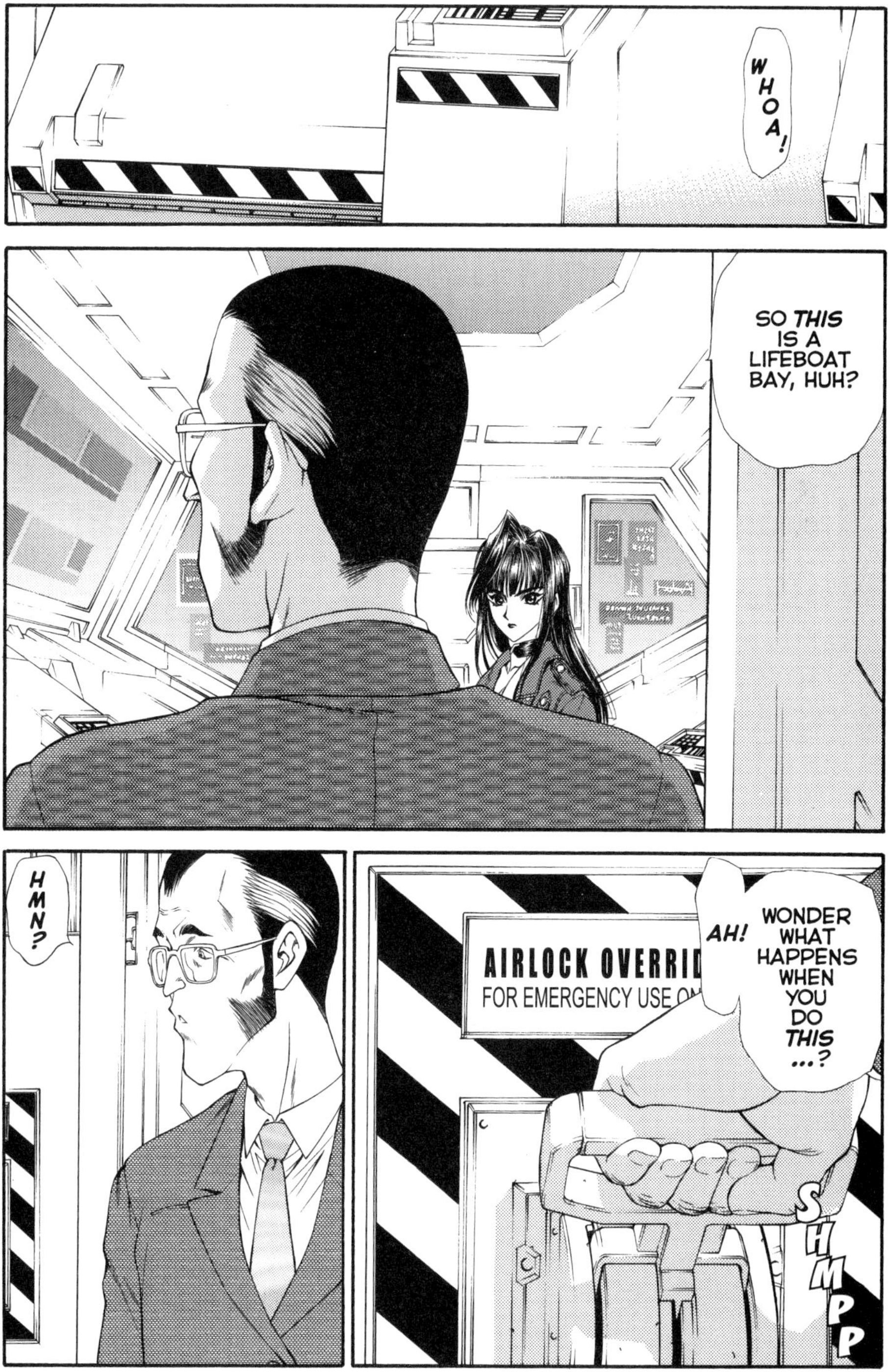
WHOA!
SO THIS IS A LIFEBOAT BAY, HUH?
HMN?
AH!
WONDER WHAT HAPPENS WHEN YOU DO THIS ...?
AIRLOCK OVERRID
FOR EMERGENCY USE ON
SHMPP

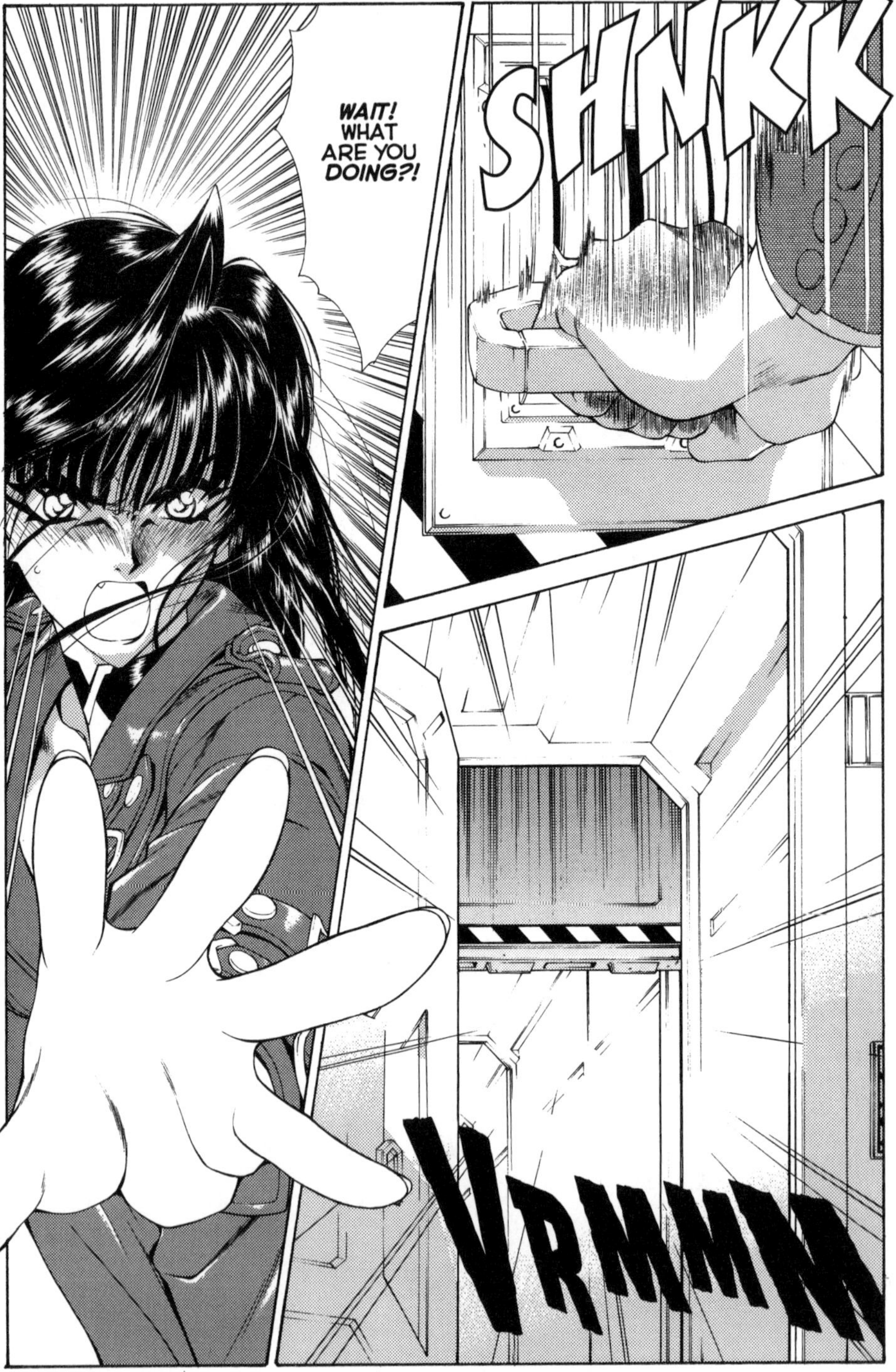
SHNKK
VRMMKK
WAIT! WHAT ARE YOU DOING?!

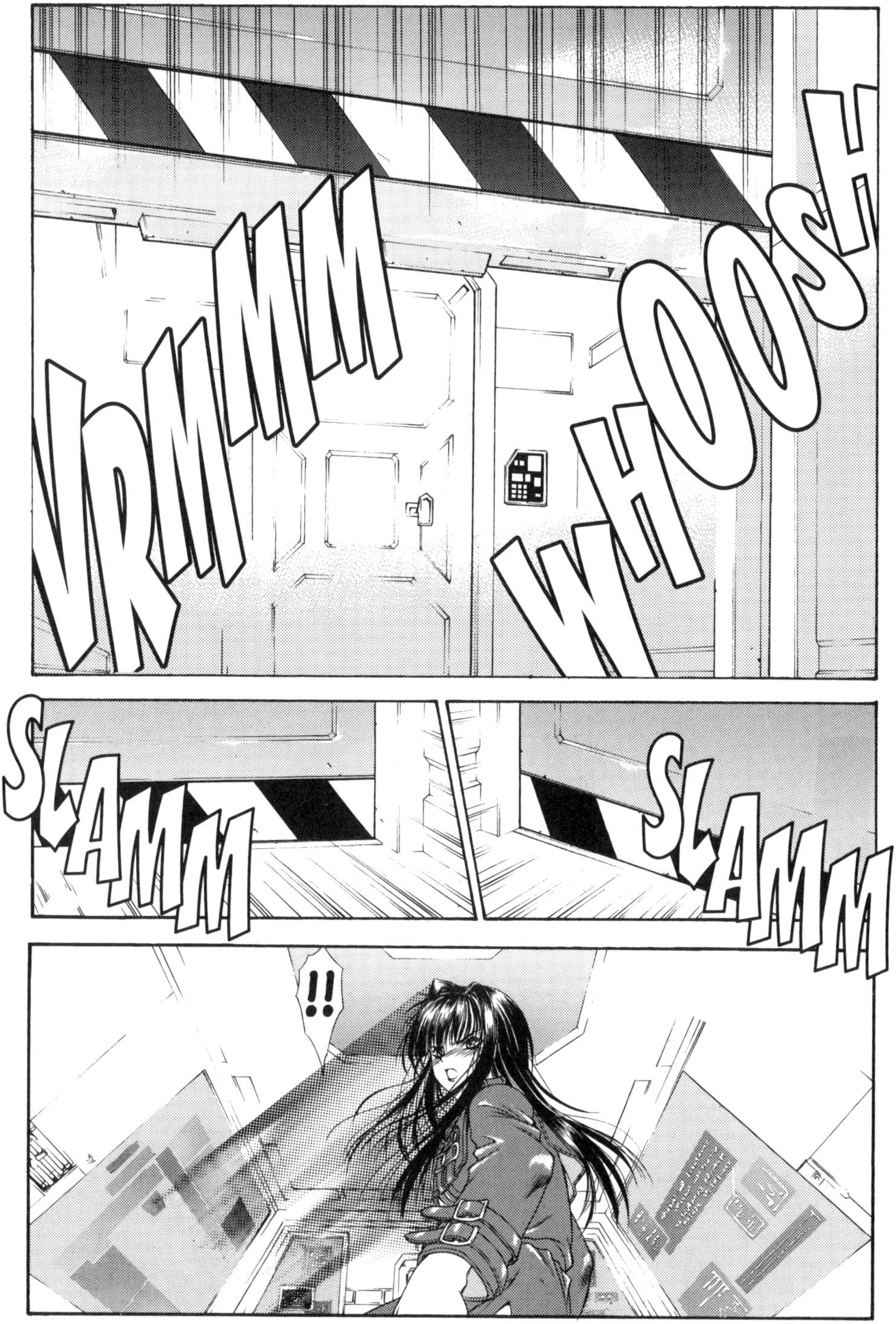
WHOOSH
VRMMMM
SLAMM
SLAMM
!!

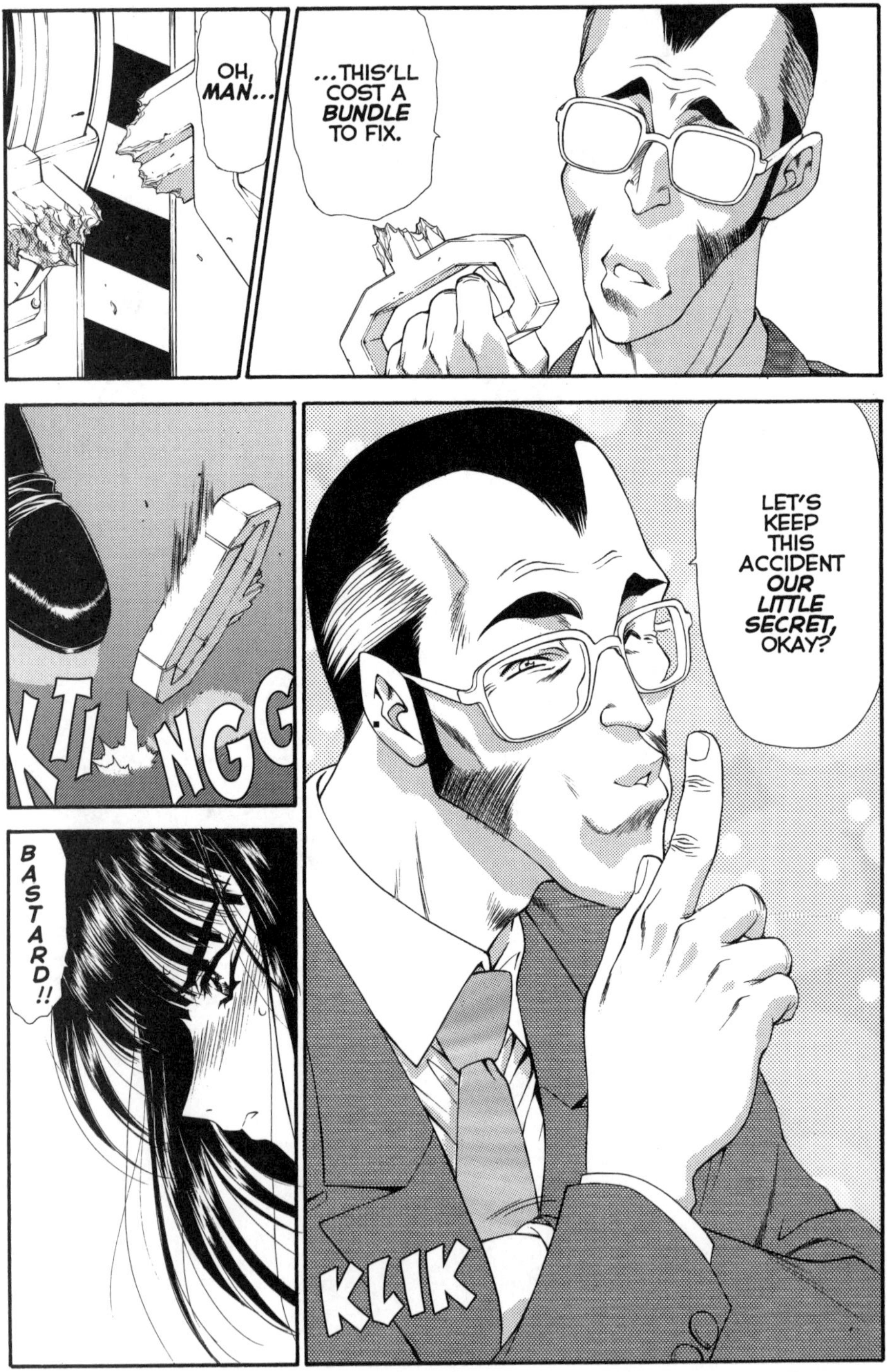
OH, MAN...
...THIS'LL COST A BUNDLE TO FIX.
KTINGG
BASTARD!!
LET'S KEEP THIS ACCIDENT OUR LITTLE SECRET, OKAY?
KLIK

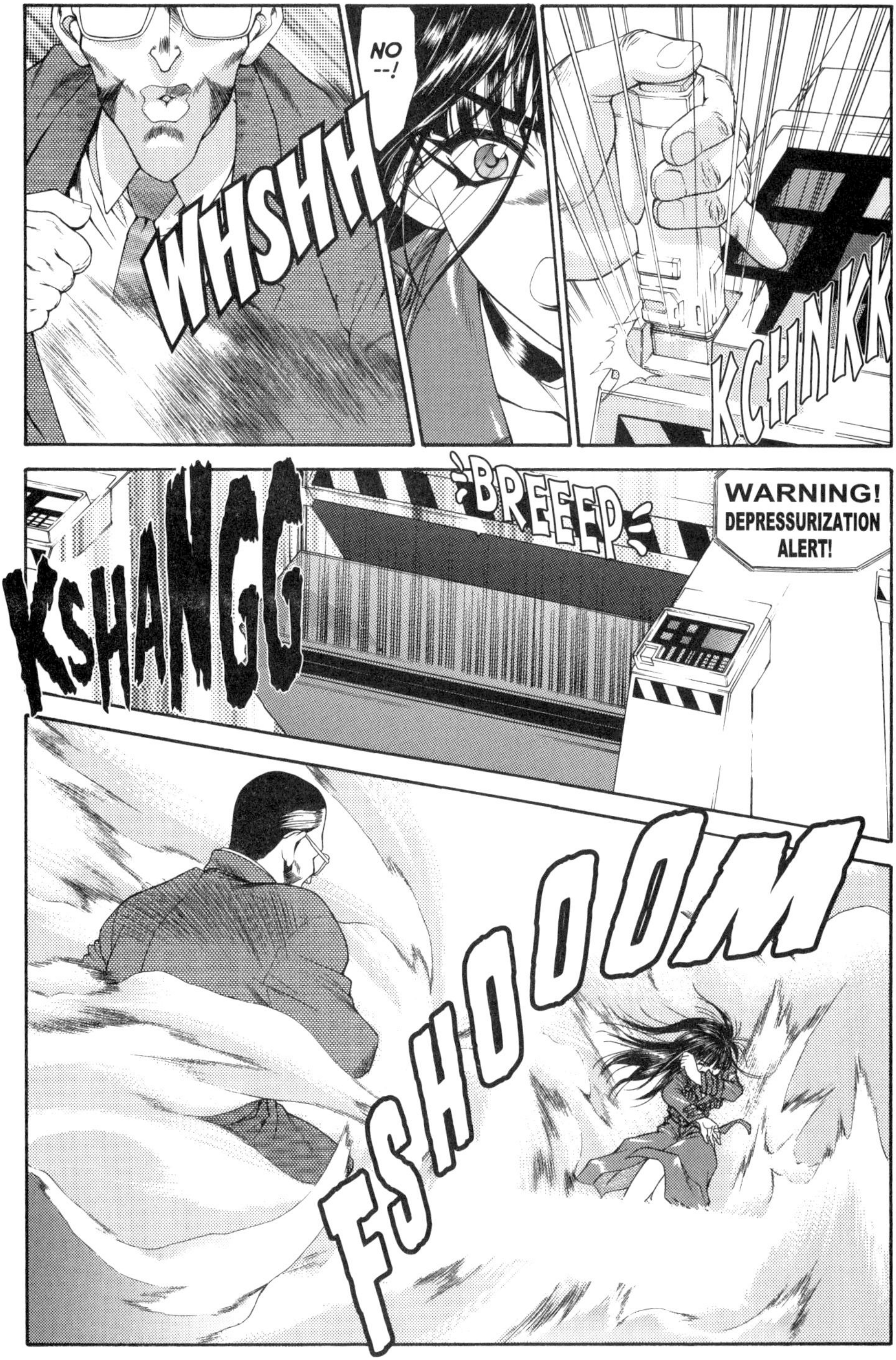
KCHNKK
NO --!
WHSHH
WARNING! DEPRESSURIZATION ALERT!
BREEEP
KSHANGG
FSHOOOM

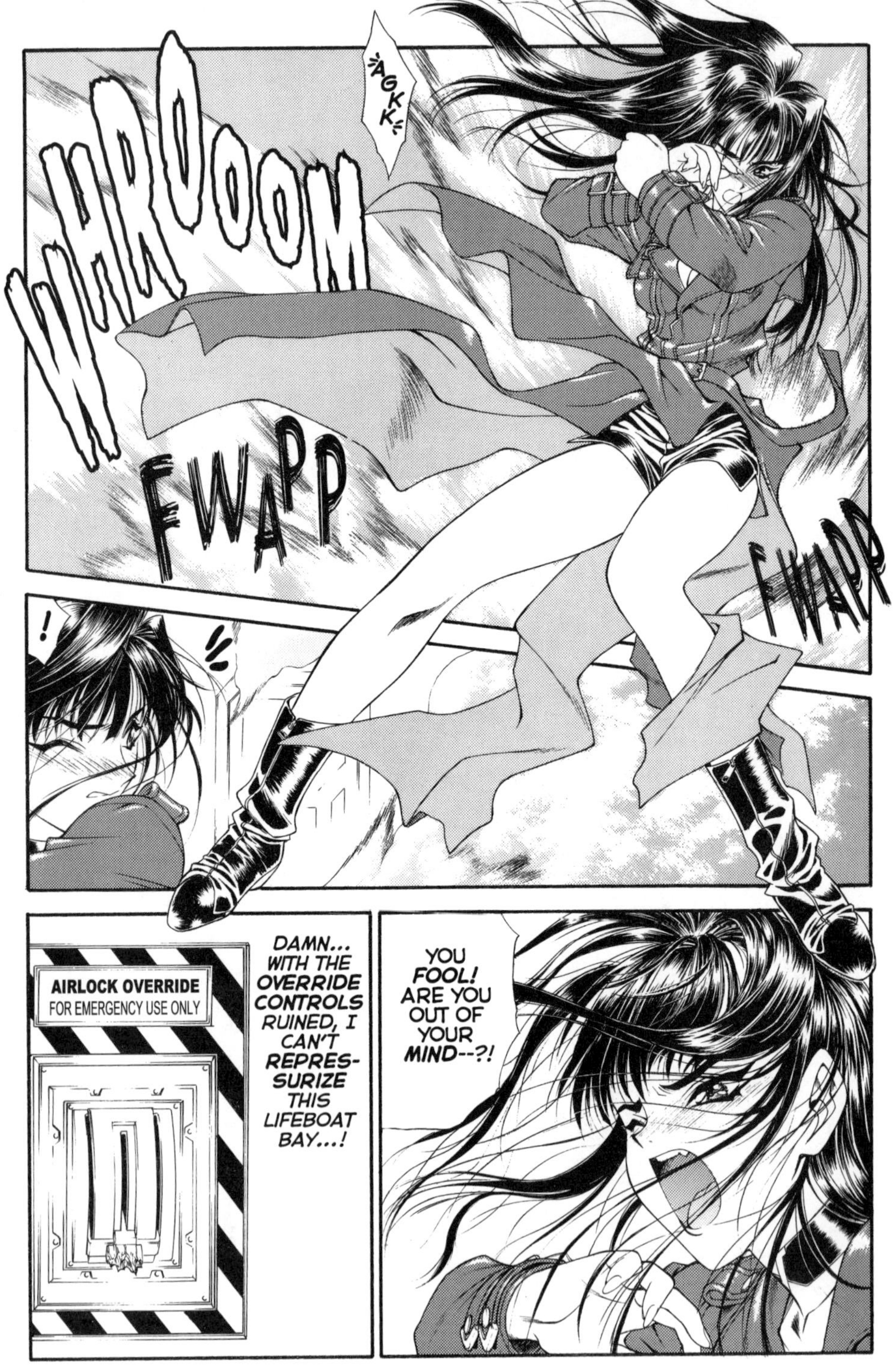

WHROOOM
AGKK
FWAPP
FWAPP
!
!
AIRLOCK OVERRIDE
FOR EMERGENCY USE ONLY
DAMN... WITH THE OVERRIDE CONTROLS RUINED, I CAN'T REPRES-SURIZE THIS LIFEBOAT BAY...!
YOU FOOL! ARE YOU OUT OF YOUR MIND--?!

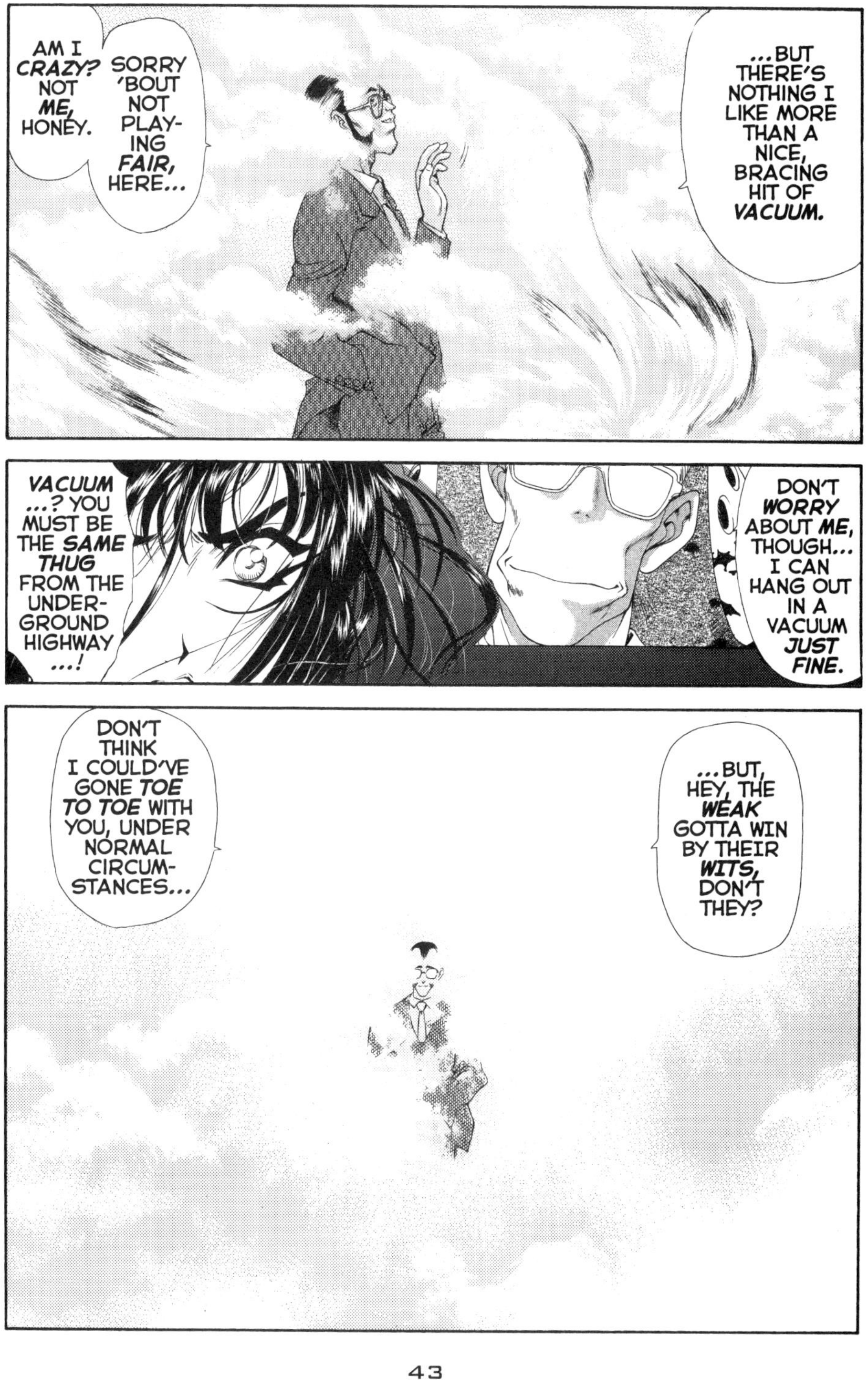
AM I CRAZY? NOT ME, HONEY.
SORRY 'BOUT NOT PLAYING FAIR, HERE...
...BUT THERE'S NOTHING I LIKE MORE THAN A NICE, BRACING HIT OF VACUUM.
VACUUM ...? YOU MUST BE THE SAME THUG FROM THE UNDERGROUND HIGHWAY ...!
DON'T WORRY ABOUT ME, THOUGH... I CAN HANG OUT IN A VACUUM JUST FINE.
DON'T THINK I COULD'VE GONE TOE TO TOE WITH YOU, UNDER NORMAL CIRCUMSTANCES...
...BUT, HEY, THE WEAK GOTTA WIN BY THEIR WITS, DON'T THEY?

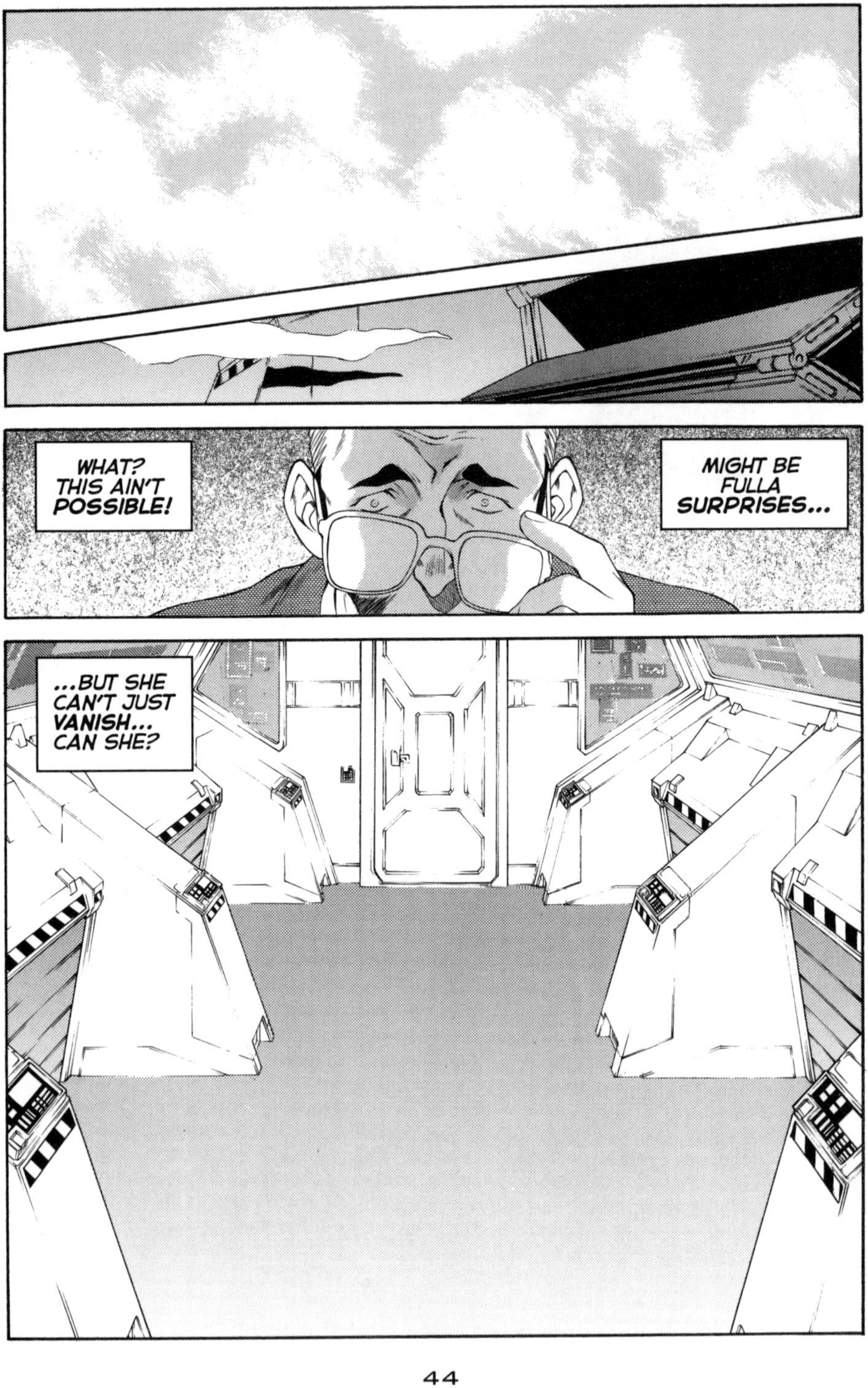
MIGHT BE FULLA SURPRISES...
WHAT? THIS AIN'T POSSIBLE!
...BUT SHE CAN'T JUST VANISH... CAN SHE?

Act 60

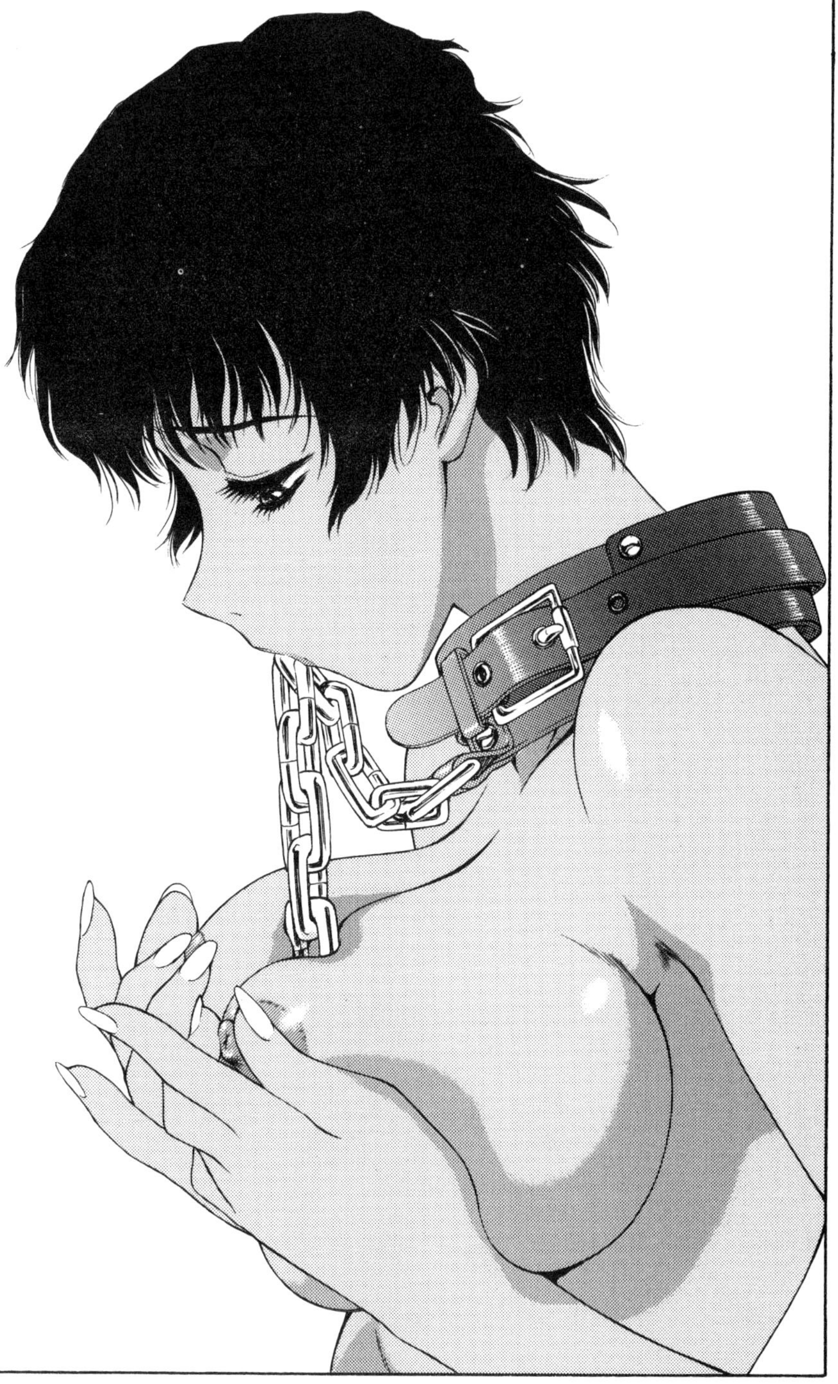

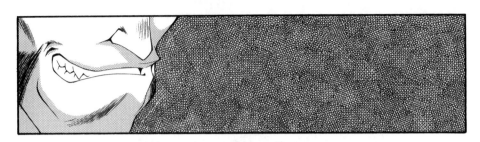

HEY,
HEY...

...SO NOW
WE'RE
PLAYING
HIDE AND
SEEK,
ARE WE?

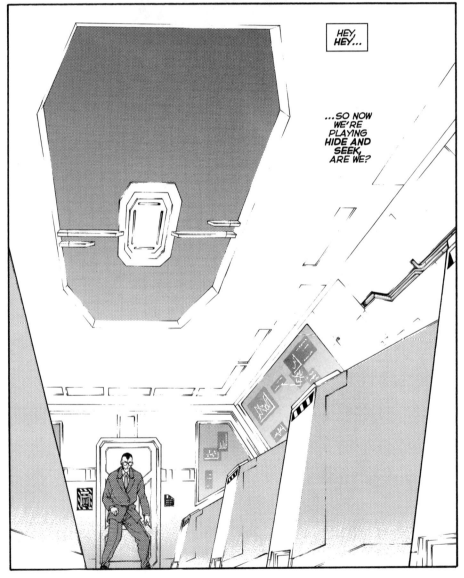

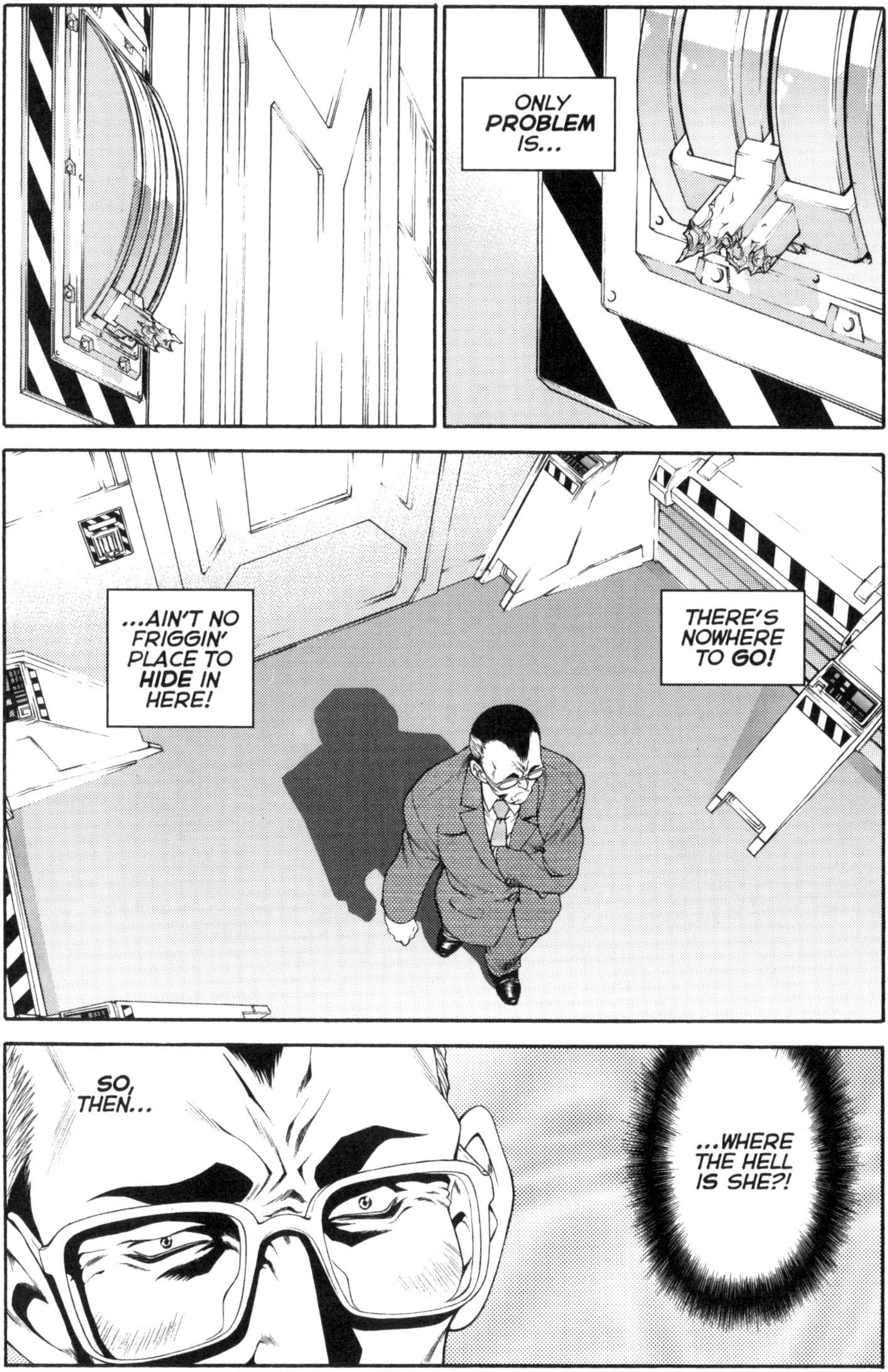
ONLY PROBLEM IS...
...AIN'T NO FRIGGIN' PLACE TO HIDE IN HERE!
THERE'S NOWHERE TO GO!
SO, THEN...
...WHERE THE HELL IS SHE?!

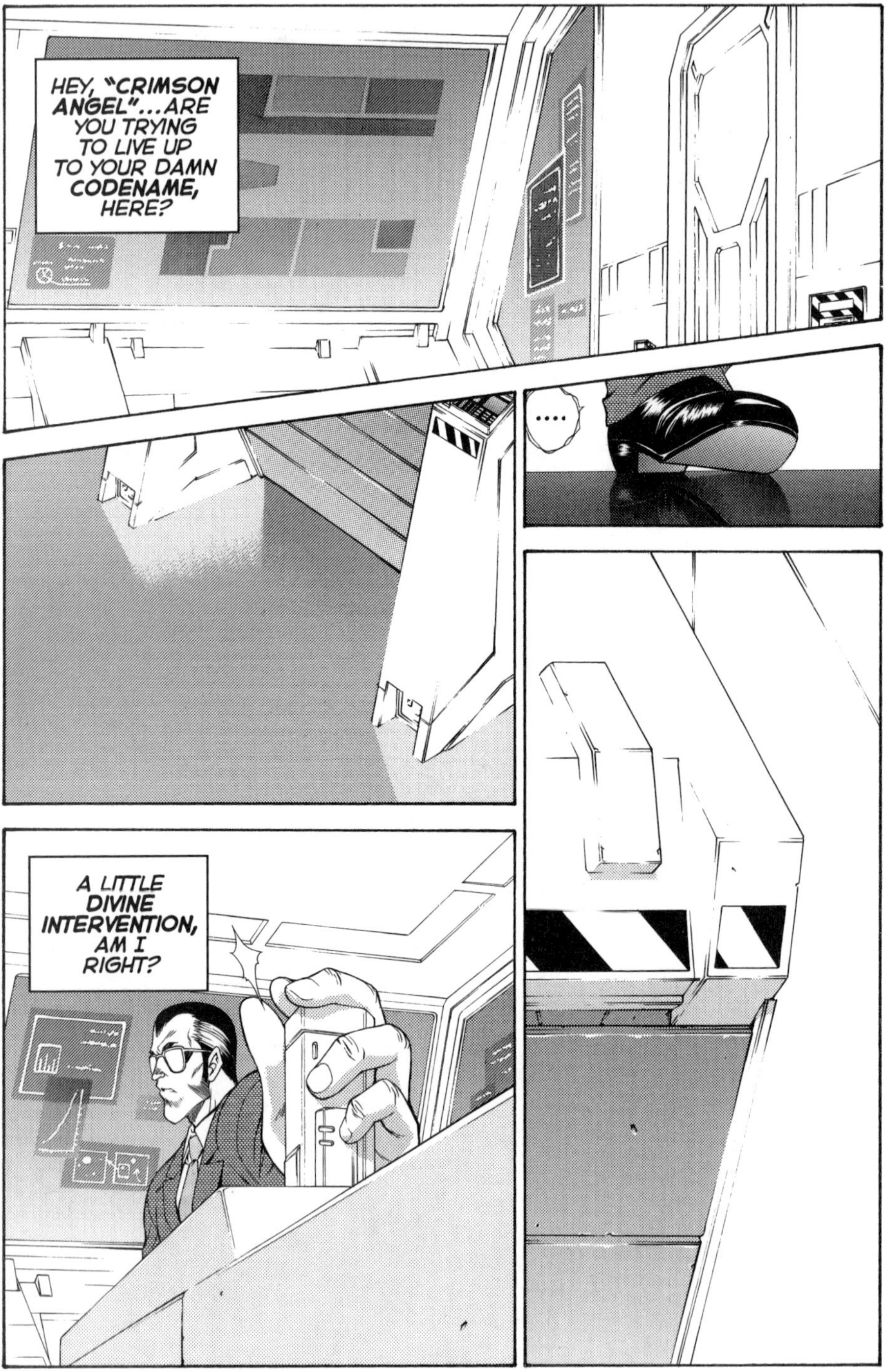
HEY, "CRIMSON ANGEL"...ARE YOU TRYING TO LIVE UP TO YOUR DAMN CODENAME, HERE?
....
A LITTLE DIVINE INTERVENTION, AM I RIGHT?

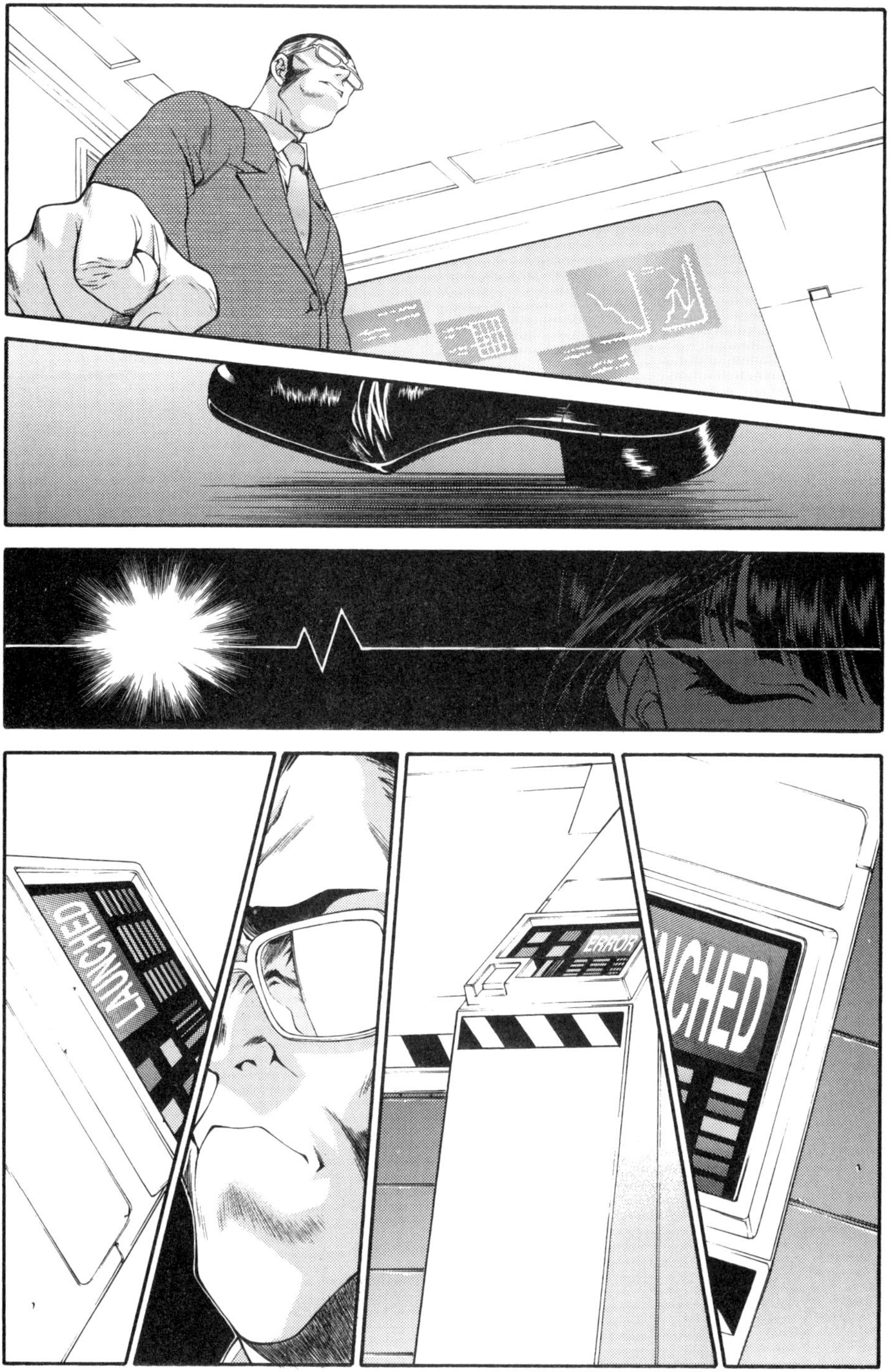
ERROR
LAUNCHED

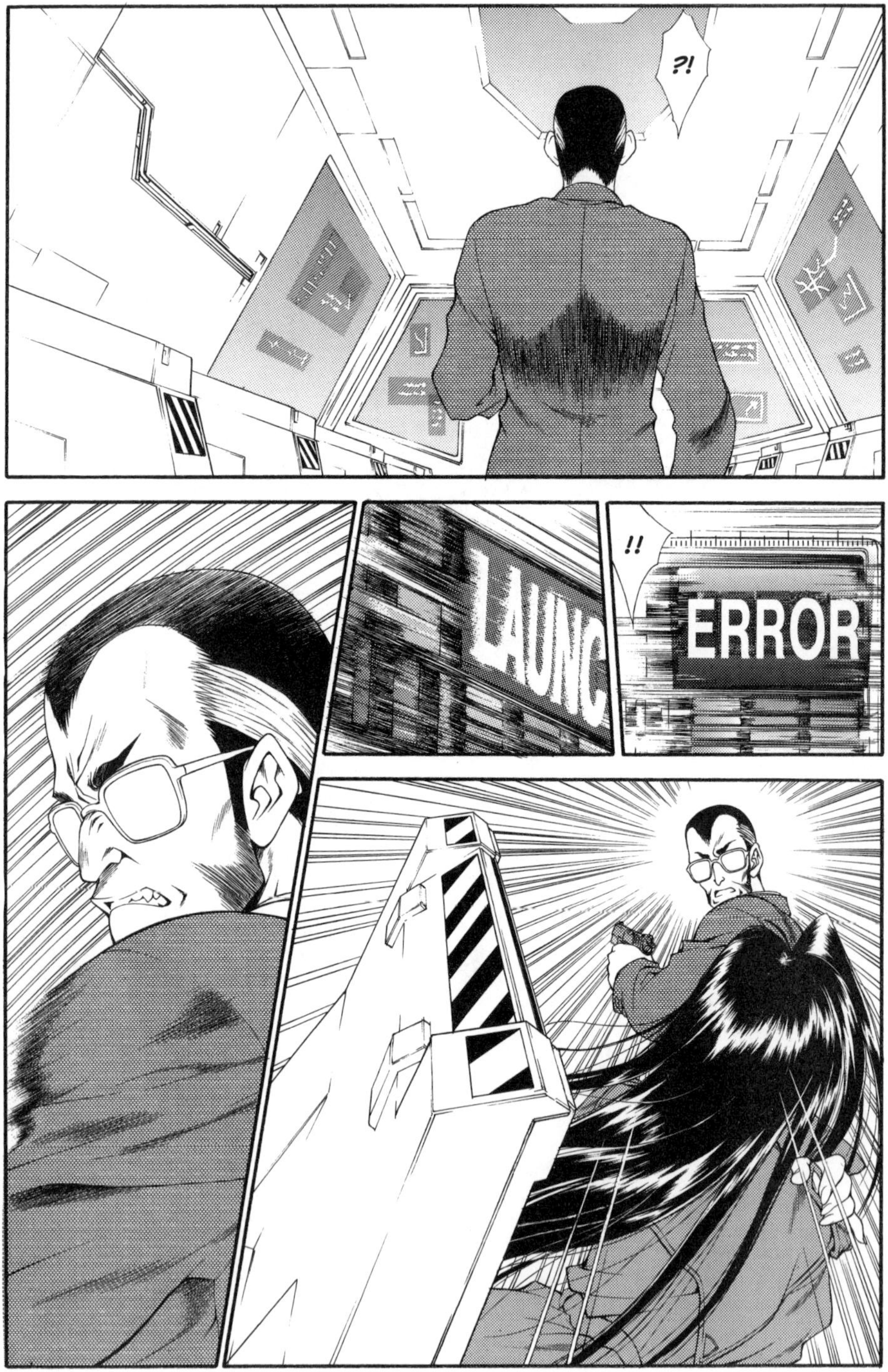
?!
!!
ERROR
LAUNC

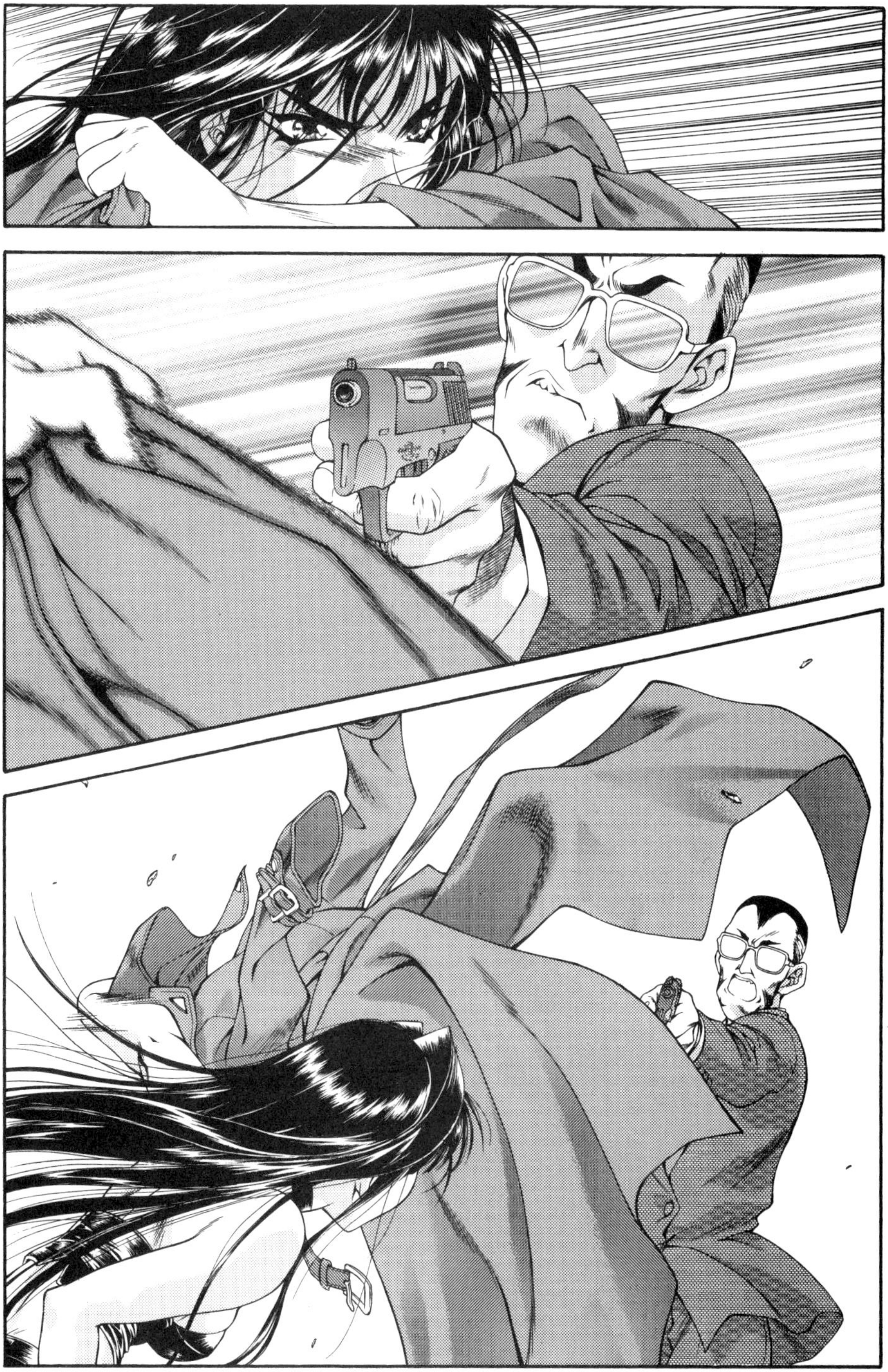

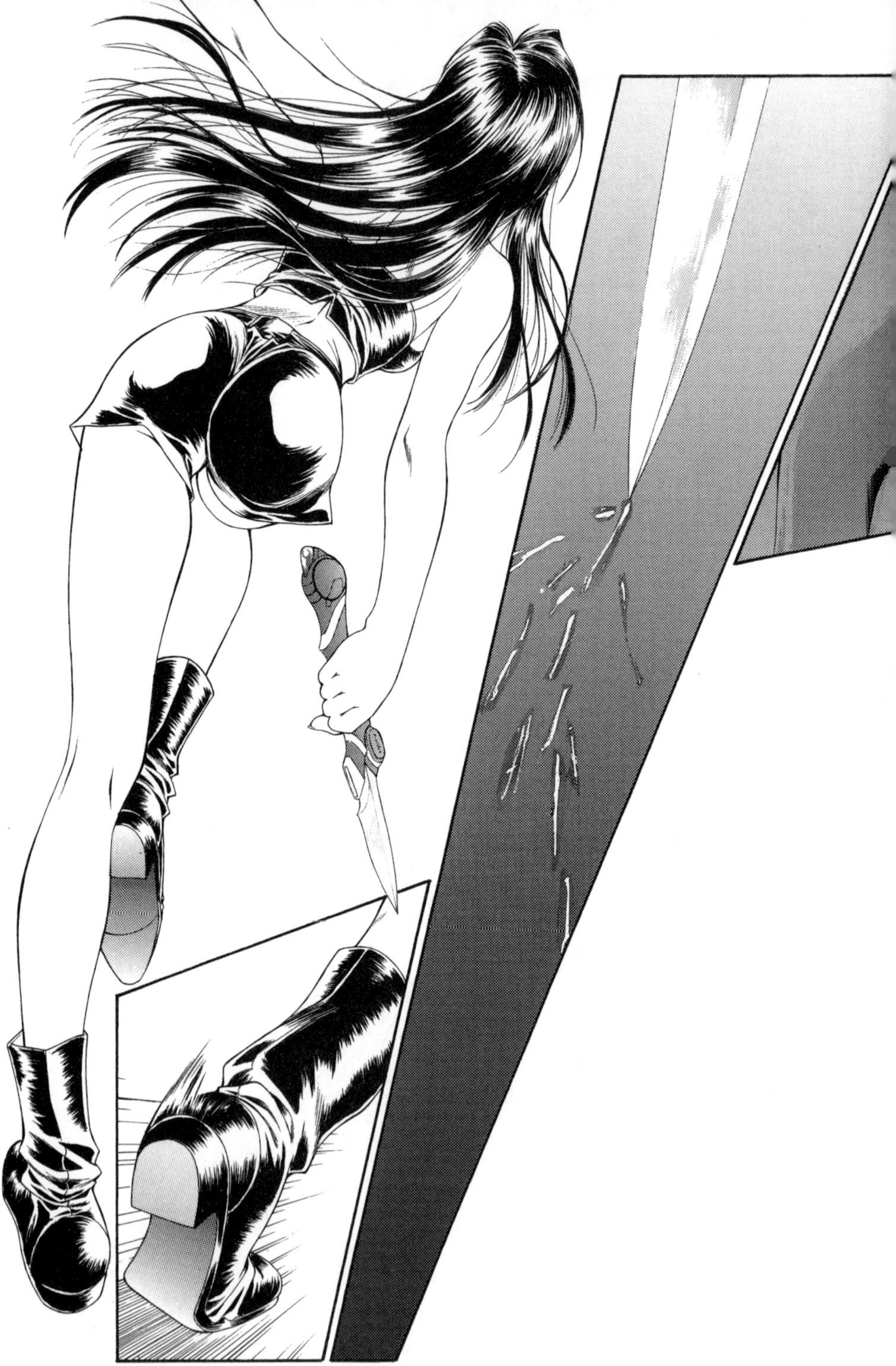

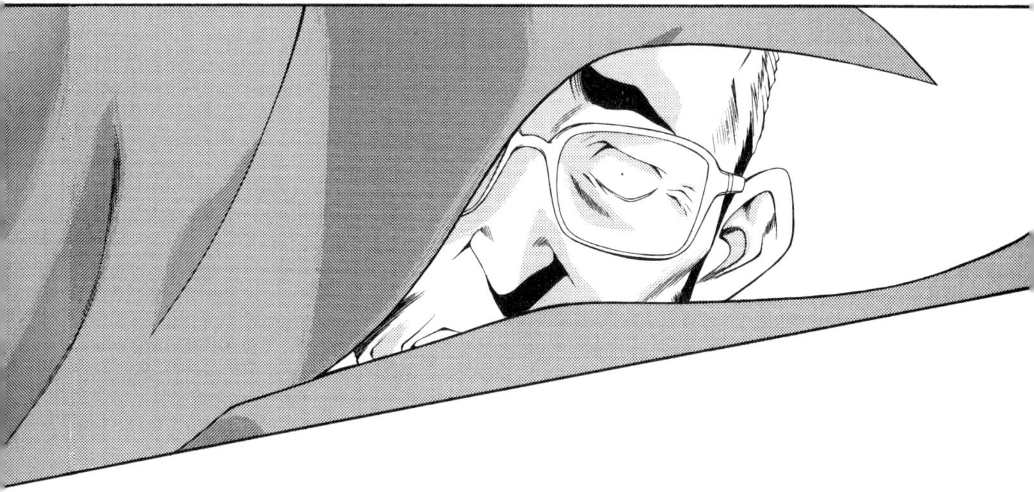

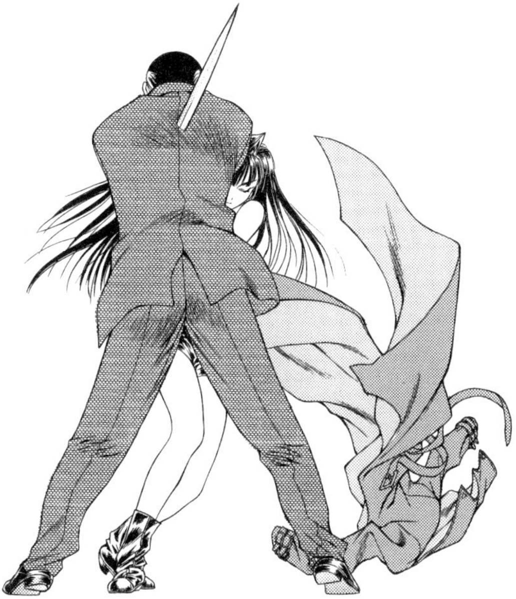

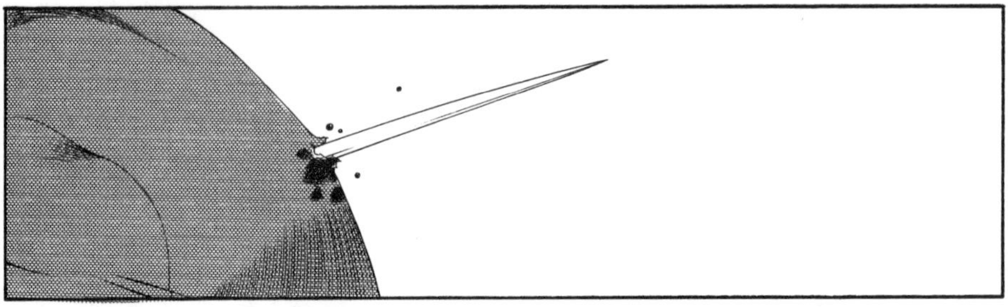

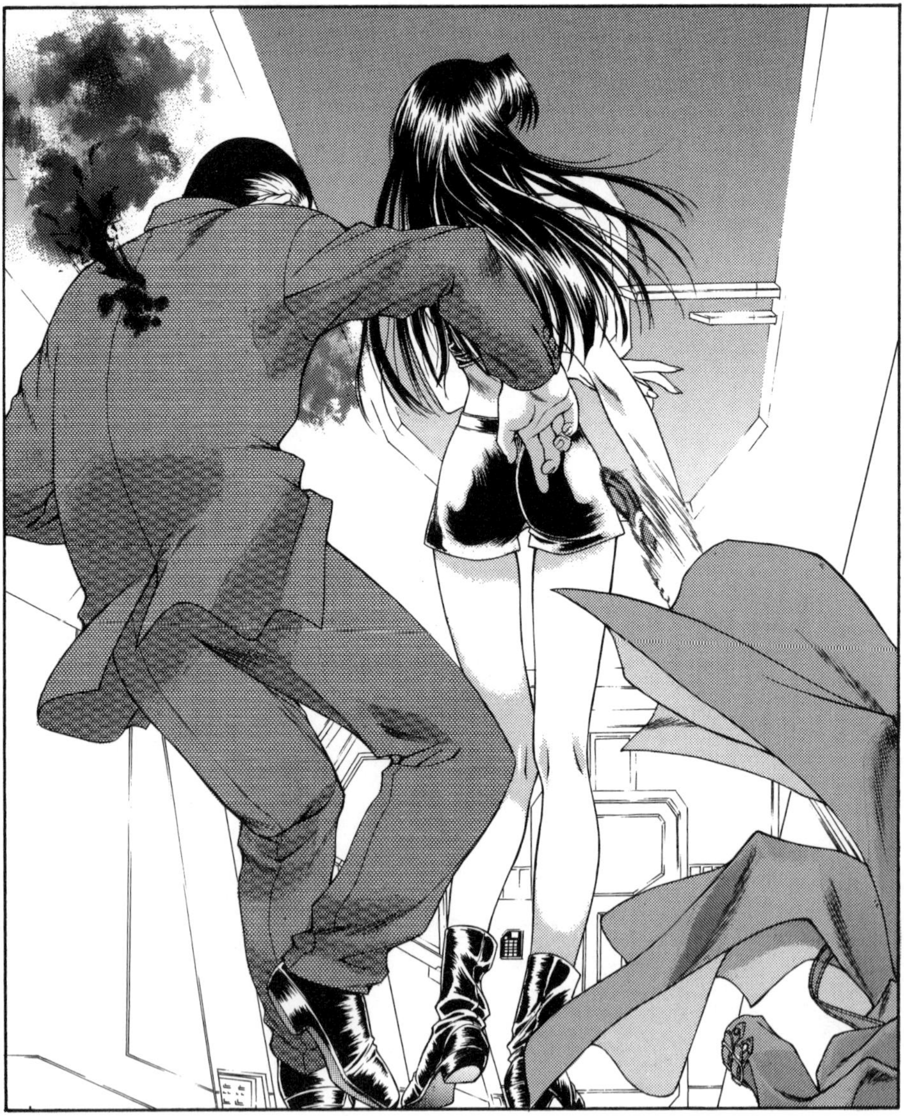

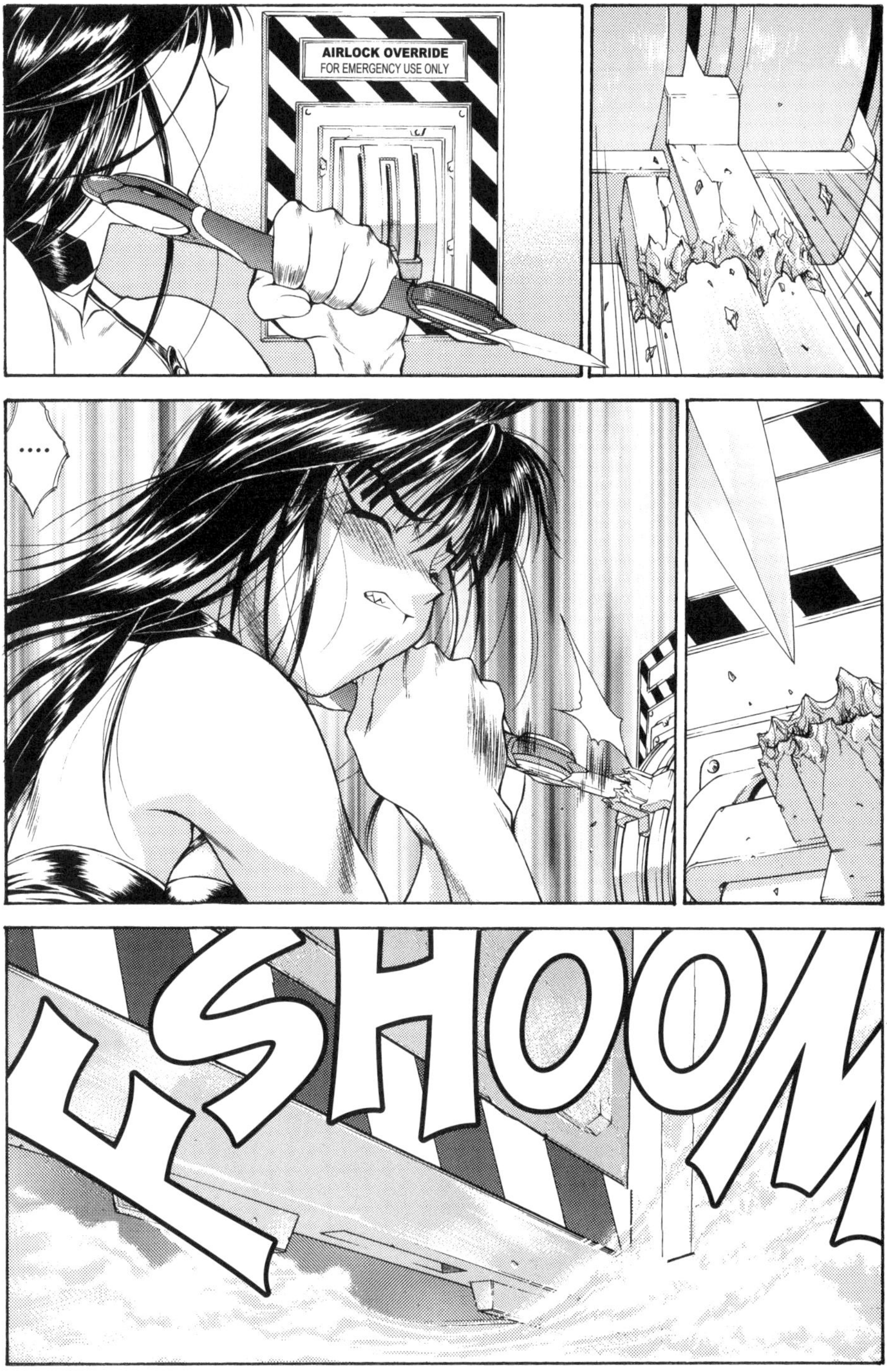
AIRLOCK OVERRIDE
FOR EMERGENCY USE ONLY
....
SHOOM

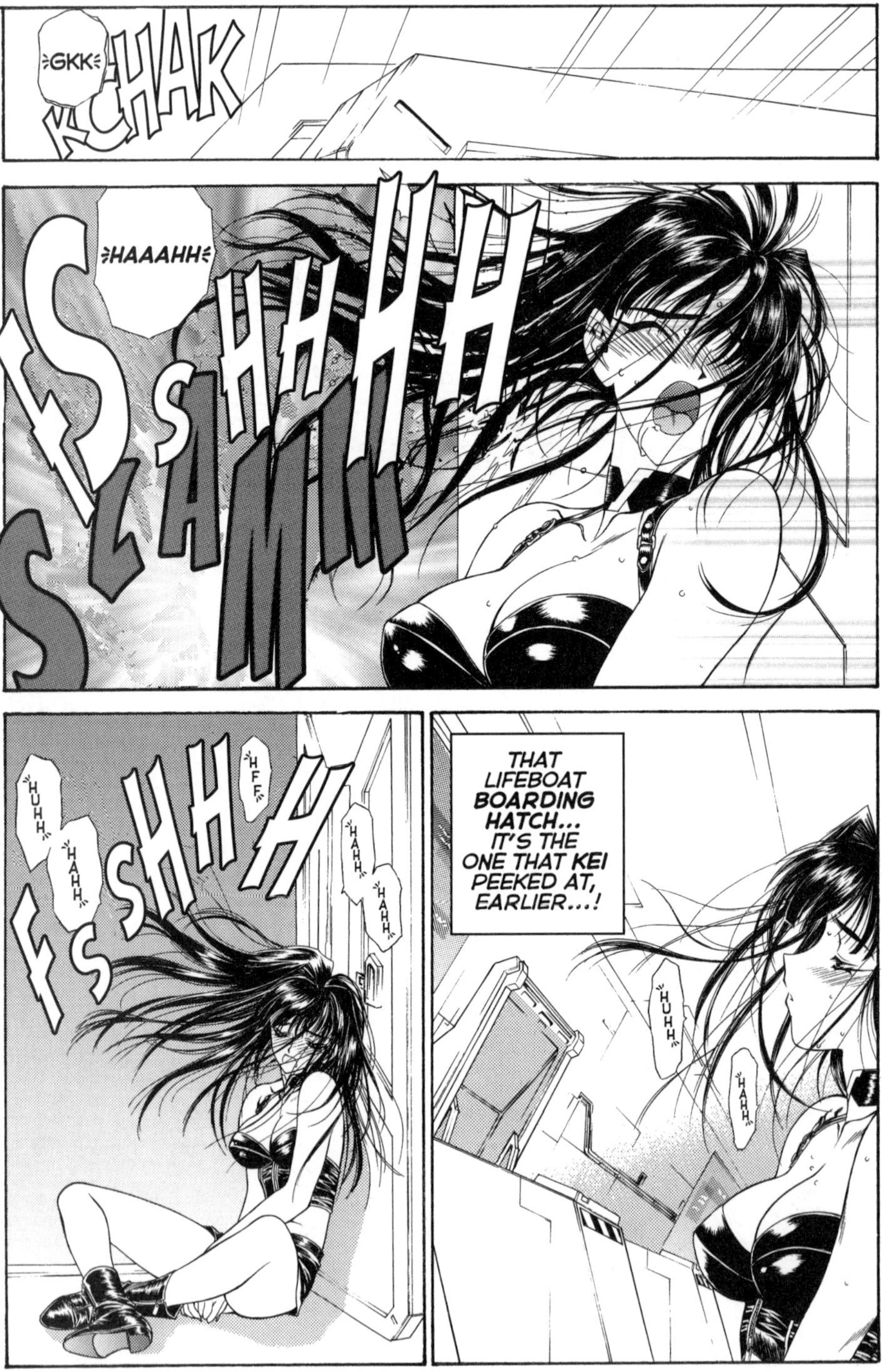
GKK
KCHAK
HAAAHH
FSSHHHHH
SLAMM
THAT LIFEBOAT BOARDING HATCH... IT'S THE ONE THAT KEI PEEKED AT, EARLIER...!
HUHH
HAHH
HFF
HAHH
HAHH
HUHH
HAHH
FSSHHH

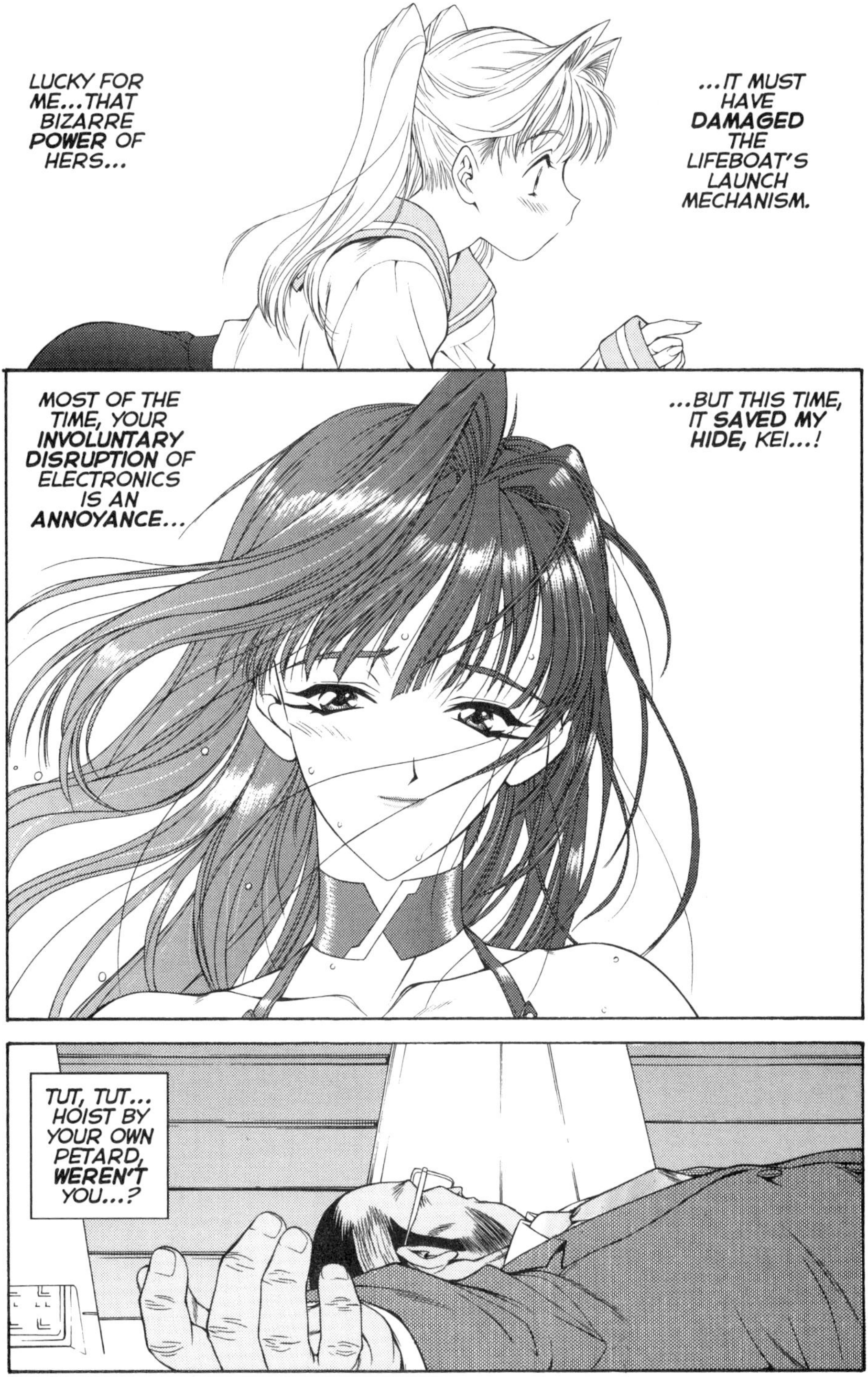
LUCKY FOR ME...THAT BIZARRE **POWER** OF HERS...
...IT MUST HAVE **DAMAGED** THE LIFEBOAT'S LAUNCH MECHANISM.
MOST OF THE TIME, YOUR **INVOLUNTARY DISRUPTION** OF ELECTRONICS IS AN **ANNOYANCE**...
...BUT THIS TIME, IT **SAVED MY HIDE**, KEI...!
TUT, TUT... HOIST BY YOUR OWN PETARD, **WEREN'T** YOU...?

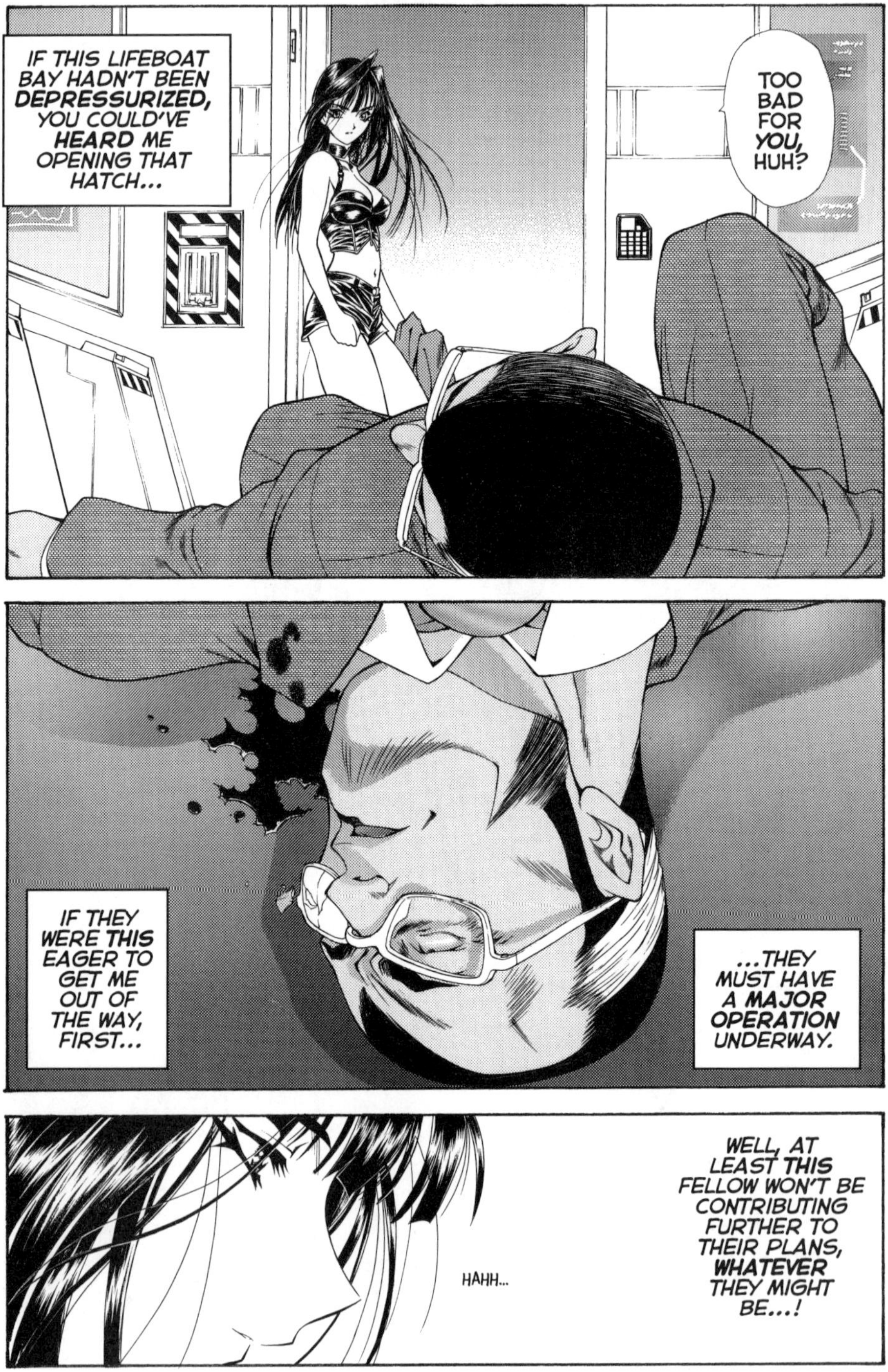
IF THIS LIFEBOAT BAY HADN'T BEEN DEPRESSURIZED, YOU COULD'VE HEARD ME OPENING THAT HATCH...
TOO BAD FOR YOU, HUH?
IF THEY WERE THIS EAGER TO GET ME OUT OF THE WAY, FIRST...
...THEY MUST HAVE A MAJOR OPERATION UNDERWAY.
HAHH...
WELL, AT LEAST THIS FELLOW WON'T BE CONTRIBUTING FURTHER TO THEIR PLANS, WHATEVER THEY MIGHT BE...!

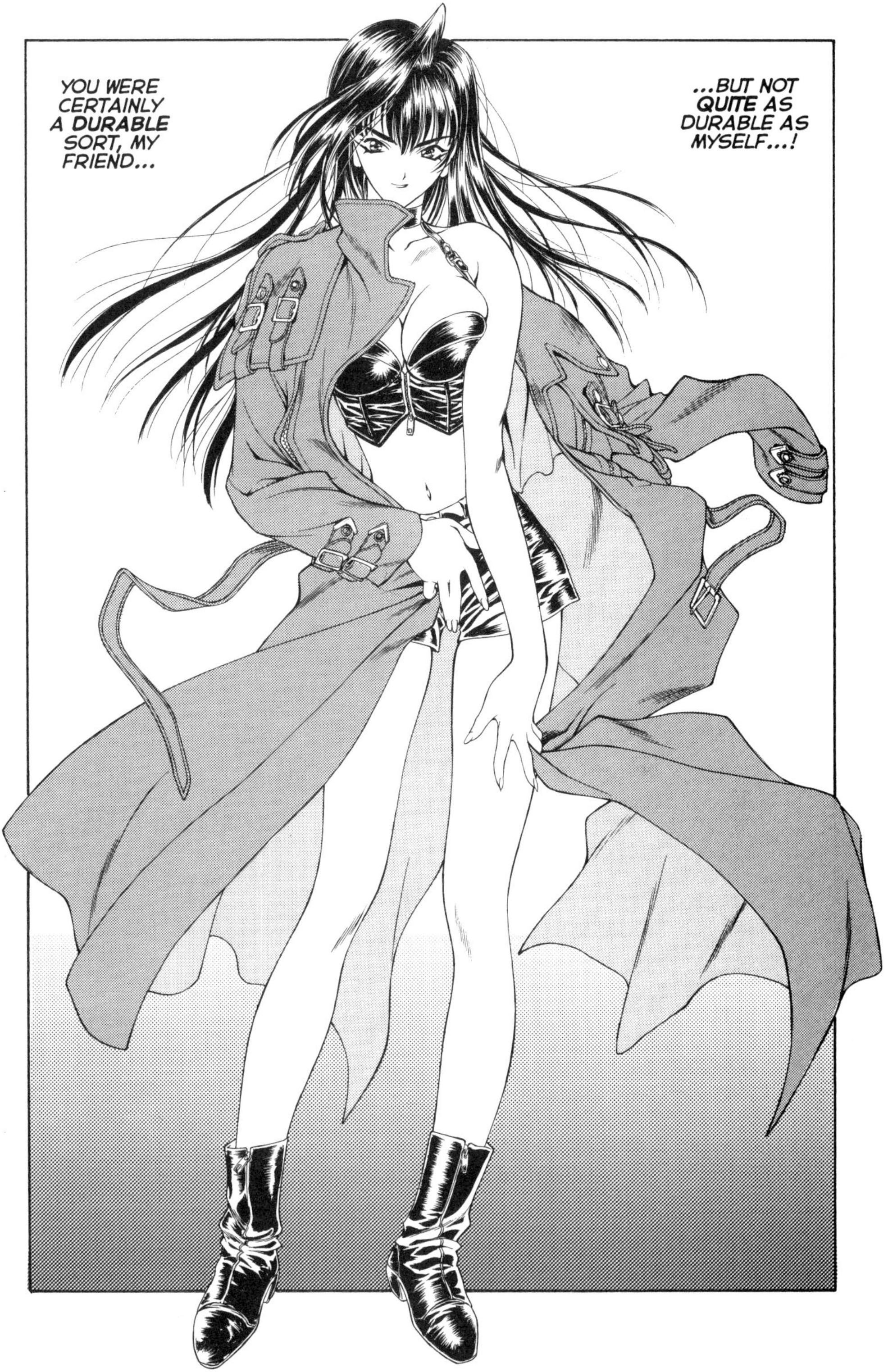
...BUT NOT QUITE AS DURABLE AS MYSELF...!
YOU WERE CERTAINLY A DURABLE SORT, MY FRIEND...

KLAK
KLAK
KLAK
......

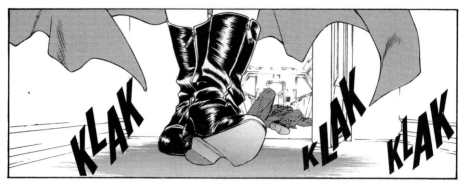

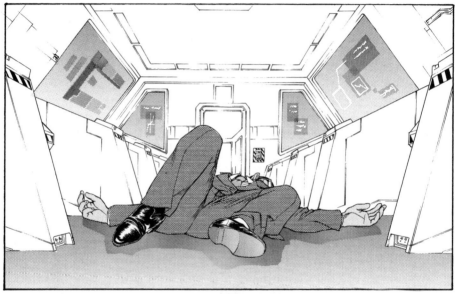

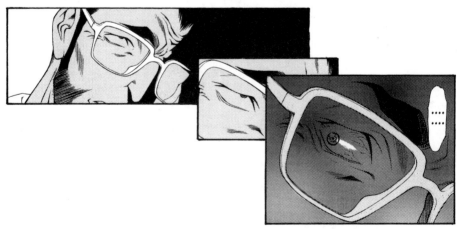

ACT 61

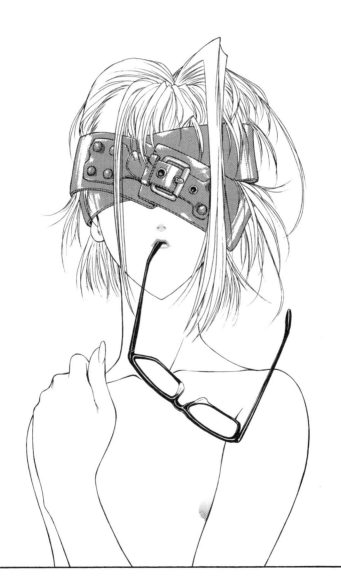

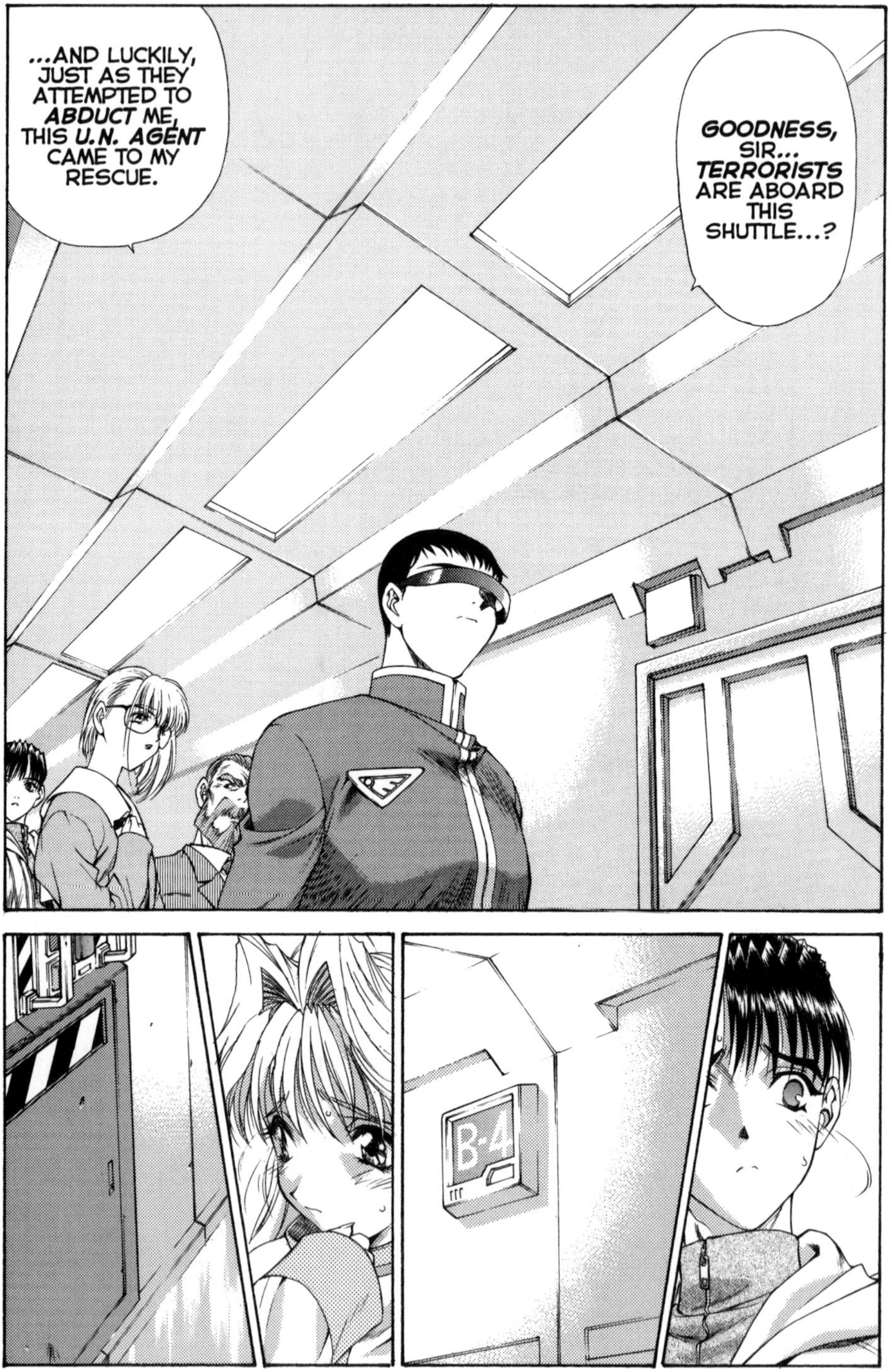
GOODNESS, SIR... TERRORISTS ARE ABOARD THIS SHUTTLE...?
...AND LUCKILY, JUST AS THEY ATTEMPTED TO ABDUCT ME, THIS U.N. AGENT CAME TO MY RESCUE.
B-4

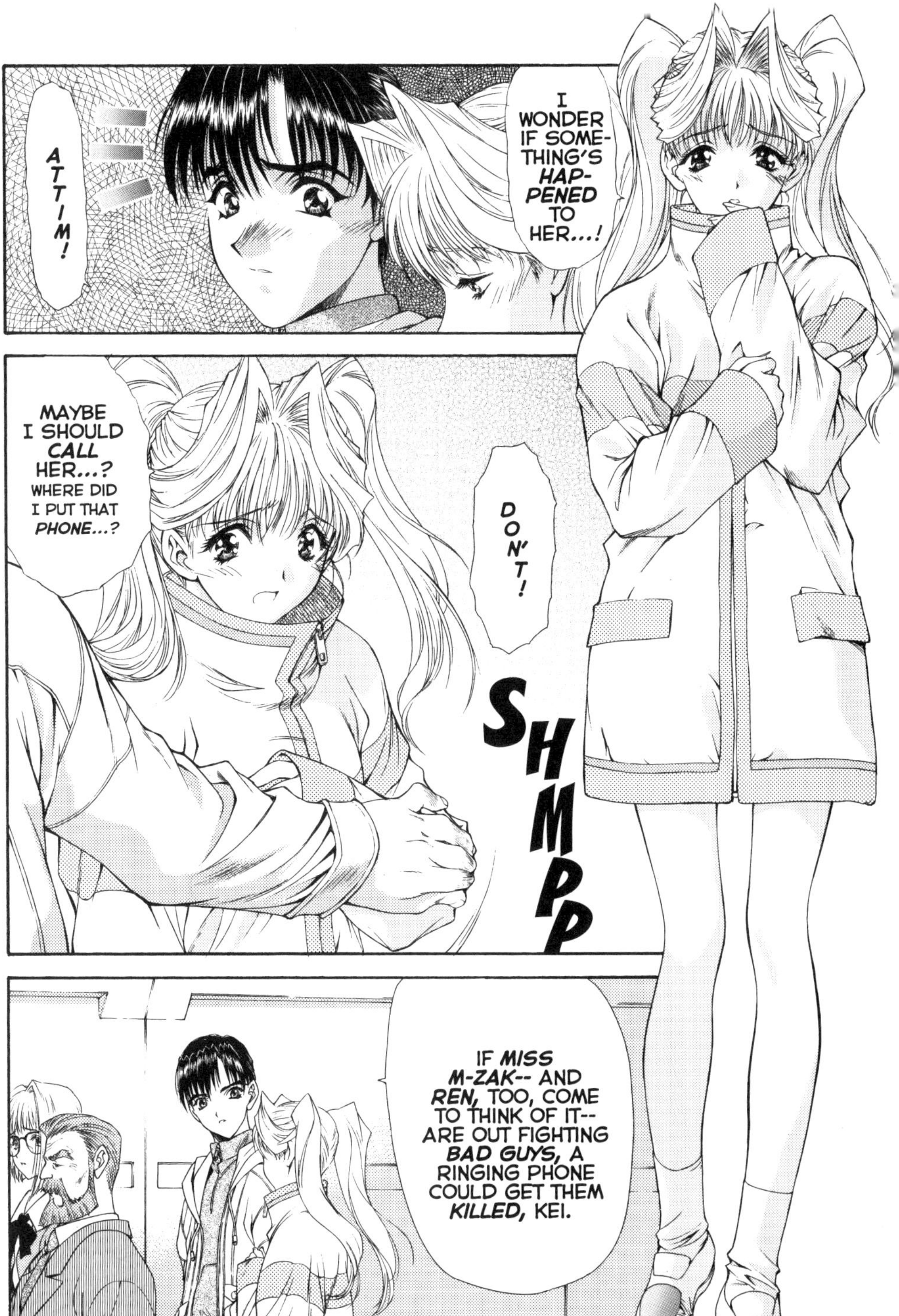
ATTIM!
I WONDER IF SOMETHING'S *HAPPENED* TO HER...!
MAYBE I SHOULD *CALL* HER...? WHERE DID I PUT THAT *PHONE*...?
DON'T!
SHMPP
IF *MISS M-ZAK*-- AND *REN,* TOO, COME TO THINK OF IT-- ARE OUT FIGHTING *BAD GUYS,* A RINGING PHONE COULD GET THEM *KILLED,* KEI.

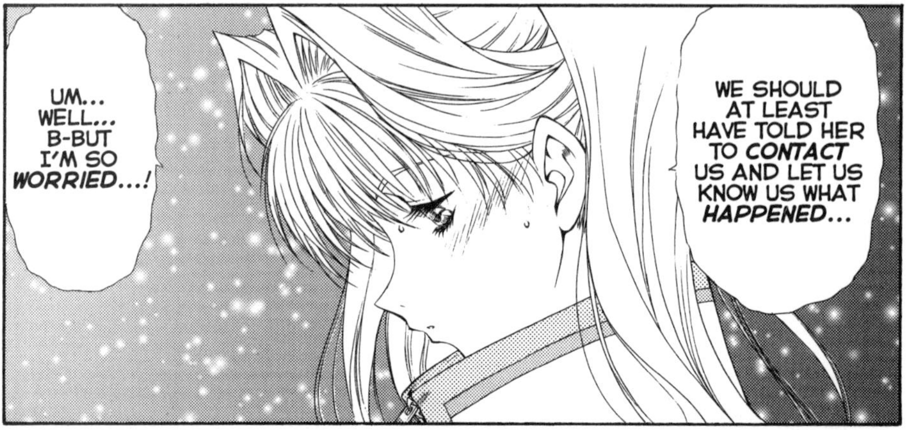
UM... WELL... B-BUT I'M SO WORRIED...!
WE SHOULD AT LEAST HAVE TOLD HER TO CONTACT US AND LET US KNOW US WHAT HAPPENED...

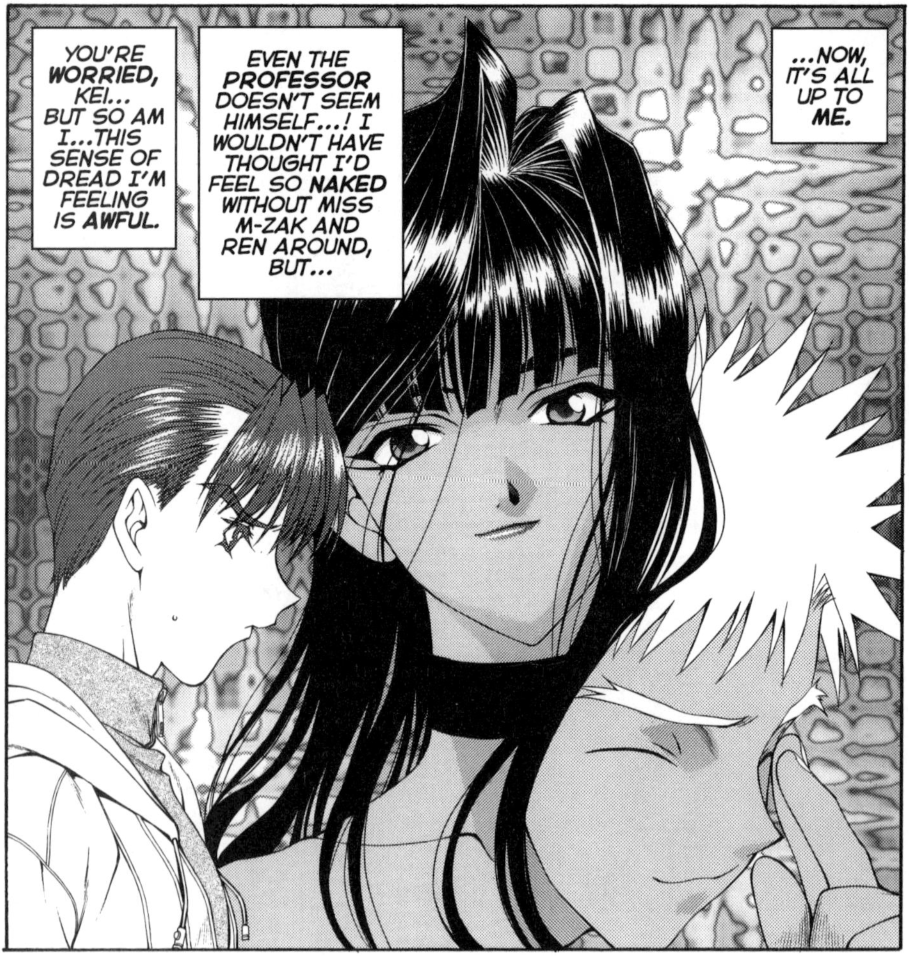
YOU'RE WORRIED, KEI... BUT SO AM I...THIS SENSE OF DREAD I'M FEELING IS AWFUL.
EVEN THE PROFESSOR DOESN'T SEEM HIMSELF...! I WOULDN'T HAVE THOUGHT I'D FEEL SO NAKED WITHOUT MISS M-ZAK AND REN AROUND, BUT...
...NOW, IT'S ALL UP TO ME.

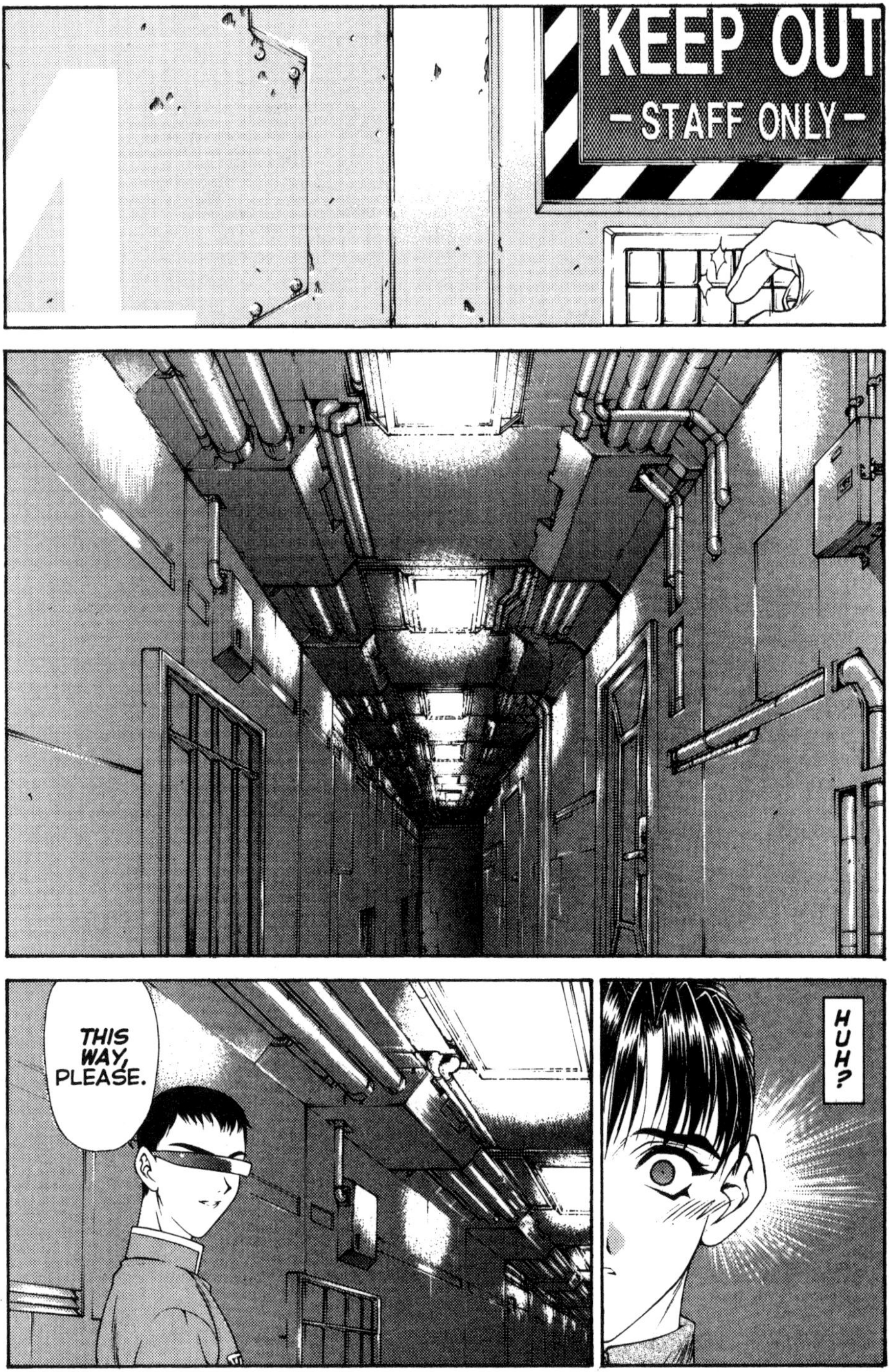
KEEP OUT
-STAFF ONLY-
THIS WAY, PLEASE.
HUH?

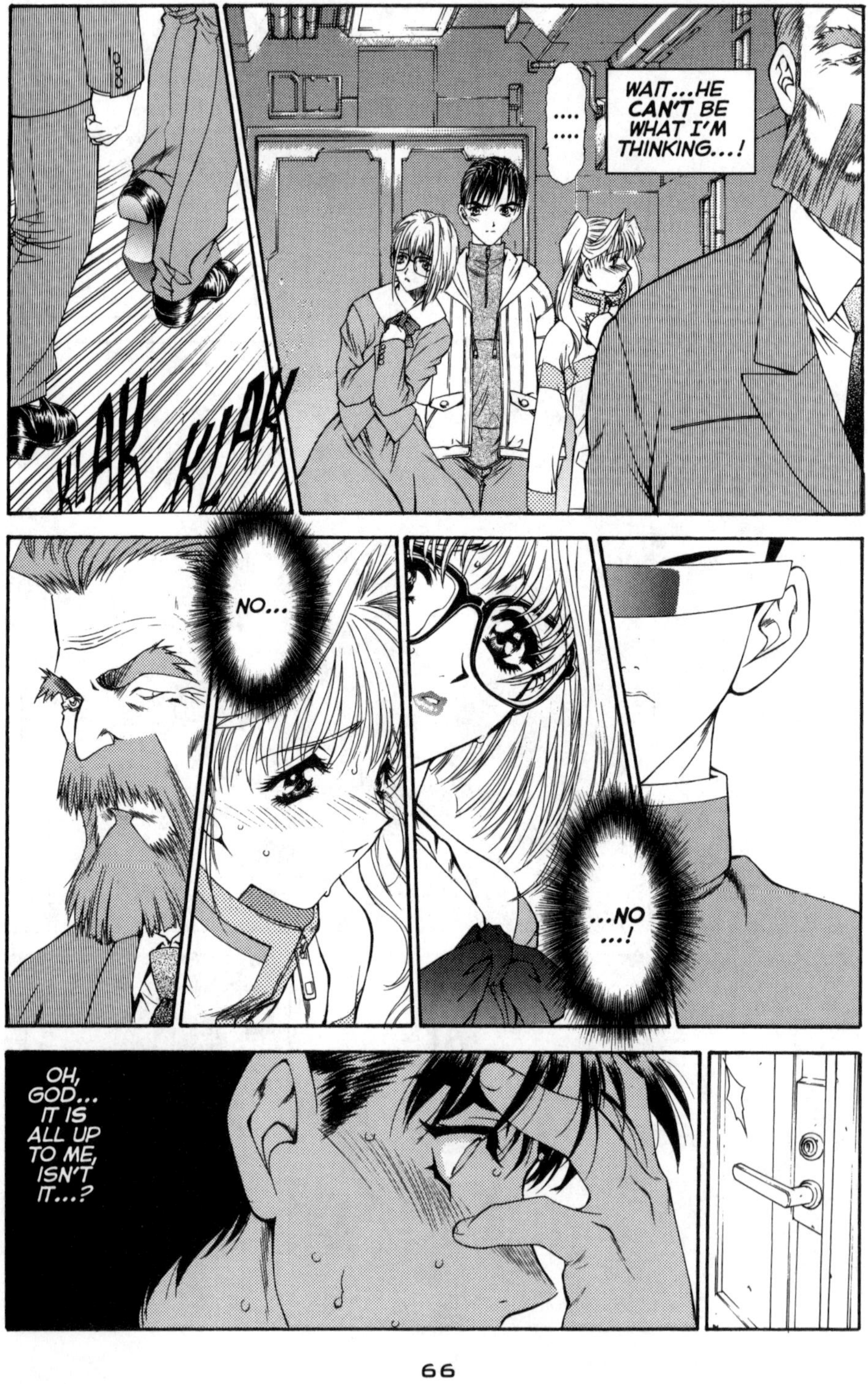
WAIT...HE CAN'T BE WHAT I'M THINKING...!
....
....
KLAK KLAK
...NO ...!
NO...
OH, GOD... IT IS ALL UP TO ME, ISN'T IT...?

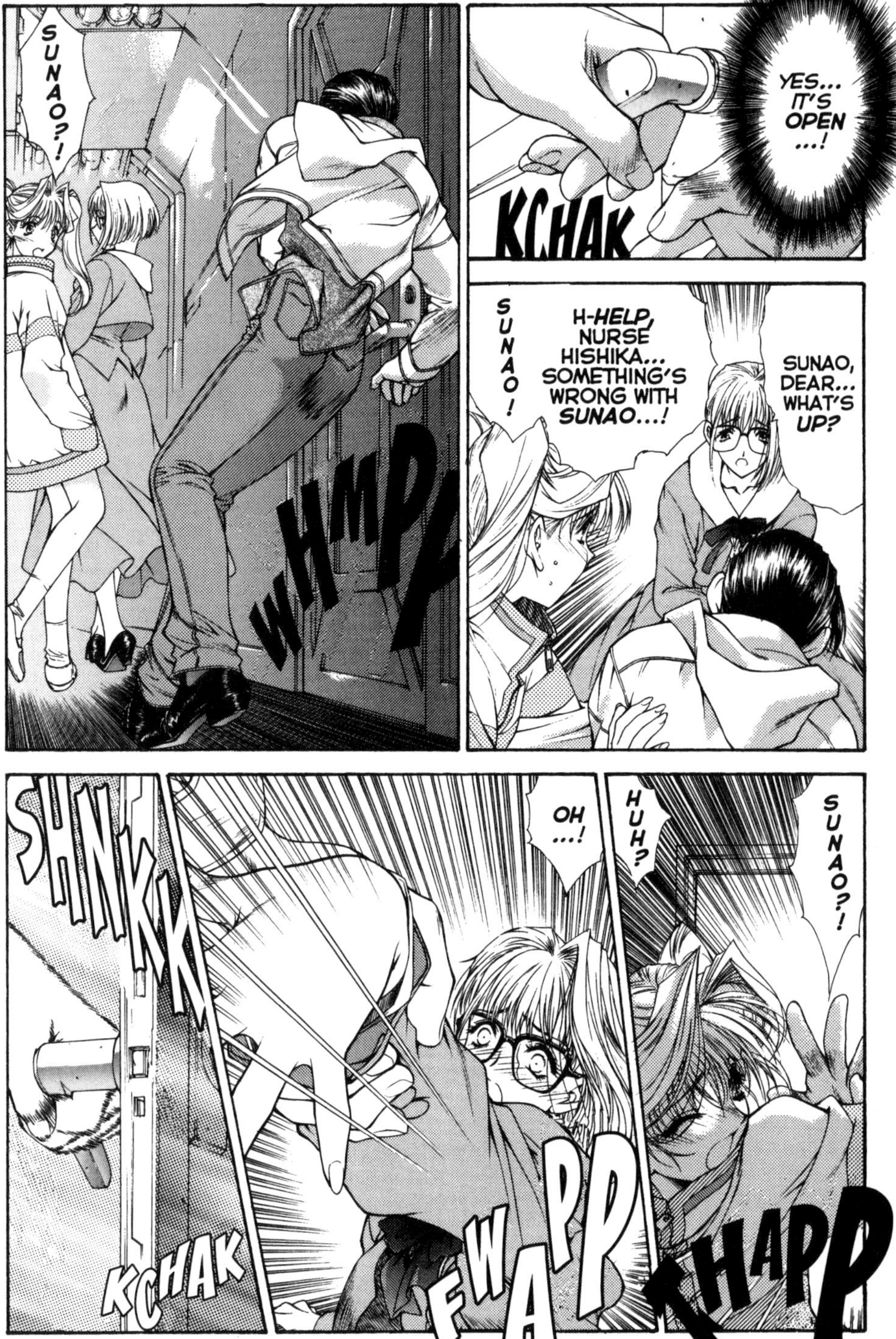

YES... IT'S OPEN ...!
KCHAK
SUNAO, DEAR... WHAT'S UP?
H-HELP, NURSE HISHIKA... SOMETHING'S WRONG WITH SUNAO...!
SUNAO!
SUNAO?!
WHMPP
SUNAO?!
THAPP
HUH?
OH ...!
FWAPP
SHNKK
KCHAK

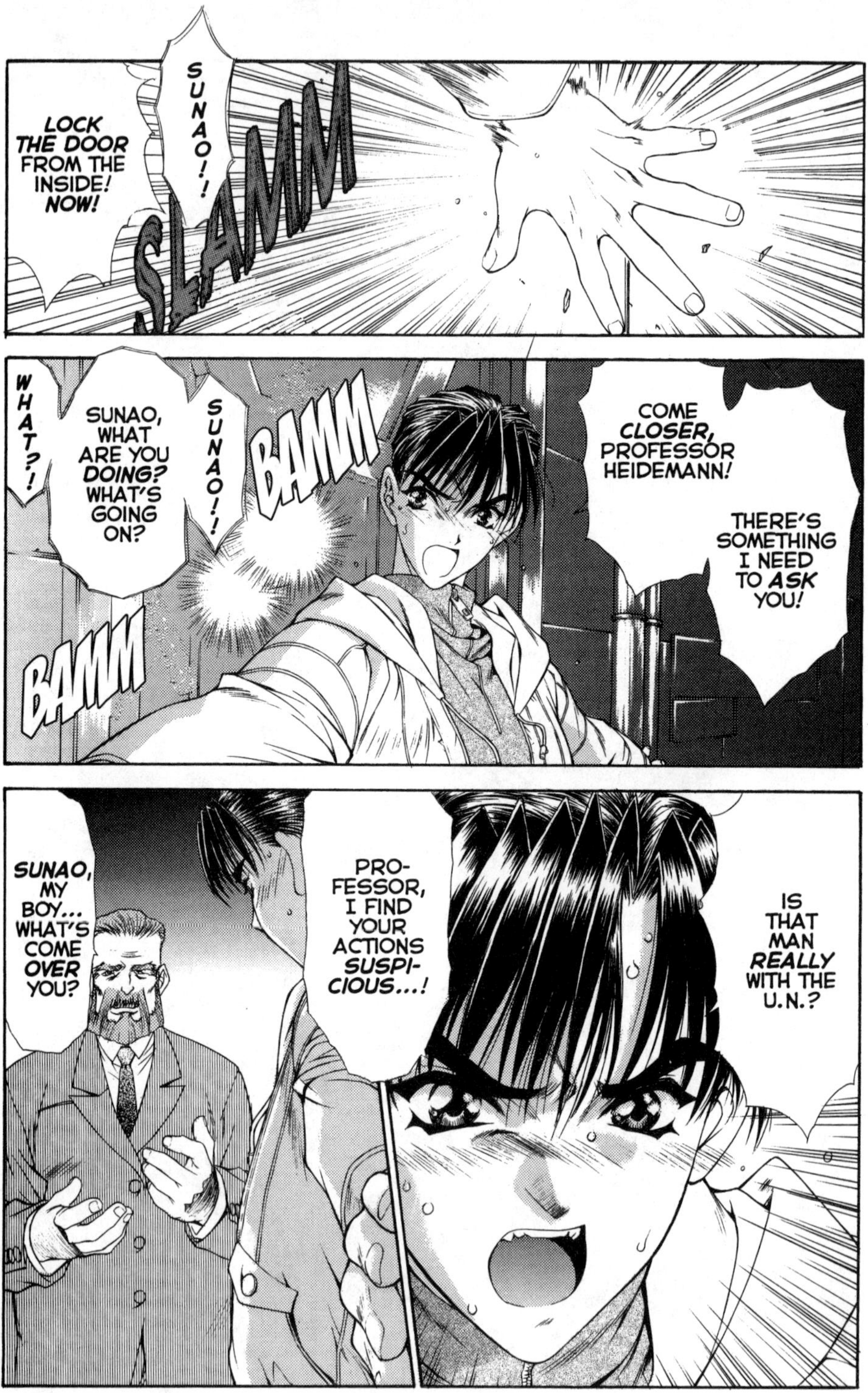
SLAMM
SUNAO!!
LOCK THE DOOR FROM THE INSIDE! NOW!
COME CLOSER, PROFESSOR HEIDEMANN!
THERE'S SOMETHING I NEED TO ASK YOU!
BAMM
SUNAO!!
SUNAO, WHAT ARE YOU DOING? WHAT'S GOING ON?
WHAT?!
BAMM
IS THAT MAN REALLY WITH THE U.N.?
PROFESSOR, I FIND YOUR ACTIONS SUSPICIOUS...!
SUNAO, MY BOY... WHAT'S COME OVER YOU?

Act 62

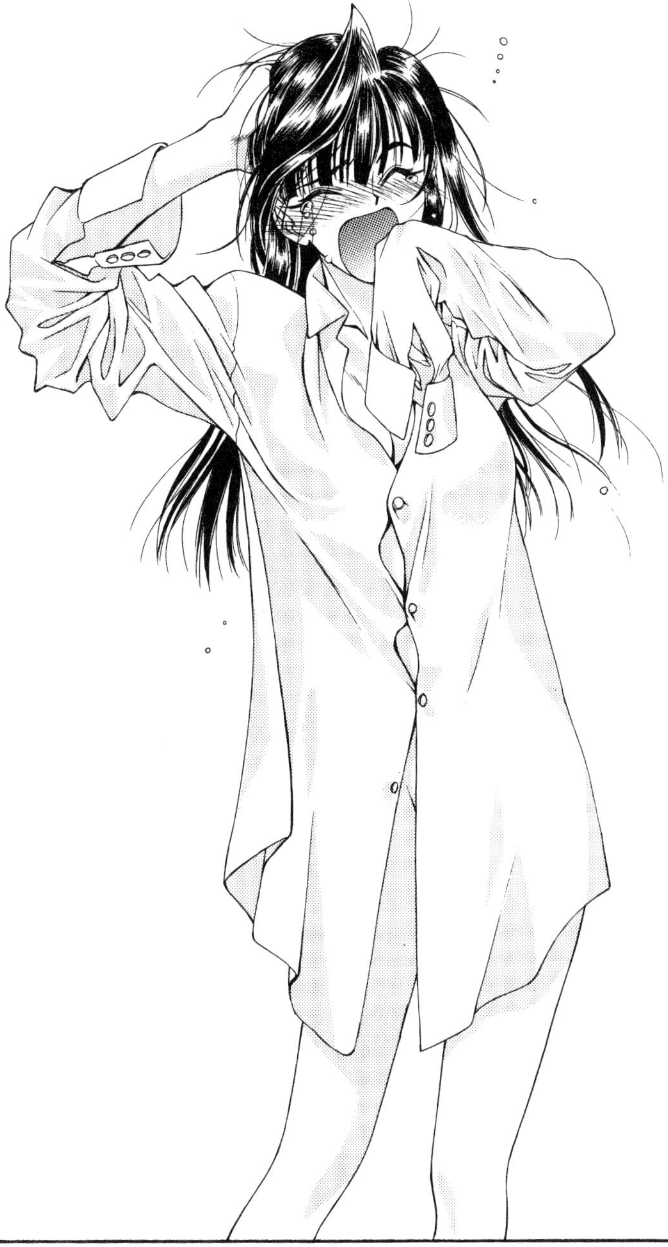

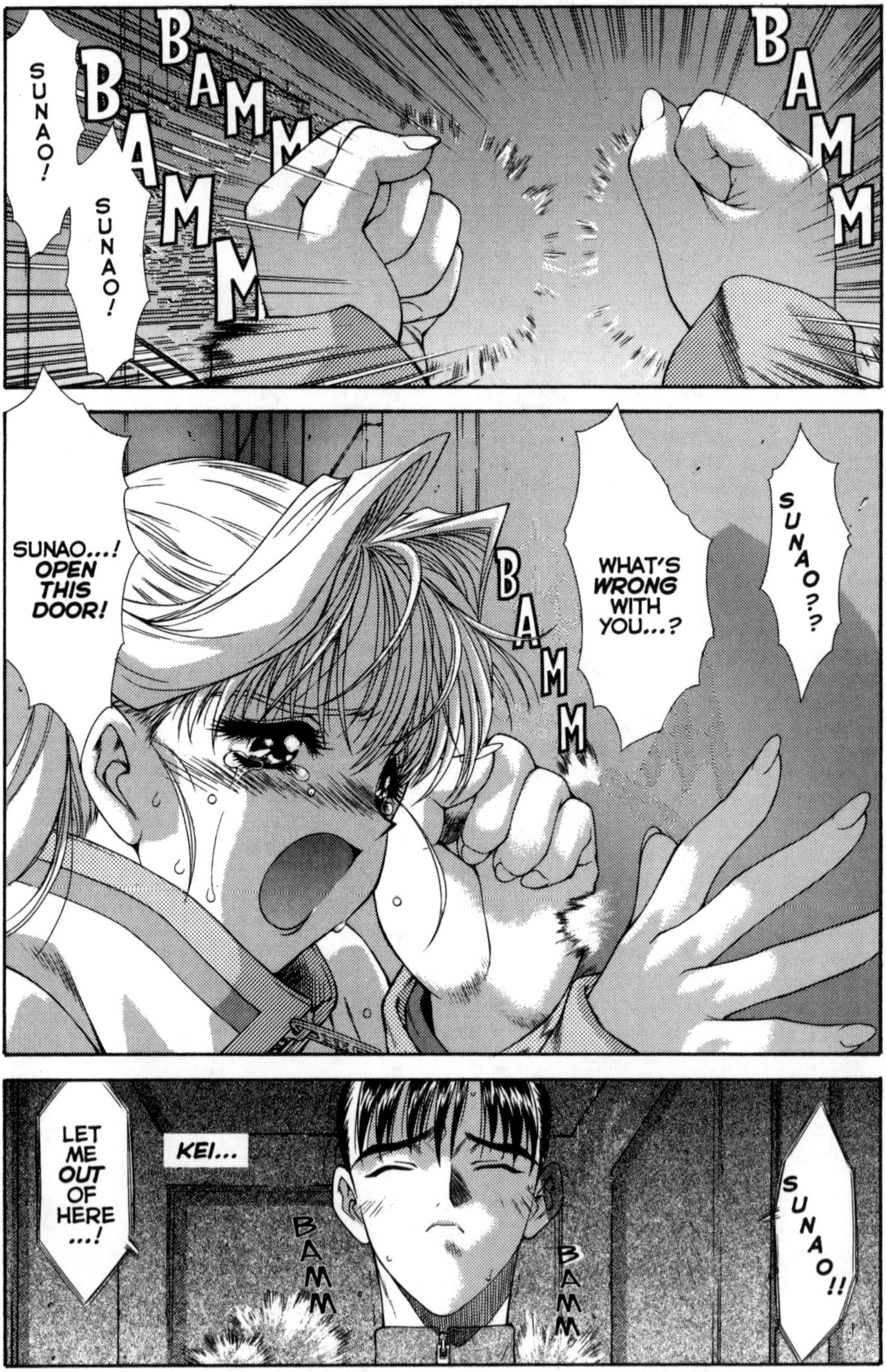
BAMM
BAMMM
BAMM
SUNAO!
SUNAO!
SUNAO??
WHAT'S WRONG WITH YOU...?
BAMM
SUNAO...! OPEN THIS DOOR!
SUNAO!!
BAMM
BAMM
KEI...
LET ME OUT OF HERE...!

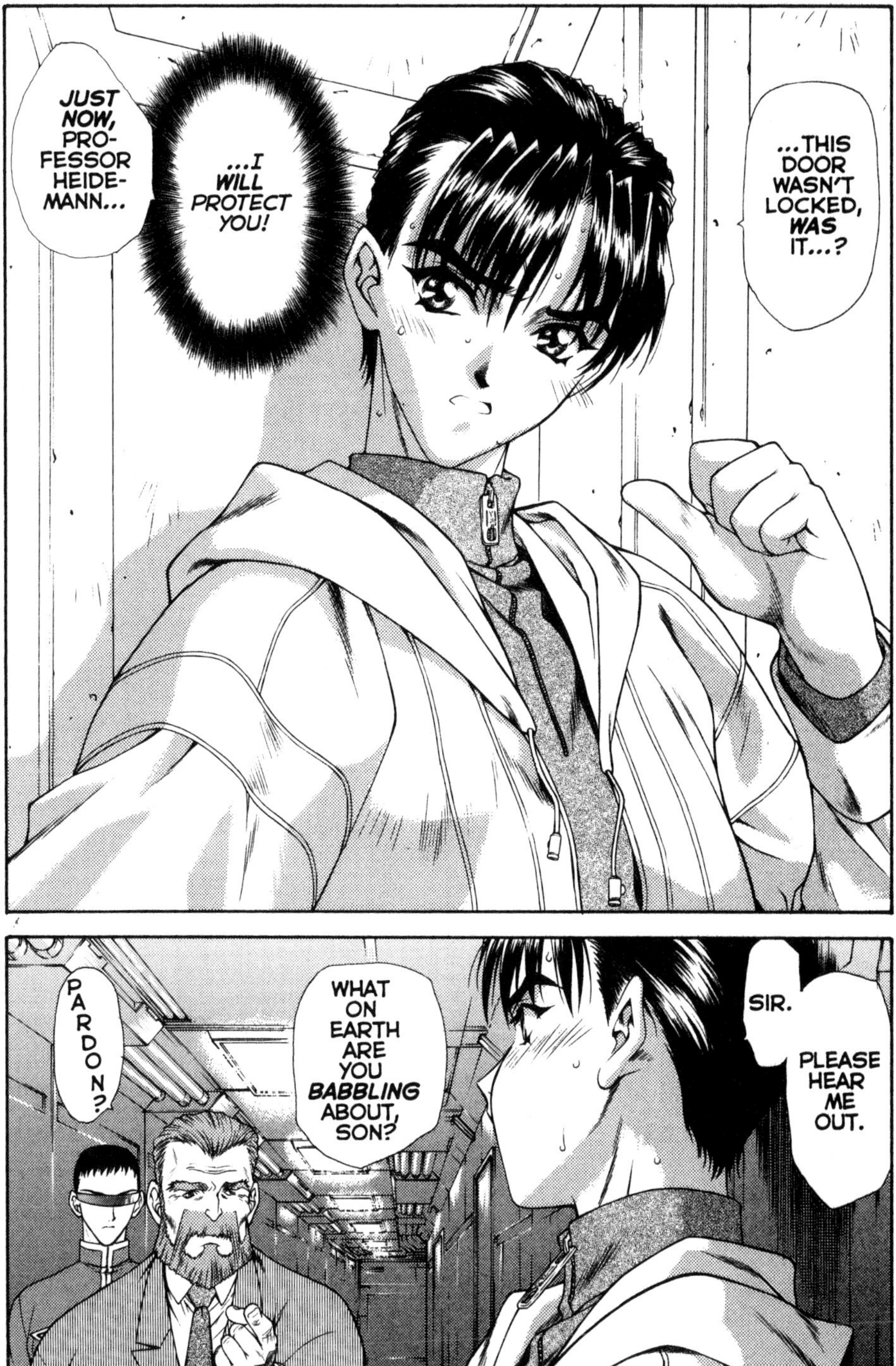
...THIS DOOR WASN'T LOCKED, WAS IT...?
...I WILL PROTECT YOU!
JUST NOW, PRO-FESSOR HEIDE-MANN...
SIR.
PLEASE HEAR ME OUT.
WHAT ON EARTH ARE YOU BABBLING ABOUT, SON?
PARDON?

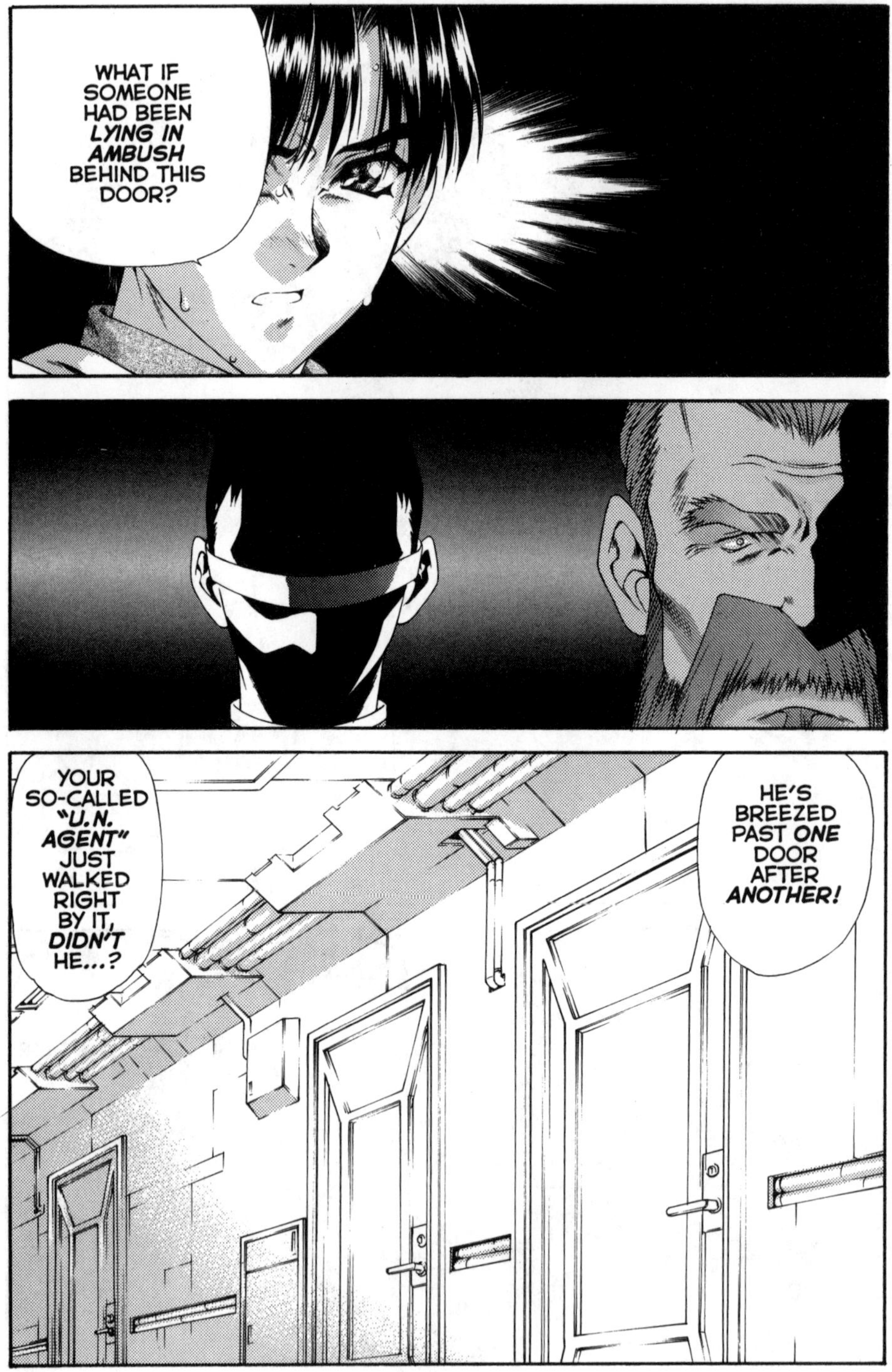
WHAT IF SOMEONE HAD BEEN *LYING IN AMBUSH* BEHIND THIS DOOR?
YOUR SO-CALLED *"U.N. AGENT"* JUST WALKED RIGHT BY IT, *DIDN'T* HE...?
HE'S BREEZED PAST *ONE* DOOR AFTER *ANOTHER!*

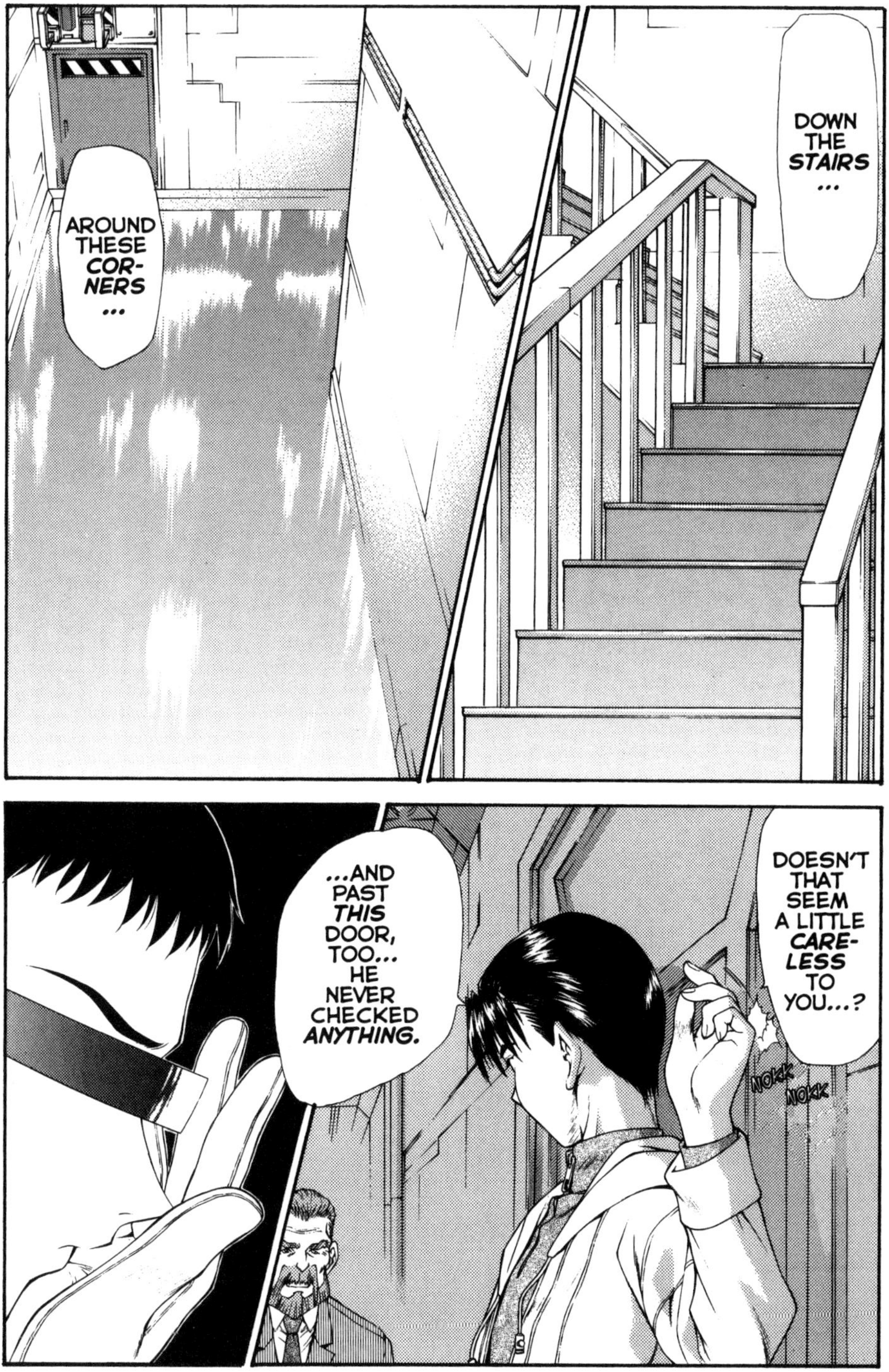
AROUND THESE *CORNERS* ...
DOWN THE *STAIRS* ...
...AND PAST *THIS* DOOR, TOO... HE NEVER CHECKED *ANYTHING.*
DOESN'T THAT SEEM A LITTLE *CARELESS* TO YOU...?
NOKK NOKK

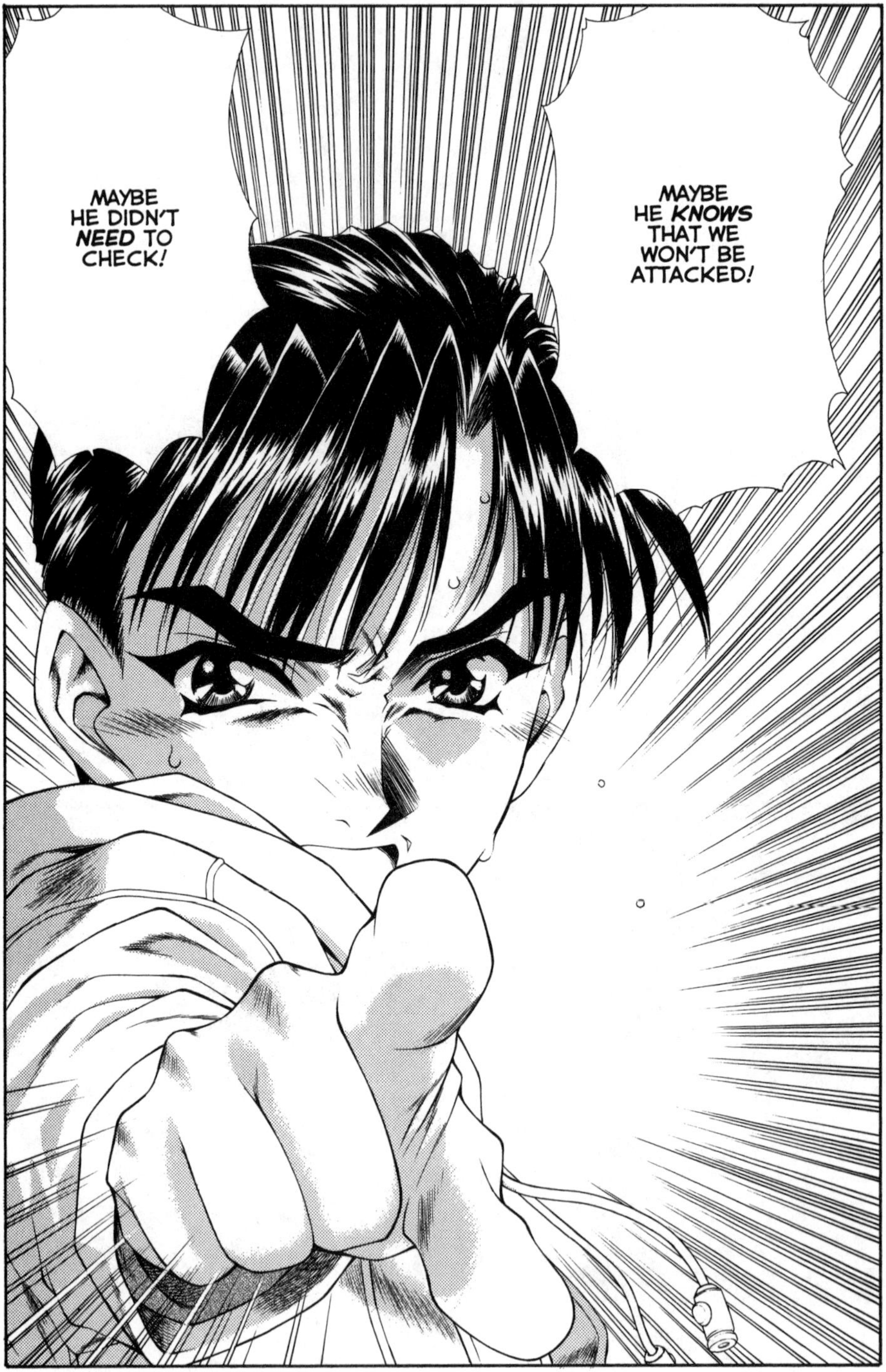
MAYBE HE ***KNOWS*** THAT WE WON'T BE ATTACKED!
MAYBE HE DIDN'T ***NEED*** TO CHECK!

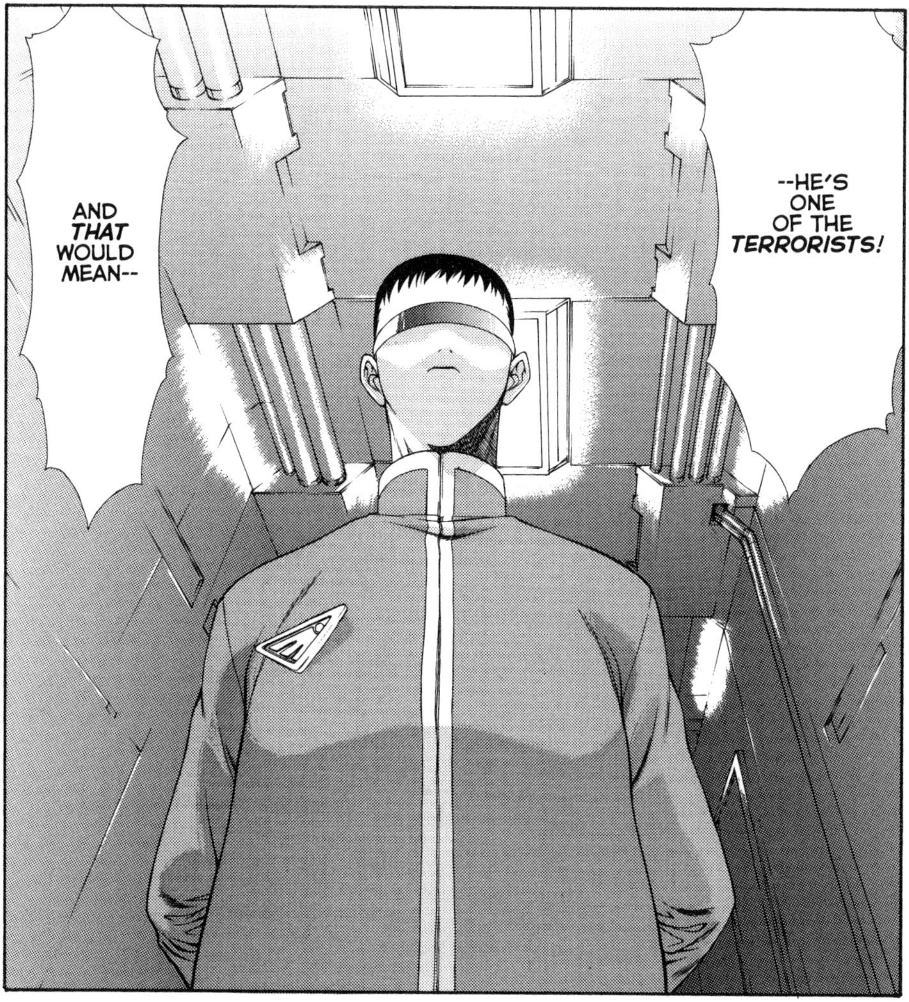
AND *THAT* WOULD MEAN--
--HE'S ONE OF THE *TERRORISTS!*
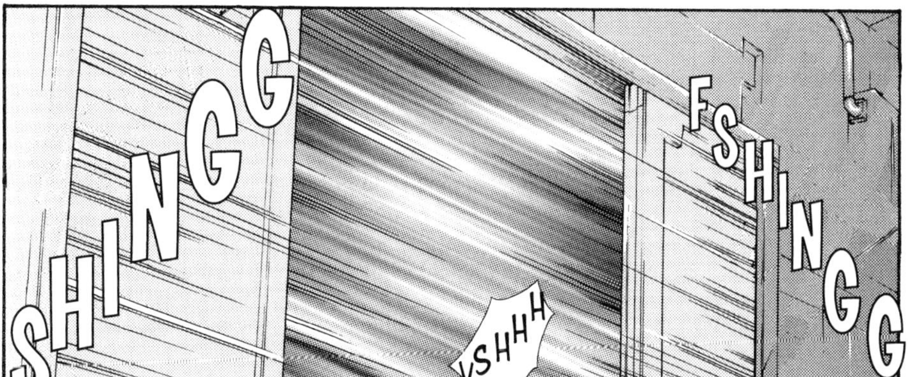
SHINGG
VSHHH
FSHINGG

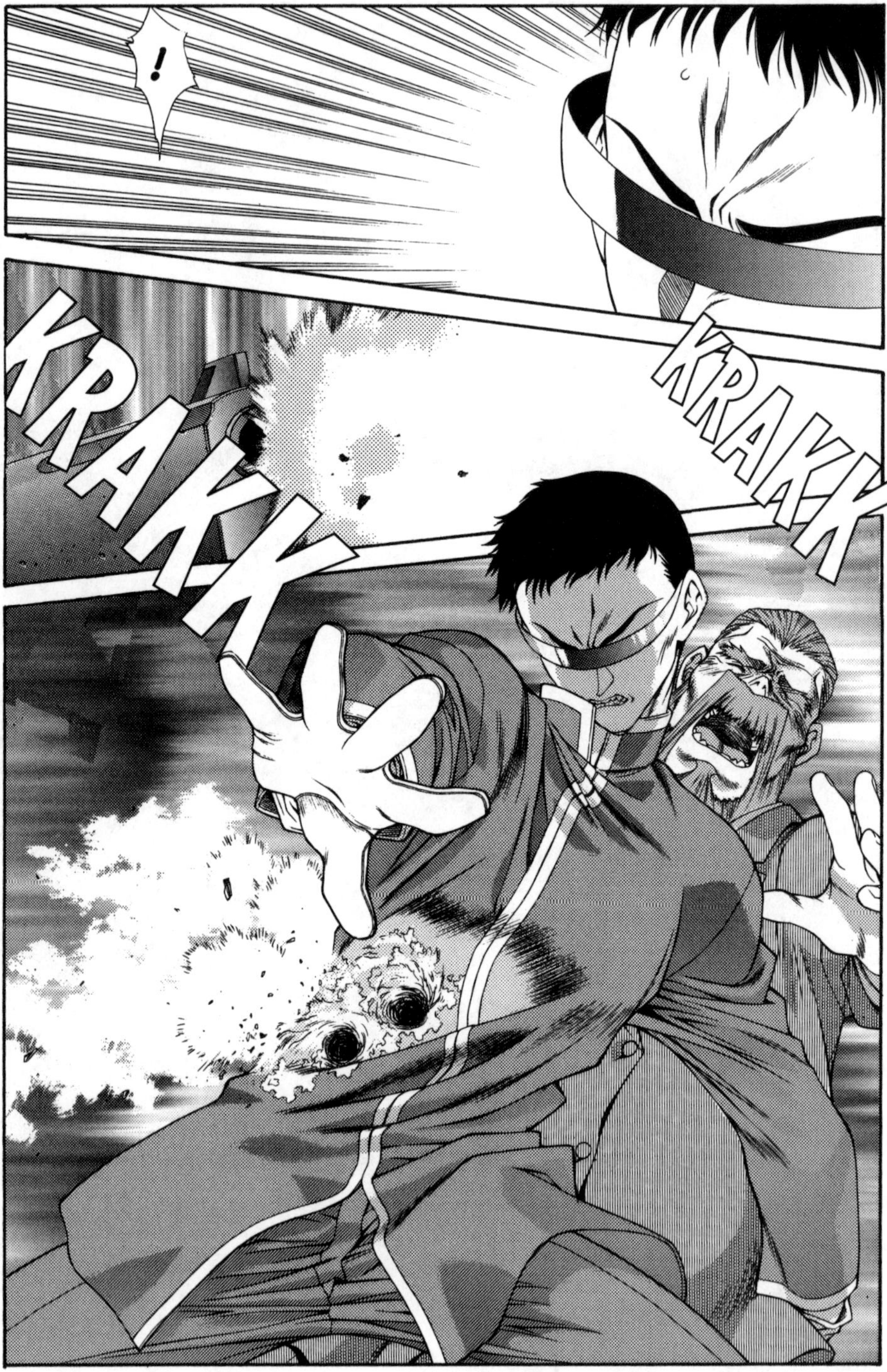
!
KRAKK
KRAKK

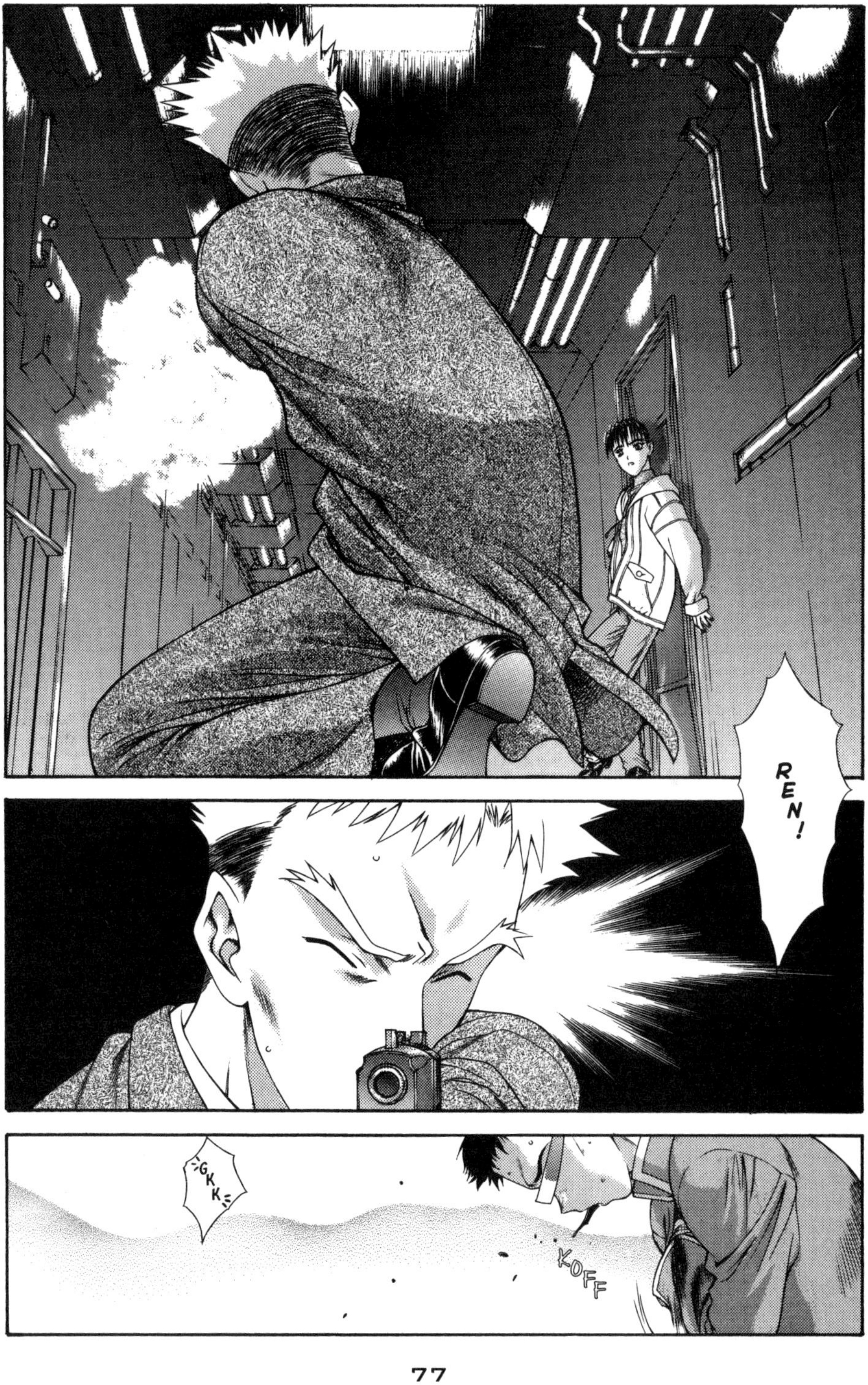
REN!
KOFF
GKK

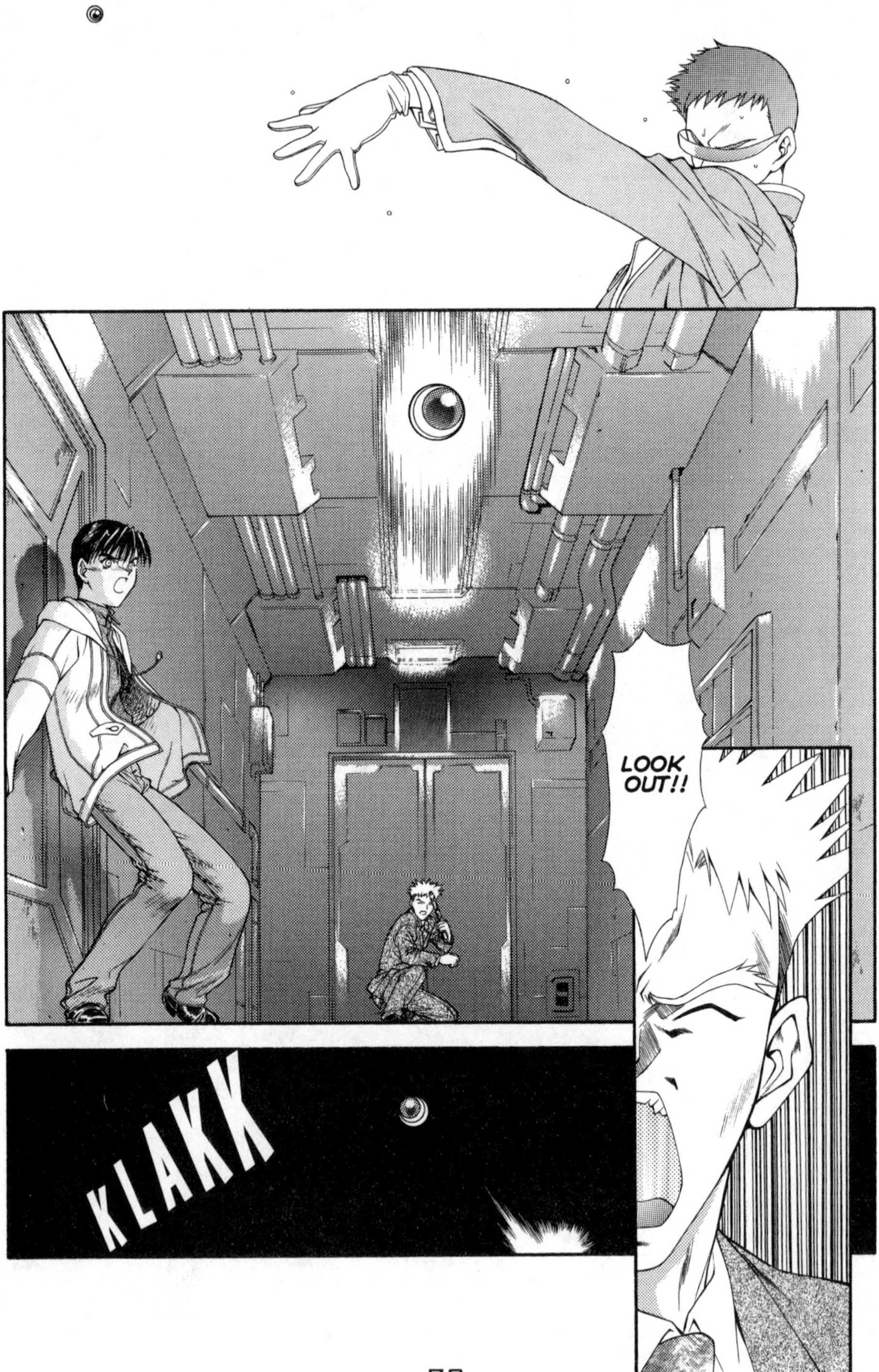
LOOK OUT!!
KLAKK

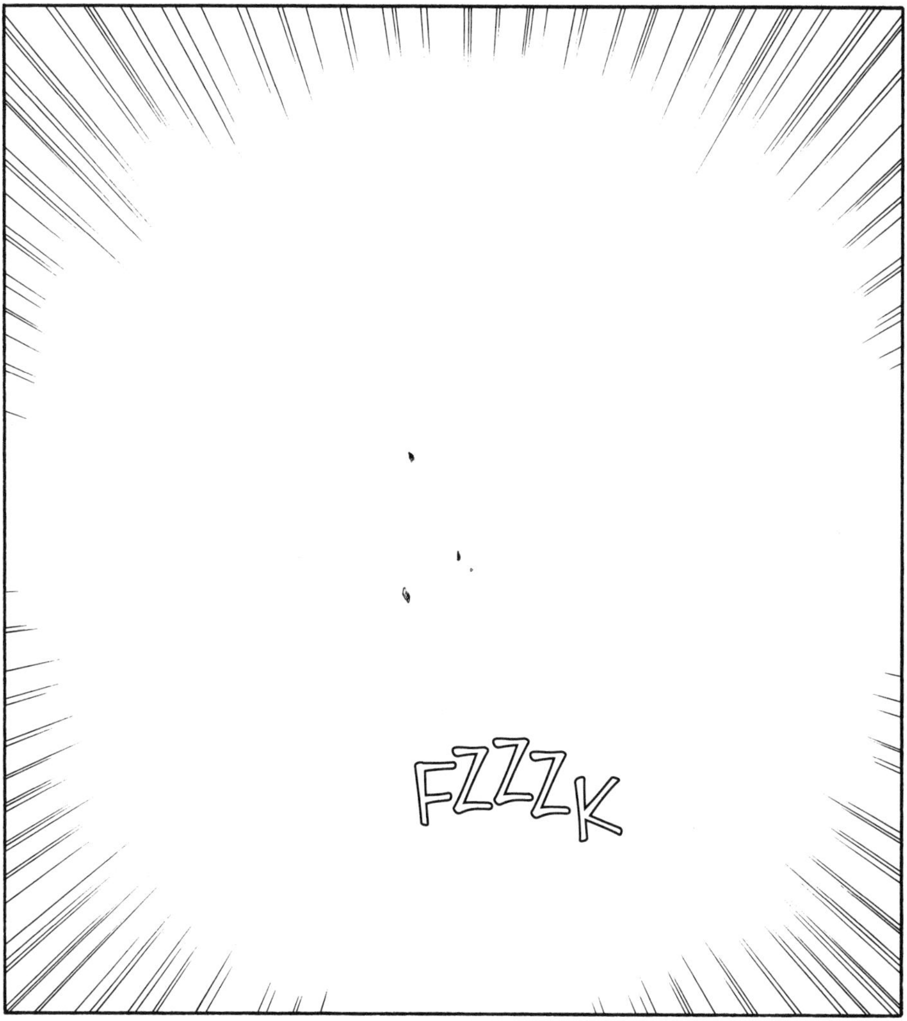
FZZZK
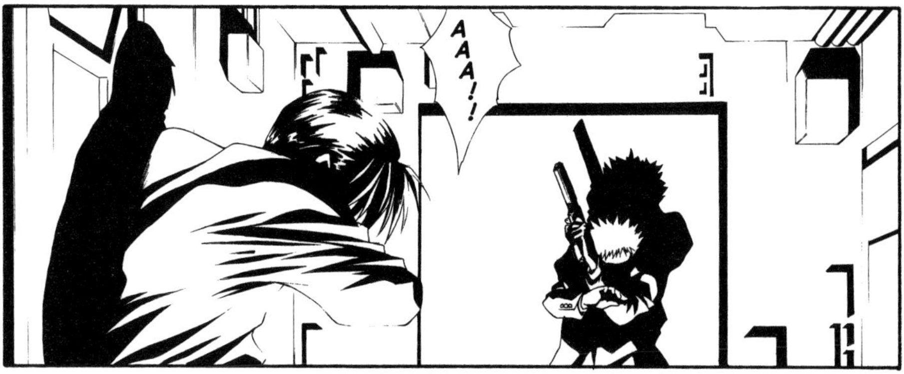
AAA!!

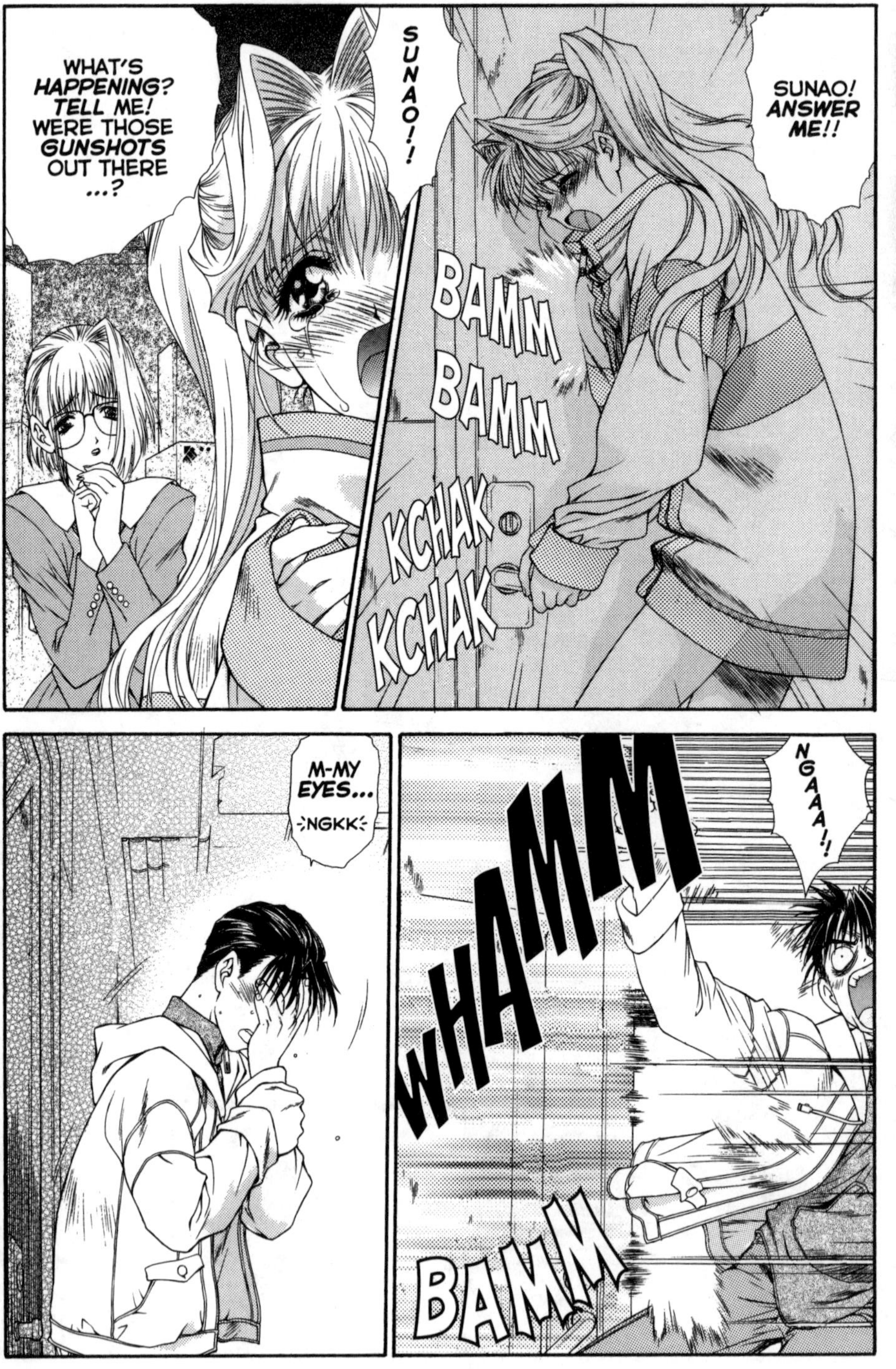
SUNAO! ANSWER ME!!
BAMM BAMM
KCHAK KCHAK
SUNAO!!
WHAT'S HAPPENING? TELL ME! WERE THOSE GUNSHOTS OUT THERE ...?
NGAAA!!
WHAMM
BAMM
M-MY EYES...
NGKK

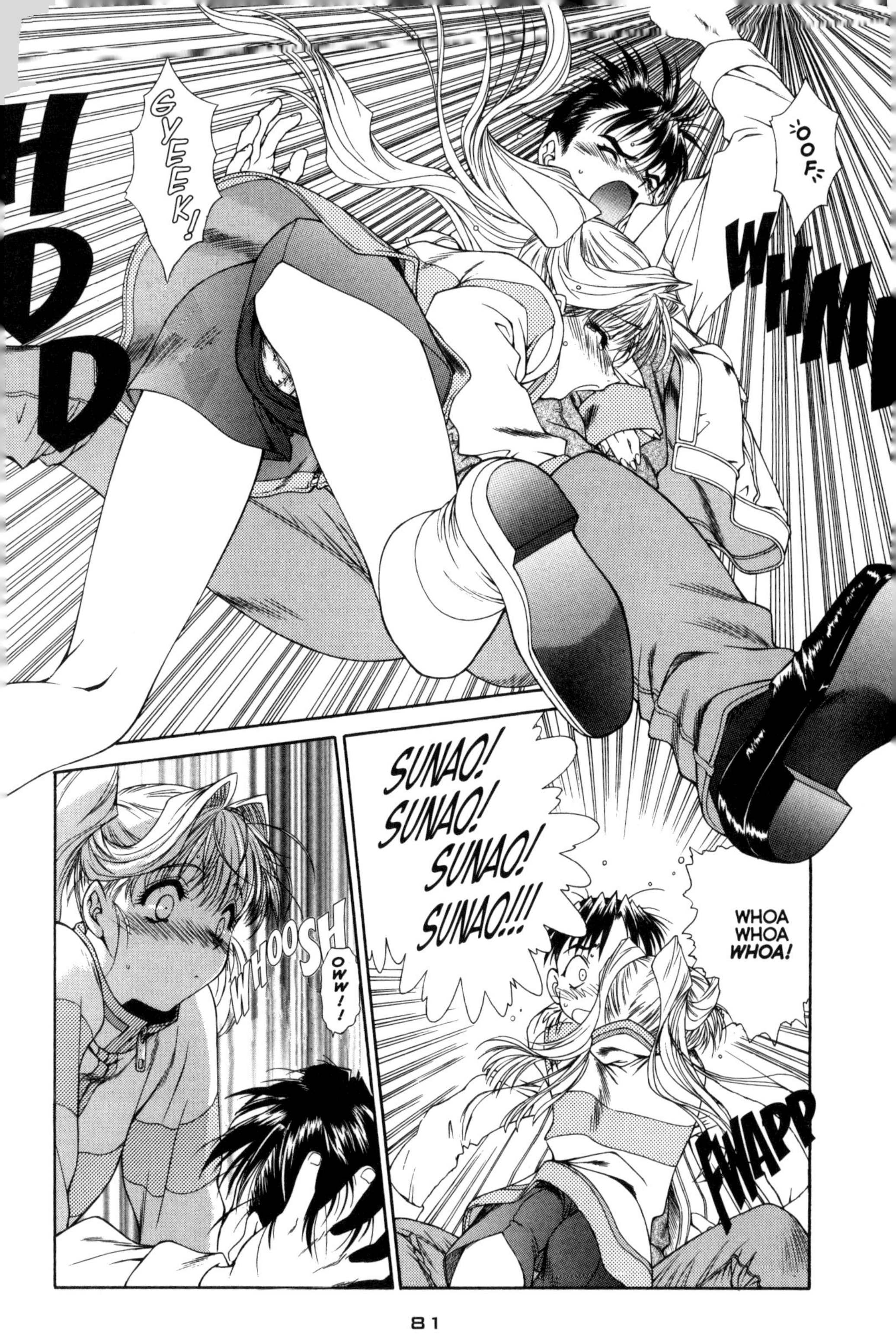
OOF
WHMP
GYEEK!
HDD
SUNAO! SUNAO! SUNAO! SUNAO!!!
WHOA WHOA WHOA!
FWAPP
WHOOSH
OWW!!

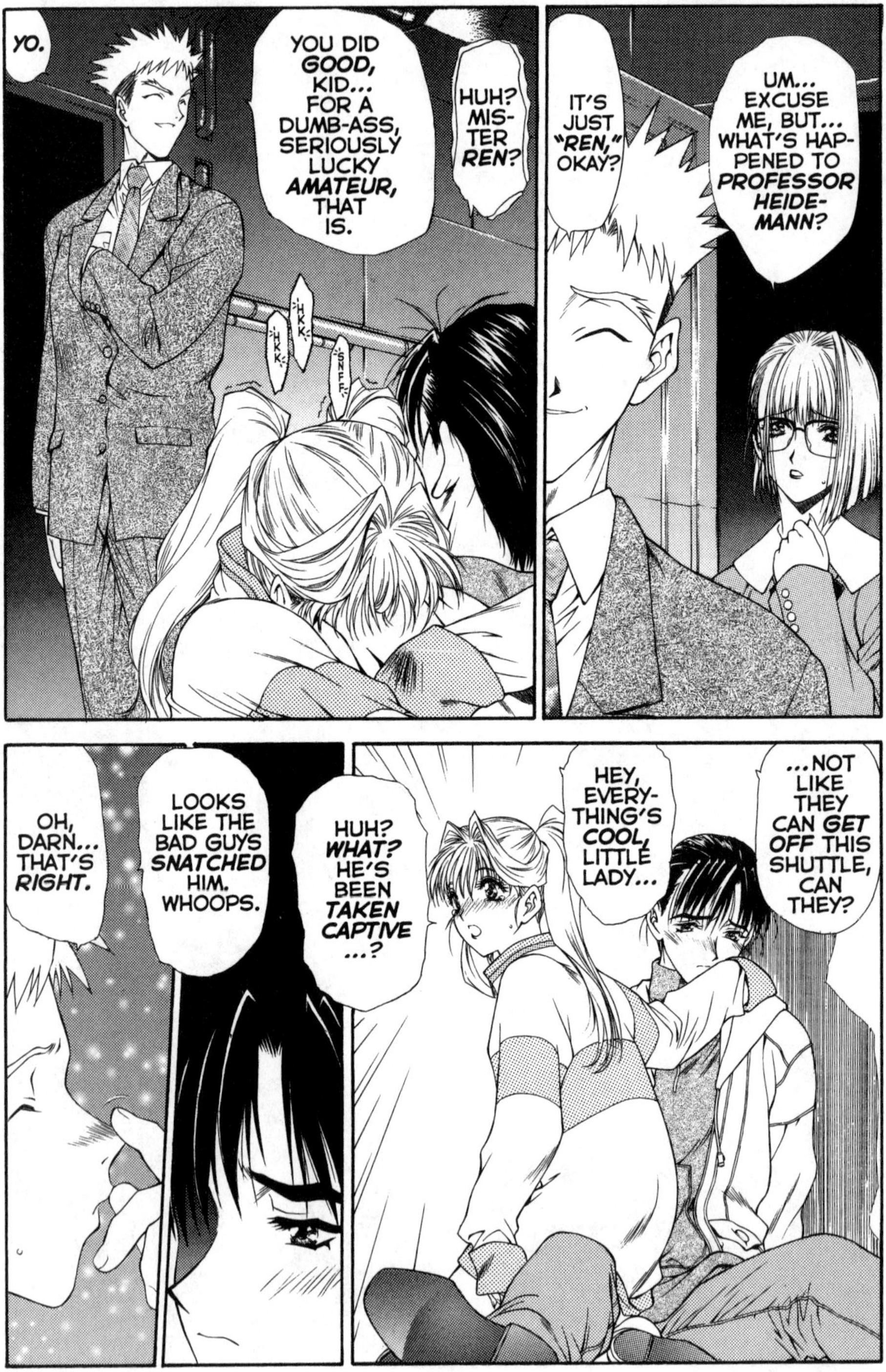
YO.
YOU DID GOOD, KID... FOR A DUMB-ASS, SERIOUSLY LUCKY AMATEUR, THAT IS.
HKK
HKK
SNFF
HUH? MIS-TER REN?
IT'S JUST "REN," OKAY?
UM... EXCUSE ME, BUT... WHAT'S HAP-PENED TO PROFESSOR HEIDE-MANN?
OH, DARN... THAT'S RIGHT.
LOOKS LIKE THE BAD GUYS SNATCHED HIM. WHOOPS.
HUH? WHAT? HE'S BEEN TAKEN CAPTIVE ...?
HEY, EVERY-THING'S COOL, LITTLE LADY...
...NOT LIKE THEY CAN GET OFF THIS SHUTTLE, CAN THEY?

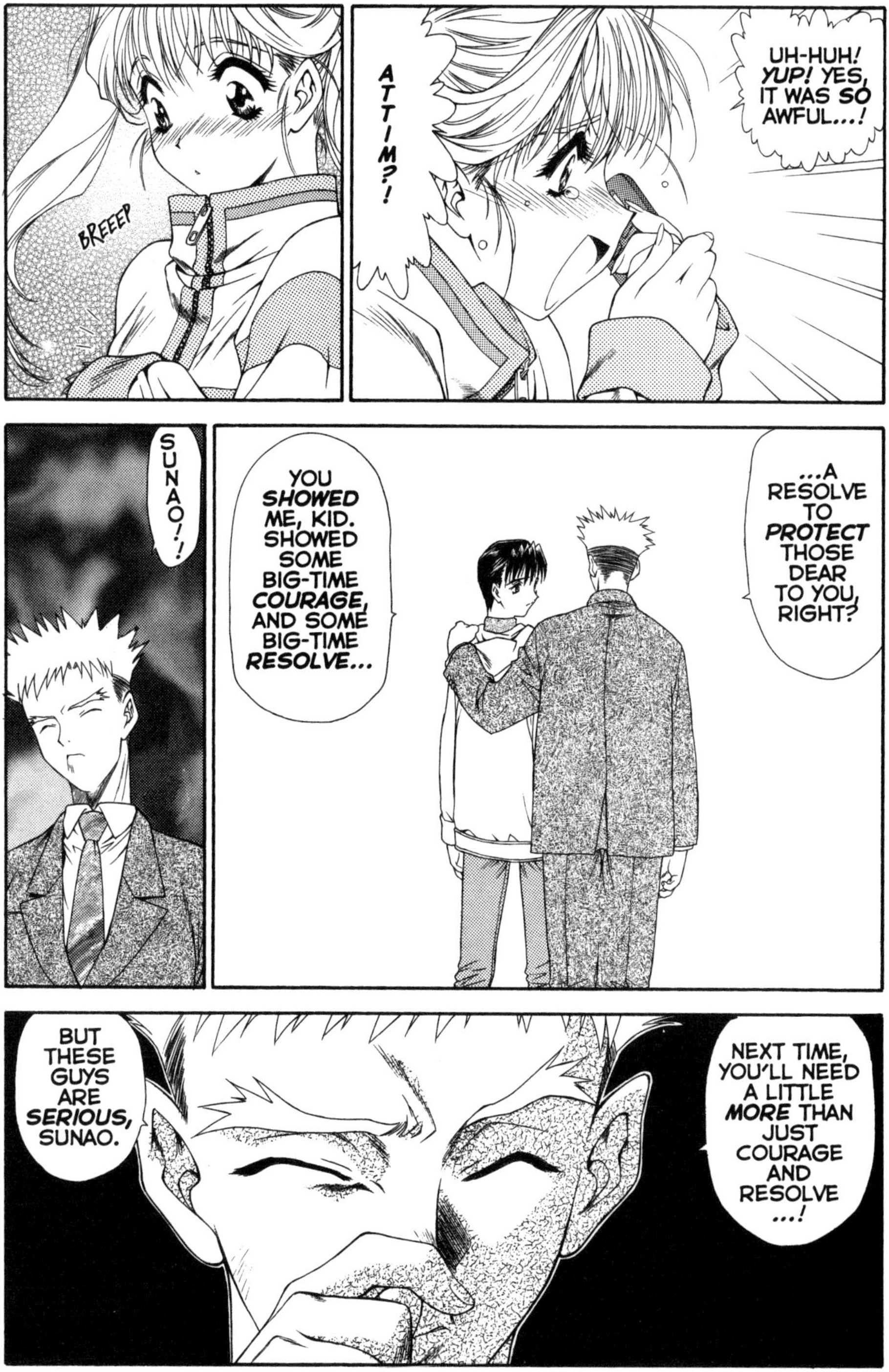
BREEEP
ATTIM?!
UH-HUH! YUP! YES, IT WAS SO AWFUL...!
SUNAO!!
YOU SHOWED ME, KID. SHOWED SOME BIG-TIME COURAGE, AND SOME BIG-TIME RESOLVE...
...A RESOLVE TO PROTECT THOSE DEAR TO YOU, RIGHT?
BUT THESE GUYS ARE SERIOUS, SUNAO.
NEXT TIME, YOU'LL NEED A LITTLE MORE THAN JUST COURAGE AND RESOLVE ...!

UM... LIKE *WHAT*...?

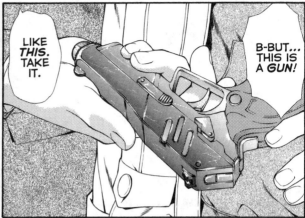

LIKE *THIS.* TAKE IT.

B-BUT... THIS IS A *GUN!*

REMEMBER THE *"RESOLVE"* THING, KID...

...'*CAUSE YOU MAY NEED TO KILL TO PROTECT YOUR OWN*...

UM... ER... WELL...

...ATTIM SAID THAT WE SHOULD GET BACK TO THE STATEROOM...

...AND SHE *ALSO* SAID...AND I DON'T UNDERSTAND THIS *AT ALL*...

...BUT SHE SAID THAT I *SAVED HER LIFE,* SOMEHOW!

ACT 63

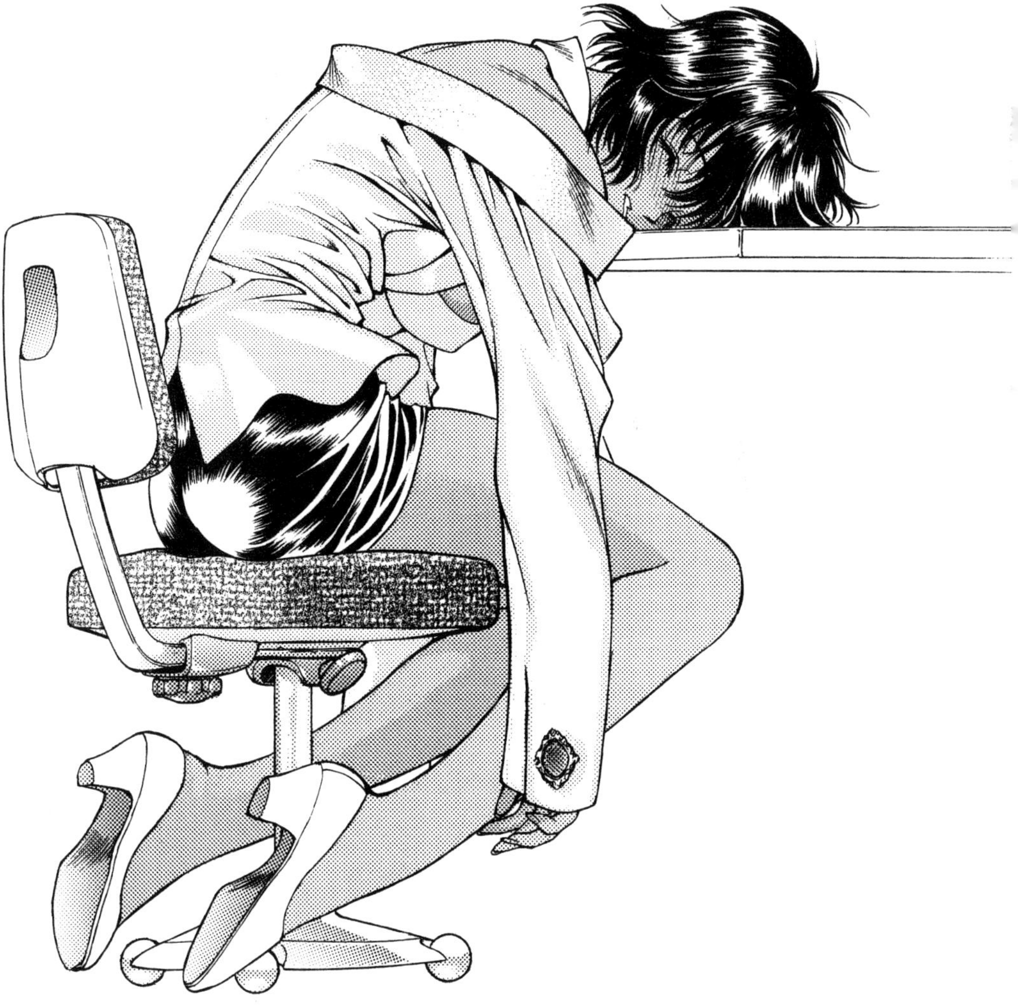

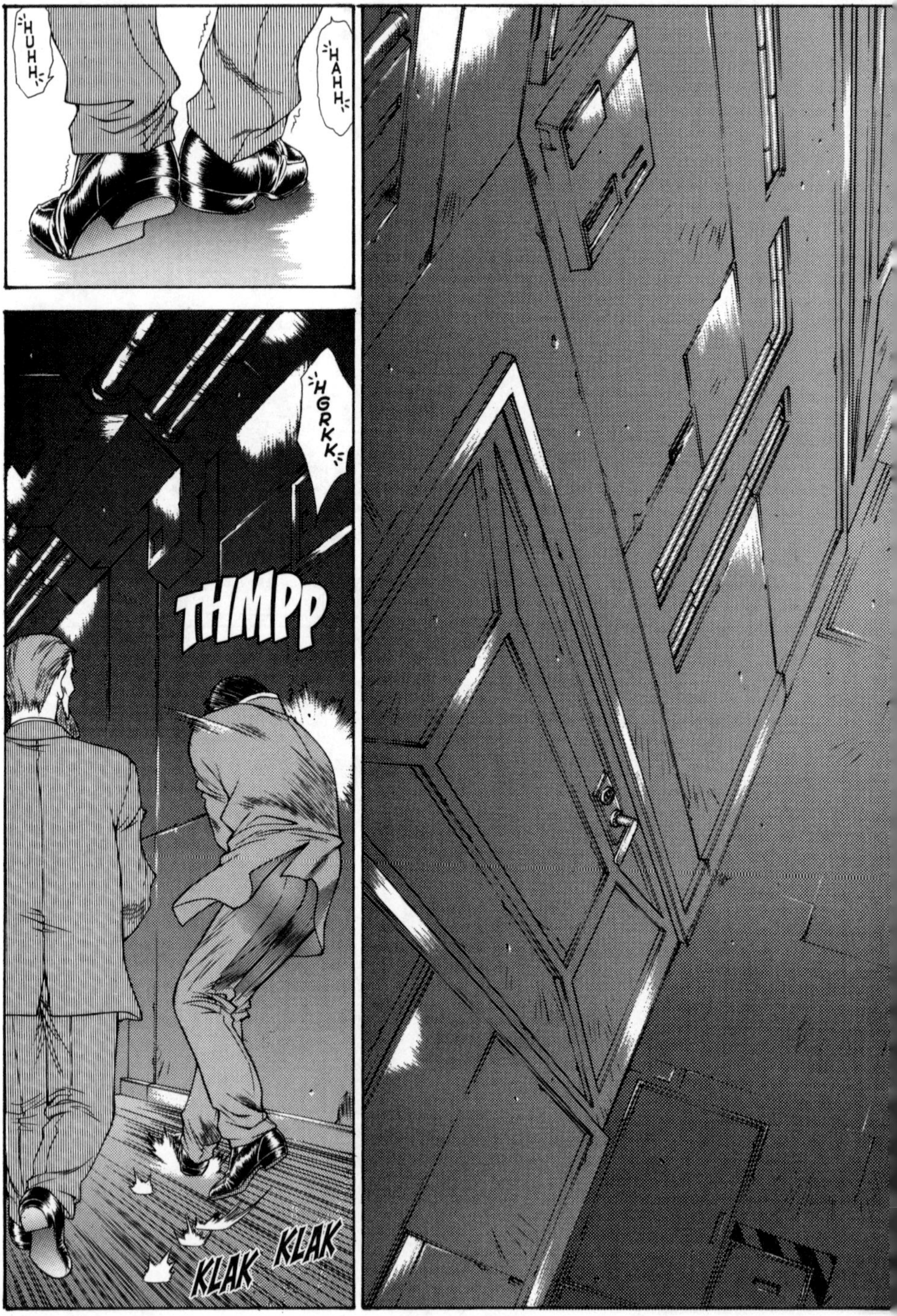
HAHH
HUHH
HGRKK
THMPP
KLAK
KLAK

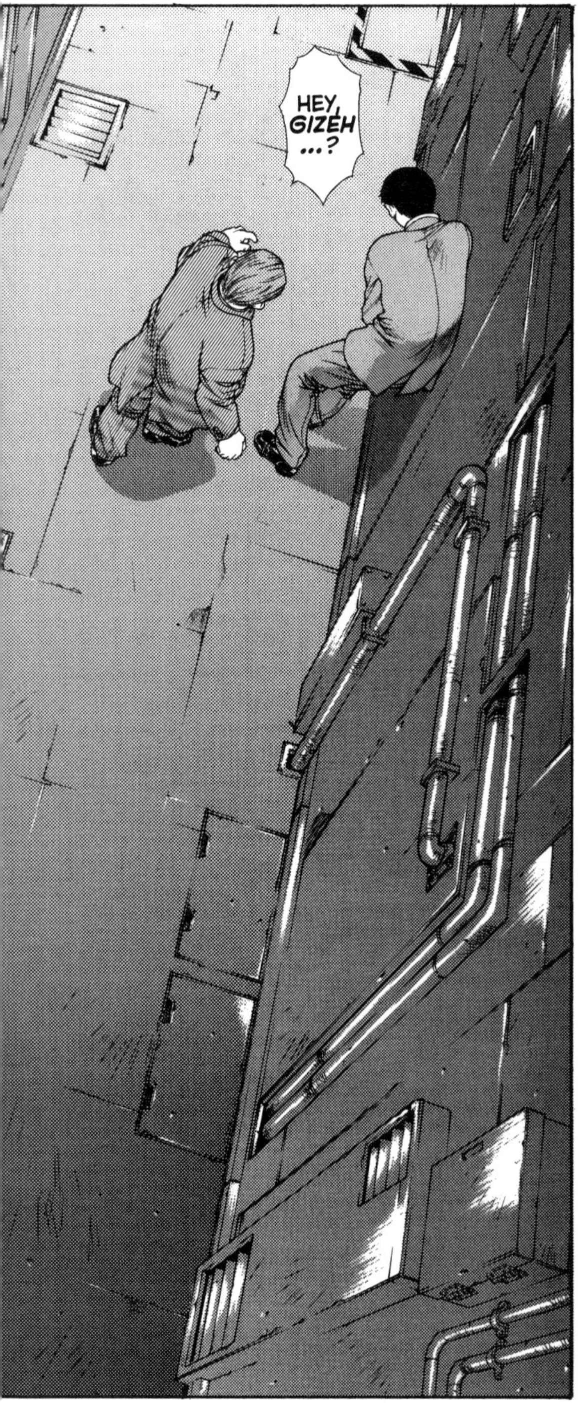
HEY, GIZEH ...?

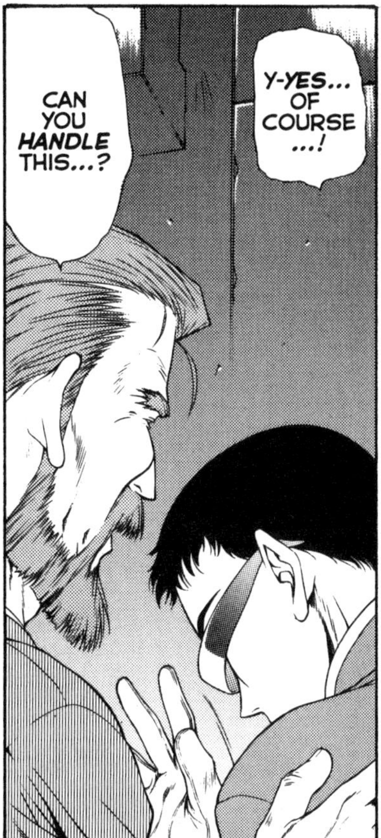
CAN YOU *HANDLE* THIS...?
Y-*YES*... OF COURSE ...!

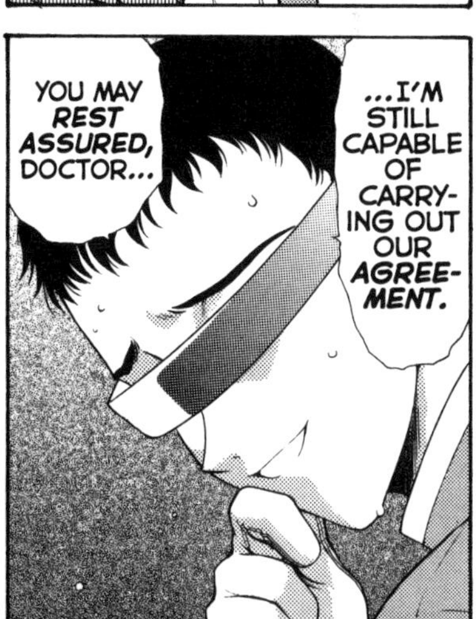
YOU *MAY* ***REST ASSURED,*** DOCTOR...
...I'M STILL CAPABLE OF CARRYING OUT OUR ***AGREEMENT.***

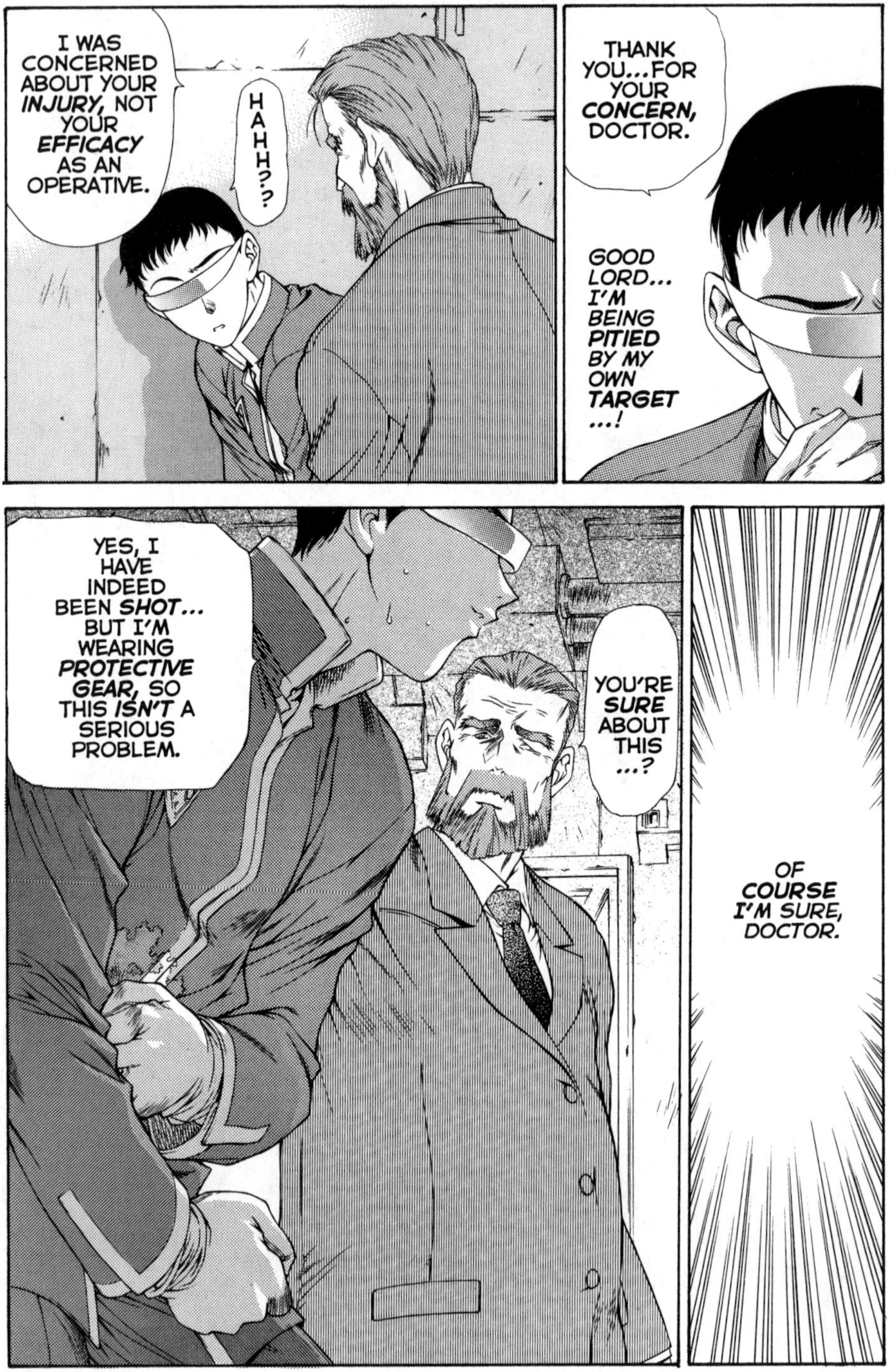
I WAS CONCERNED ABOUT YOUR INJURY, NOT YOUR EFFICACY AS AN OPERATIVE.
HAHH??
THANK YOU...FOR YOUR CONCERN, DOCTOR.
GOOD LORD... I'M BEING PITIED BY MY OWN TARGET ...!
YES, I HAVE INDEED BEEN SHOT... BUT I'M WEARING PROTECTIVE GEAR, SO THIS ISN'T A SERIOUS PROBLEM.
YOU'RE SURE ABOUT THIS ...?
OF COURSE I'M SURE, DOCTOR.

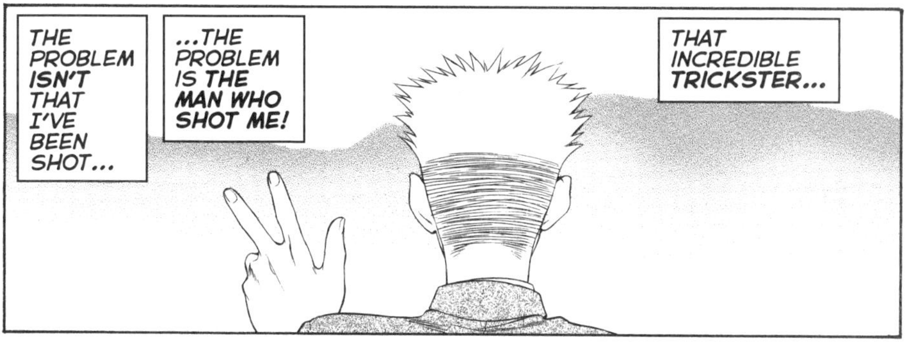
THE PROBLEM **ISN'T** THAT I'VE BEEN SHOT...
...THE PROBLEM IS **THE MAN WHO SHOT ME!**
THAT INCREDIBLE **TRICKSTER...**

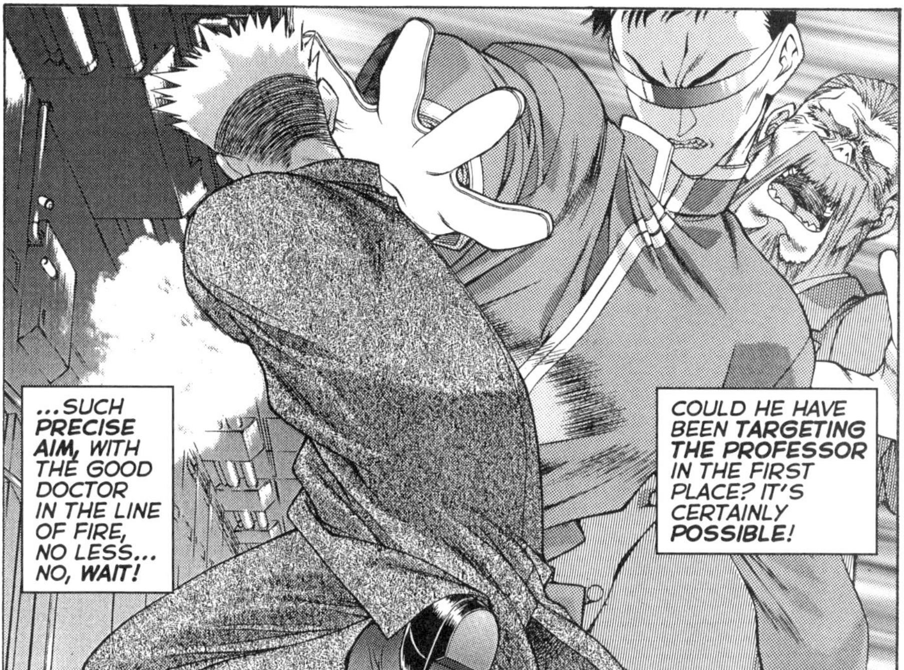
...SUCH **PRECISE AIM,** WITH THE GOOD DOCTOR IN THE LINE OF FIRE, NO LESS... NO, **WAIT!**
COULD HE HAVE BEEN **TARGETING THE PROFESSOR** IN THE FIRST PLACE? IT'S CERTAINLY **POSSIBLE!**

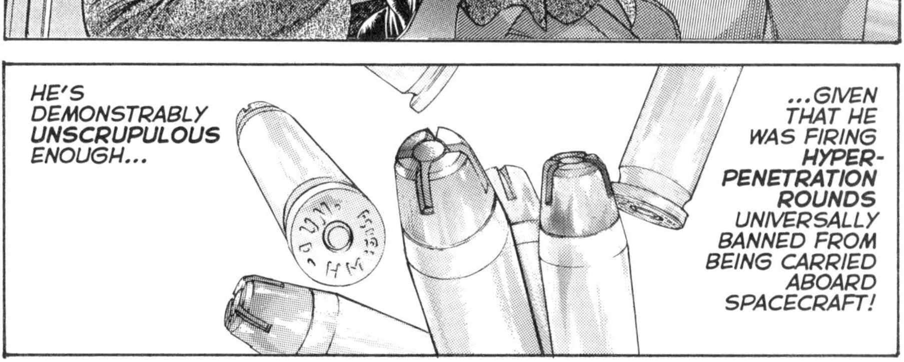
HE'S DEMONSTRABLY **UNSCRUPULOUS** ENOUGH...
...GIVEN THAT HE WAS FIRING **HYPER-PENETRATION ROUNDS** UNIVERSALLY BANNED FROM BEING CARRIED ABOARD SPACECRAFT!

DOES THE U.N. SIMPLY NOT **NEED** HEIDEMANN ANY LONGER?

OR WILL THEY DO **ANYTHING** TO PREVENT FURTHER **DEFECTIONS?**

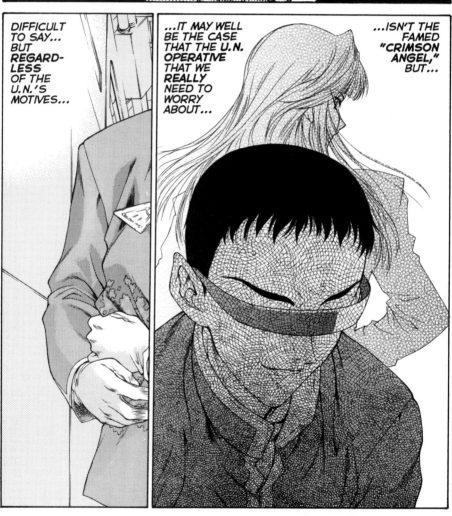

DIFFICULT TO SAY... BUT **REGARDLESS** OF THE U.N.'S MOTIVES...

...IT MAY WELL BE THE CASE THAT THE U.N. OPERATIVE THAT WE **REALLY** NEED TO WORRY ABOUT...

...ISN'T THE FAMED *"CRIMSON ANGEL,"* BUT...

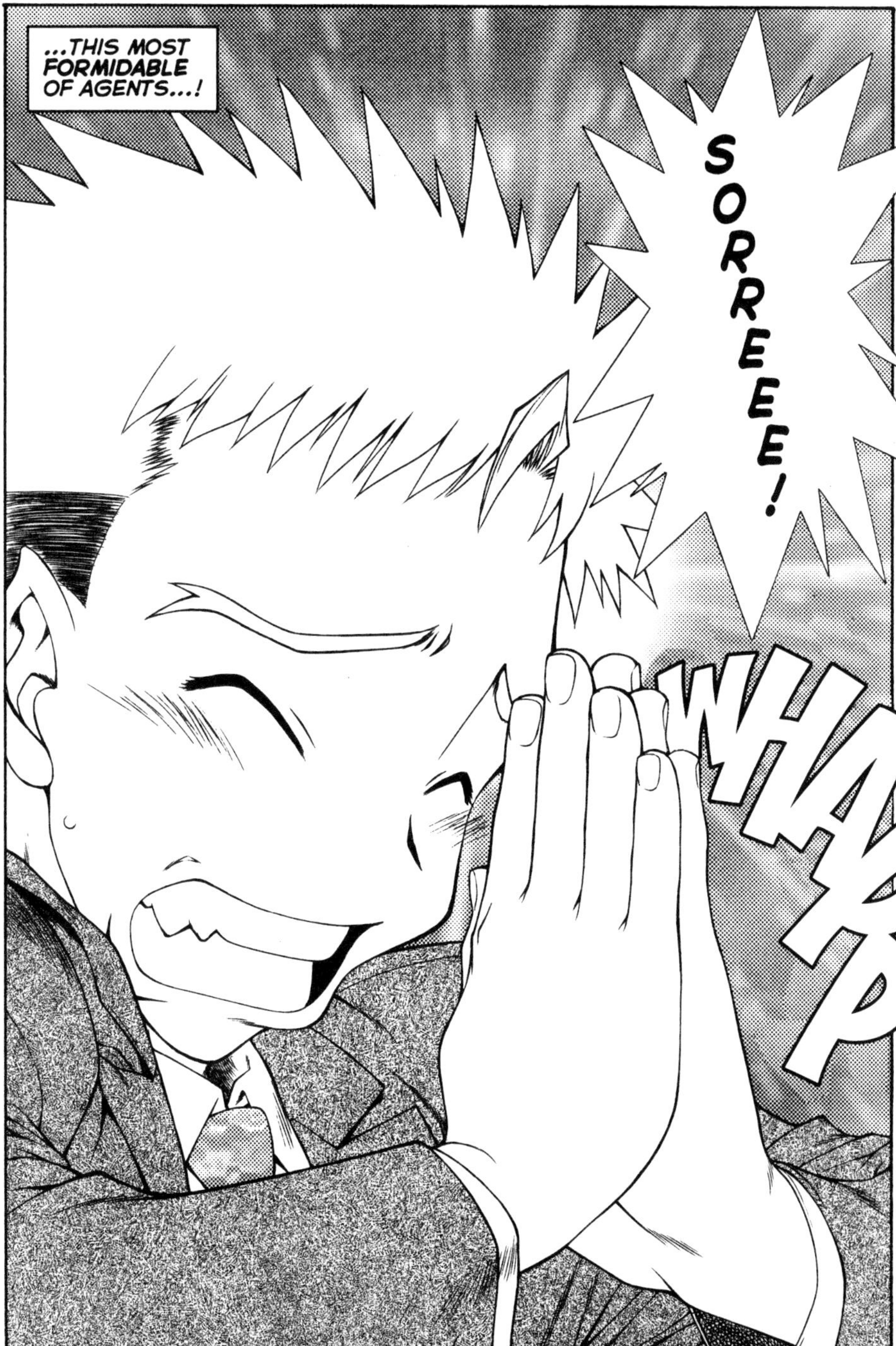
...THIS MOST FORMIDABLE OF AGENTS...!
SORREEE!
WHAP

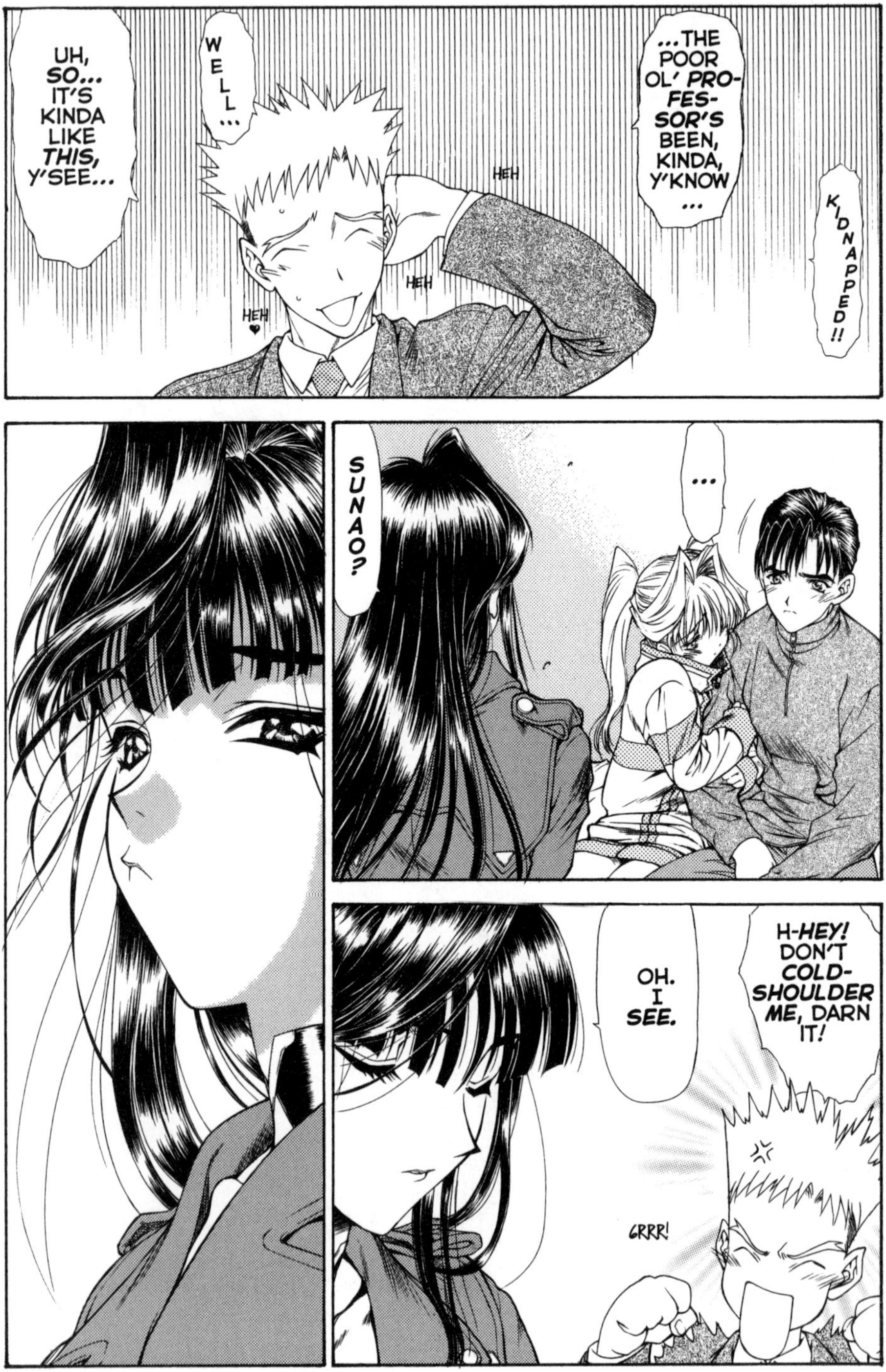
UH, SO... IT'S KINDA LIKE THIS, Y'SEE...
WELL...
HEH
HEH
HEH
...THE POOR OL' PROFESSOR'S BEEN, KINDA, Y'KNOW...
KIDNAPPED!!
SUNAO?
...
OH. I SEE.
H-HEY! DON'T COLD-SHOULDER ME, DARN IT!
GRRR!

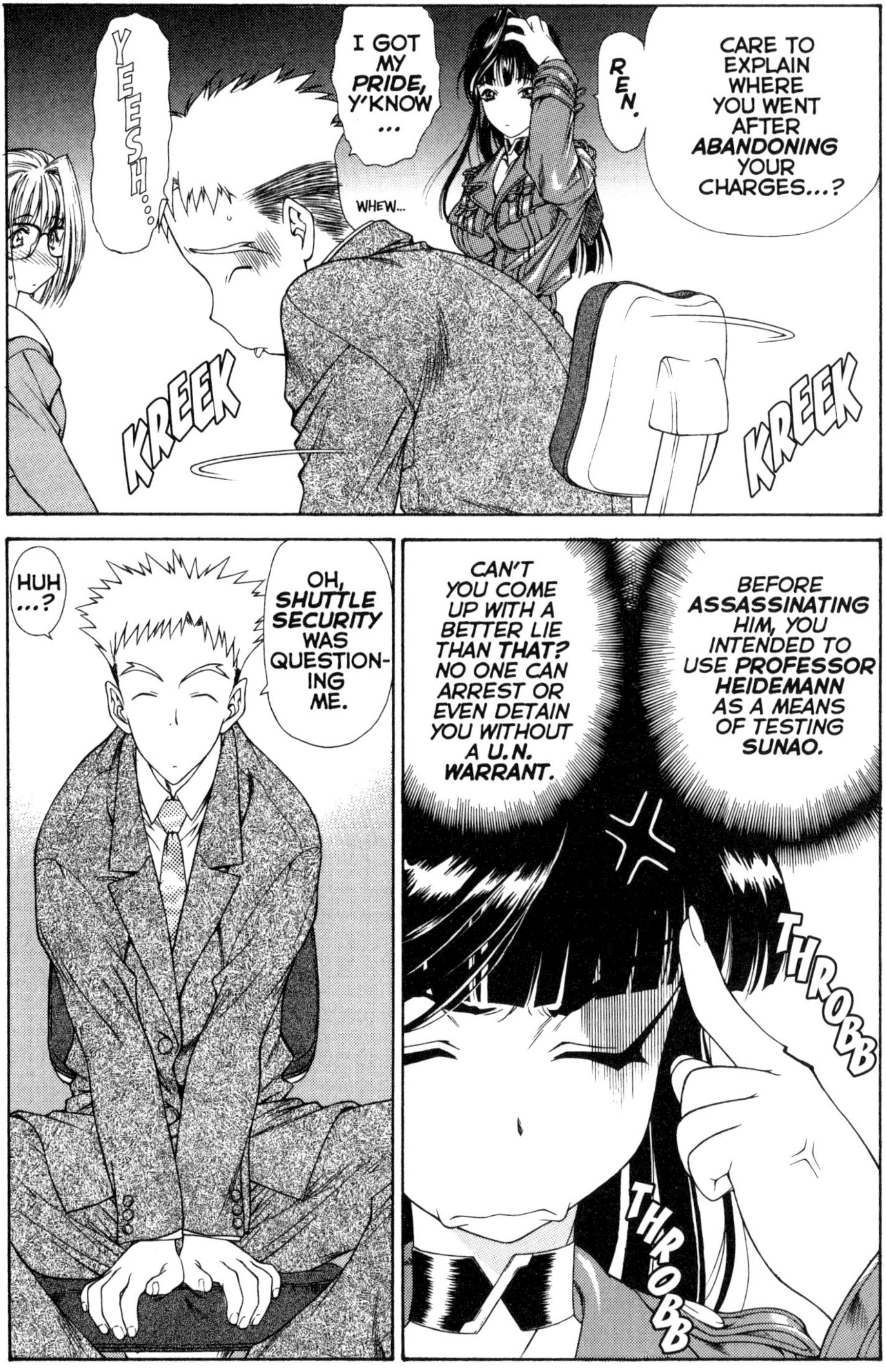
YEESH...
I GOT MY PRIDE, Y'KNOW...
WHEW...
REN.
CARE TO EXPLAIN WHERE YOU WENT AFTER ABANDONING YOUR CHARGES...?
KREEK
KREEK
HUH...?
OH, SHUTTLE SECURITY WAS QUESTIONING ME.
CAN'T YOU COME UP WITH A BETTER LIE THAN THAT? NO ONE CAN ARREST OR EVEN DETAIN YOU WITHOUT A U.N. WARRANT.
BEFORE ASSASSINATING HIM, YOU INTENDED TO USE PROFESSOR HEIDEMANN AS A MEANS OF TESTING SUNAO.
THROBB
THROBB

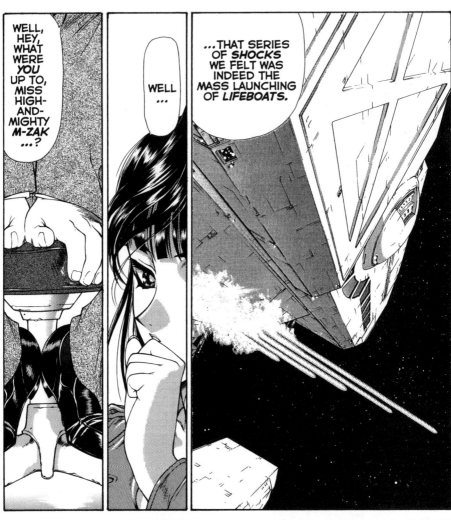

WELL, HEY, WHAT WERE *YOU* UP TO, MISS HIGH-AND-MIGHTY *M-ZAK*...?

WELL...

...THAT SERIES OF *SHOCKS* WE FELT WAS INDEED THE MASS LAUNCHING OF *LIFEBOATS.*

YES, *ALL* OF THE LIFEBOATS HAD LAUNCHED, I FOUND...

...EXCEPT *ONE*...

Lifeboat 4	Lifeboat 5	Life...
LAUNCHED	LAUNCHED	LAUNCHED

Lifeboat 9	Lifeboat 10	Lifeboat 11	Lifeboat 12
LAUNCHED	LAUNCHED	LAUNCHED	LAUNCHED

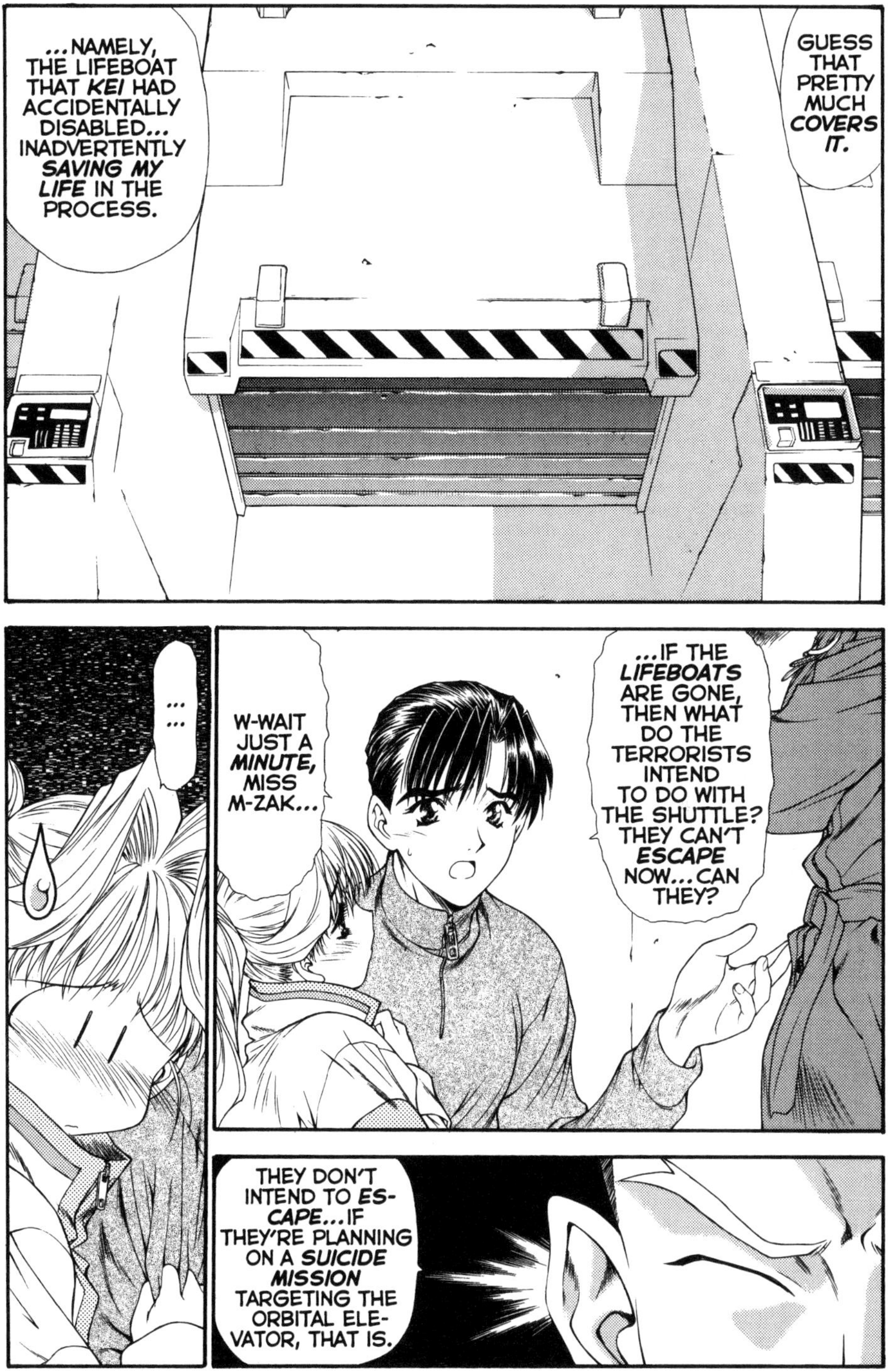
...NAMELY, THE LIFEBOAT THAT KEI HAD ACCIDENTALLY DISABLED... INADVERTENTLY SAVING MY LIFE IN THE PROCESS.
GUESS THAT PRETTY MUCH COVERS IT.
......
W-WAIT JUST A MINUTE, MISS M-ZAK...
...IF THE LIFEBOATS ARE GONE, THEN WHAT DO THE TERRORISTS INTEND TO DO WITH THE SHUTTLE? THEY CAN'T ESCAPE NOW... CAN THEY?
THEY DON'T INTEND TO ES-CAPE... IF THEY'RE PLANNING ON A SUICIDE MISSION TARGETING THE ORBITAL ELE-VATOR, THAT IS.

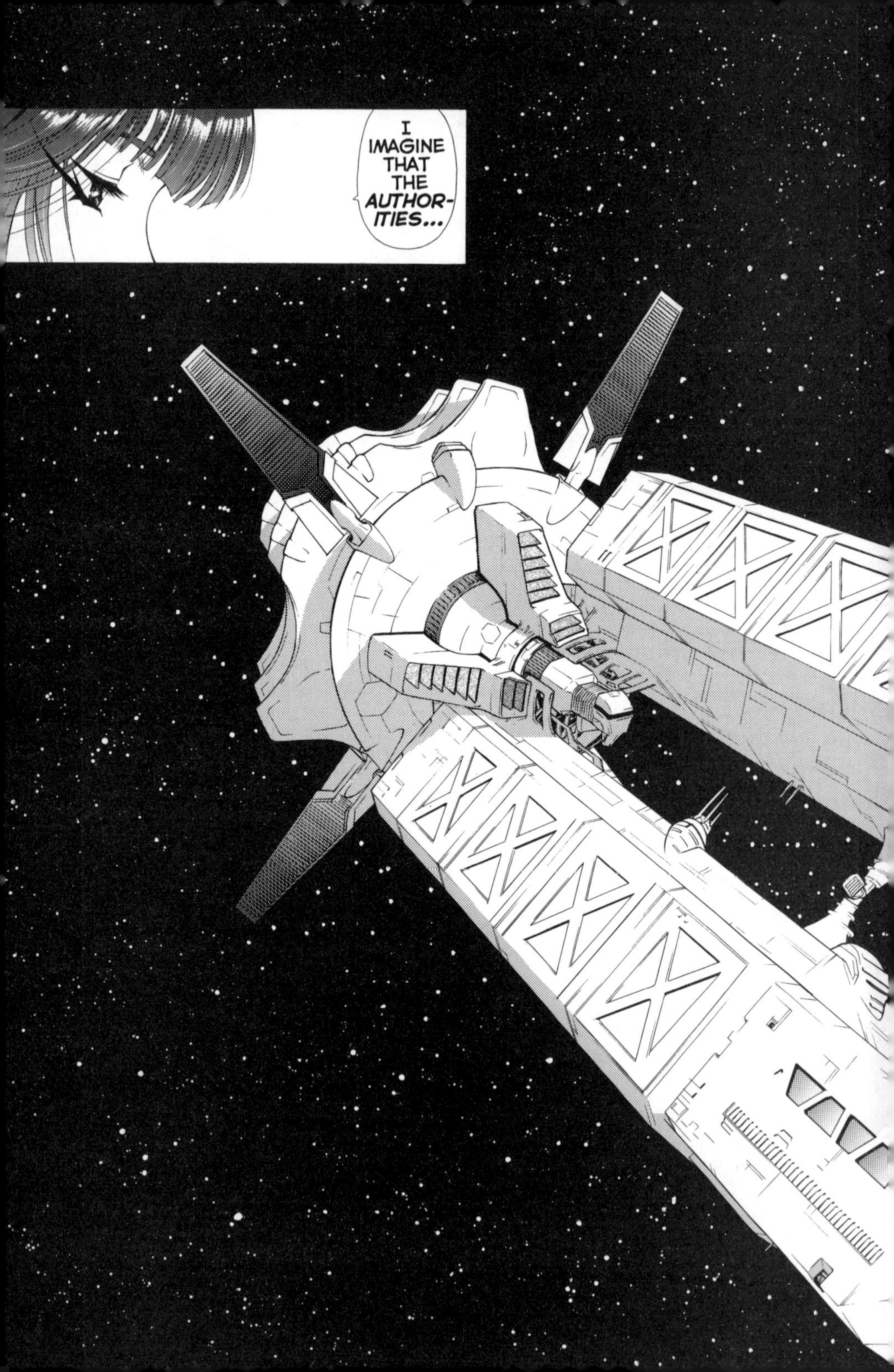
I IMAGINE THAT THE AUTHORITIES...

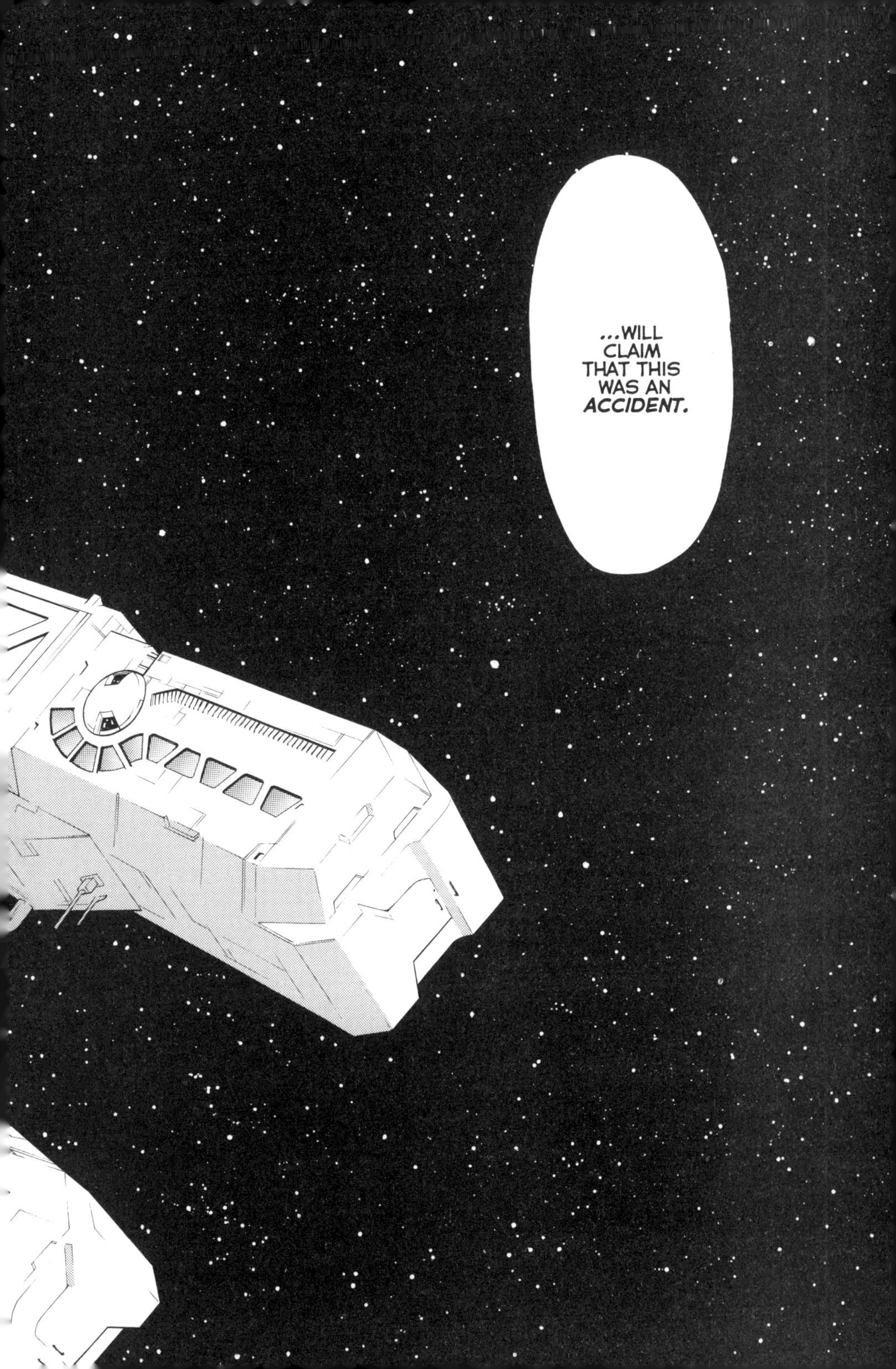
...WILL CLAIM THAT THIS WAS AN *ACCIDENT.*

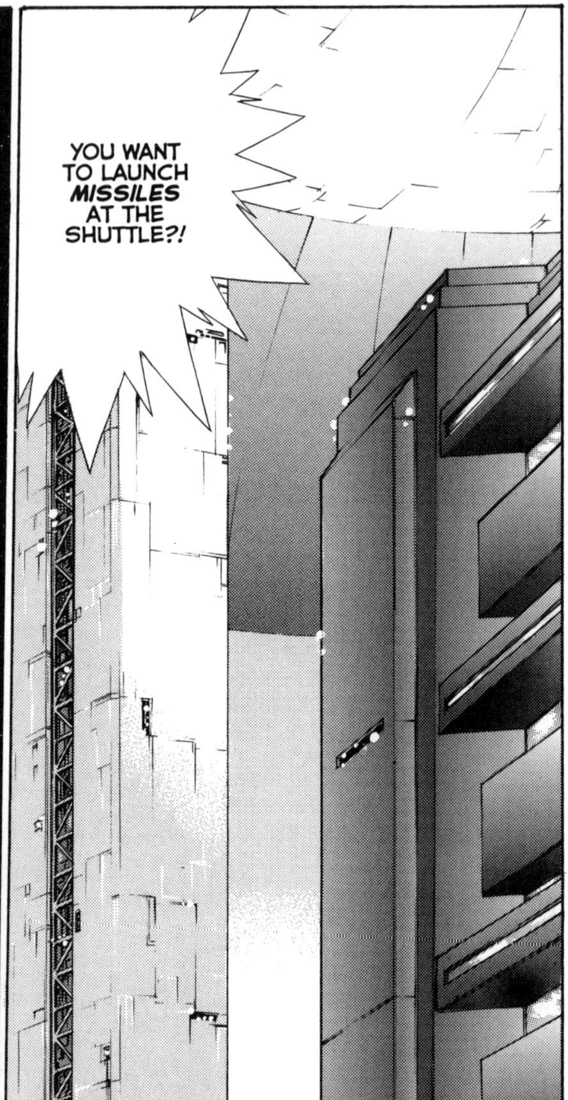
YOU WANT TO LAUNCH *MISSILES* AT THE SHUTTLE?!

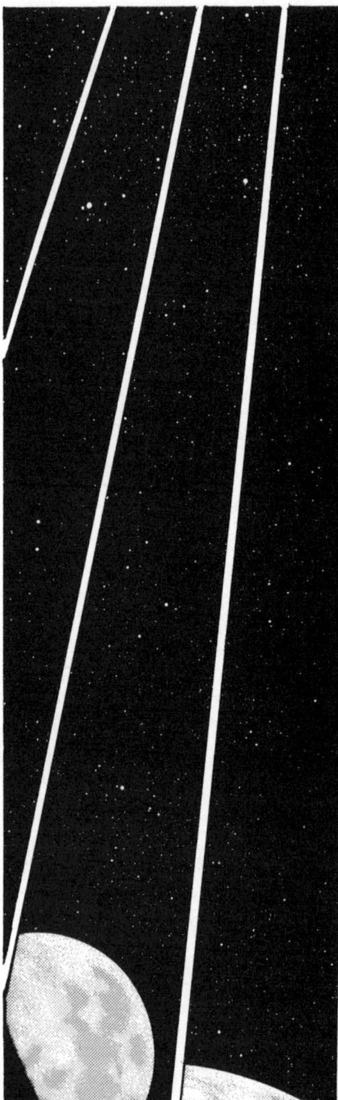

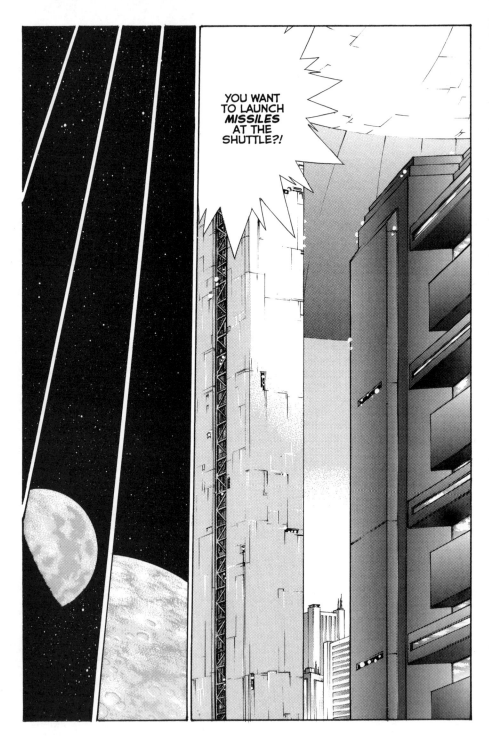

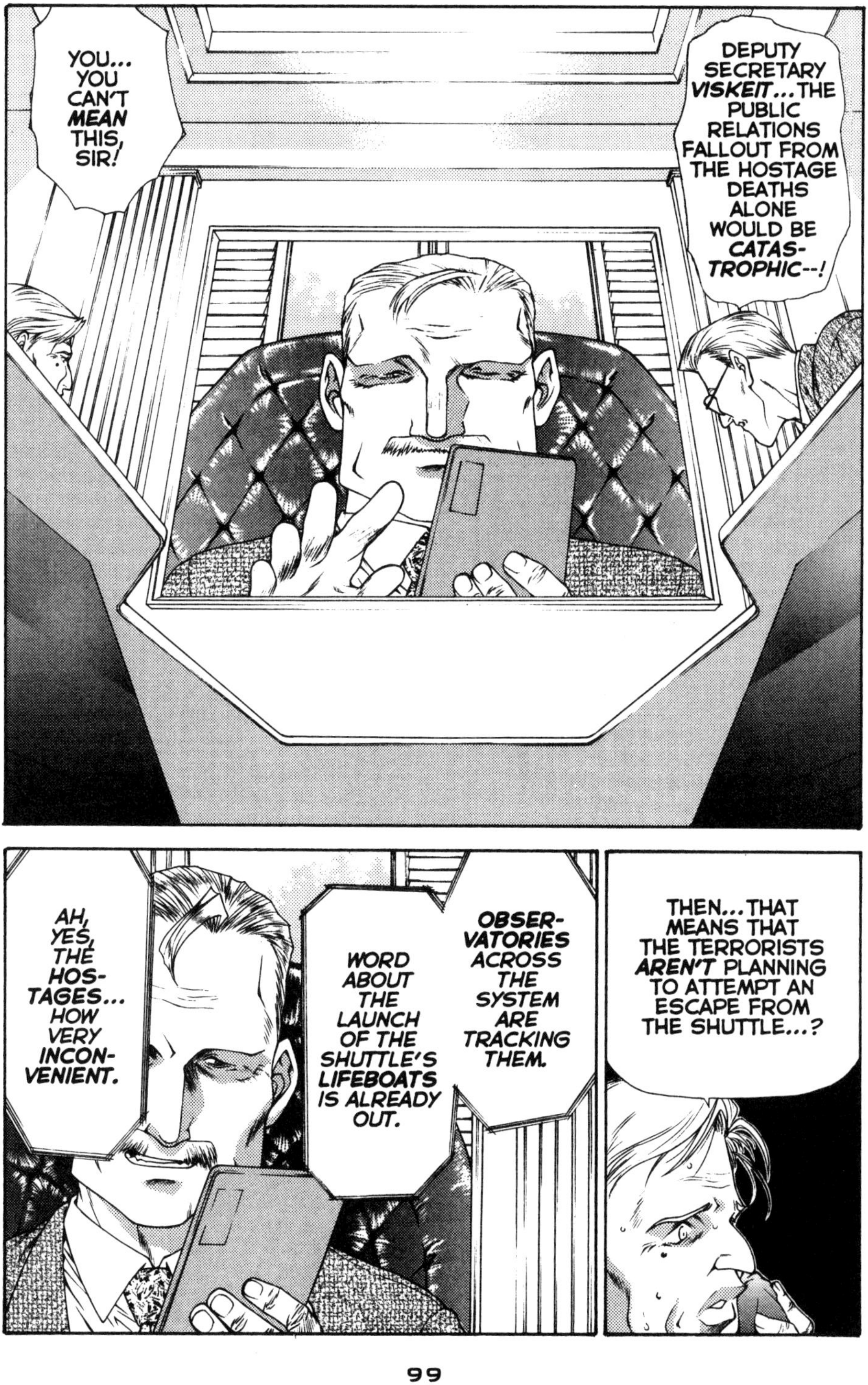
YOU... YOU CAN'T *MEAN* THIS, SIR!
DEPUTY SECRETARY *VISKEIT*... THE PUBLIC RELATIONS FALLOUT FROM THE HOSTAGE DEATHS ALONE WOULD BE *CATASTROPHIC*--!
AH, YES, THE HOSTAGES... HOW VERY INCONVENIENT.
WORD ABOUT THE LAUNCH OF THE SHUTTLE'S *LIFEBOATS* IS ALREADY OUT.
OBSERVATORIES ACROSS THE SYSTEM ARE TRACKING THEM.
THEN... THAT MEANS THAT THE TERRORISTS *AREN'T* PLANNING TO ATTEMPT AN ESCAPE FROM THE SHUTTLE...?

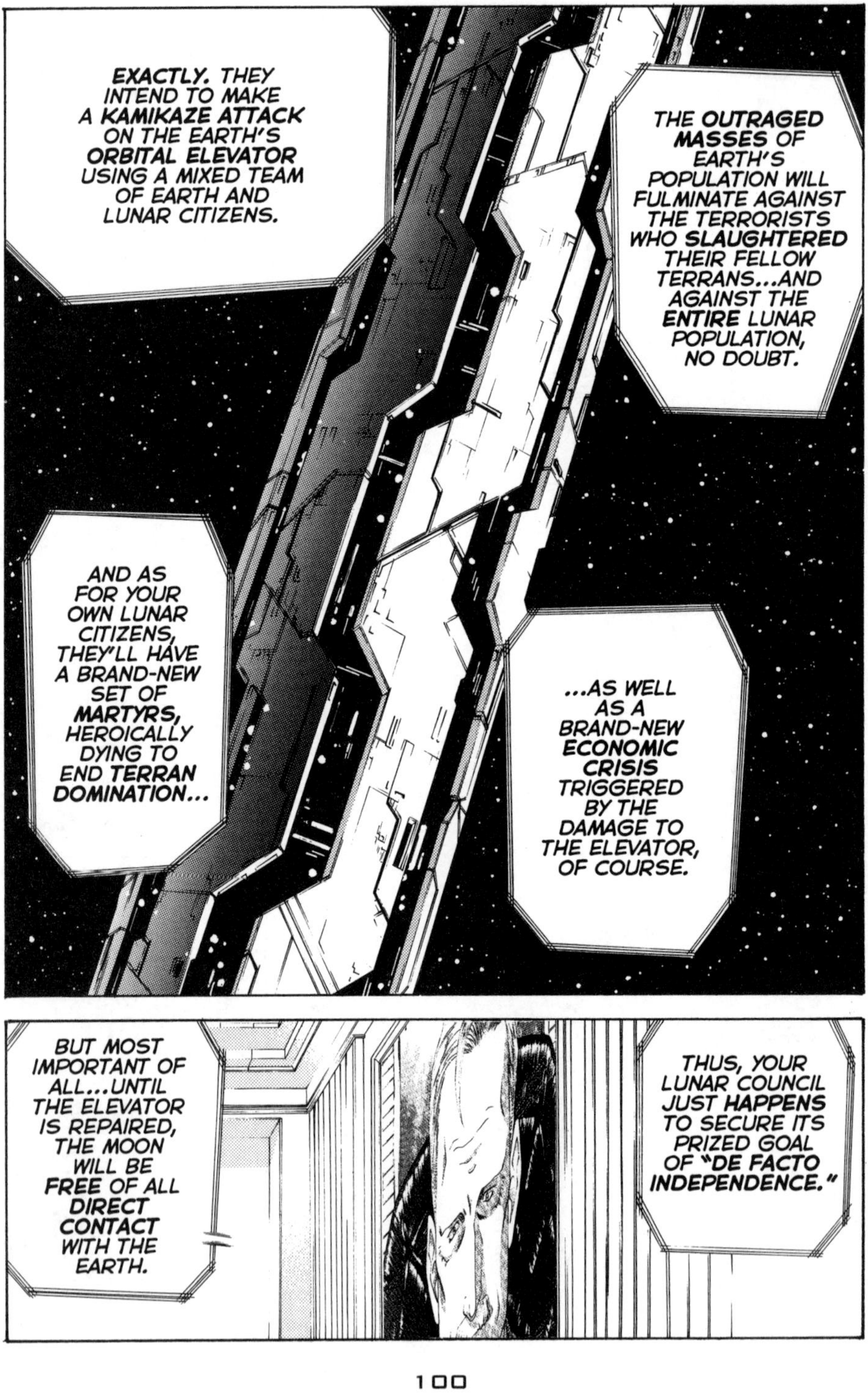
EXACTLY. THEY INTEND TO MAKE A KAMIKAZE ATTACK ON THE EARTH'S ORBITAL ELEVATOR USING A MIXED TEAM OF EARTH AND LUNAR CITIZENS.
THE OUTRAGED MASSES OF EARTH'S POPULATION WILL FULMINATE AGAINST THE TERRORISTS WHO SLAUGHTERED THEIR FELLOW TERRANS...AND AGAINST THE ENTIRE LUNAR POPULATION, NO DOUBT.
AND AS FOR YOUR OWN LUNAR CITIZENS, THEY'LL HAVE A BRAND-NEW SET OF MARTYRS, HEROICALLY DYING TO END TERRAN DOMINATION...
...AS WELL AS A BRAND-NEW ECONOMIC CRISIS TRIGGERED BY THE DAMAGE TO THE ELEVATOR, OF COURSE.
BUT MOST IMPORTANT OF ALL...UNTIL THE ELEVATOR IS REPAIRED, THE MOON WILL BE FREE OF ALL DIRECT CONTACT WITH THE EARTH.
THUS, YOUR LUNAR COUNCIL JUST HAPPENS TO SECURE ITS PRIZED GOAL OF "DE FACTO INDEPENDENCE."

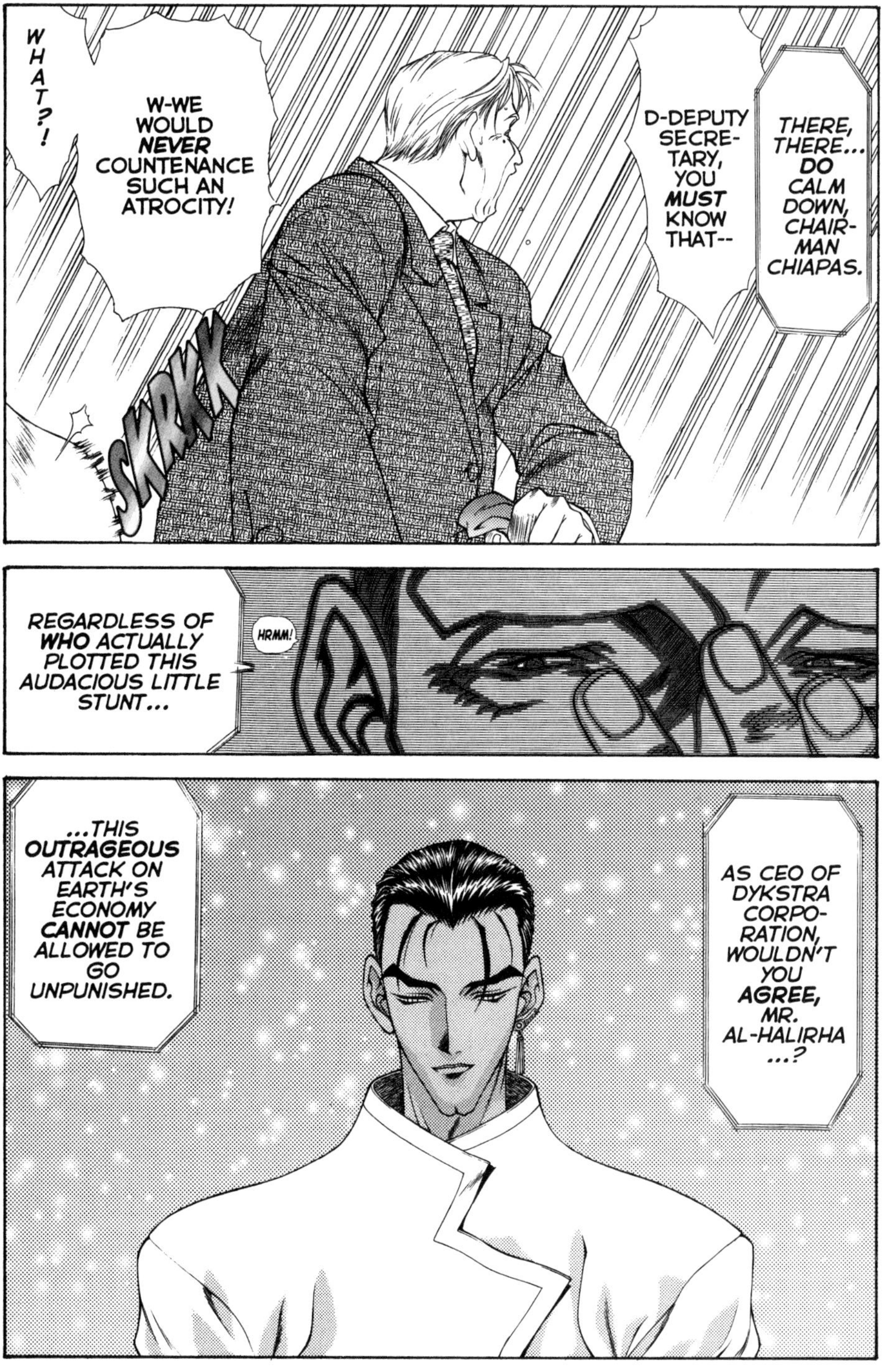
WHAT?!
W-WE WOULD **NEVER** COUNTENANCE SUCH AN ATROCITY!
SKRKK
D-DEPUTY SECRETARY, YOU **MUST** KNOW THAT--
THERE, THERE... **DO** CALM DOWN, CHAIRMAN CHIAPAS.
REGARDLESS OF **WHO** ACTUALLY PLOTTED THIS AUDACIOUS LITTLE STUNT...
HRMM!
...THIS **OUTRAGEOUS** ATTACK ON EARTH'S ECONOMY **CANNOT** BE ALLOWED TO GO UNPUNISHED.
AS CEO OF DYKSTRA CORPORATION, WOULDN'T YOU **AGREE**, MR. AL-HALIRHA ...?

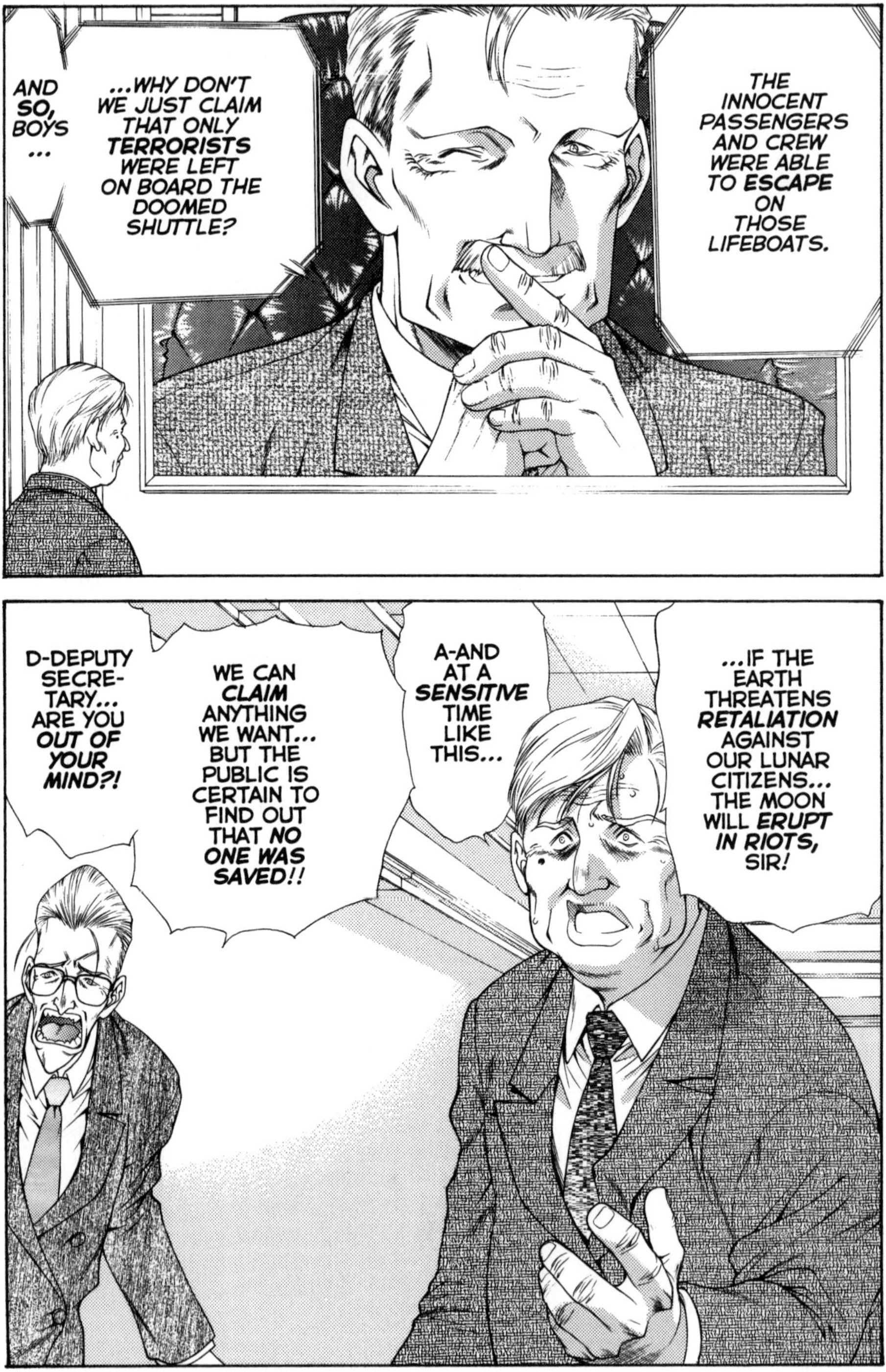
AND SO, BOYS ...
...WHY DON'T WE JUST CLAIM THAT ONLY TERRORISTS WERE LEFT ON BOARD THE DOOMED SHUTTLE?
THE INNOCENT PASSENGERS AND CREW WERE ABLE TO ESCAPE ON THOSE LIFEBOATS.
D-DEPUTY SECRETARY... ARE YOU OUT OF YOUR MIND?!
WE CAN CLAIM ANYTHING WE WANT... BUT THE PUBLIC IS CERTAIN TO FIND OUT THAT NO ONE WAS SAVED!!
A-AND AT A SENSITIVE TIME LIKE THIS...
...IF THE EARTH THREATENS RETALIATION AGAINST OUR LUNAR CITIZENS... THE MOON WILL ERUPT IN RIOTS, SIR!

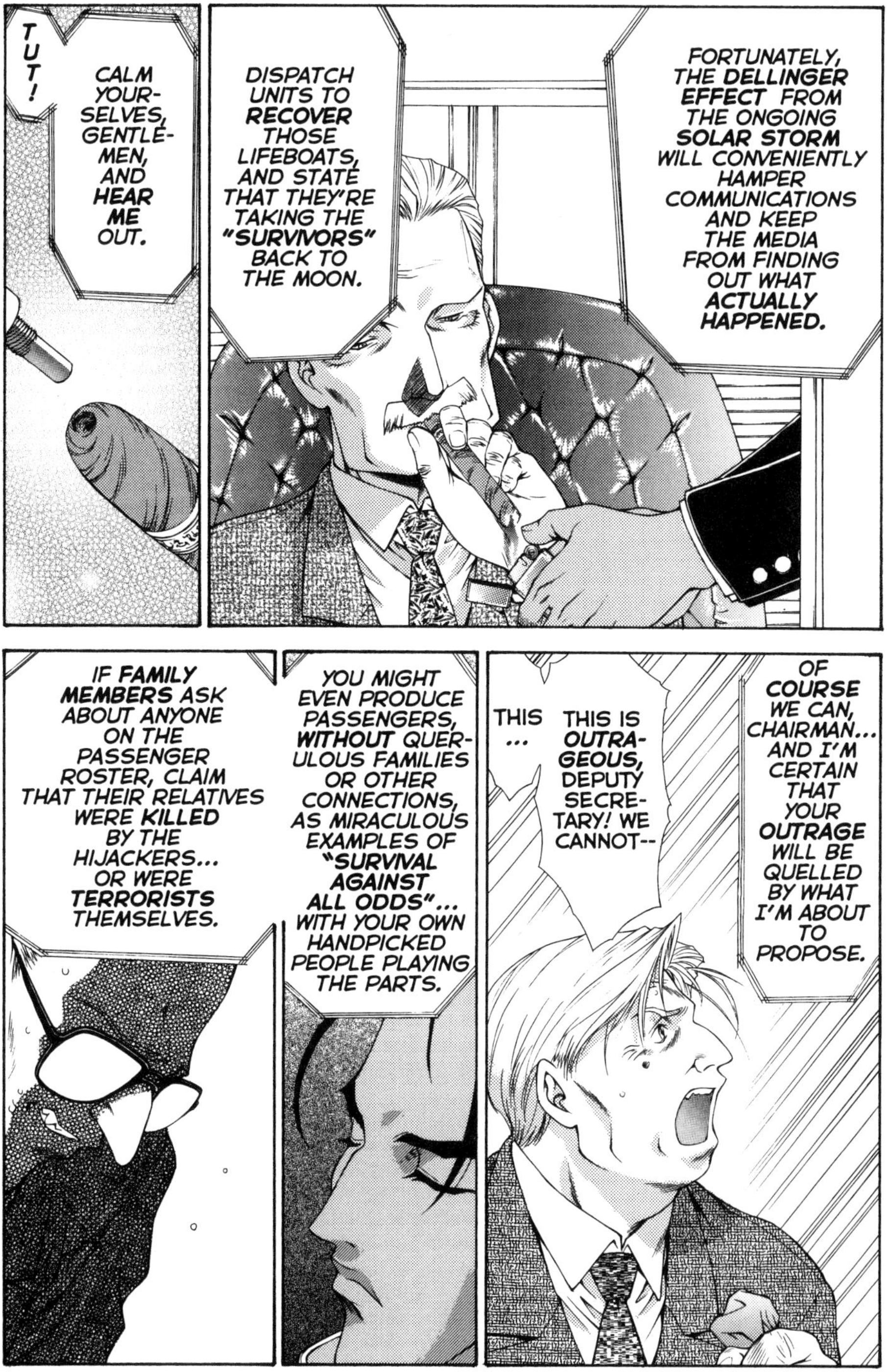
TUT!
CALM YOURSELVES, GENTLEMEN, AND HEAR ME OUT.
DISPATCH UNITS TO RECOVER THOSE LIFEBOATS, AND STATE THAT THEY'RE TAKING THE "SURVIVORS" BACK TO THE MOON.
FORTUNATELY, THE DELLINGER EFFECT FROM THE ONGOING SOLAR STORM WILL CONVENIENTLY HAMPER COMMUNICATIONS AND KEEP THE MEDIA FROM FINDING OUT WHAT ACTUALLY HAPPENED.
IF FAMILY MEMBERS ASK ABOUT ANYONE ON THE PASSENGER ROSTER, CLAIM THAT THEIR RELATIVES WERE KILLED BY THE HIJACKERS... OR WERE TERRORISTS THEMSELVES.
YOU MIGHT EVEN PRODUCE PASSENGERS, WITHOUT QUERULOUS FAMILIES OR OTHER CONNECTIONS, AS MIRACULOUS EXAMPLES OF "SURVIVAL AGAINST ALL ODDS"... WITH YOUR OWN HANDPICKED PEOPLE PLAYING THE PARTS.
THIS...
THIS IS OUTRAGEOUS, DEPUTY SECRETARY! WE CANNOT--
OF COURSE WE CAN, CHAIRMAN... AND I'M CERTAIN THAT YOUR OUTRAGE WILL BE QUELLED BY WHAT I'M ABOUT TO PROPOSE.

NOW, GRANTING THE MOON *ABSOLUTE* INDEPENDENCE WOULD BE, SHALL WE SAY... *POLITICALLY UNTENABLE* FOR US.

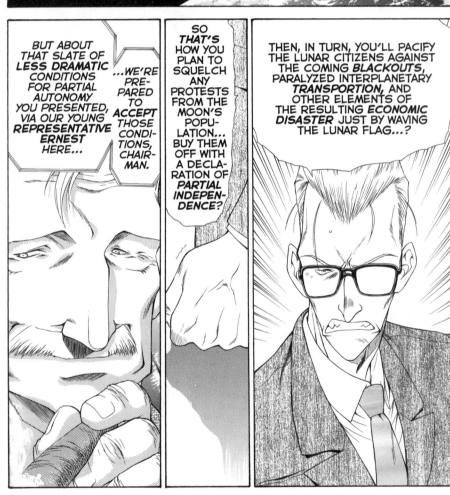

BUT ABOUT THAT SLATE OF *LESS DRAMATIC* CONDITIONS FOR PARTIAL AUTONOMY YOU PRESENTED, VIA OUR YOUNG *REPRESENTATIVE ERNEST* HERE...

...WE'RE PREPARED TO *ACCEPT* THOSE CONDITIONS, CHAIRMAN.

SO *THAT'S* HOW YOU PLAN TO SQUELCH ANY PROTESTS FROM THE MOON'S POPULATION... BUY THEM OFF WITH A DECLARATION OF *PARTIAL INDEPENDENCE*?

THEN, IN TURN, YOU'LL PACIFY THE LUNAR CITIZENS AGAINST THE COMING *BLACKOUTS*, PARALYZED INTERPLANETARY *TRANSPORTION*, AND OTHER ELEMENTS OF THE RESULTING *ECONOMIC DISASTER* JUST BY WAVING THE LUNAR FLAG...?

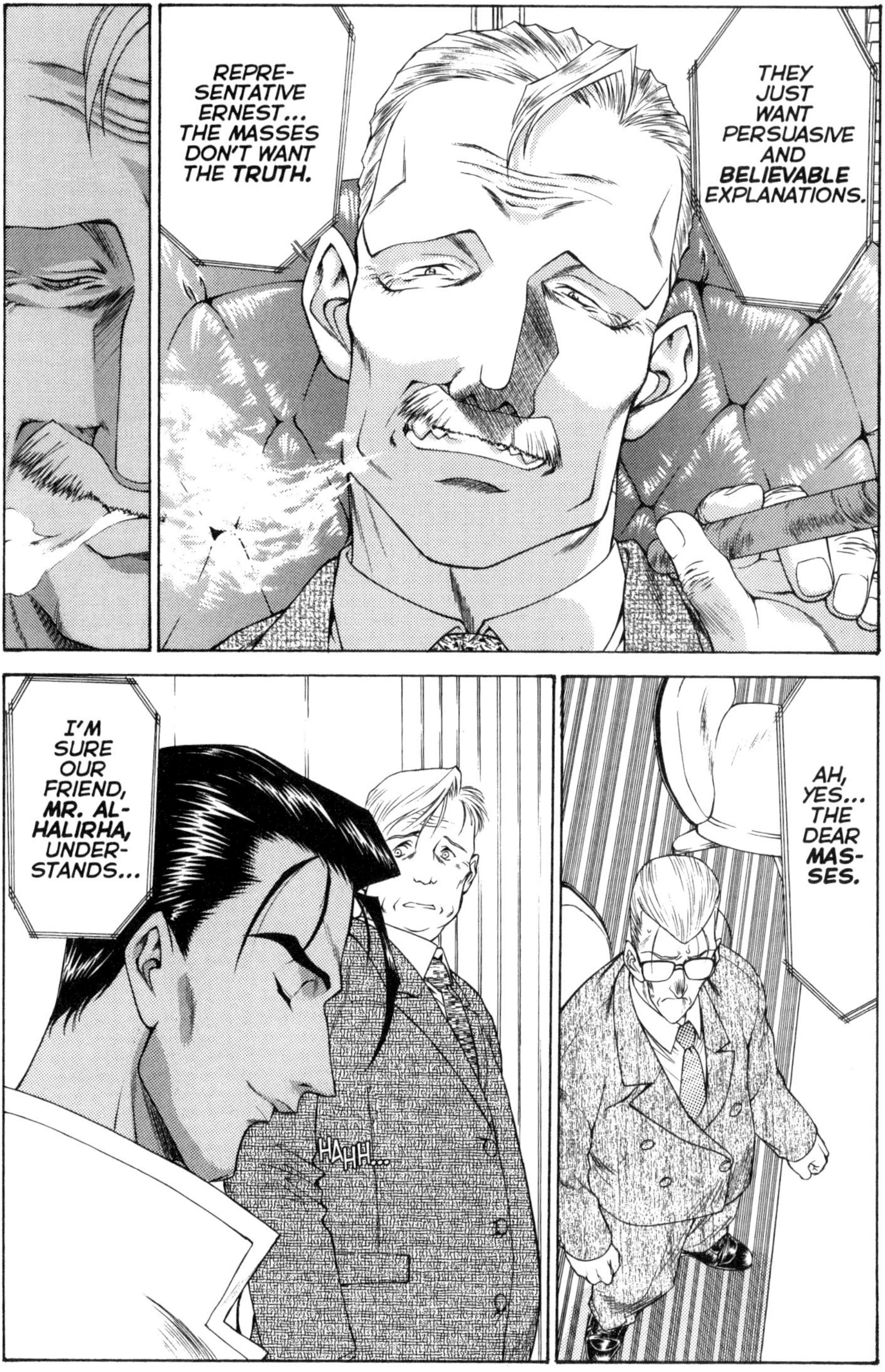
REPRE-SENTATIVE ERNEST... THE MASSES DON'T WANT THE TRUTH.
THEY JUST WANT PERSUASIVE AND BELIEVABLE EXPLANATIONS.
I'M SURE OUR FRIEND, MR. AL-HALIRHA, UNDER-STANDS...
HAHH...
AH, YES... THE DEAR MAS-SES.

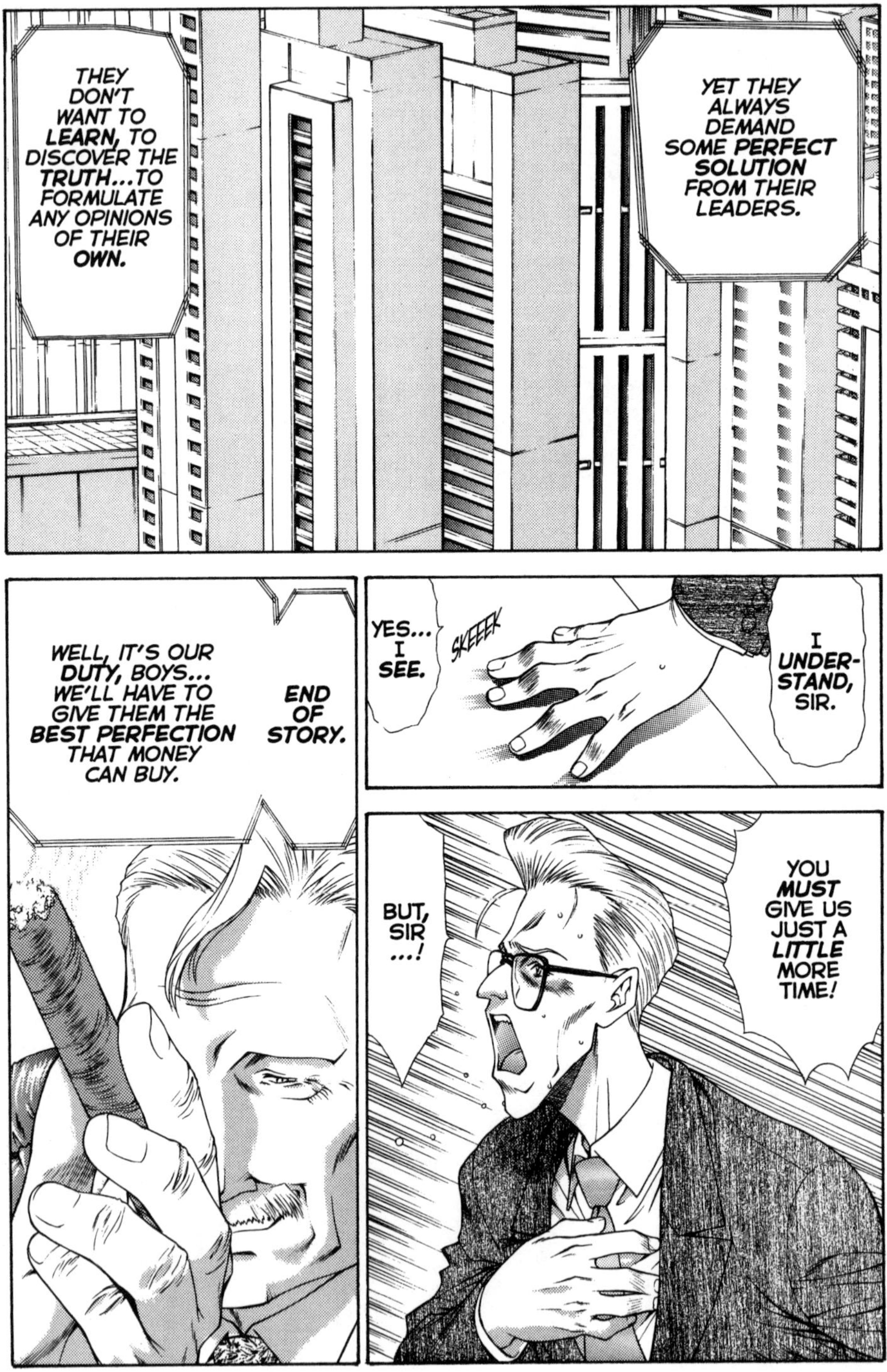
THEY DON'T WANT TO LEARN, TO DISCOVER THE TRUTH...TO FORMULATE ANY OPINIONS OF THEIR OWN.
YET THEY ALWAYS DEMAND SOME PERFECT SOLUTION FROM THEIR LEADERS.
WELL, IT'S OUR DUTY, BOYS... WE'LL HAVE TO GIVE THEM THE BEST PERFECTION THAT MONEY CAN BUY.
END OF STORY.
YES... I SEE.
SKEEEK
I UNDERSTAND, SIR.
BUT, SIR ...!
YOU MUST GIVE US JUST A LITTLE MORE TIME!

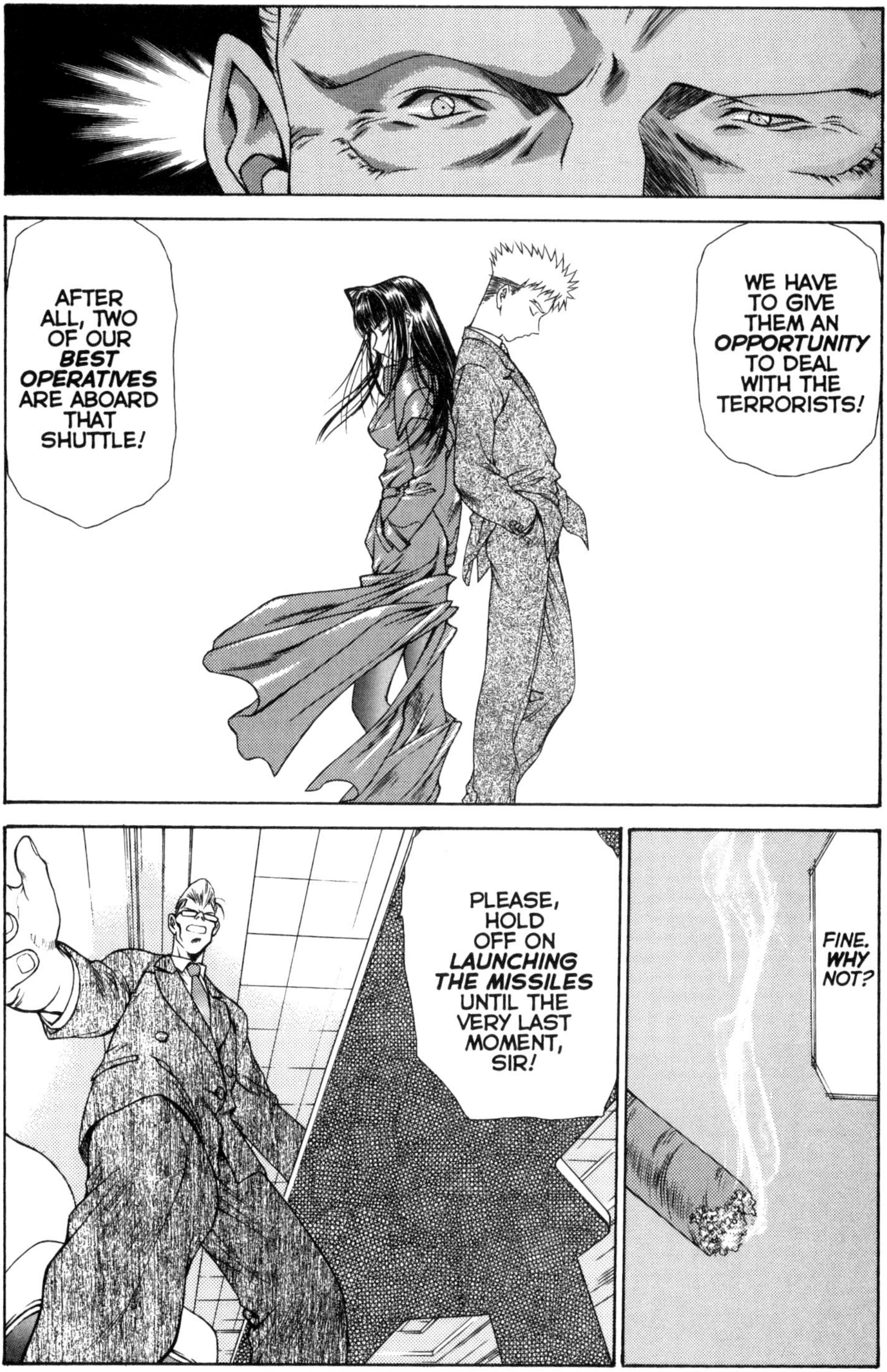
AFTER ALL, TWO OF OUR BEST OPERATIVES ARE ABOARD THAT SHUTTLE!
WE HAVE TO GIVE THEM AN OPPORTUNITY TO DEAL WITH THE TERRORISTS!
PLEASE, HOLD OFF ON LAUNCHING THE MISSILES UNTIL THE VERY LAST MOMENT, SIR!
FINE. WHY NOT?

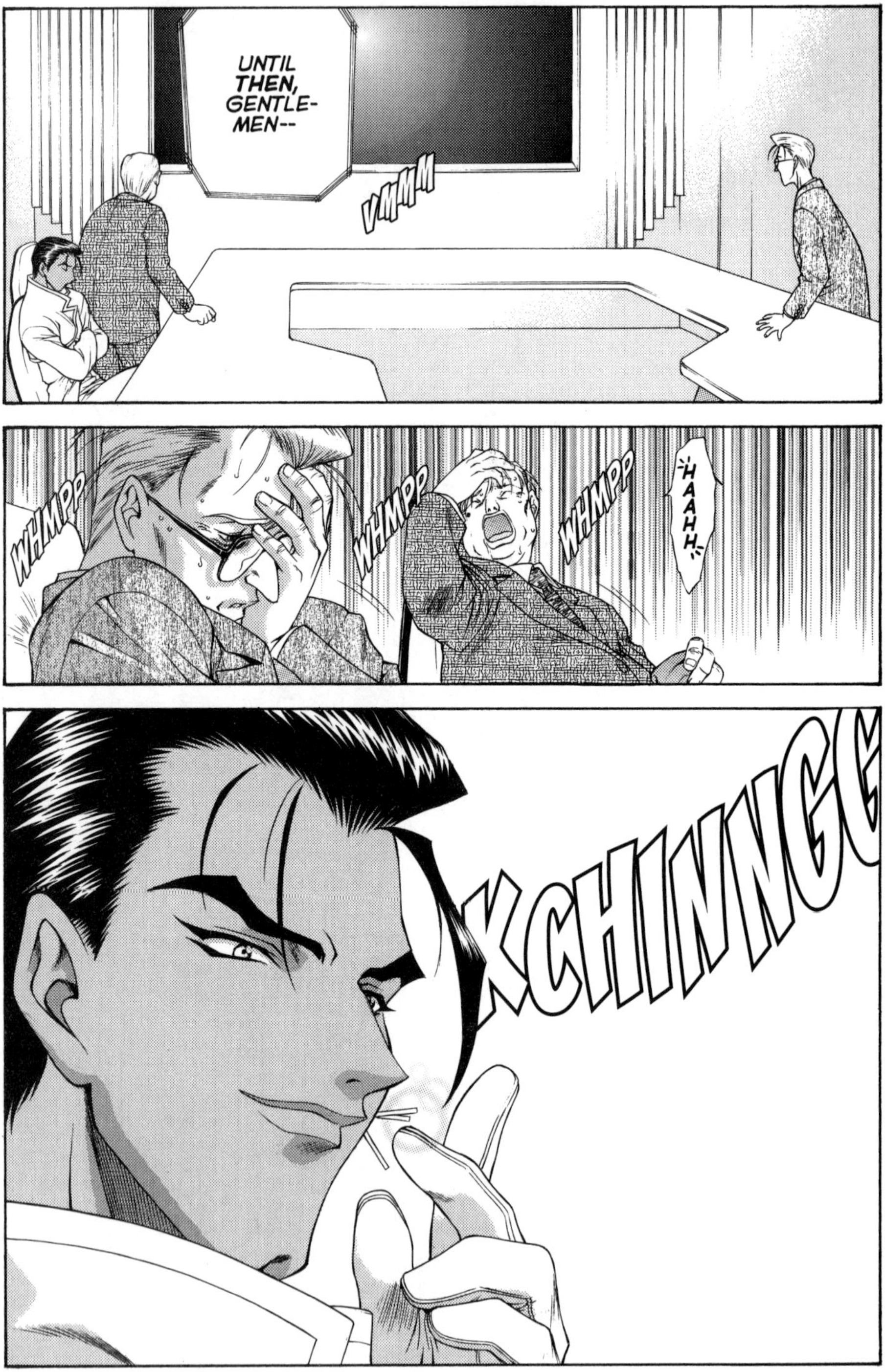
UNTIL THEN, GENTLE-MEN--
VMMM
WHMPP
WHMPP
WHMPP
HAAAHH
KCHINNGG

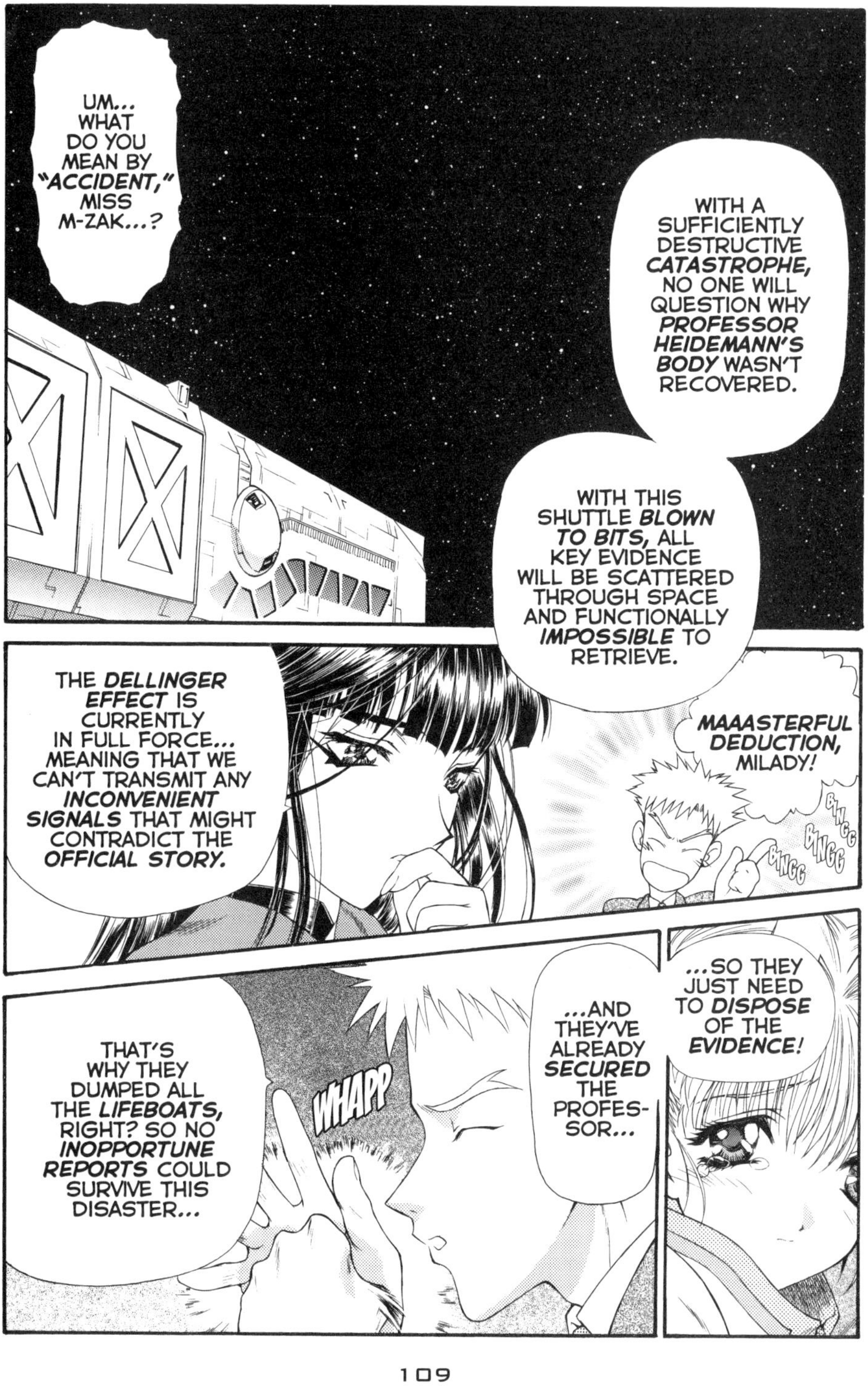
UM... WHAT DO YOU MEAN BY "ACCIDENT," MISS M-ZAK...?
WITH A SUFFICIENTLY DESTRUCTIVE CATASTROPHE, NO ONE WILL QUESTION WHY PROFESSOR HEIDEMANN'S BODY WASN'T RECOVERED.
WITH THIS SHUTTLE BLOWN TO BITS, ALL KEY EVIDENCE WILL BE SCATTERED THROUGH SPACE AND FUNCTIONALLY IMPOSSIBLE TO RETRIEVE.
THE DELLINGER EFFECT IS CURRENTLY IN FULL FORCE... MEANING THAT WE CAN'T TRANSMIT ANY INCONVENIENT SIGNALS THAT MIGHT CONTRADICT THE OFFICIAL STORY.
MAAASTERFUL DEDUCTION, MILADY!
BINGG BINGG BINGG
THAT'S WHY THEY DUMPED ALL THE LIFEBOATS, RIGHT? SO NO INOPPORTUNE REPORTS COULD SURVIVE THIS DISASTER...
WHAPP
...AND THEY'VE ALREADY SECURED THE PROFES-SOR...
...SO THEY JUST NEED TO DISPOSE OF THE EVIDENCE!

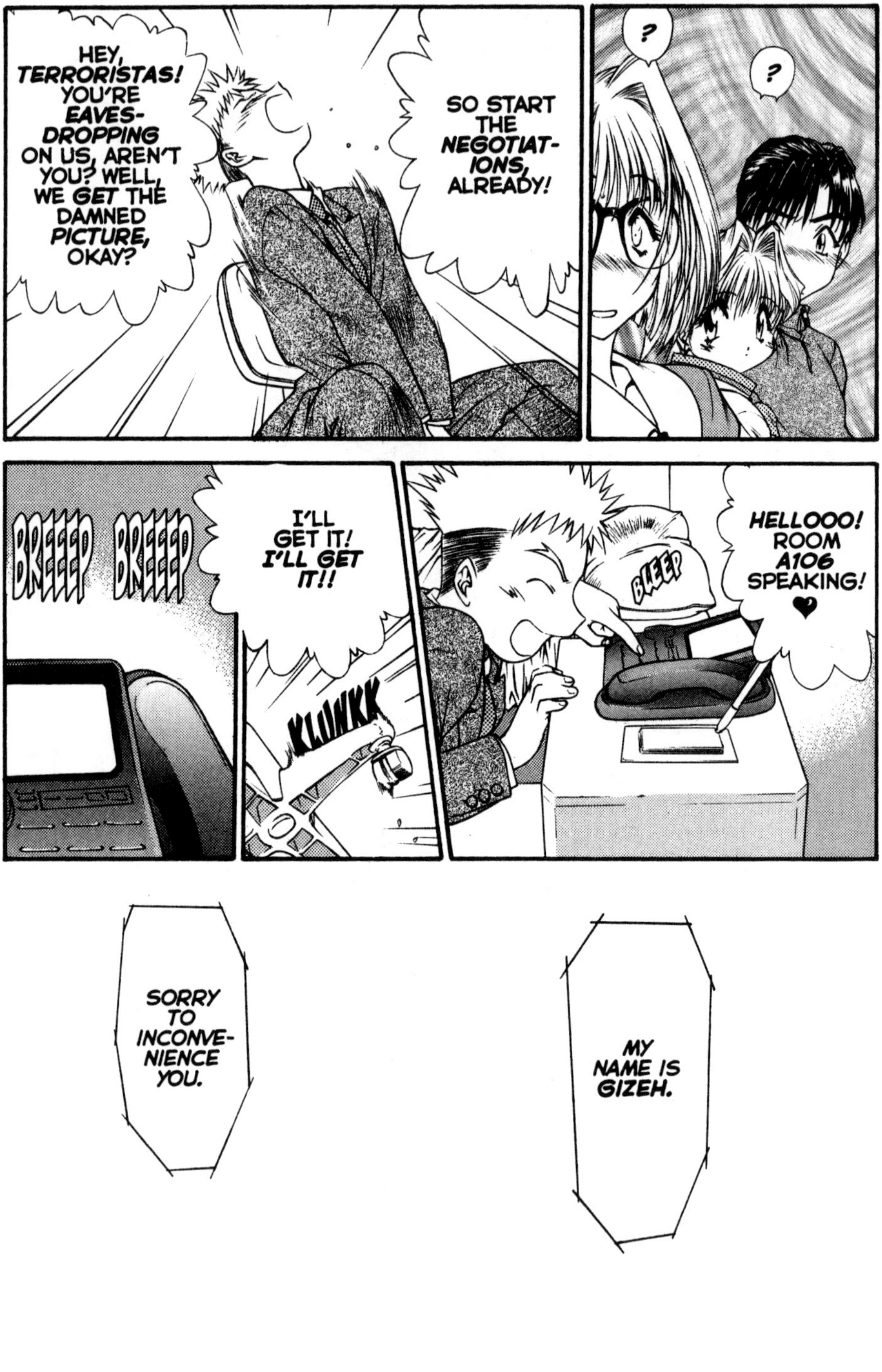
HEY, TERRORISTAS! YOU'RE EAVES-DROPPING ON US, AREN'T YOU? WELL, WE GET THE DAMNED PICTURE, OKAY?
SO START THE NEGOTIAT-IONS, ALREADY!
?
?
BREEEP BREEEP
I'LL GET IT! I'LL GET IT!!
KLUNKK
BLEEP
HELLOOO! ROOM A106 SPEAKING! ❤
SORRY TO INCONVE-NIENCE YOU.
MY NAME IS GIZEH.

Act 64

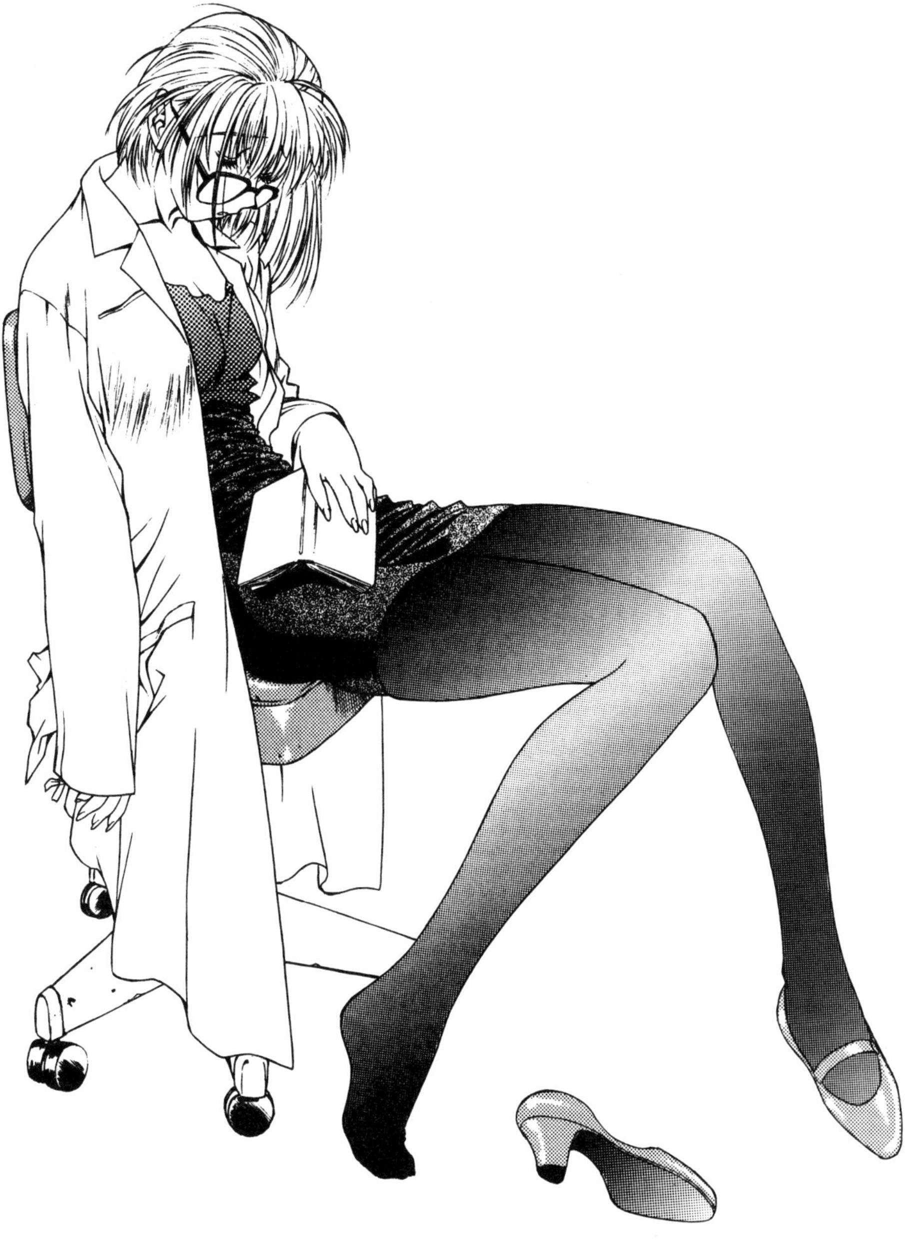

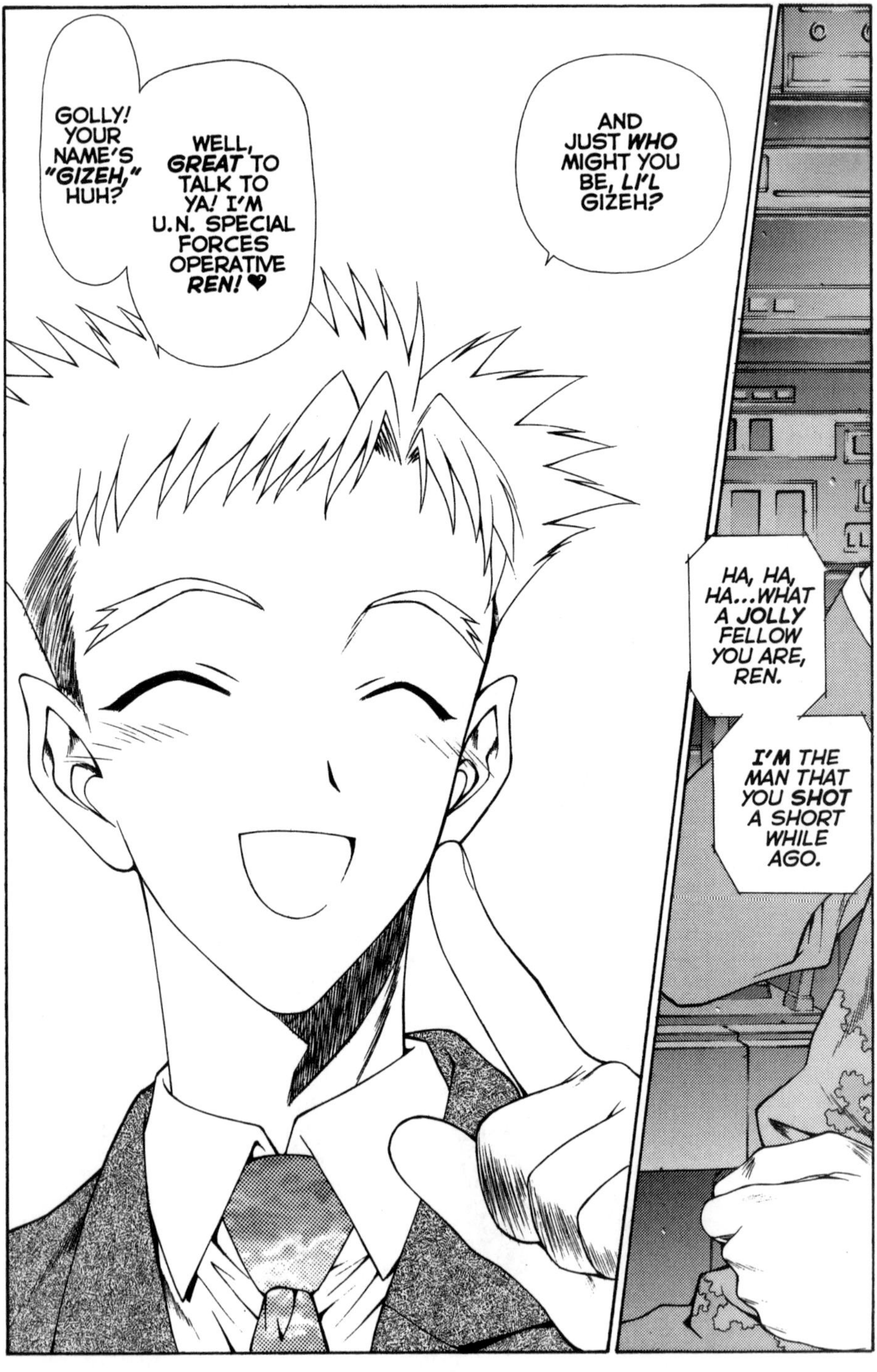
GOLLY! YOUR NAME'S "GIZEH," HUH?
WELL, GREAT TO TALK TO YA! I'M U.N. SPECIAL FORCES OPERATIVE REN! ❤
AND JUST WHO MIGHT YOU BE, LI'L GIZEH?
HA, HA, HA...WHAT A JOLLY FELLOW YOU ARE, REN.
I'M THE MAN THAT YOU SHOT A SHORT WHILE AGO.

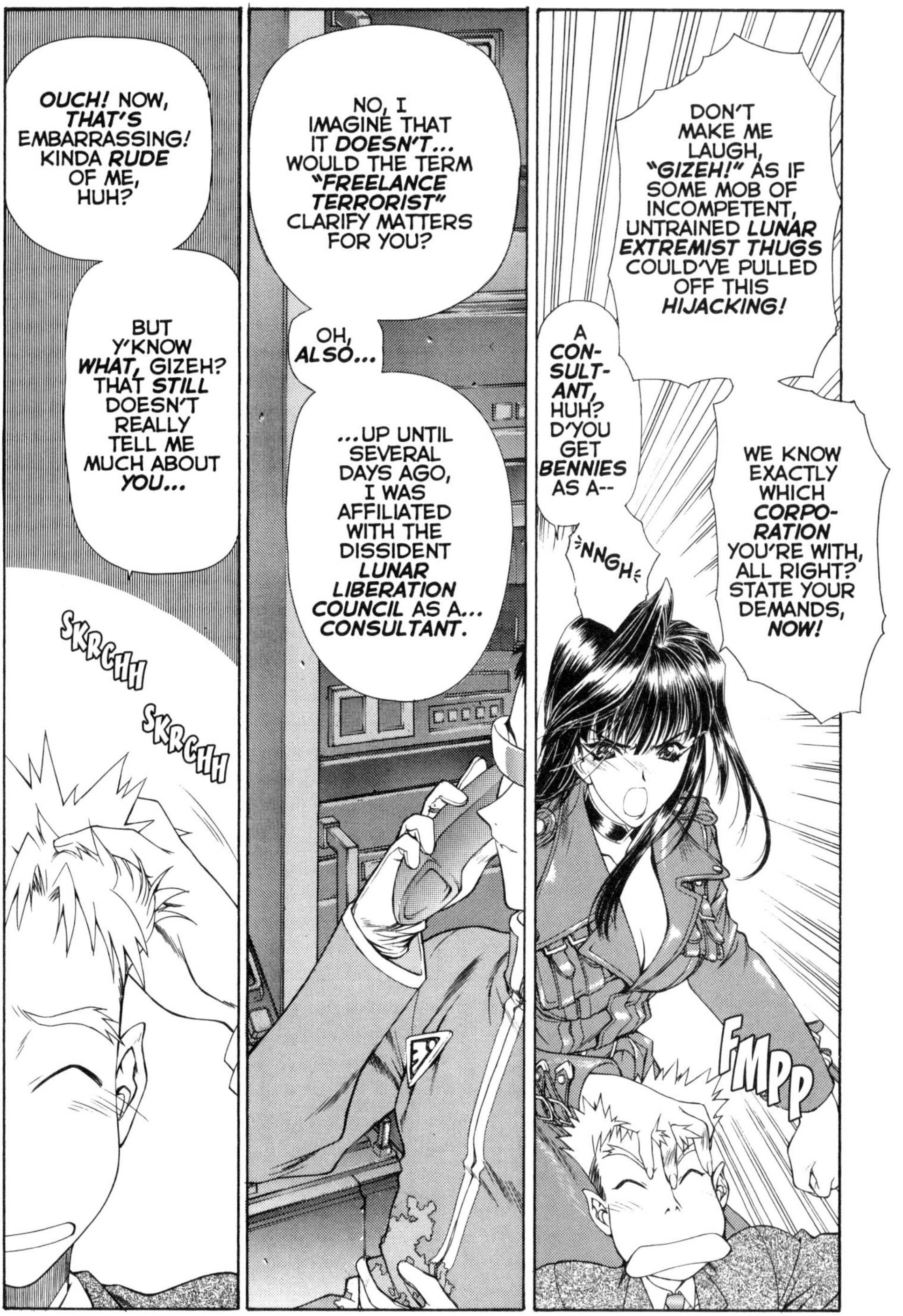

OUCH! NOW, THAT'S EMBARRASSING! KINDA RUDE OF ME, HUH?
BUT Y'KNOW WHAT, GIZEH? THAT STILL DOESN'T REALLY TELL ME MUCH ABOUT YOU...
SKRCHH
SKRCHH
NO, I IMAGINE THAT IT DOESN'T... WOULD THE TERM "FREELANCE TERRORIST" CLARIFY MATTERS FOR YOU?
OH, ALSO...
...UP UNTIL SEVERAL DAYS AGO, I WAS AFFILIATED WITH THE DISSIDENT LUNAR LIBERATION COUNCIL AS A... CONSULTANT.
A CON-SULT-ANT, HUH? D'YOU GET BENNIES AS A--
NNGH
DON'T MAKE ME LAUGH, "GIZEH!" AS IF SOME MOB OF INCOMPETENT, UNTRAINED LUNAR EXTREMIST THUGS COULD'VE PULLED OFF THIS HIJACKING!
WE KNOW EXACTLY WHICH CORPO-RATION YOU'RE WITH, ALL RIGHT? STATE YOUR DEMANDS, NOW!
FMPP

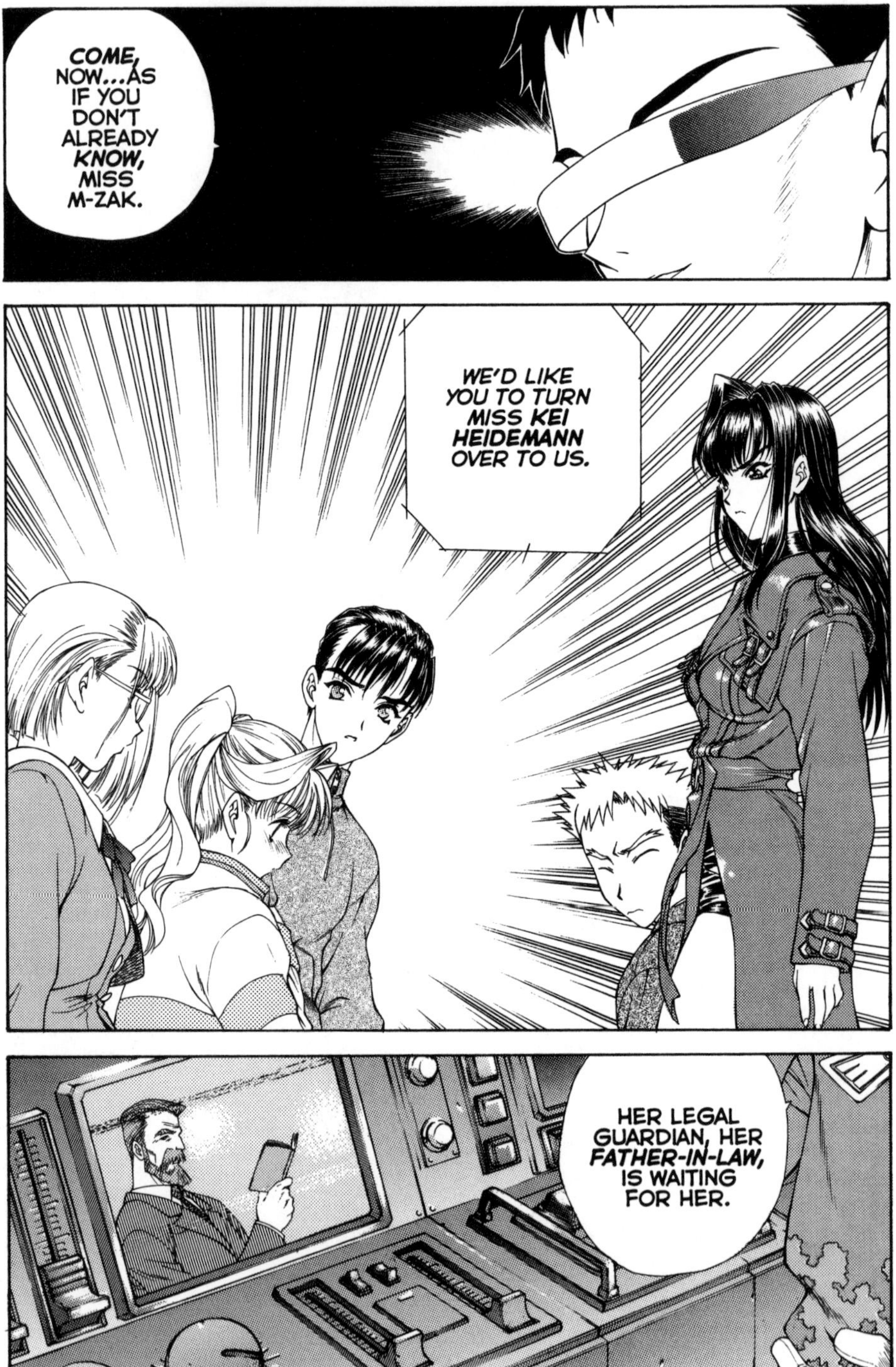
COME, NOW...AS IF YOU DON'T ALREADY KNOW, MISS M-ZAK.
WE'D LIKE YOU TO TURN MISS KEI HEIDEMANN OVER TO US.
HER LEGAL GUARDIAN, HER FATHER-IN-LAW, IS WAITING FOR HER.

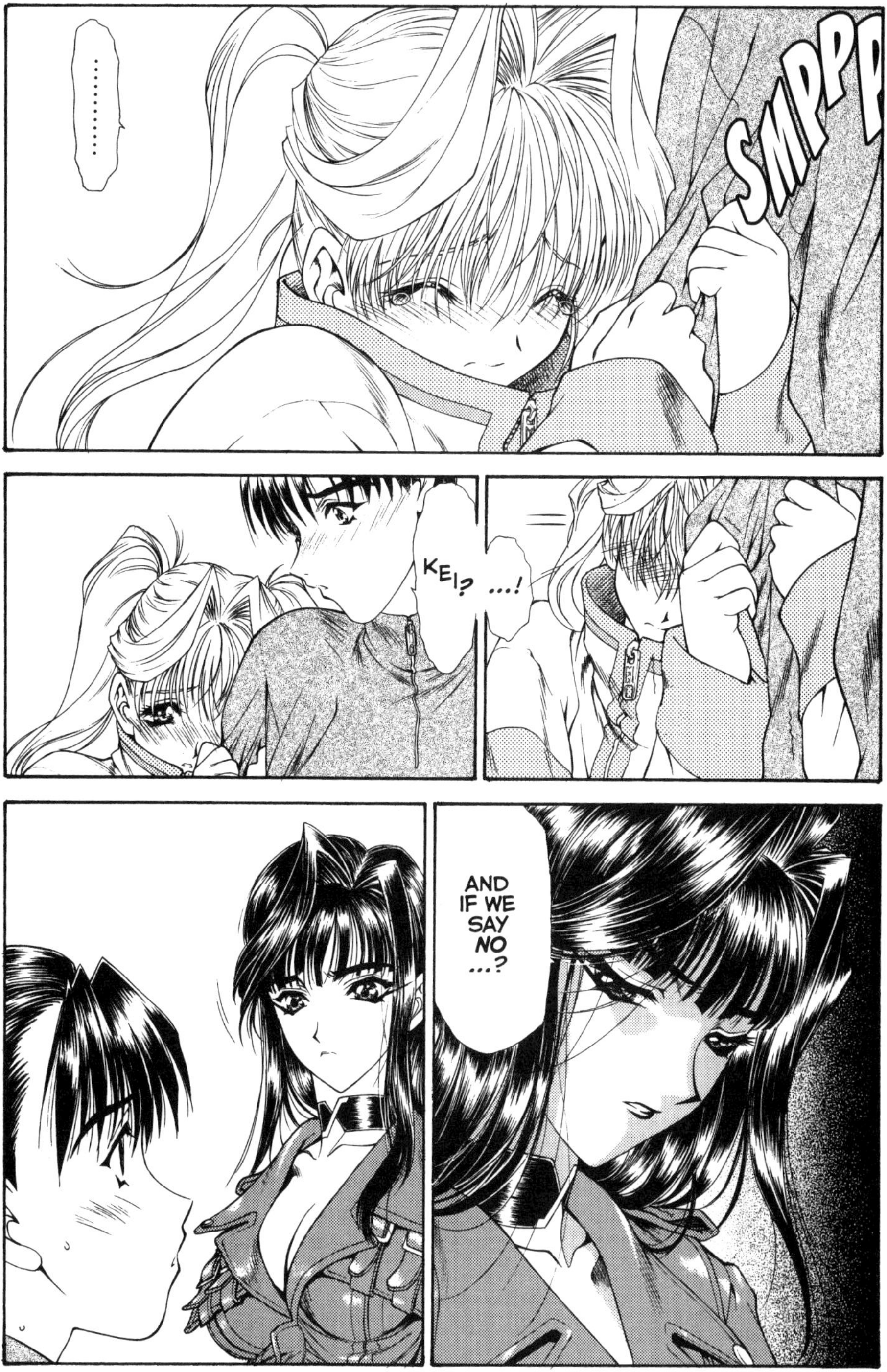
......
SMPPP
KEI?
...!
AND IF WE SAY NO ...?

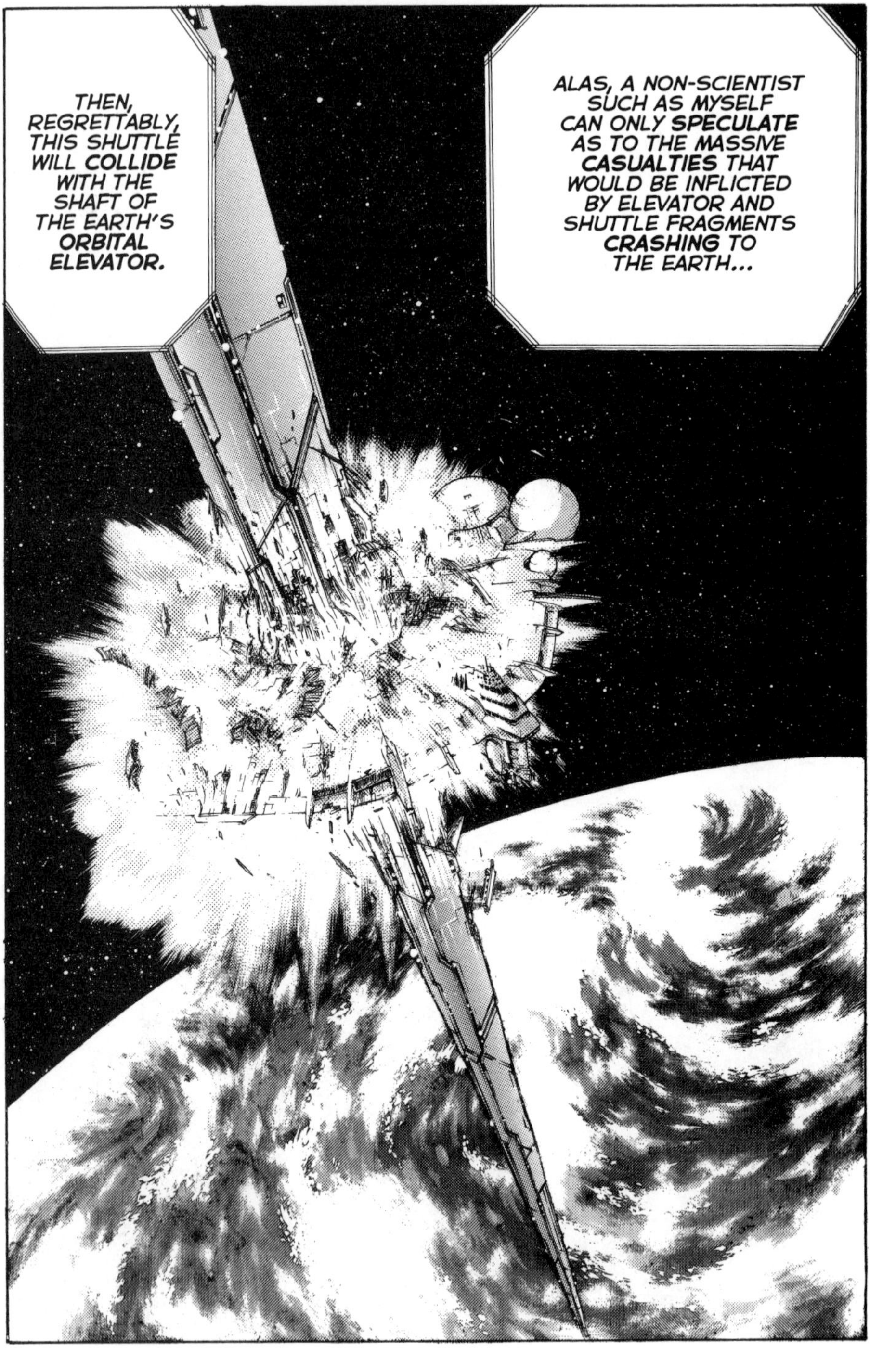
ALAS, A NON-SCIENTIST SUCH AS MYSELF CAN ONLY SPECULATE AS TO THE MASSIVE CASUALTIES THAT WOULD BE INFLICTED BY ELEVATOR AND SHUTTLE FRAGMENTS CRASHING TO THE EARTH...
THEN, REGRETTABLY, THIS SHUTTLE WILL COLLIDE WITH THE SHAFT OF THE EARTH'S ORBITAL ELEVATOR.

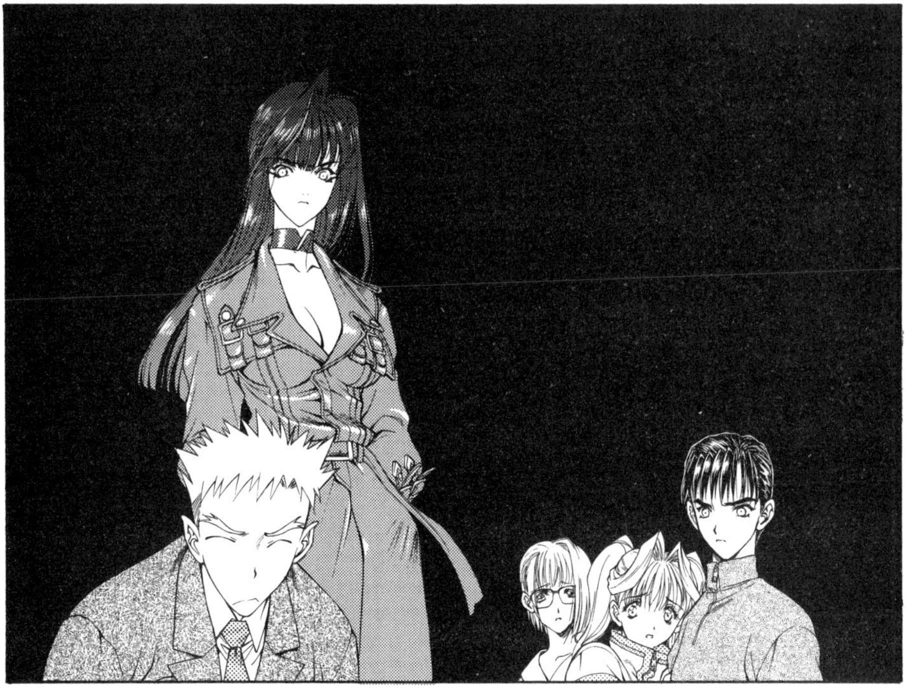

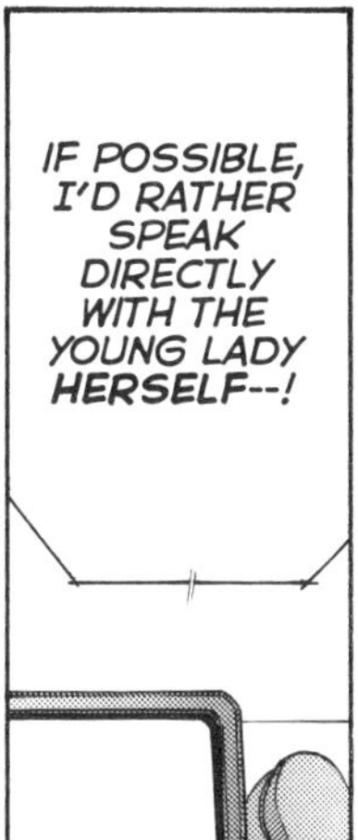
IF POSSIBLE, I'D RATHER SPEAK DIRECTLY WITH THE YOUNG LADY **HERSELF**--!

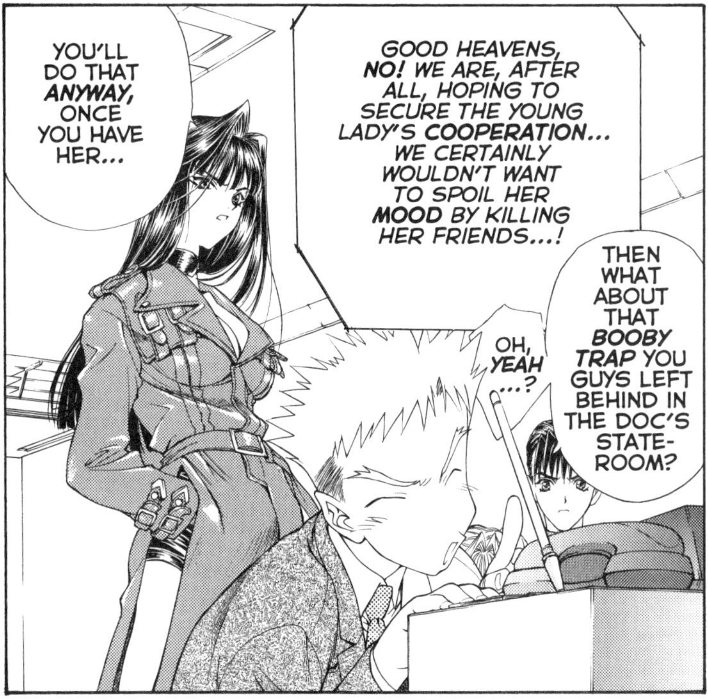
GOOD HEAVENS, **NO!** WE ARE, AFTER ALL, HOPING TO SECURE THE YOUNG LADY'S **COOPERATION...** WE CERTAINLY WOULDN'T WANT TO SPOIL HER **MOOD** BY KILLING HER FRIENDS...!
YOU'LL DO THAT **ANYWAY,** ONCE YOU HAVE HER...
OH, ***YEAH***...?
THEN WHAT ABOUT THAT ***BOOBY TRAP*** YOU GUYS LEFT BEHIND IN THE DOC'S STATE-ROOM?

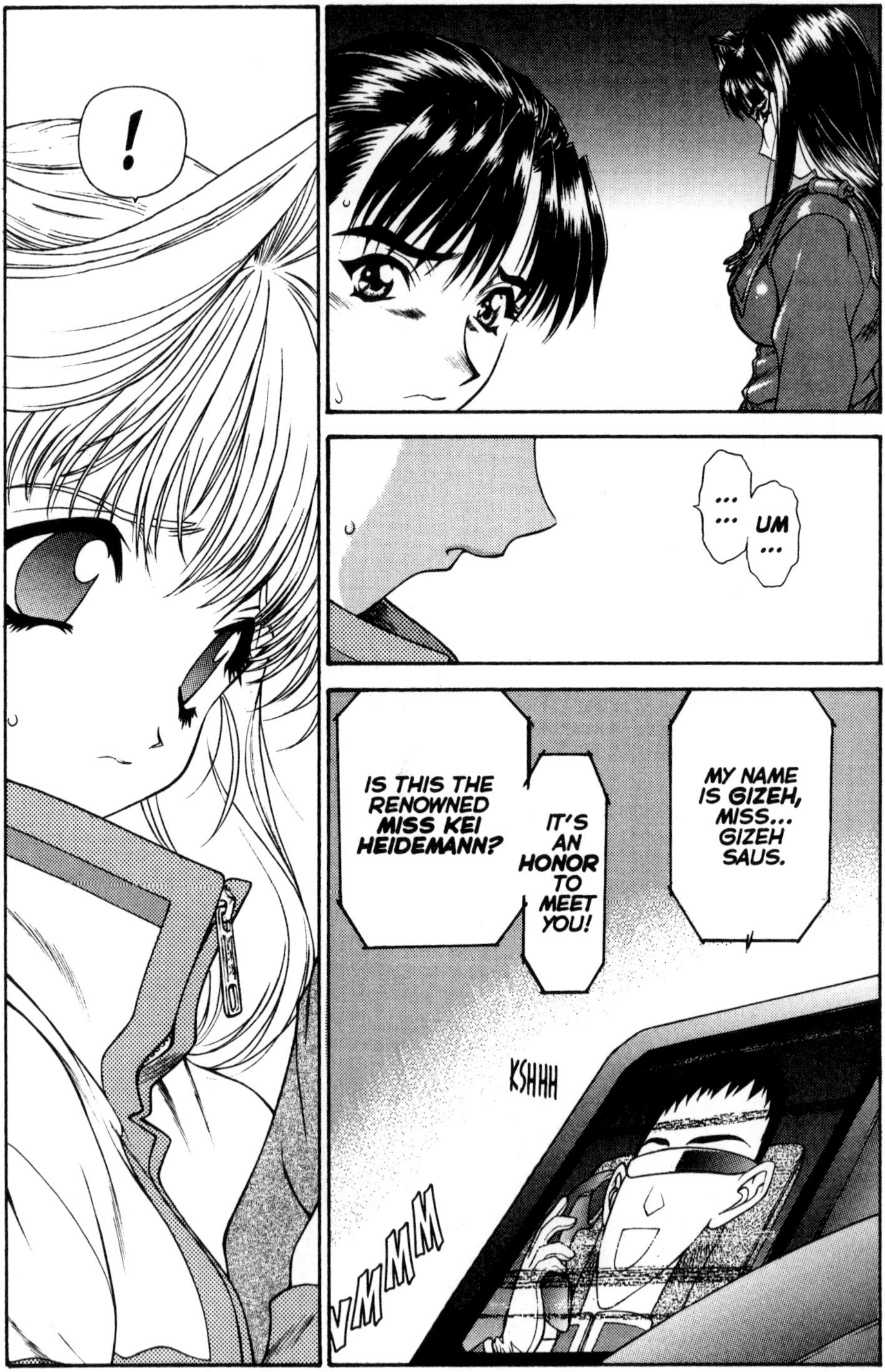
... ...
UM ...
MY NAME IS GIZEH, MISS... GIZEH SAUS.
IT'S AN HONOR TO MEET YOU!
IS THIS THE RENOWNED MISS KEI HEIDEMANN?
KSHHH
VMMMM
!

SO...I GATHER THAT YOU **UNDERSTAND** THE SITUATION ...?

Y E S ...

IT'S **TERRIBLY** UNFORTUNATE THAT THINGS TURNED OUT THIS WAY...

...BUT FOR THE GOOD OF ALL **LUNAR** MANKIND ...

...WE **DESPERATELY** NEED YOUR COOPERATION, MISS HEIDEMANN.

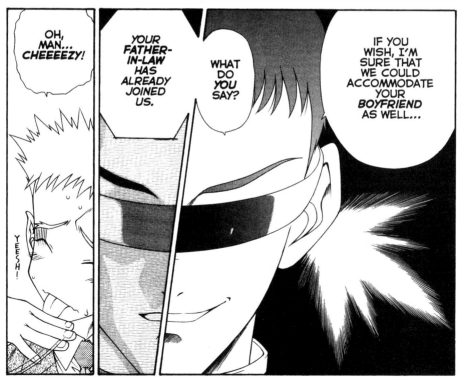

OH, MAN... **CHEEEEZY!**

YEESH!

YOUR **FATHER-IN-LAW** HAS ALREADY JOINED US.

WHAT DO **YOU** SAY?

IF YOU WISH, I'M SURE THAT WE COULD ACCOMMODATE YOUR **BOYFRIEND** AS WELL...

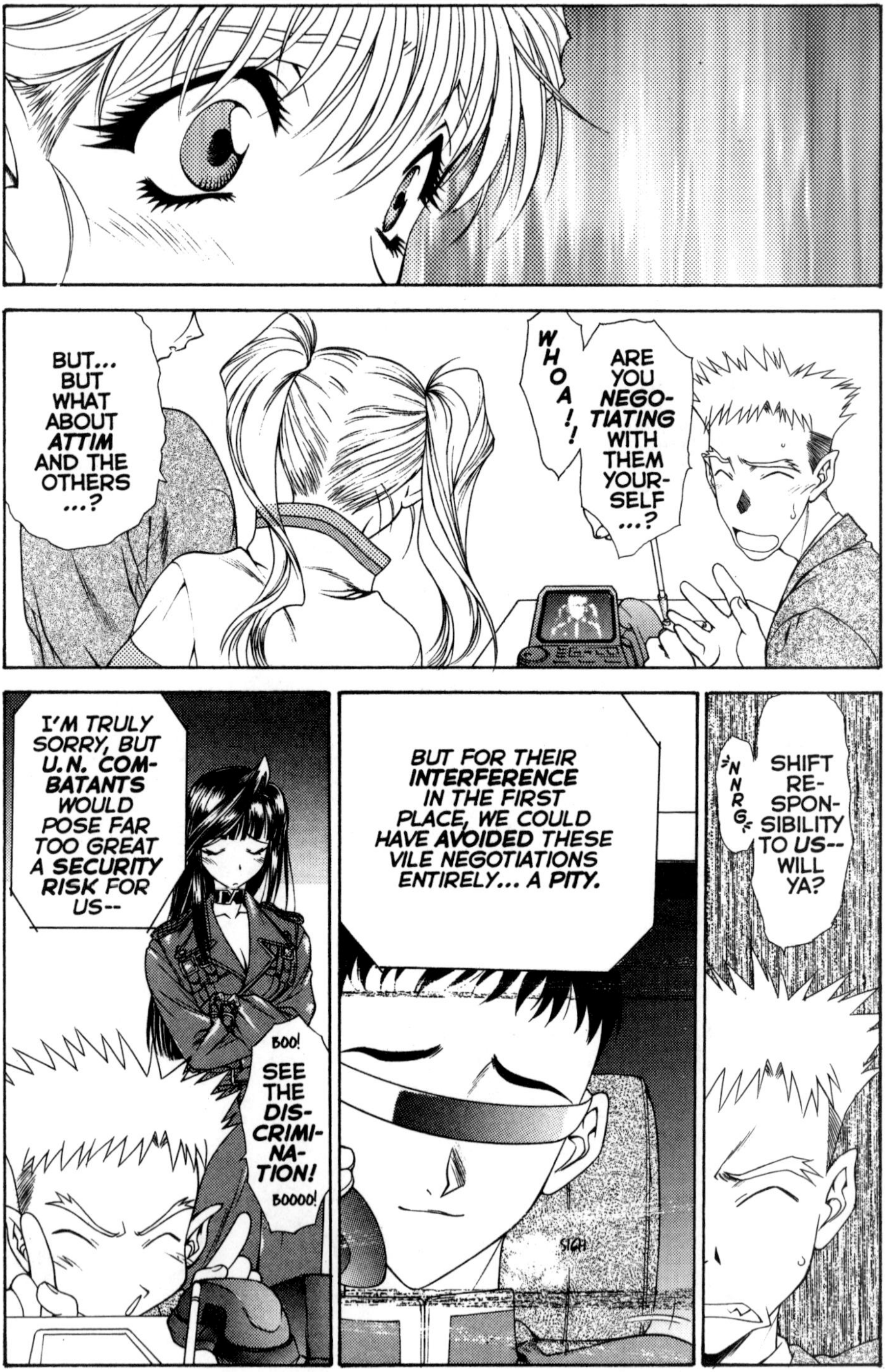
WHOA!!
ARE YOU NEGO-TIATING WITH THEM YOUR-SELF ...?
BUT... BUT WHAT ABOUT ATTIM AND THE OTHERS ...?
SHIFT RE-SPON-SIBILITY TO US-- WILL YA?
NNRG
BUT FOR THEIR INTERFERENCE IN THE FIRST PLACE, WE COULD HAVE AVOIDED THESE VILE NEGOTIATIONS ENTIRELY... A PITY.
SIGH
I'M TRULY SORRY, BUT U.N. COM-BATANTS WOULD POSE FAR TOO GREAT A SECURITY RISK FOR US--
BOO!
SEE THE DIS-CRIMI-NA-TION!
BOOOO!

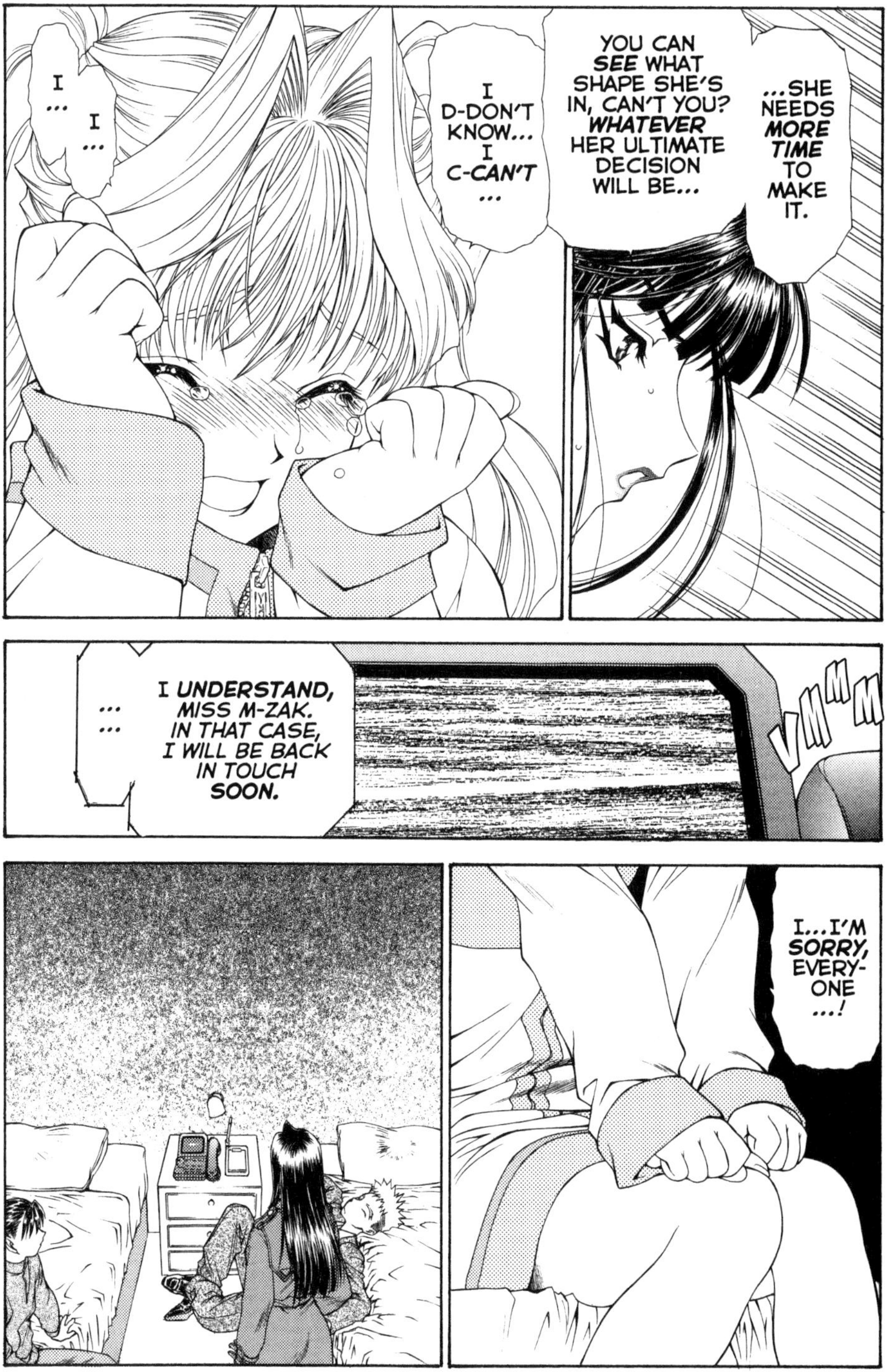
YOU CAN SEE WHAT SHAPE SHE'S IN, CAN'T YOU? WHATEVER HER ULTIMATE DECISION WILL BE...
...SHE NEEDS MORE TIME TO MAKE IT.
I D-DON'T KNOW... I C-CAN'T...
I ... I ...
VMMMM
I UNDERSTAND, MISS M-ZAK. IN THAT CASE, I WILL BE BACK IN TOUCH SOON.
... ...
I...I'M SORRY, EVERY-ONE...!

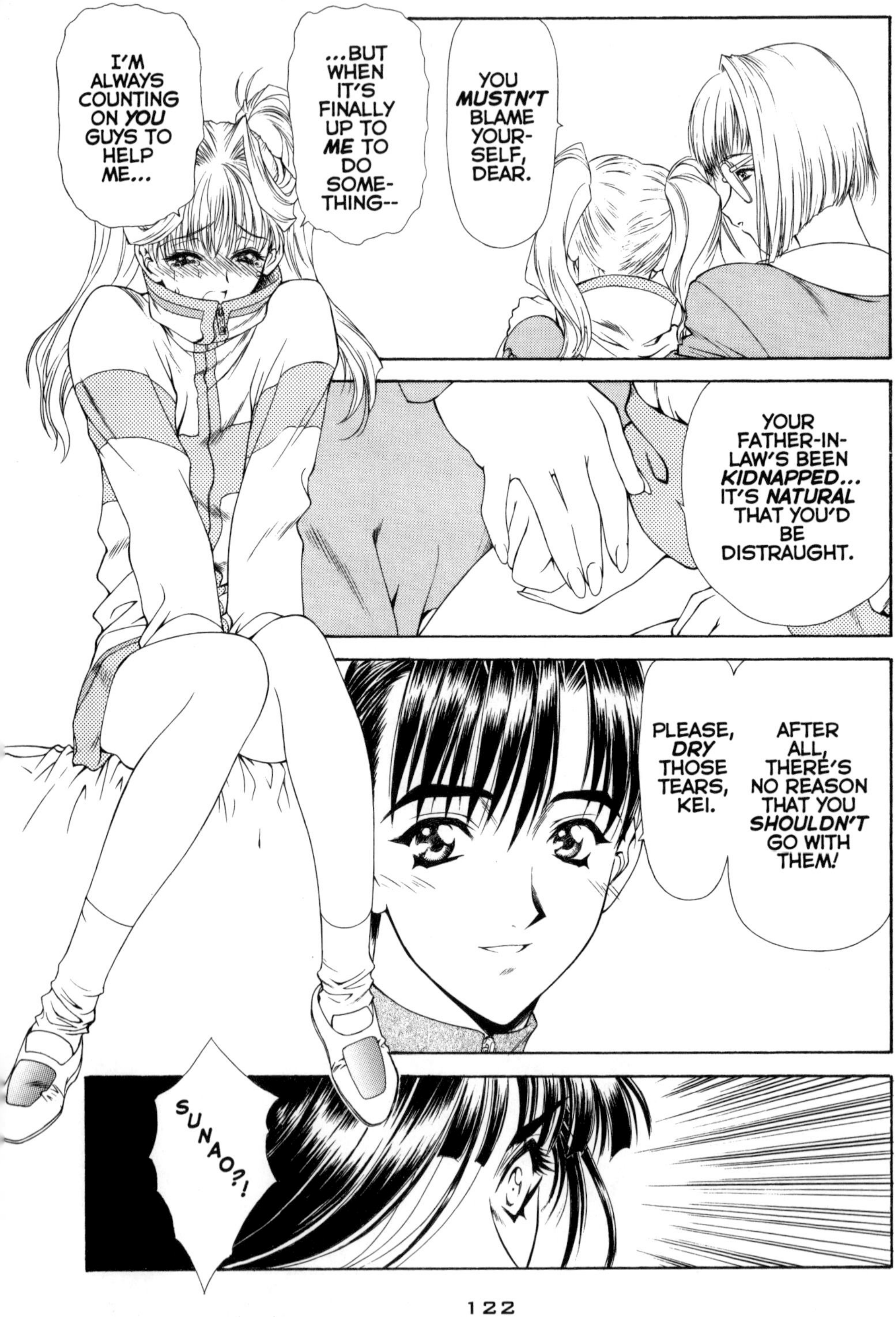
I'M ALWAYS COUNTING ON YOU GUYS TO HELP ME...
...BUT WHEN IT'S FINALLY UP TO ME TO DO SOME-THING--
YOU MUSTN'T BLAME YOUR-SELF, DEAR.
YOUR FATHER-IN-LAW'S BEEN KIDNAPPED... IT'S NATURAL THAT YOU'D BE DISTRAUGHT.
AFTER ALL, THERE'S NO REASON THAT YOU SHOULDN'T GO WITH THEM!
PLEASE, DRY THOSE TEARS, KEI.
SUNAO?!

Act 65

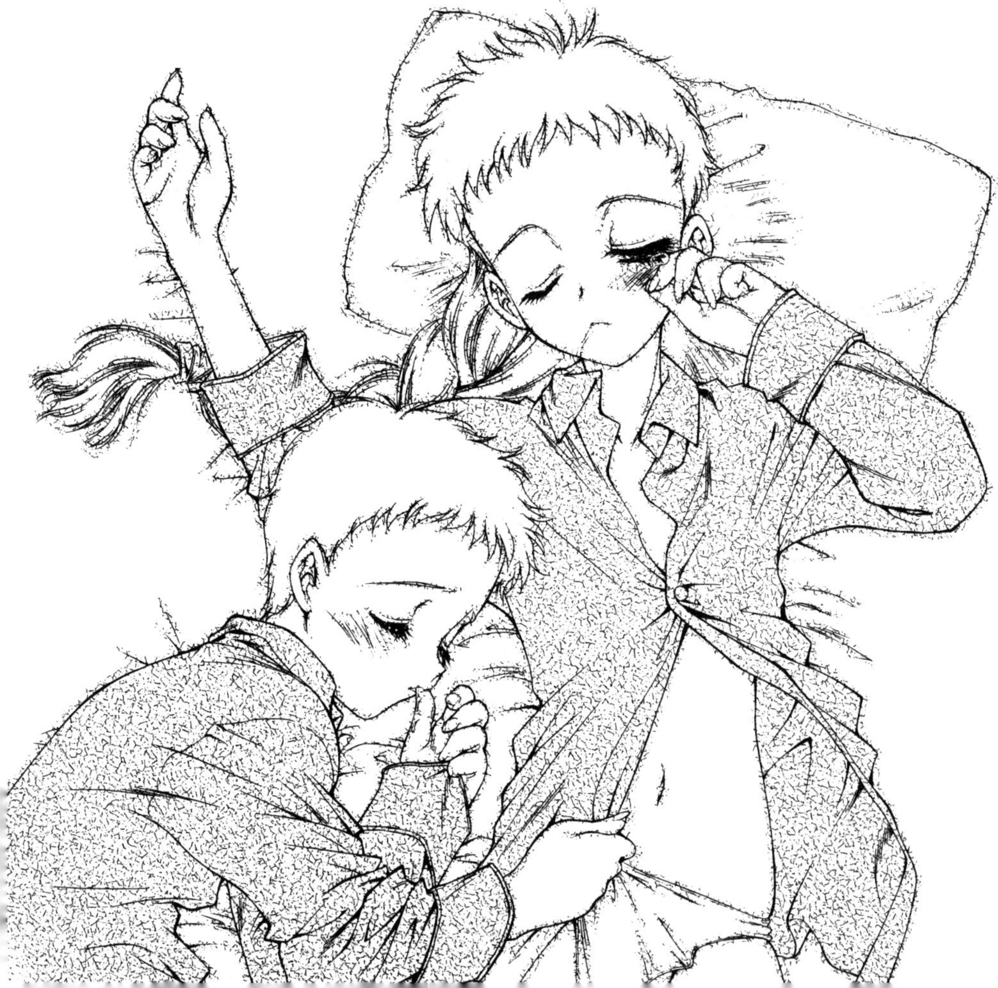

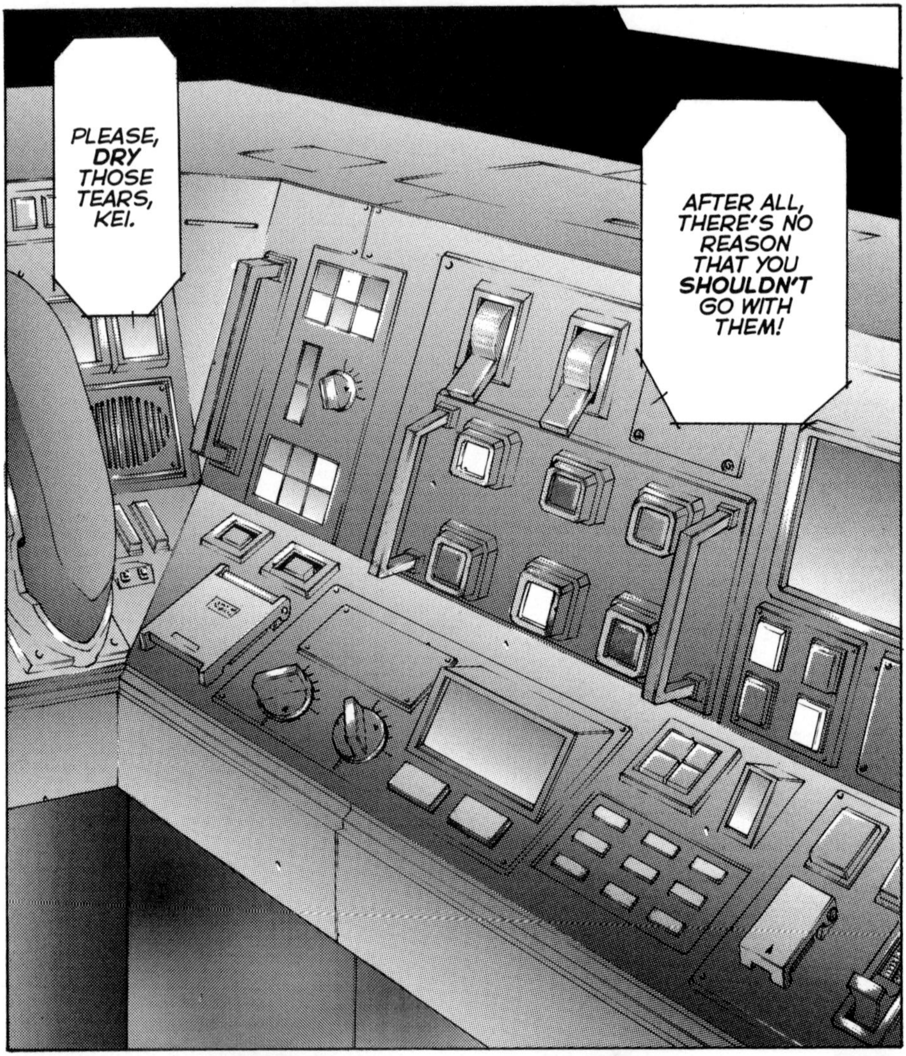
PLEASE, DRY THOSE TEARS, KEI.
AFTER ALL, THERE'S NO REASON THAT YOU SHOULDN'T GO WITH THEM!

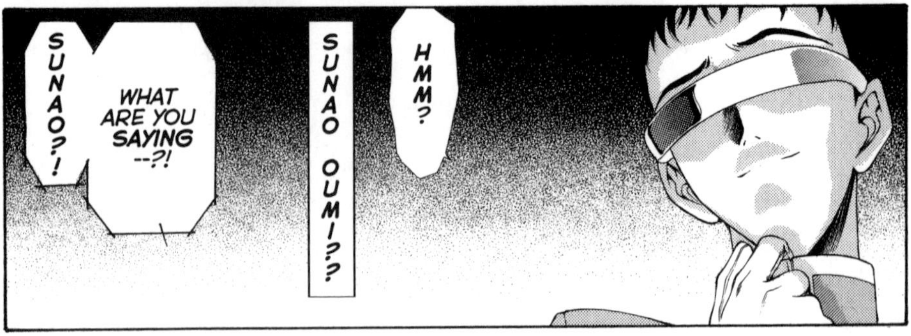
HMM?
SUNAO OUMI?!?
WHAT ARE YOU SAYING --?!
SUNAO?!

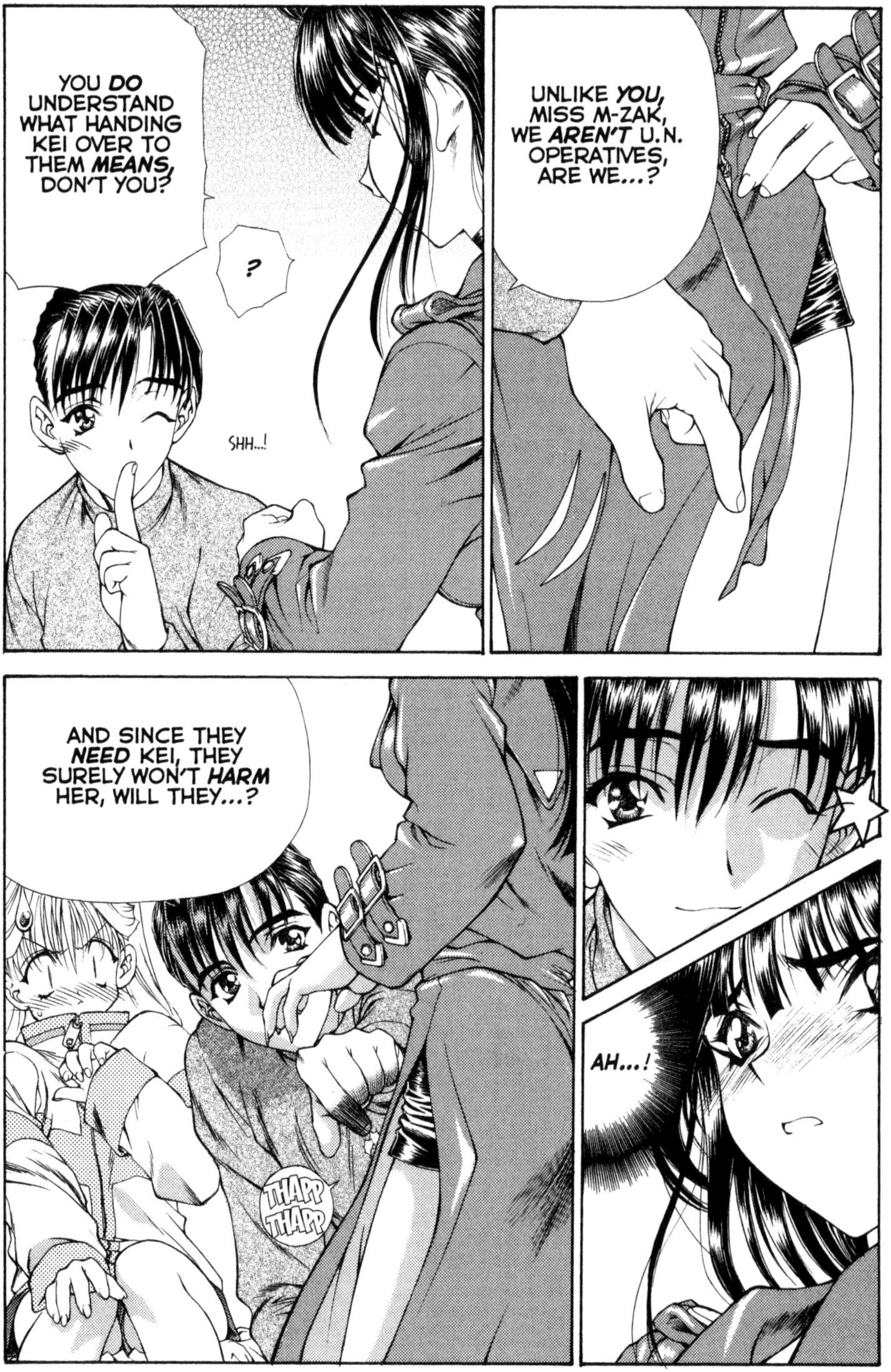
YOU **DO** UNDERSTAND WHAT HANDING KEI OVER TO THEM **MEANS,** DON'T YOU?
?
SHH...!
UNLIKE **YOU,** MISS M-ZAK, WE **AREN'T** U.N. OPERATIVES, ARE WE...?
AND SINCE THEY **NEED** KEI, THEY SURELY WON'T **HARM** HER, WILL THEY...?
THAPP THAPP
AH...!

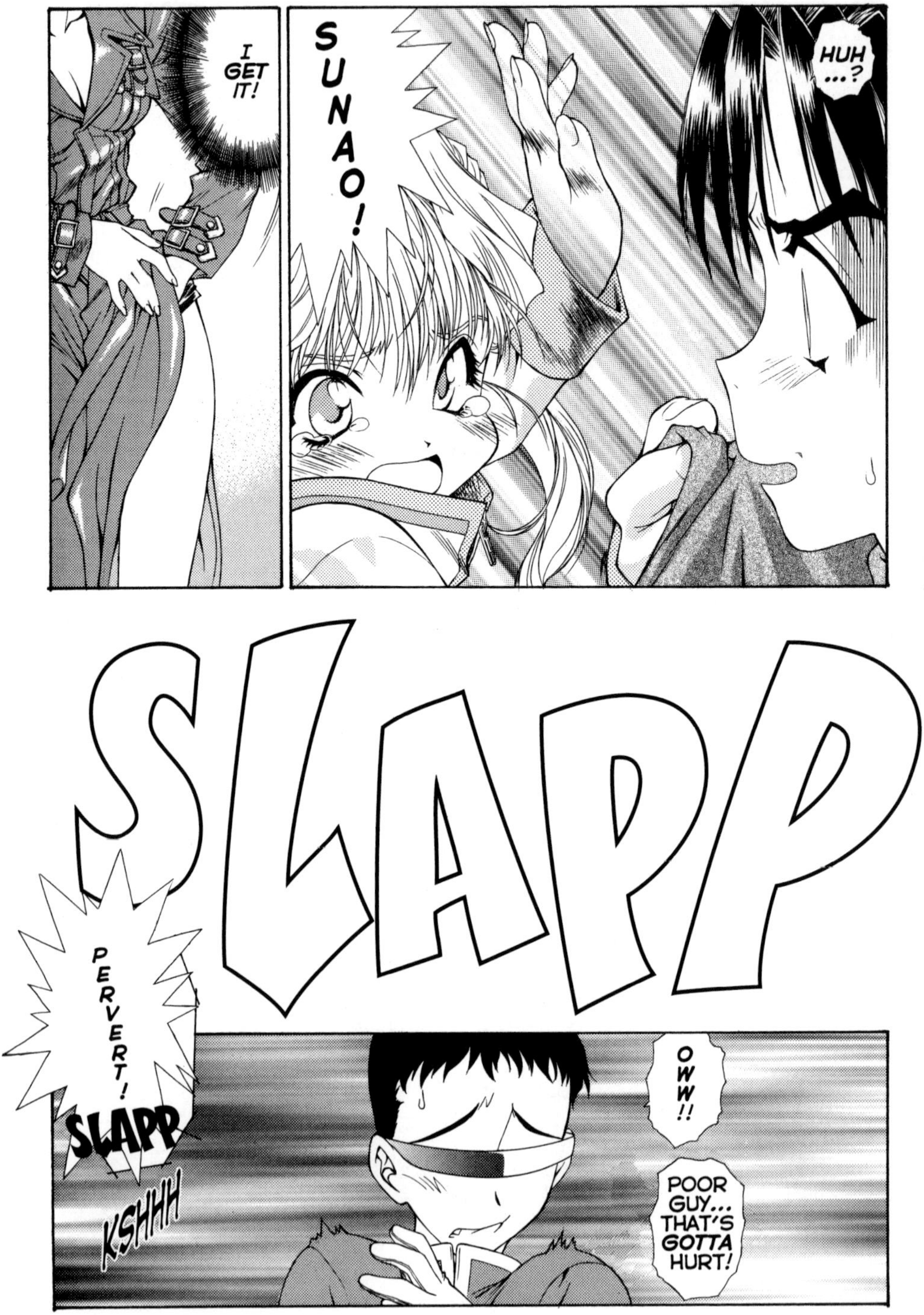
HUH ...?
SUNAO!
I GET IT!
SLAPP
OWW!!
POOR GUY... THAT'S GOTTA HURT!
PERVERT!
SLAPP
KSHHH

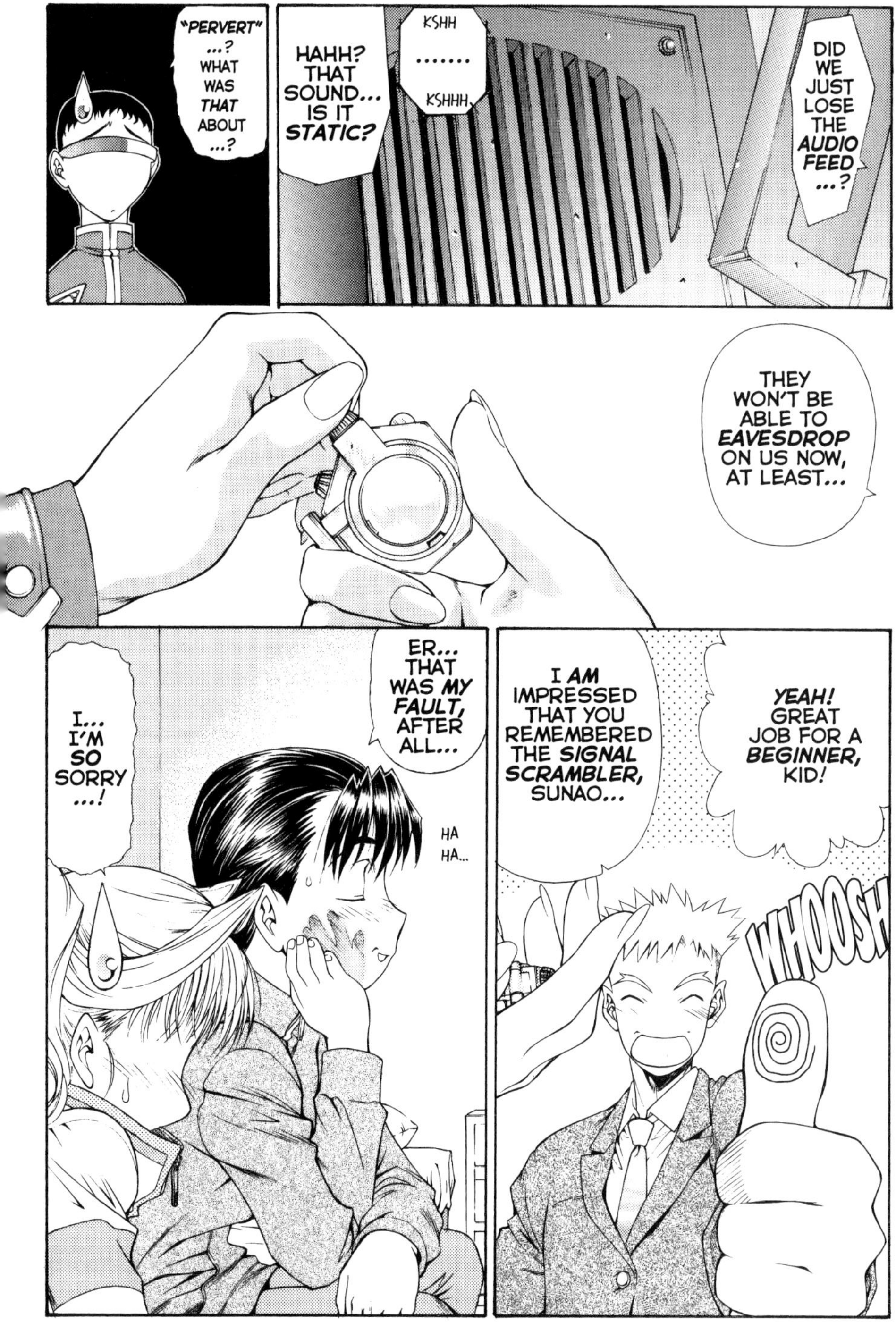
DID WE JUST LOSE THE AUDIO FEED...?
KSHH .... KSHHH
HAHH? THAT SOUND... IS IT STATIC?
"PERVERT" ...? WHAT WAS THAT ABOUT ...?
THEY WON'T BE ABLE TO EAVESDROP ON US NOW, AT LEAST...
I AM IMPRESSED THAT YOU REMEMBERED THE SIGNAL SCRAMBLER, SUNAO...
YEAH! GREAT JOB FOR A BEGINNER, KID!
WHOOSH
ER... THAT WAS MY FAULT, AFTER ALL...
HA HA...
I... I'M SO SORRY ...!

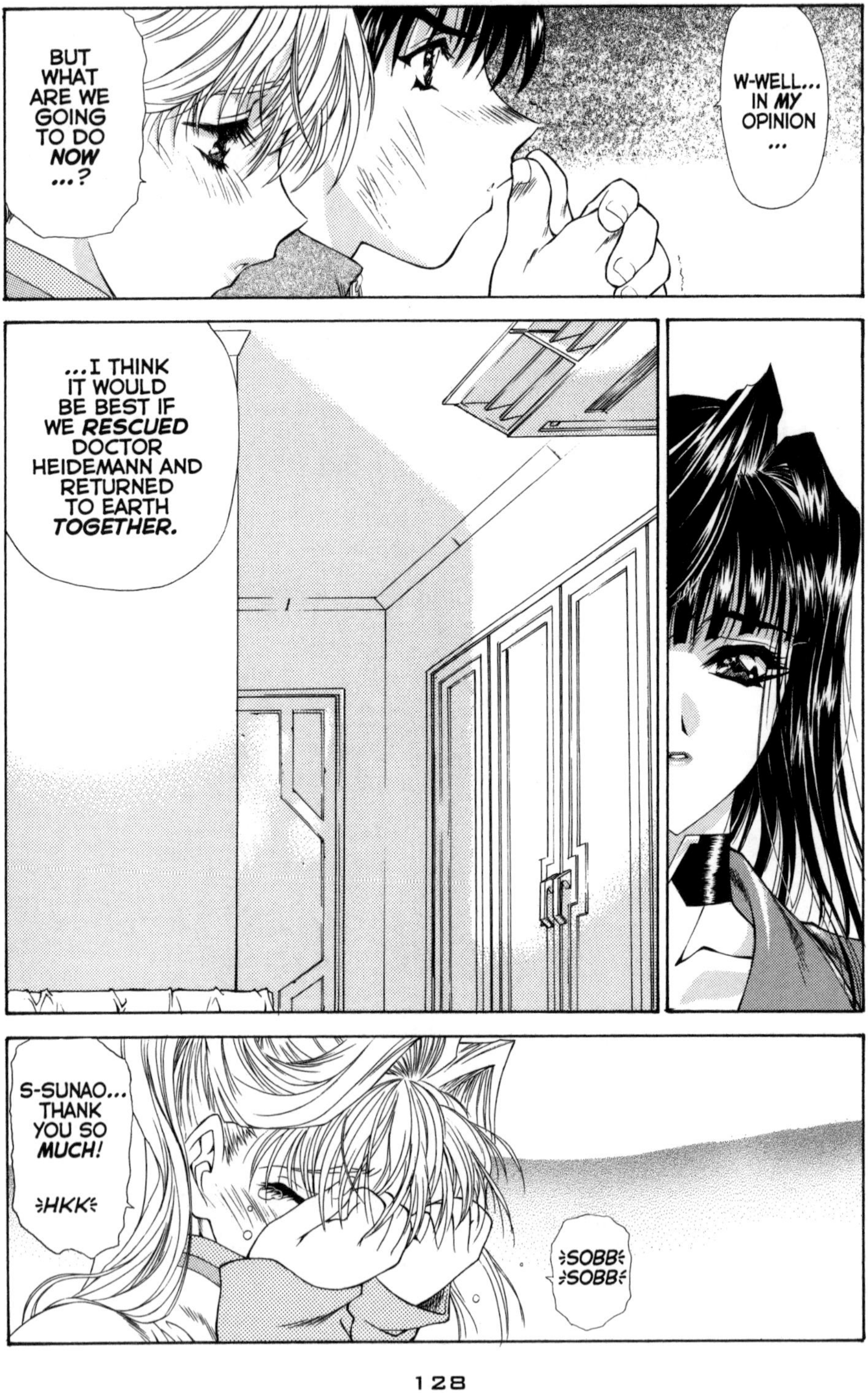
BUT WHAT ARE WE GOING TO DO *NOW*...?
W-WELL... IN *MY* OPINION...
...I THINK IT WOULD BE BEST IF WE *RESCUED* DOCTOR HEIDEMANN AND RETURNED TO EARTH *TOGETHER.*
S-SUNAO... THANK YOU SO *MUCH!*
HKK
SOBB *SOBB*

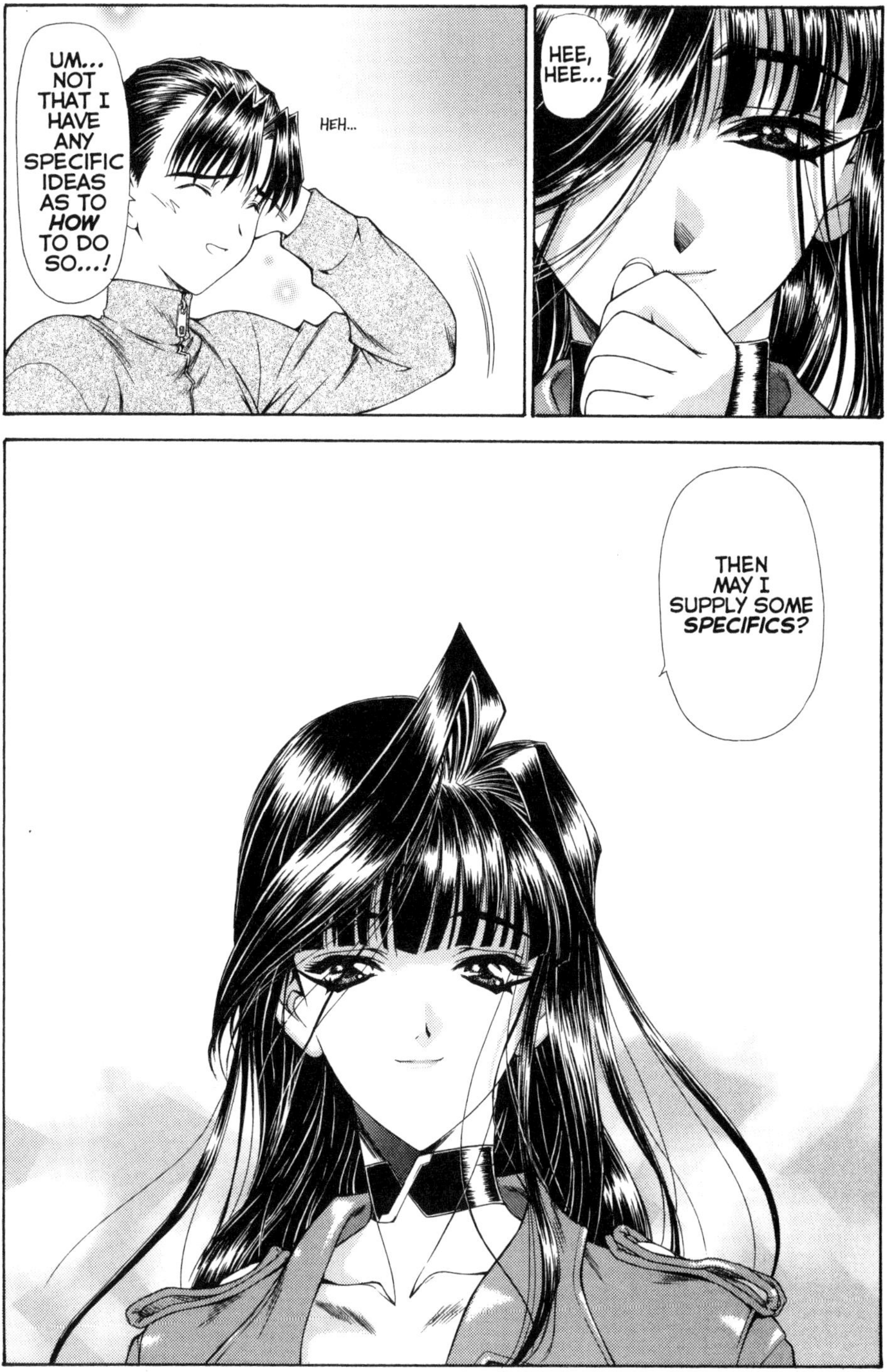
UM... NOT THAT I HAVE ANY SPECIFIC IDEAS AS TO *HOW* TO DO SO...!
HEH...
HEE, HEE...
THEN MAY I SUPPLY SOME *SPECIFICS?*

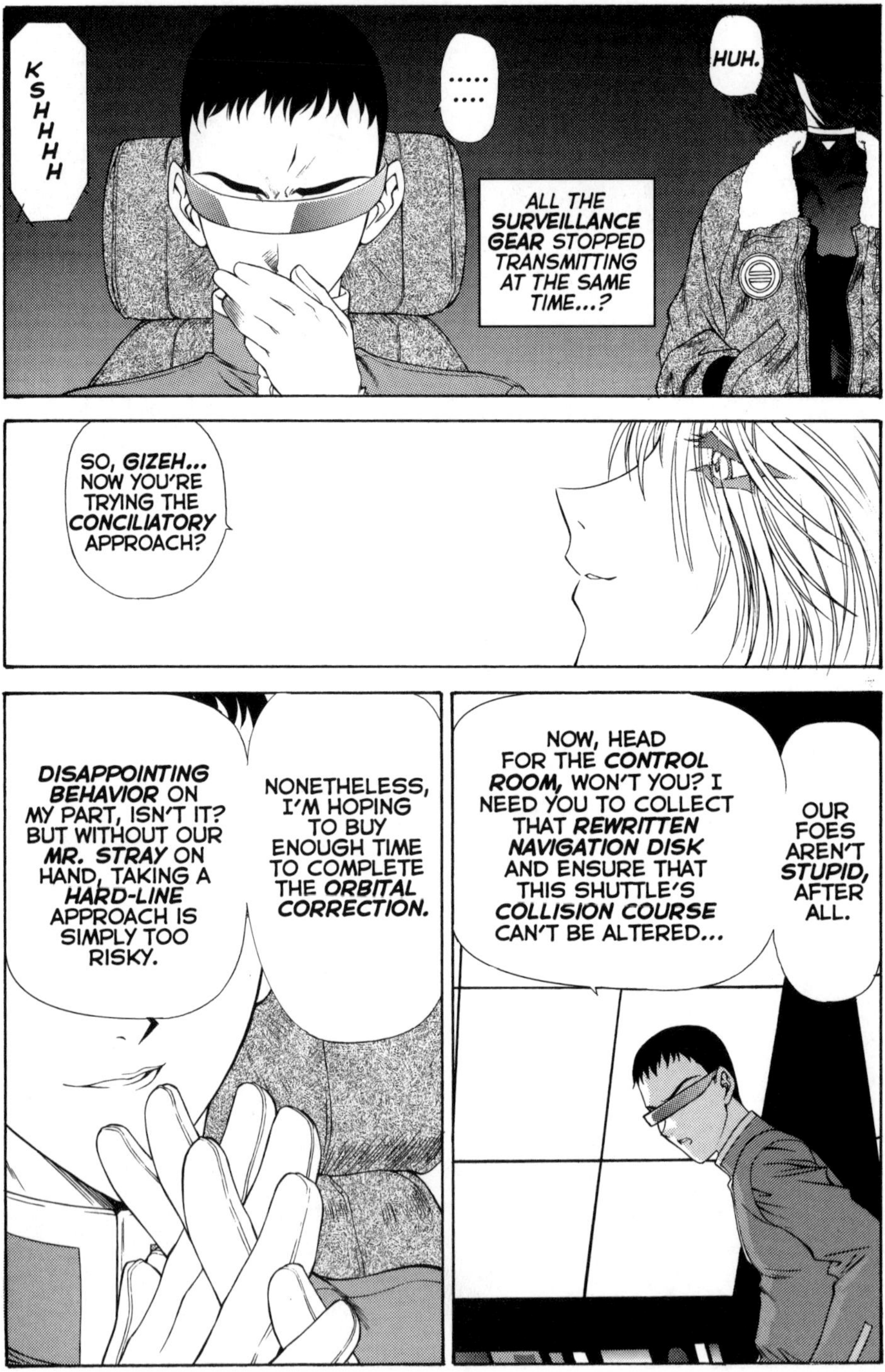
KSHHHH
......
......
ALL THE SURVEILLANCE GEAR STOPPED TRANSMITTING AT THE SAME TIME...?
HUH.
SO, GIZEH... NOW YOU'RE TRYING THE CONCILIATORY APPROACH?
DISAPPOINTING BEHAVIOR ON MY PART, ISN'T IT? BUT WITHOUT OUR MR. STRAY ON HAND, TAKING A HARD-LINE APPROACH IS SIMPLY TOO RISKY.
NONETHELESS, I'M HOPING TO BUY ENOUGH TIME TO COMPLETE THE ORBITAL CORRECTION.
NOW, HEAD FOR THE CONTROL ROOM, WON'T YOU? I NEED YOU TO COLLECT THAT REWRITTEN NAVIGATION DISK AND ENSURE THAT THIS SHUTTLE'S COLLISION COURSE CAN'T BE ALTERED...
OUR FOES AREN'T STUPID, AFTER ALL.

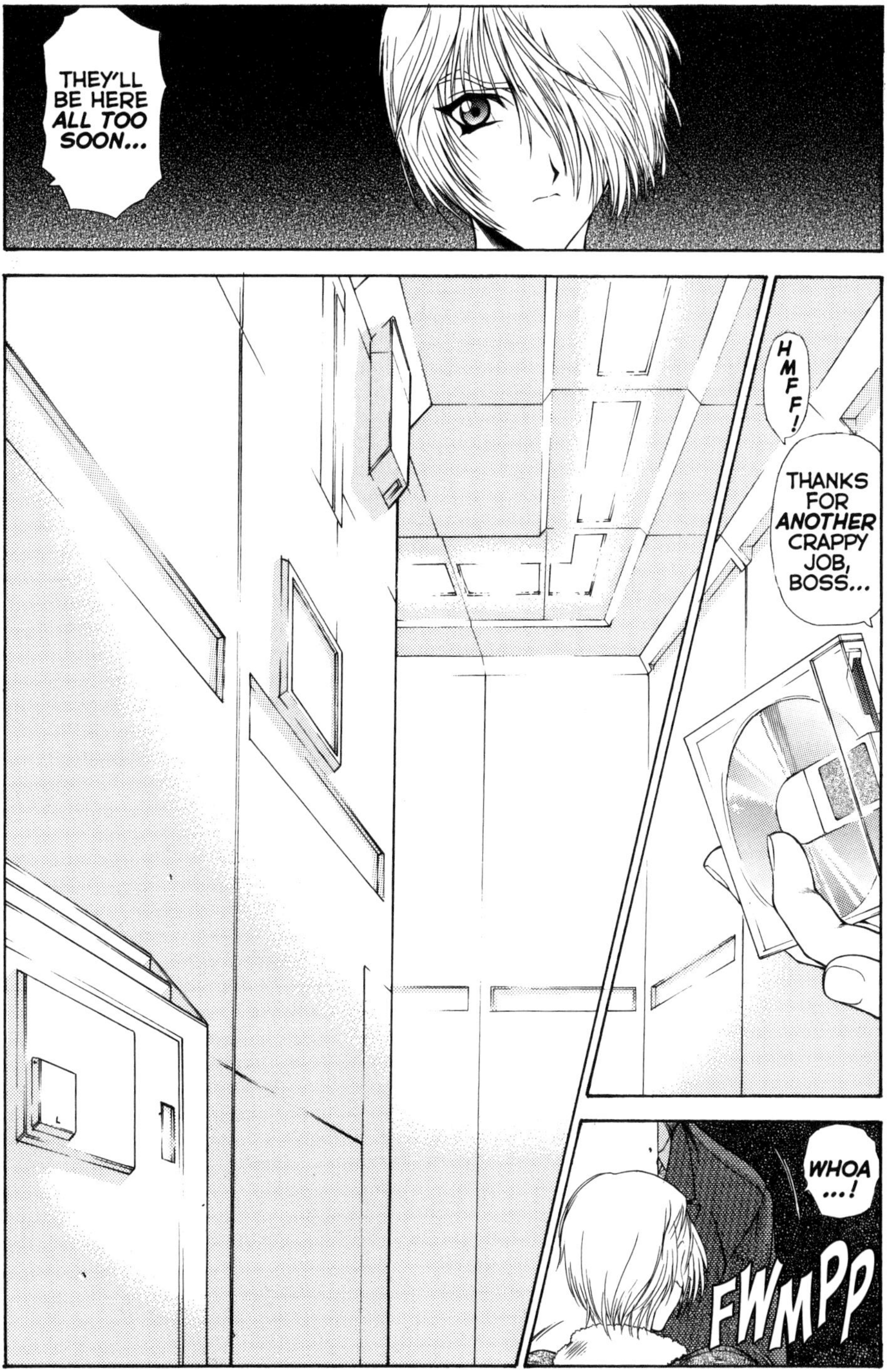
THEY'LL BE HERE ALL TOO SOON...
HMFF!
THANKS FOR ANOTHER CRAPPY JOB, BOSS...
WHOA...!
FWMPP

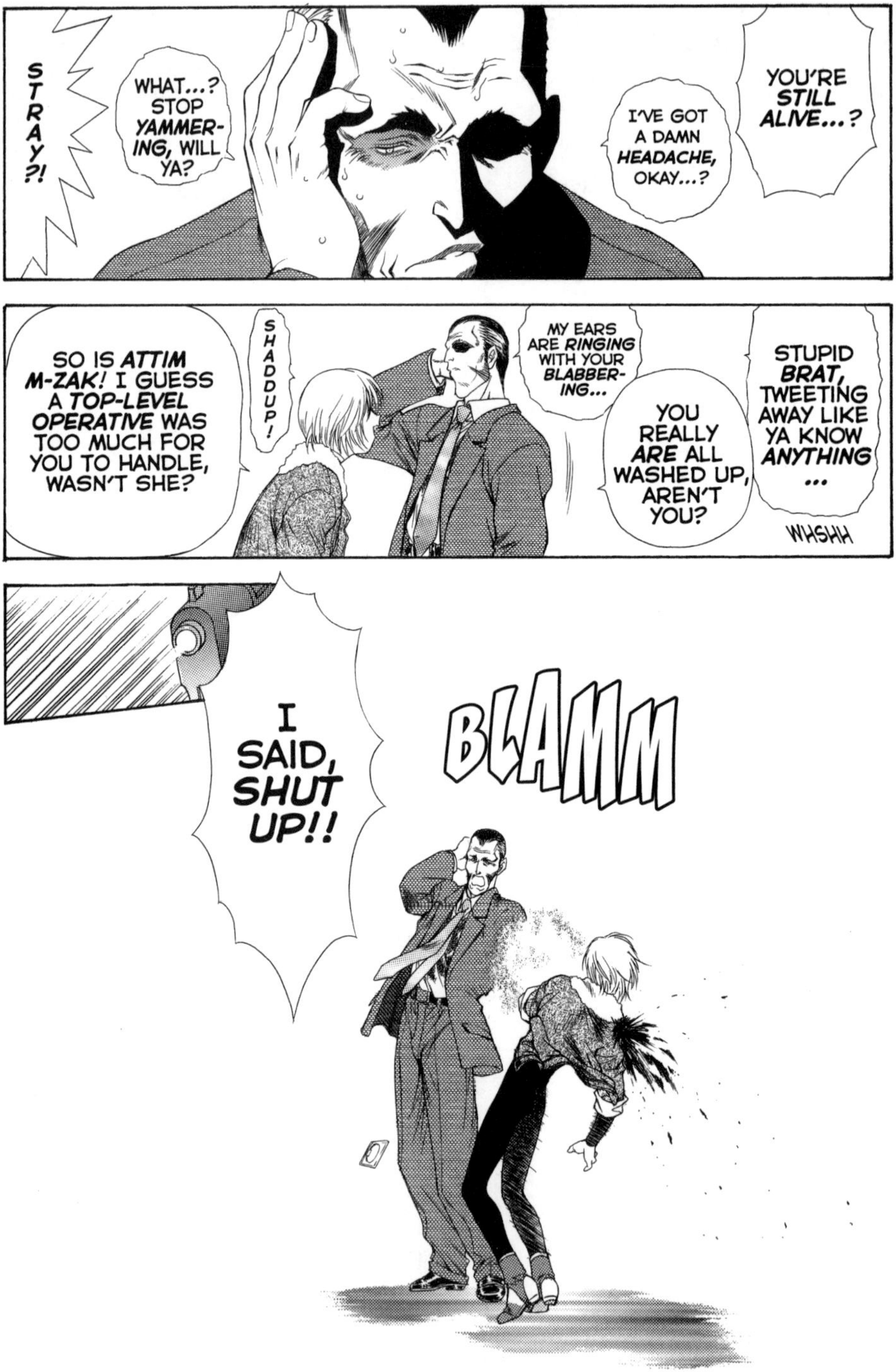

YOU'RE STILL ALIVE...?
I'VE GOT A DAMN HEADACHE, OKAY...?
WHAT...? STOP YAMMERING, WILL YA?
STRAY?!
STUPID BRAT, TWEETING AWAY LIKE YA KNOW ANYTHING...
WHSHH
MY EARS ARE RINGING WITH YOUR BLABBERING...
YOU REALLY ARE ALL WASHED UP, AREN'T YOU?
SHADDUP!
SO IS ATTIM M-ZAK! I GUESS A TOP-LEVEL OPERATIVE WAS TOO MUCH FOR YOU TO HANDLE, WASN'T SHE?
BLAMM
I SAID, SHUT UP!!

ACT 66

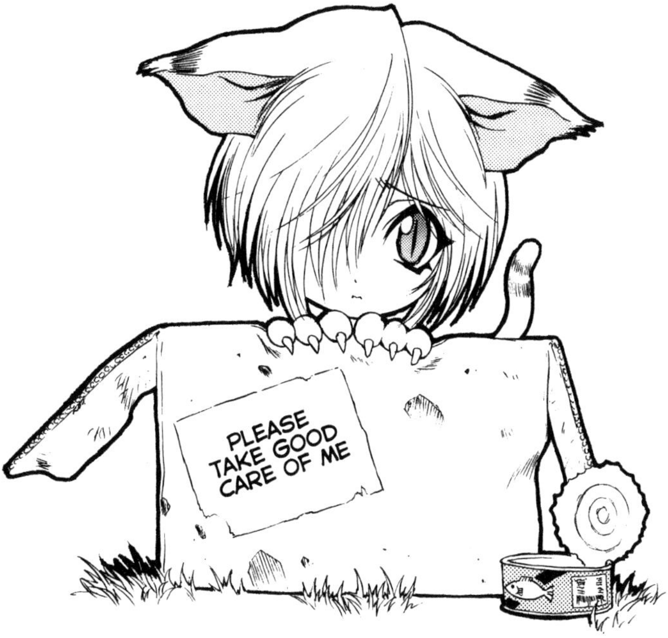
PLEASE
TAKE GOOD
CARE OF ME

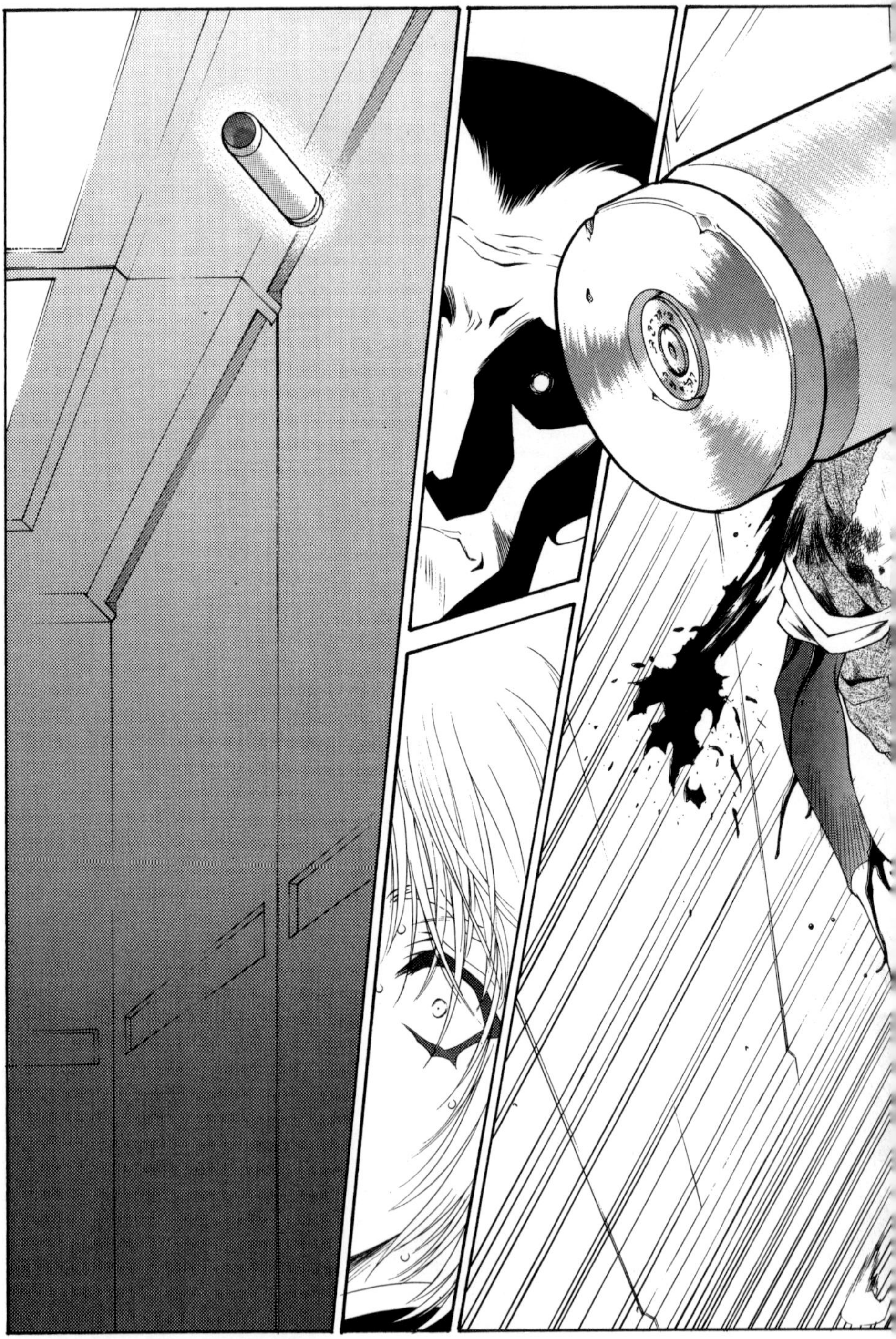

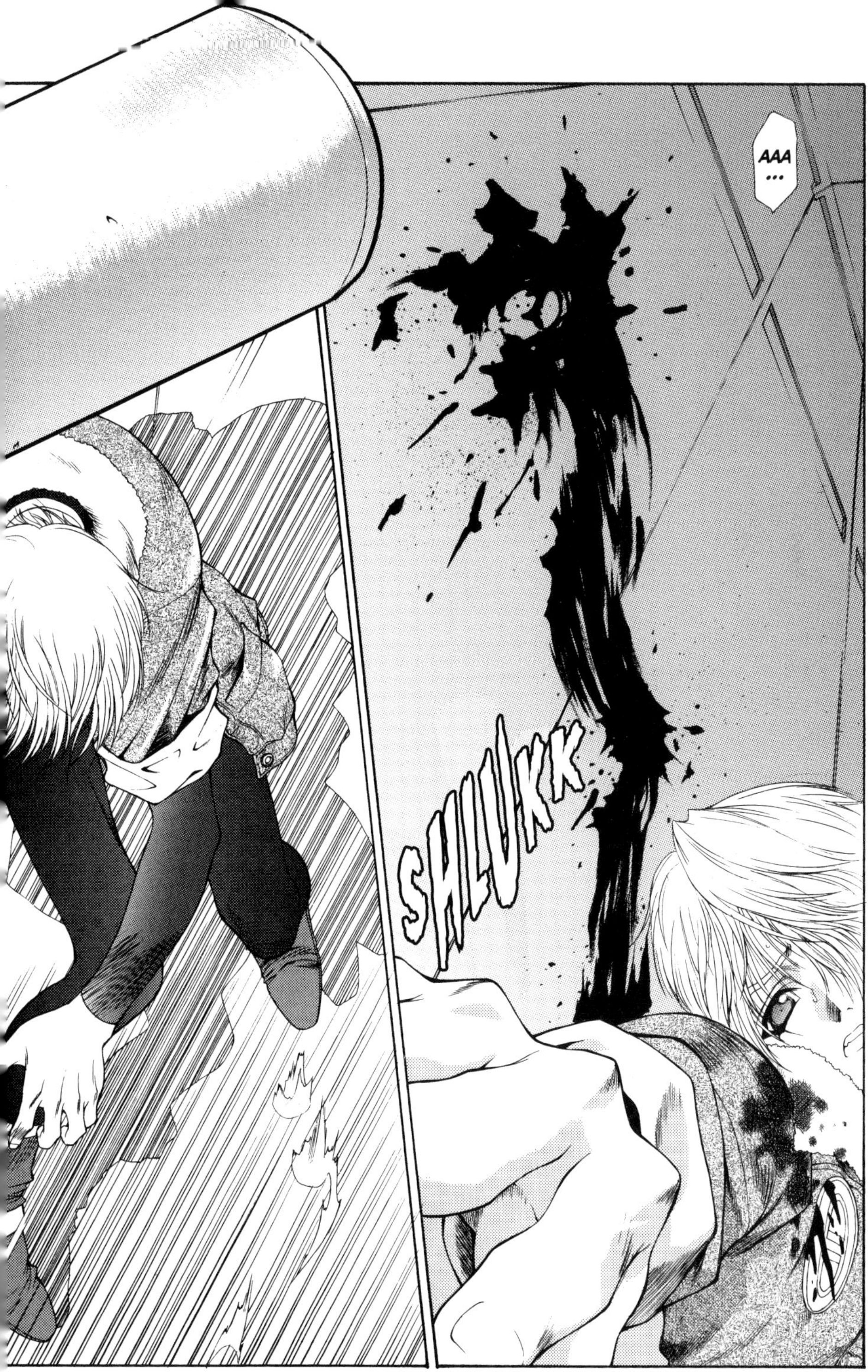
AAA...
SHLUKK

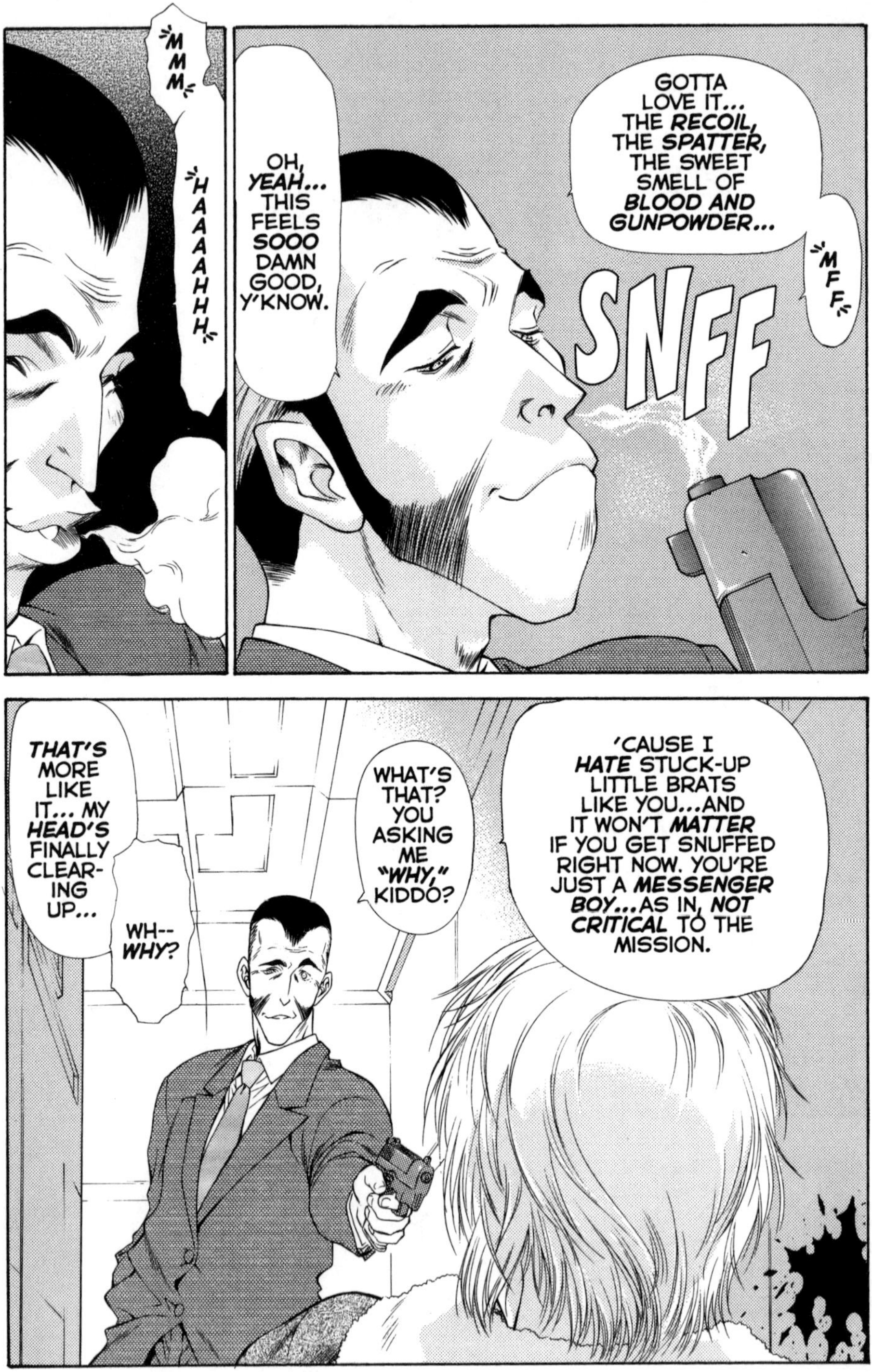
MMM
HAAAAAHHH
OH, YEAH... THIS FEELS SOOO DAMN GOOD, Y'KNOW.
GOTTA LOVE IT... THE RECOIL, THE SPATTER, THE SWEET SMELL OF BLOOD AND GUNPOWDER...
SNFF
MFF
THAT'S MORE LIKE IT... MY HEAD'S FINALLY CLEARING UP...
WH-- WHY?
WHAT'S THAT? YOU ASKING ME "WHY," KIDDO?
'CAUSE I HATE STUCK-UP LITTLE BRATS LIKE YOU...AND IT WON'T MATTER IF YOU GET SNUFFED RIGHT NOW. YOU'RE JUST A MESSENGER BOY...AS IN, NOT CRITICAL TO THE MISSION.

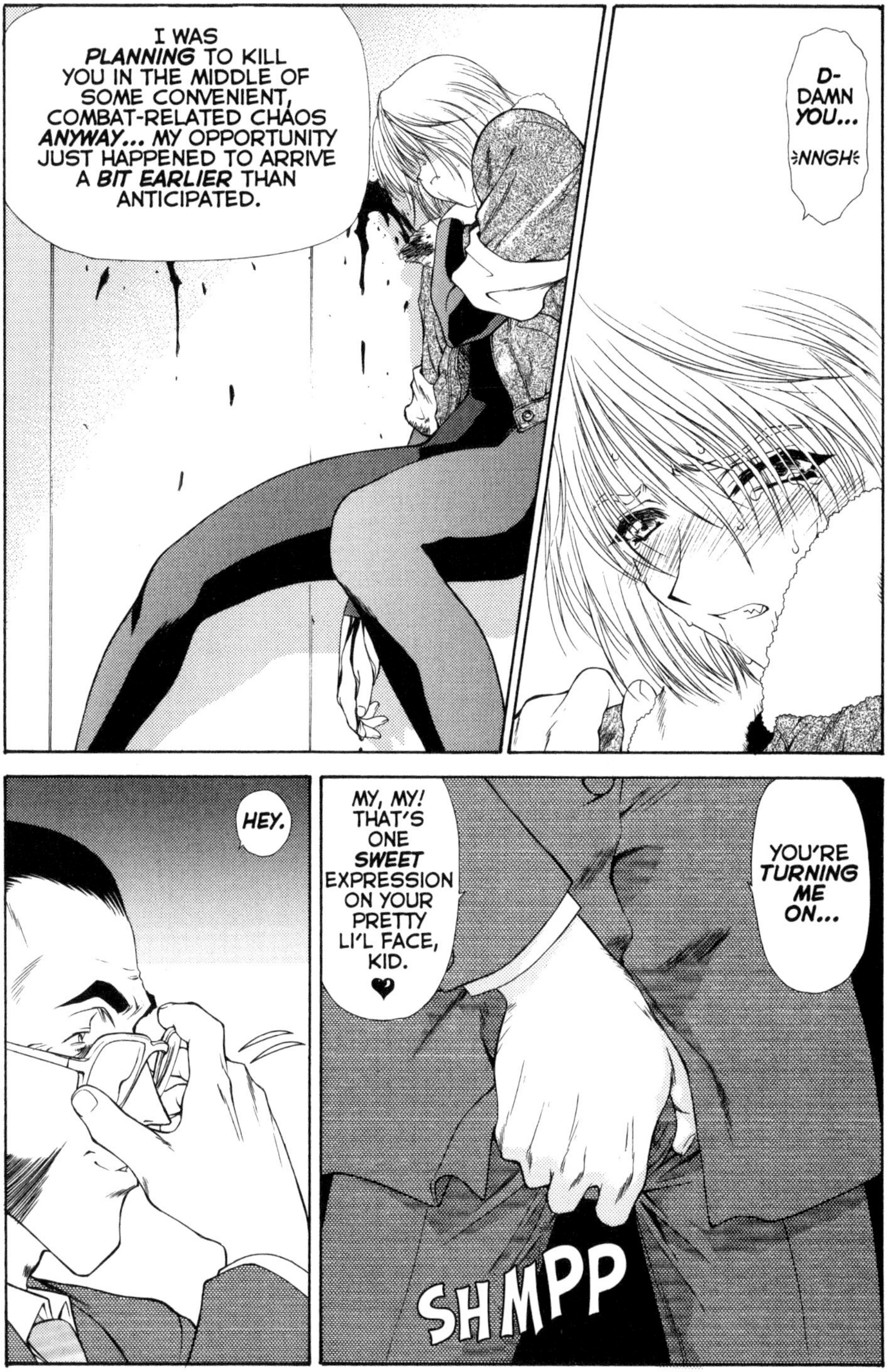
I WAS PLANNING TO KILL YOU IN THE MIDDLE OF SOME CONVENIENT, COMBAT-RELATED CHAOS ANYWAY... MY OPPORTUNITY JUST HAPPENED TO ARRIVE A BIT EARLIER THAN ANTICIPATED.
D-DAMN YOU...
NNGH
HEY.
MY, MY! THAT'S ONE SWEET EXPRESSION ON YOUR PRETTY LI'L FACE, KID. ♥
YOU'RE TURNING ME ON...
SHMPP

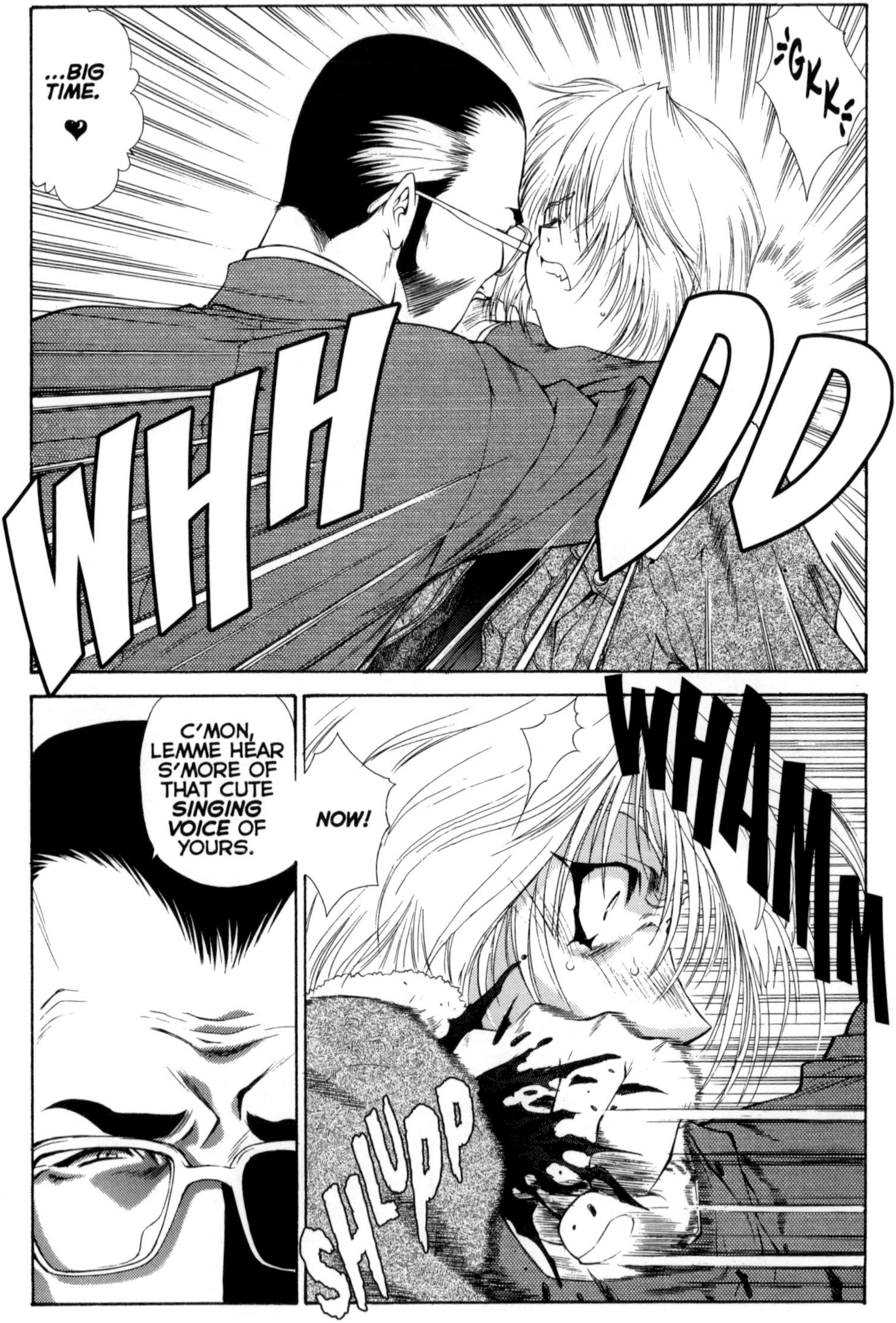
...BIG TIME. ❤
GKK
WHHDD
C'MON, LEMME HEAR S'MORE OF THAT CUTE *SINGING VOICE* OF YOURS.
NOW!
WHAMMM
SHLUPP

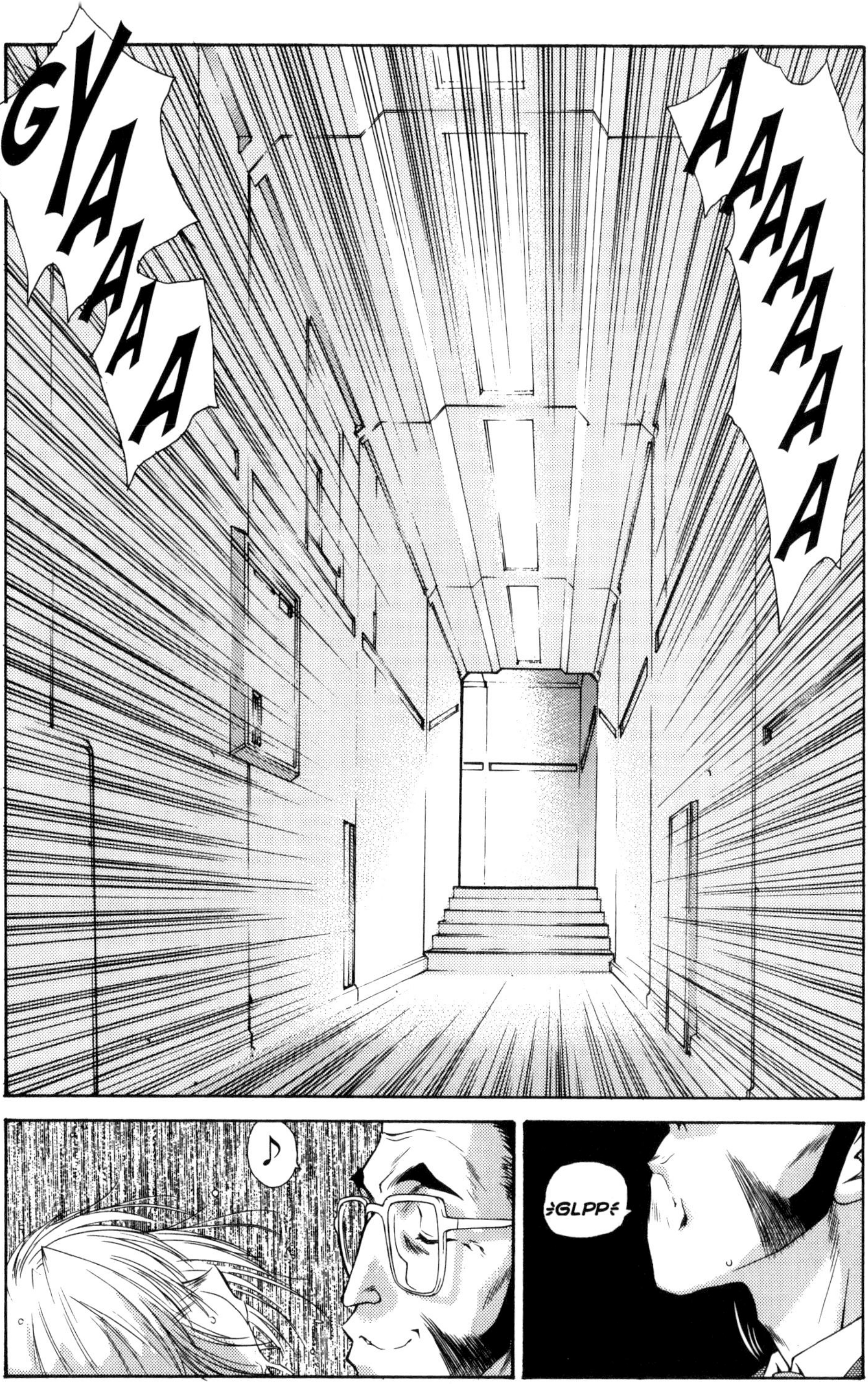
GYAAAA
AAAAAAAA
GLPP
♪

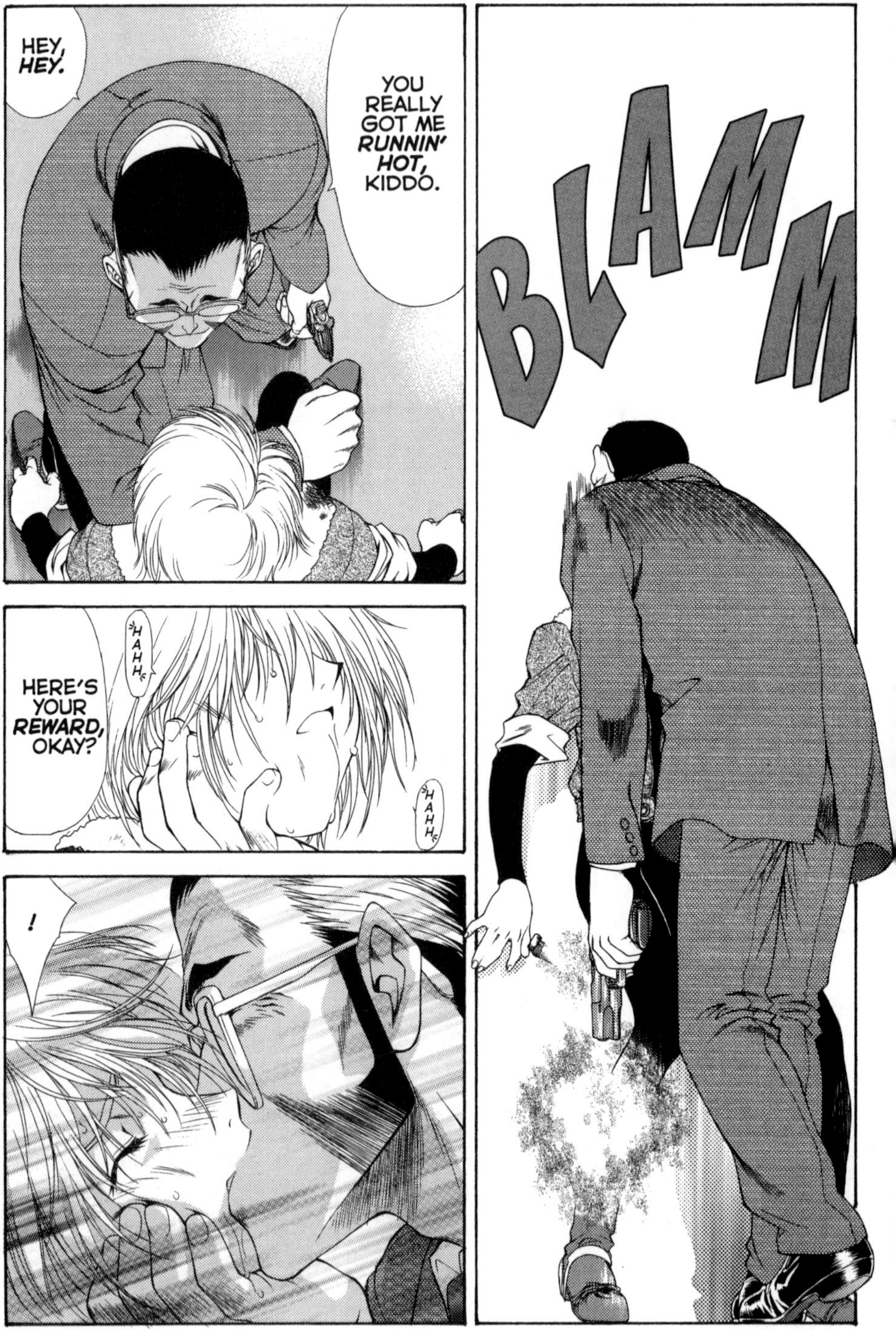
HEY, *HEY.*
YOU REALLY GOT ME *RUNNIN' HOT,* KIDDO.
HAHH
HERE'S YOUR *REWARD,* OKAY?
HAHH
!
BLAMM

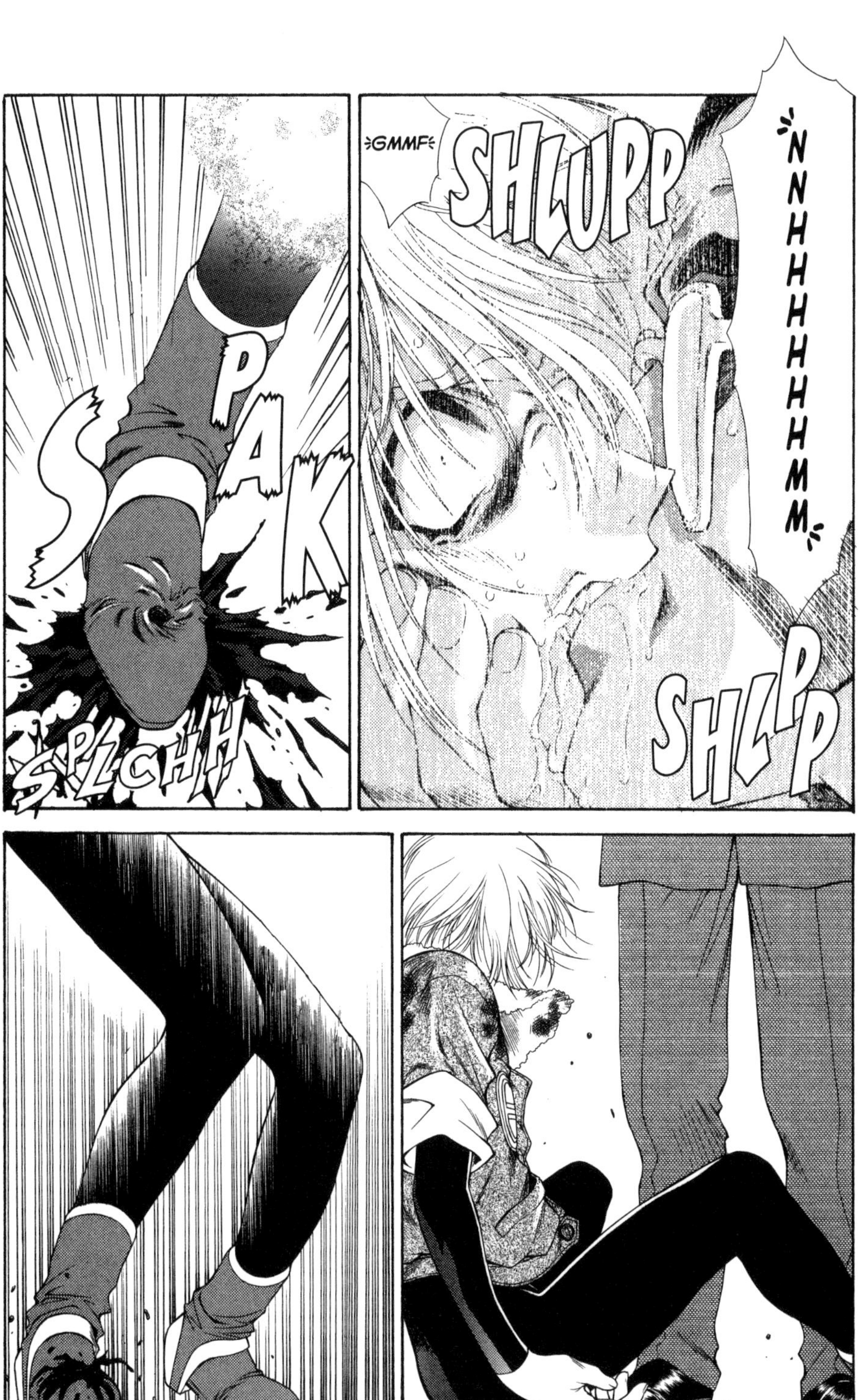
NNHHHHHHHMM
SHLUPP
GMMF
SHLPP
SPAK
SPLCHH

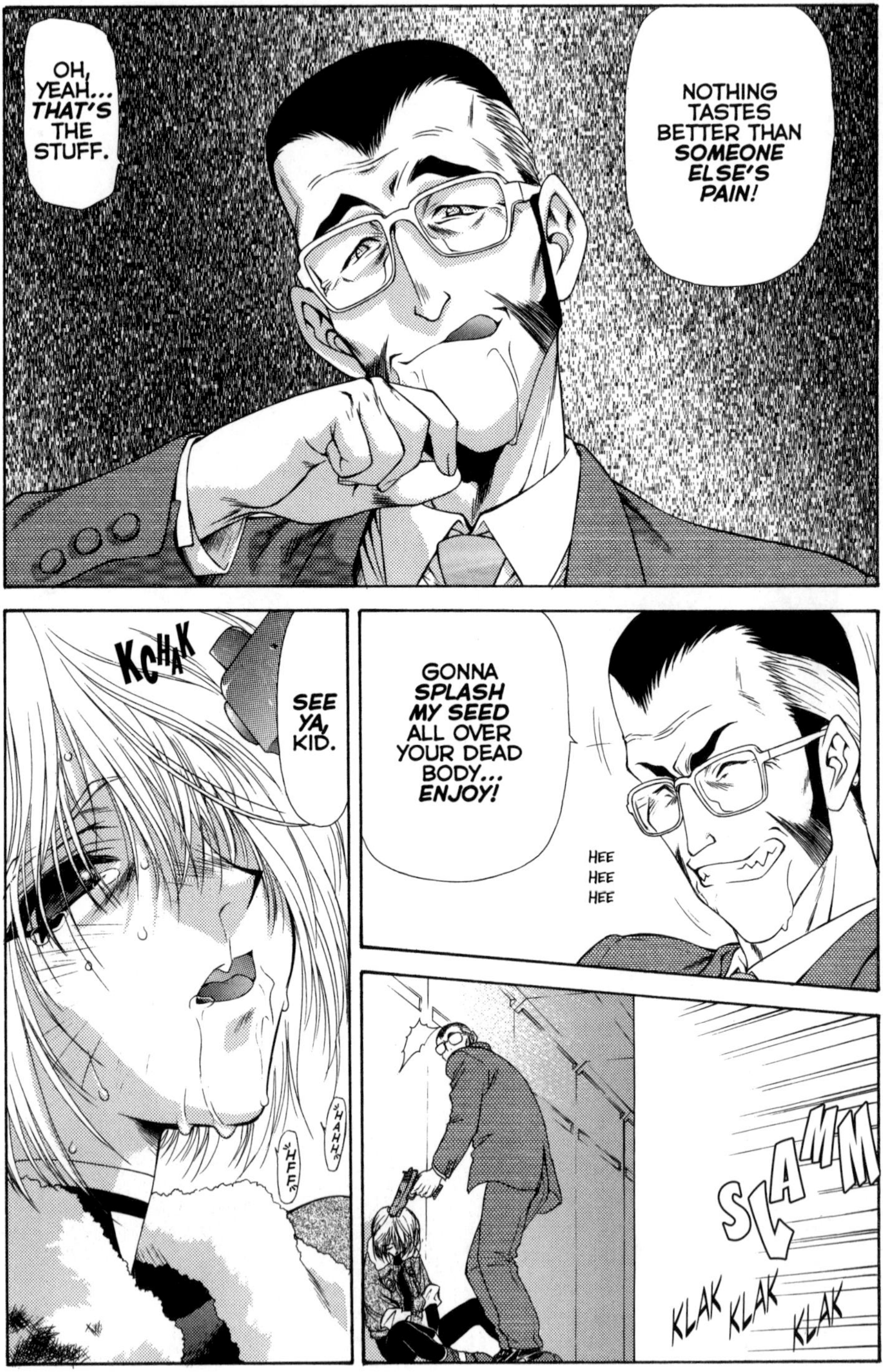
NOTHING TASTES BETTER THAN *SOMEONE ELSE'S* PAIN!
OH, YEAH... *THAT'S* THE STUFF.
GONNA *SPLASH MY SEED* ALL OVER YOUR DEAD BODY... *ENJOY!*
HEE HEE HEE
SLAMM
KLAK KLAK KLAK
KCHAK
SEE YA, KID.
HAHH
HFF

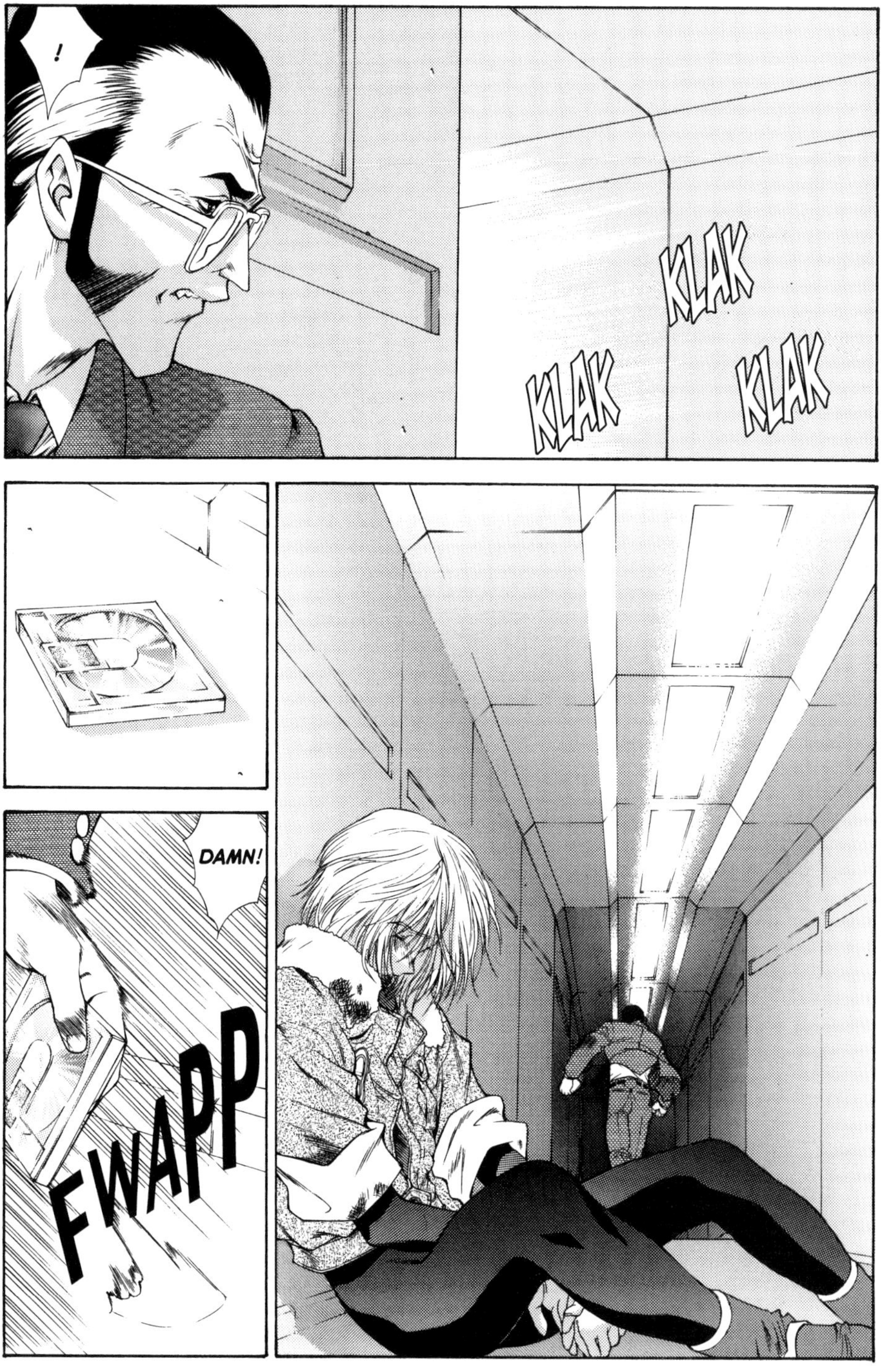
!
KLAK
KLAK
KLAK
DAMN!
FWAPP

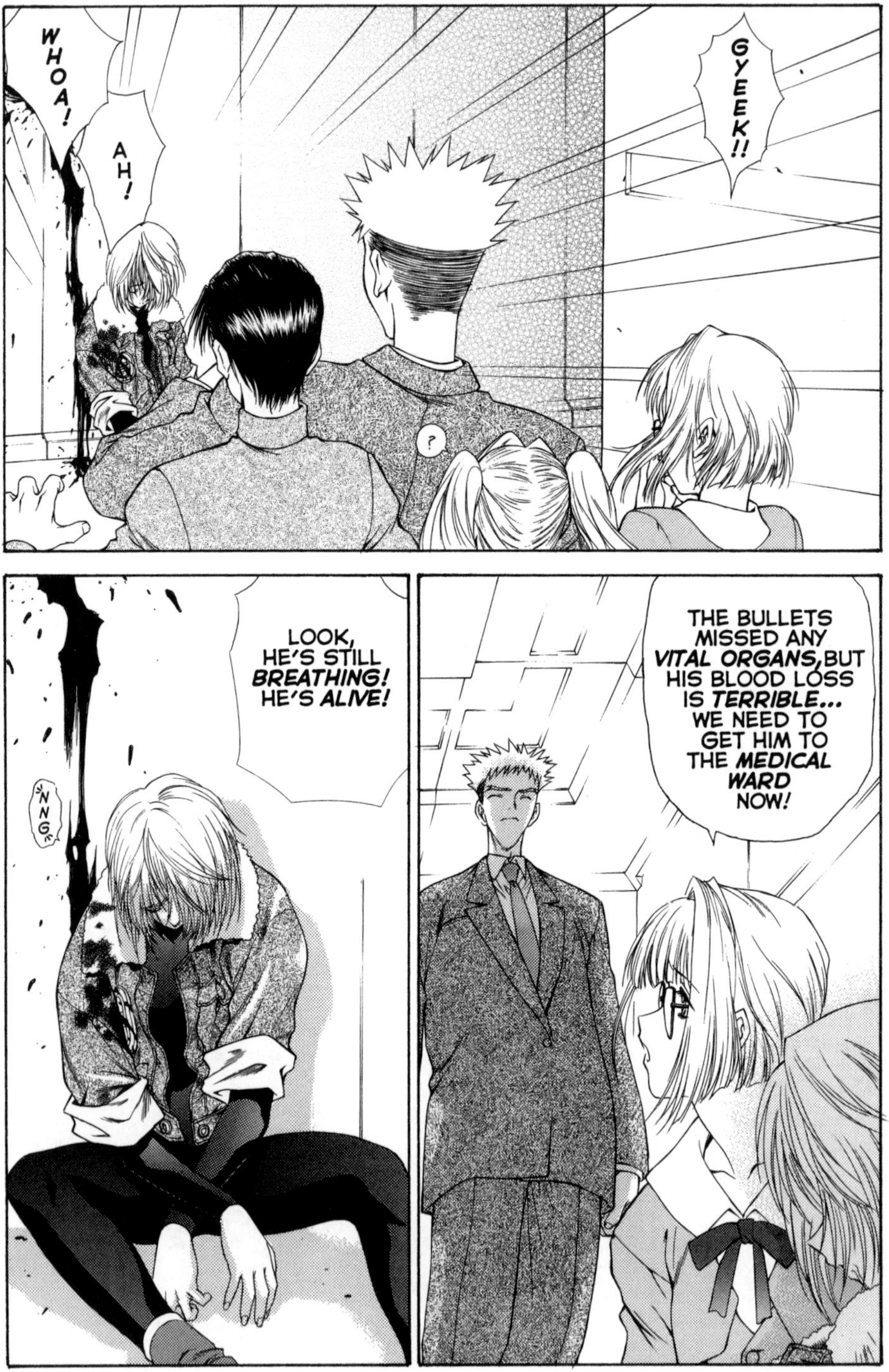
GYEEK!!
?
AH!
WHOA!
THE BULLETS MISSED ANY *VITAL ORGANS*, BUT HIS BLOOD LOSS IS *TERRIBLE...* WE NEED TO GET HIM TO THE *MEDICAL WARD* NOW!
LOOK, HE'S STILL *BREATHING!* HE'S *ALIVE!*
NNG

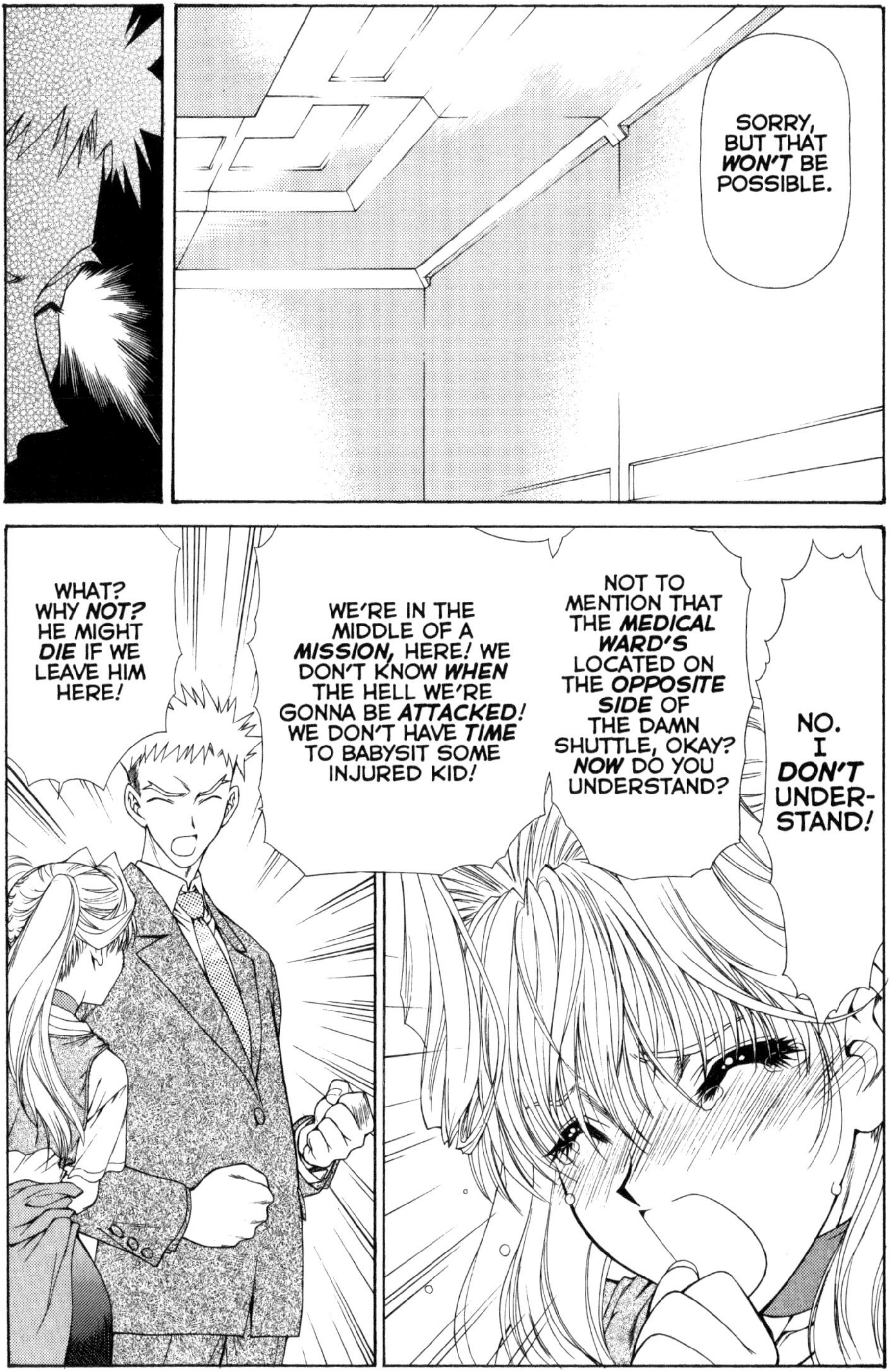
SORRY, BUT THAT ***WON'T*** BE POSSIBLE.
WHAT? WHY ***NOT?*** HE MIGHT ***DIE*** IF WE LEAVE HIM HERE!
WE'RE IN THE MIDDLE OF A ***MISSION,*** HERE! WE DON'T KNOW ***WHEN*** THE HELL WE'RE GONNA BE ***ATTACKED!*** WE DON'T HAVE ***TIME*** TO BABYSIT SOME INJURED KID!
NOT TO MENTION THAT THE ***MEDICAL WARD'S*** LOCATED ON THE ***OPPOSITE SIDE*** OF THE DAMN SHUTTLE, OKAY? ***NOW*** DO YOU UNDERSTAND?
NO. I ***DON'T*** UNDER-STAND!

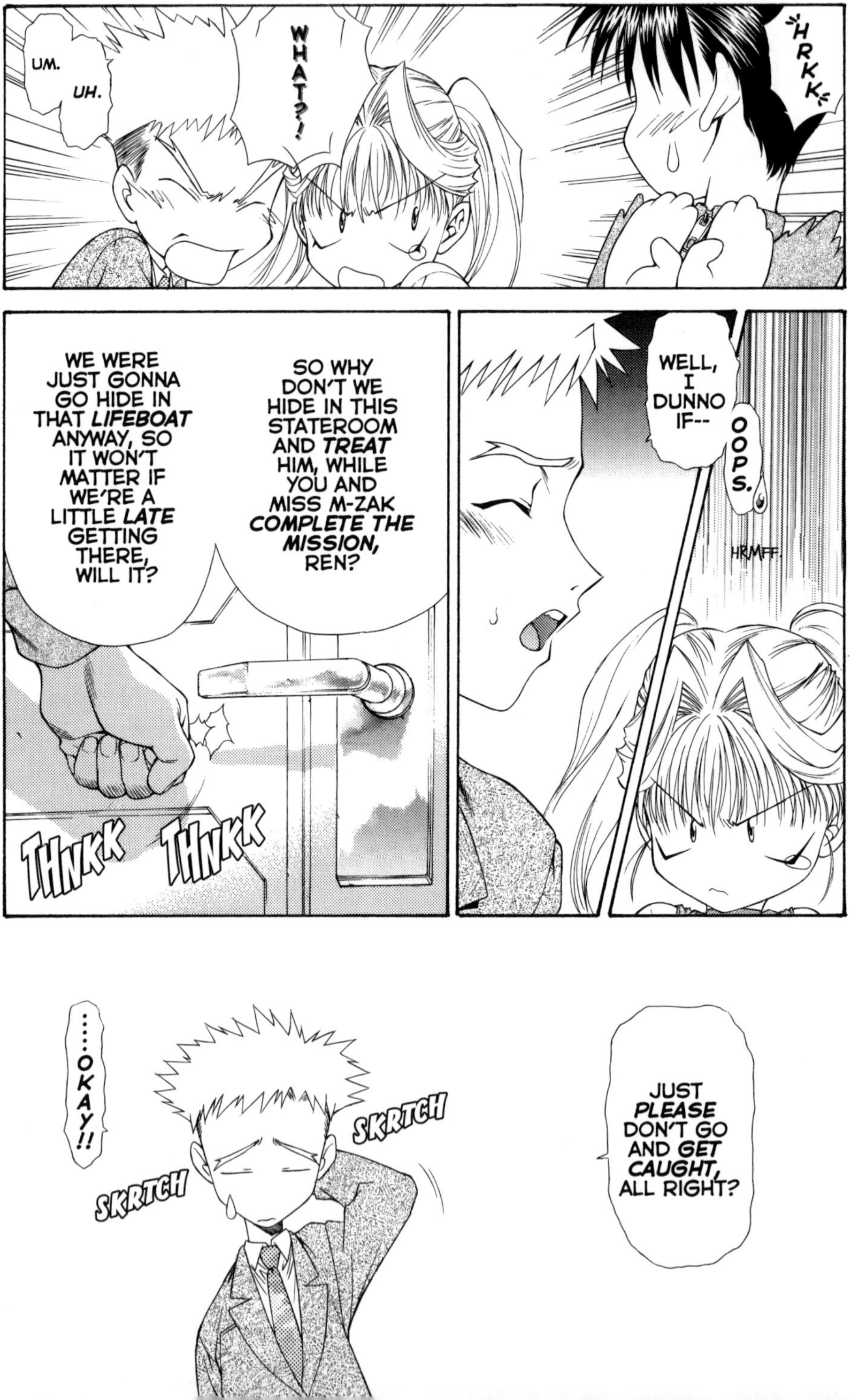
HRKK
WHAT?!
UM.
UH.
WELL, I DUNNO IF--
OOPS.
HRMFF.
SO WHY DON'T WE HIDE IN THIS STATEROOM AND TREAT HIM, WHILE YOU AND MISS M-ZAK COMPLETE THE MISSION, REN?
WE WERE JUST GONNA GO HIDE IN THAT LIFEBOAT ANYWAY, SO IT WON'T MATTER IF WE'RE A LITTLE LATE GETTING THERE, WILL IT?
THNKK
THNKK
JUST PLEASE DON'T GO AND GET CAUGHT, ALL RIGHT?
....OKAY!!
SKRTCH
SKRTCH

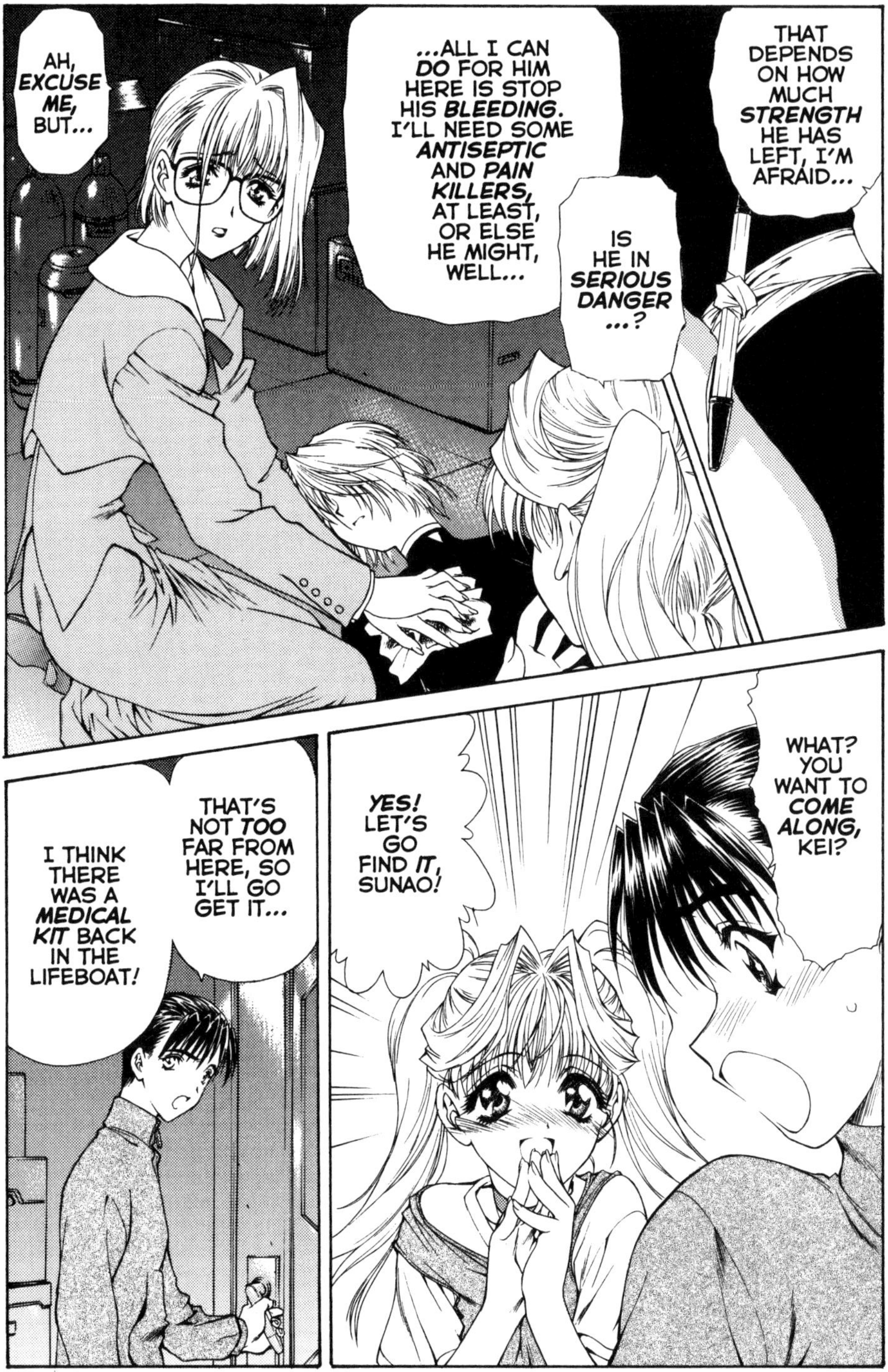
AH, EXCUSE ME, BUT...
...ALL I CAN DO FOR HIM HERE IS STOP HIS BLEEDING. I'LL NEED SOME ANTISEPTIC AND PAIN KILLERS, AT LEAST, OR ELSE HE MIGHT, WELL...
IS HE IN SERIOUS DANGER ...?
THAT DEPENDS ON HOW MUCH STRENGTH HE HAS LEFT, I'M AFRAID...
I THINK THERE WAS A MEDICAL KIT BACK IN THE LIFEBOAT!
THAT'S NOT TOO FAR FROM HERE, SO I'LL GO GET IT...
YES! LET'S GO FIND IT, SUNAO!
WHAT? YOU WANT TO COME ALONG, KEI?

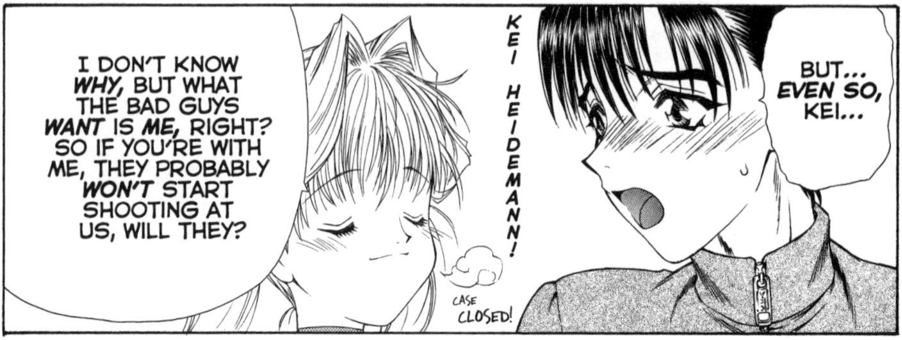
BUT... EVEN SO, KEI...
KEI HEIDEMANN!
I DON'T KNOW WHY, BUT WHAT THE BAD GUYS WANT IS ME, RIGHT? SO IF YOU'RE WITH ME, THEY PROBABLY WON'T START SHOOTING AT US, WILL THEY?
CASE CLOSED!

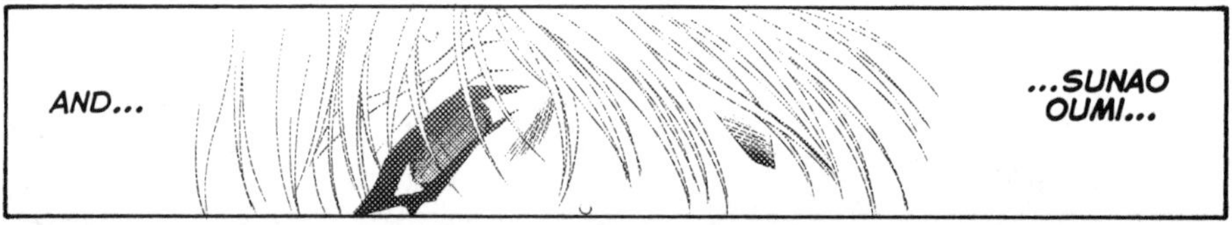
...SUNAO OUMI...
AND...

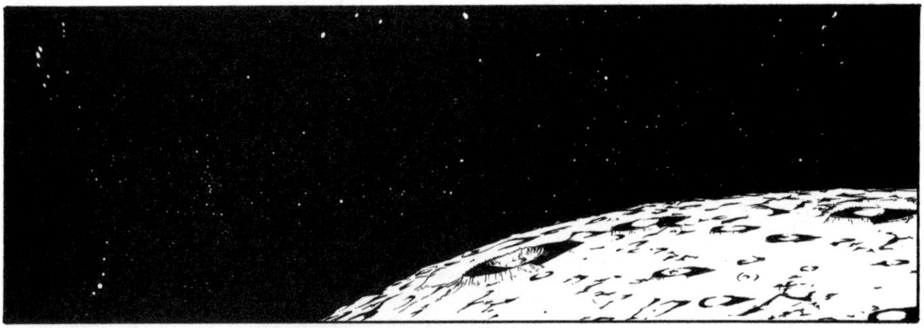

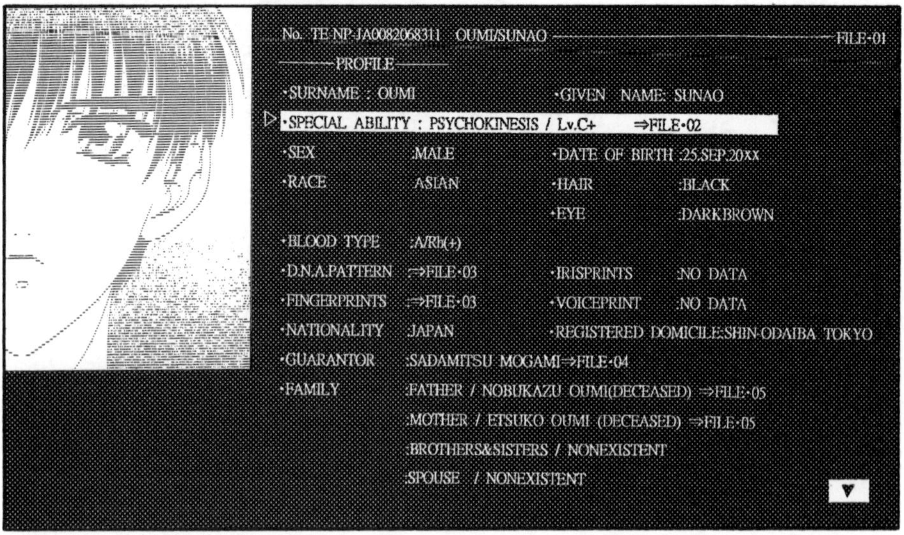
No. TE-NP-JA0082068311 OUMI/SUNAO
FILE-01
PROFILE
•SURNAME : OUMI
•GIVEN NAME: SUNAO
•SPECIAL ABILITY : PSYCHOKINESIS / Lv.C+ ⇒FILE-02
•SEX :MALE
•DATE OF BIRTH :25.SEP.20xx
•RACE :ASIAN
•HAIR :BLACK
•EYE :DARKBROWN
•BLOOD TYPE :A/Rh(+)
•D.N.A.PATTERN :⇒FILE-03
•IRISPRINTS :NO DATA
•FINGERPRINTS :⇒FILE-03
•VOICEPRINT :NO DATA
•NATIONALITY :JAPAN
•REGISTERED DOMICILE:SHIN-ODAIBA TOKYO
•GUARANTOR :SADAMITSU MOGAMI⇒FILE-04
•FAMILY :FATHER / NOBUKAZU OUMI(DECEASED) ⇒FILE-05
:MOTHER / ETSUKO OUMI (DECEASED) ⇒FILE-05
:BROTHERS&SISTERS / NONEXISTENT
:SPOUSE / NONEXISTENT

ACT 67

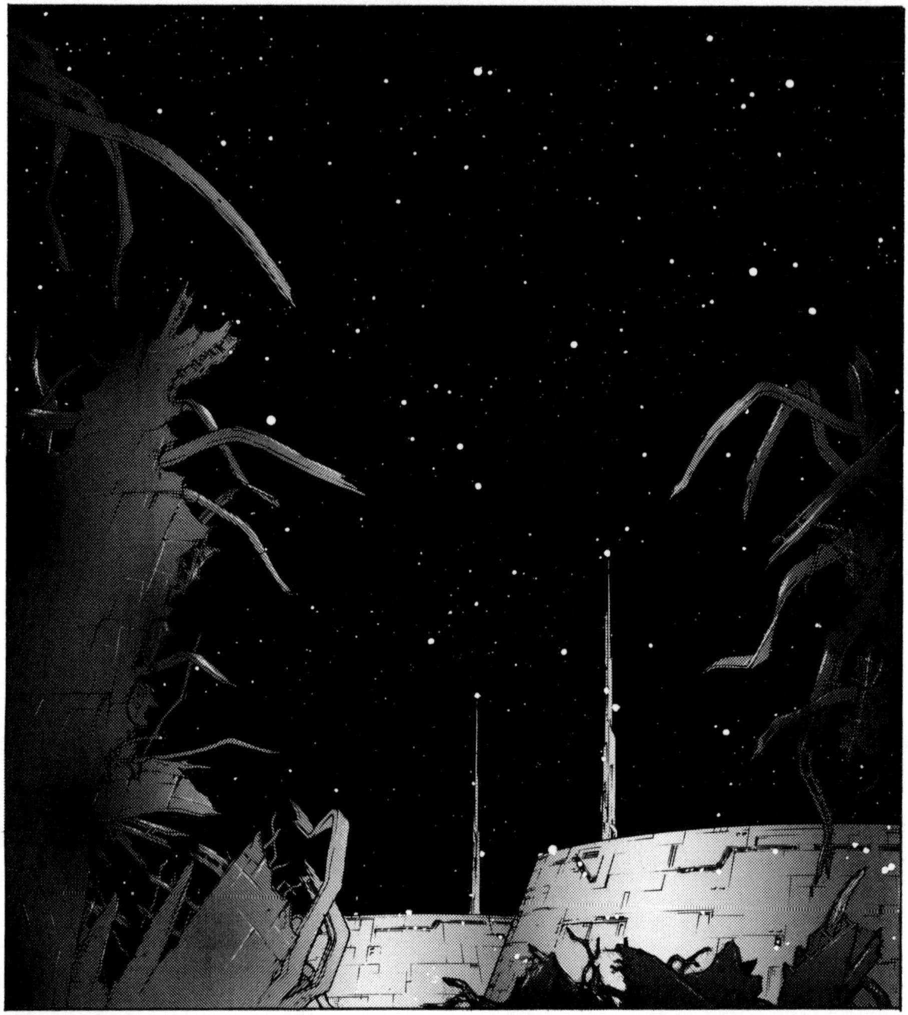

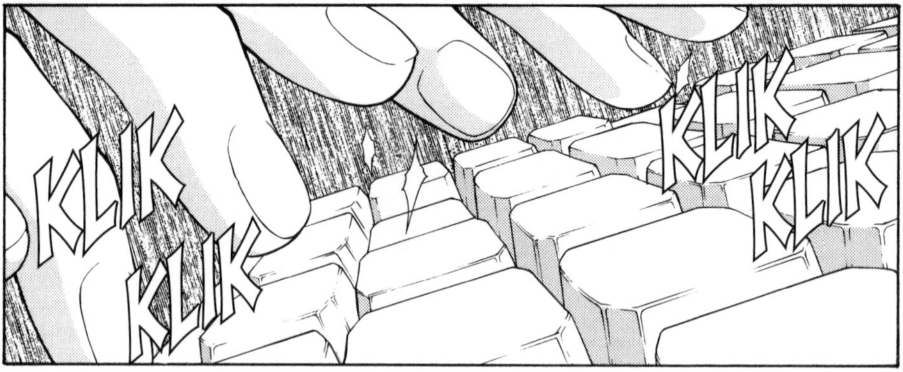
KLIK KLIK
KLIK KLIK

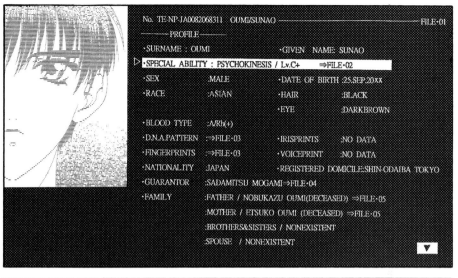

No. TE-NP-JA0082068311 OUMI/SUNAO ───────────────── FILE·01

──────── PROFILE ────────

·SURNAME : OUMI   ·GIVEN NAME: SUNAO

▷ ·SPECIAL ABILITY : PSYCHOKINESIS / Lv.C+   ⇒FILE·02

·SEX   :MALE   ·DATE OF BIRTH :25.SEP.20xx

·RACE   :ASIAN   ·HAIR   :BLACK

                                  ·EYE   :DARKBROWN

·BLOOD TYPE   :A/Rh(+)

·D.N.A.PATTERN :⇒FILE·03   ·IRISPRINTS   :NO DATA

·FINGERPRINTS   :⇒FILE·03   ·VOICEPRINT   :NO DATA

·NATIONALITY   :JAPAN   ·REGISTERED DOMICILE:SHIN-ODAIBA TOKYO

·GUARANTOR   :SADAMITSU MOGAMI⇒FILE·04

·FAMILY   :FATHER / NOBUKAZU OUMI(DECEASED) ⇒FILE·05

               :MOTHER / ETSUKO OUMI (DECEASED) ⇒FILE·05

               :BROTHERS&SISTERS / NONEXISTENT

               :SPOUSE / NONEXISTENT

▼

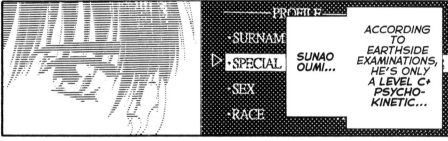

──────── PROFILE ────────

·SURNAM

▷ ·SPECIAL

·SEX

·RACE

SUNAO OUMI...

ACCORDING TO EARTHSIDE EXAMINATIONS, HE'S ONLY A LEVEL C+ PSYCHO-KINETIC...

...BUT THAT POWER...

...THE METATALENT HE USED TO DAMAGE NUMBER FOUR...

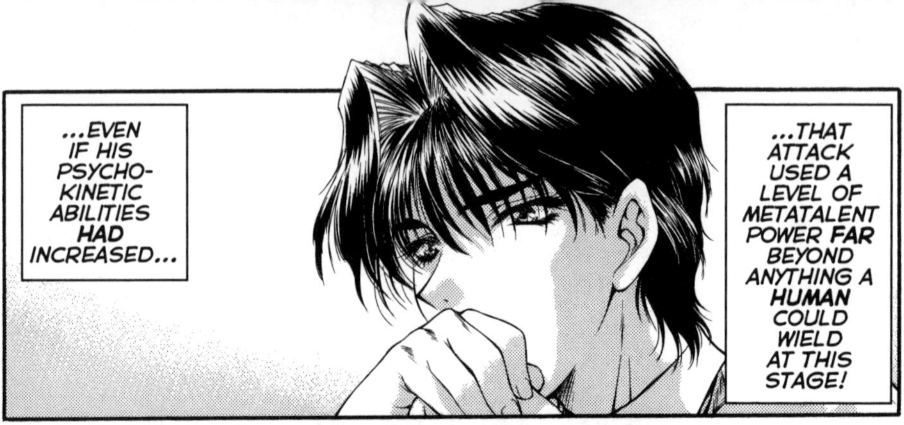
...EVEN IF HIS PSYCHO-KINETIC ABILITIES HAD INCREASED...
...THAT ATTACK USED A LEVEL OF METATALENT POWER FAR BEYOND ANYTHING A HUMAN COULD WIELD AT THIS STAGE!

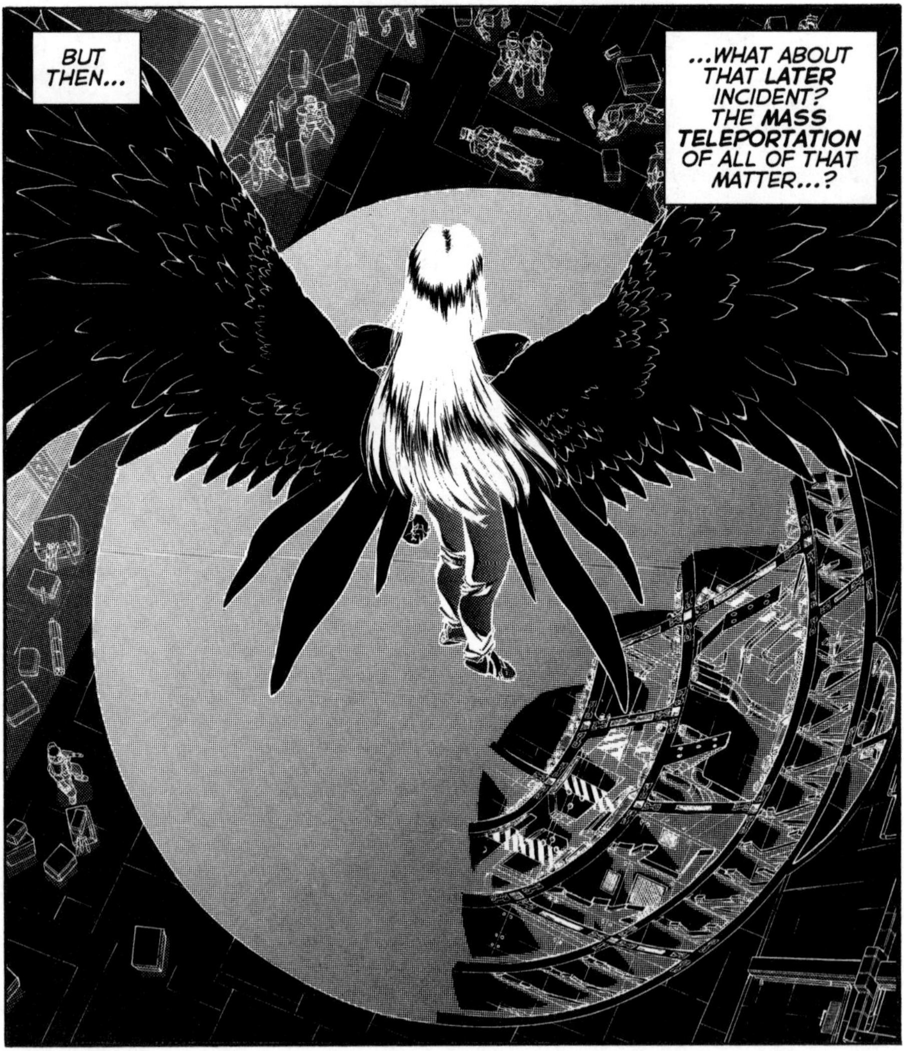
BUT THEN...
...WHAT ABOUT THAT LATER INCIDENT? THE MASS TELEPORTATION OF ALL OF THAT MATTER...?

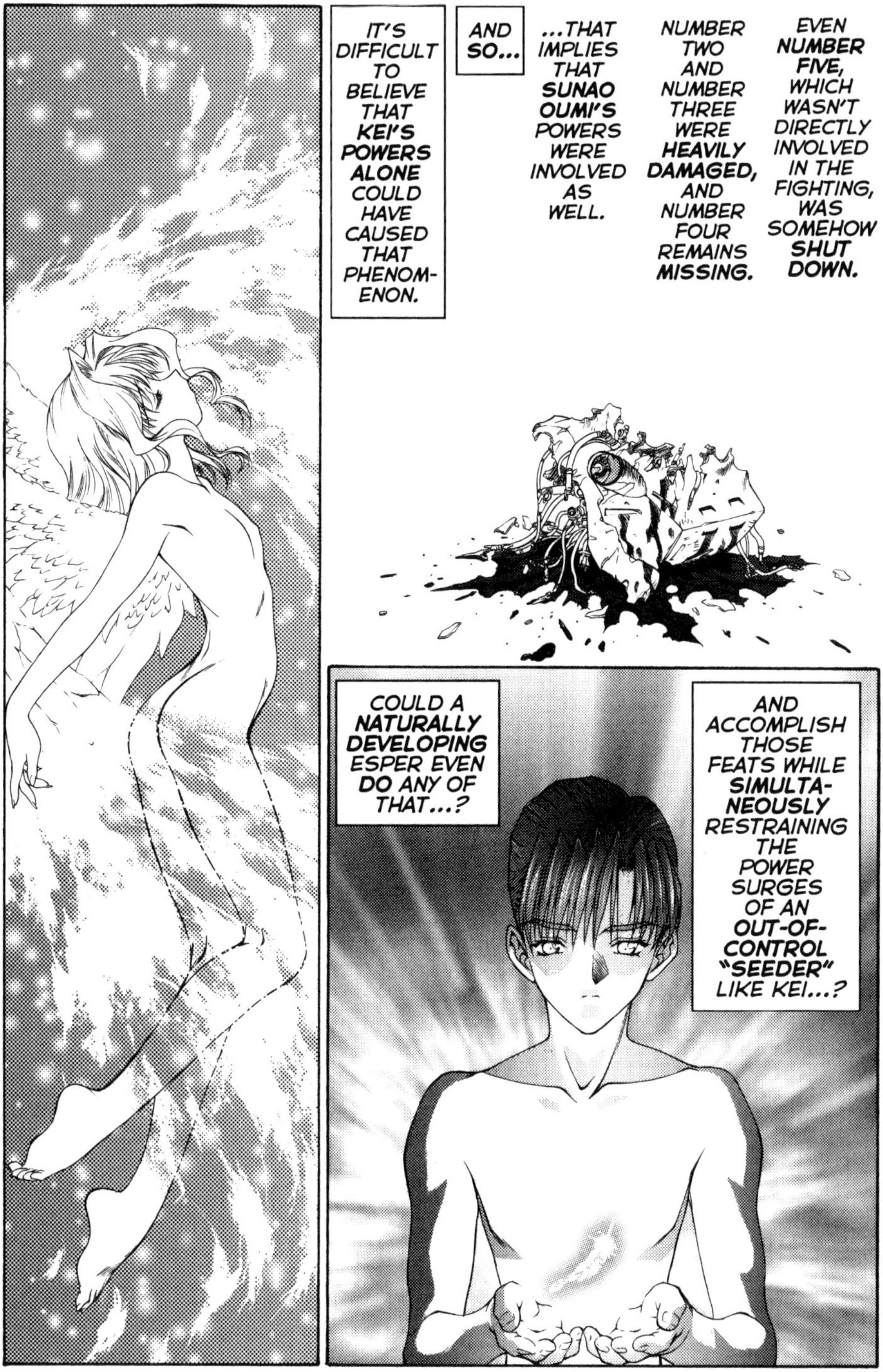
IT'S DIFFICULT TO BELIEVE THAT KEI'S POWERS ALONE COULD HAVE CAUSED THAT PHENOMENON.
AND SO...
...THAT IMPLIES THAT SUNAO OUMI'S POWERS WERE INVOLVED AS WELL.
NUMBER TWO AND NUMBER THREE WERE HEAVILY DAMAGED, AND NUMBER FOUR REMAINS MISSING.
EVEN NUMBER FIVE, WHICH WASN'T DIRECTLY INVOLVED IN THE FIGHTING, WAS SOMEHOW SHUT DOWN.
COULD A NATURALLY DEVELOPING ESPER EVEN DO ANY OF THAT...?
AND ACCOMPLISH THOSE FEATS WHILE SIMULTANEOUSLY RESTRAINING THE POWER SURGES OF AN OUT-OF-CONTROL "SEEDER" LIKE KEI...?

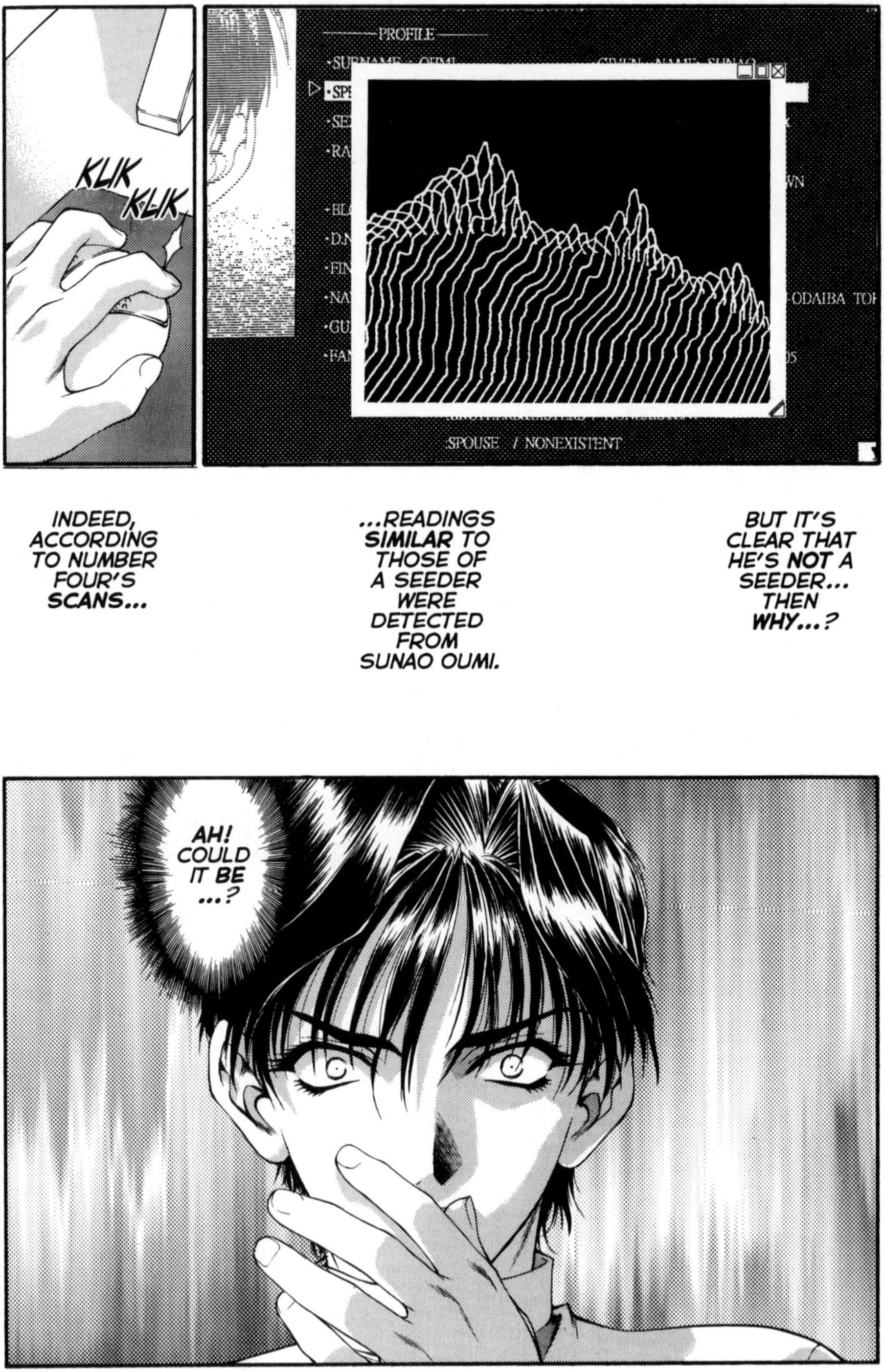
KLIK KLIK
PROFILE
SPOUSE / NONEXISTENT
INDEED, ACCORDING TO NUMBER FOUR'S **SCANS...**
...READINGS **SIMILAR** TO THOSE OF A SEEDER WERE DETECTED FROM SUNAO OUMI.
BUT IT'S CLEAR THAT HE'S **NOT** A SEEDER... THEN **WHY...?**
AH! COULD IT **BE** ...?

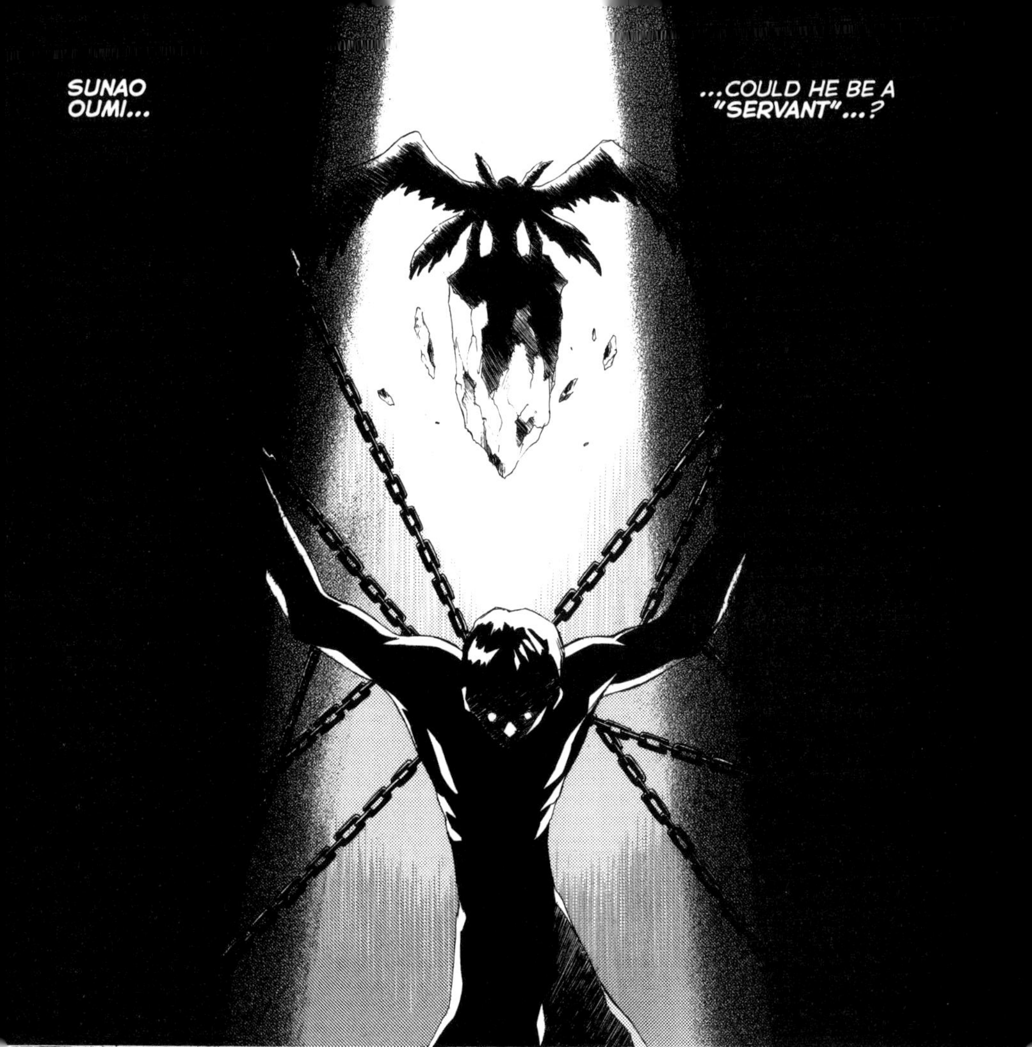
SUNAO OUMI...
...COULD HE BE A "SERVANT"...?
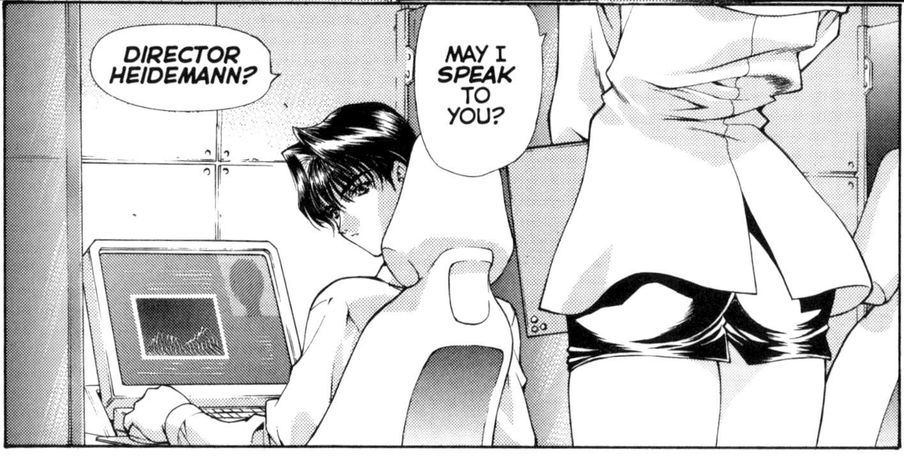
DIRECTOR HEIDEMANN?
MAY I SPEAK TO YOU?

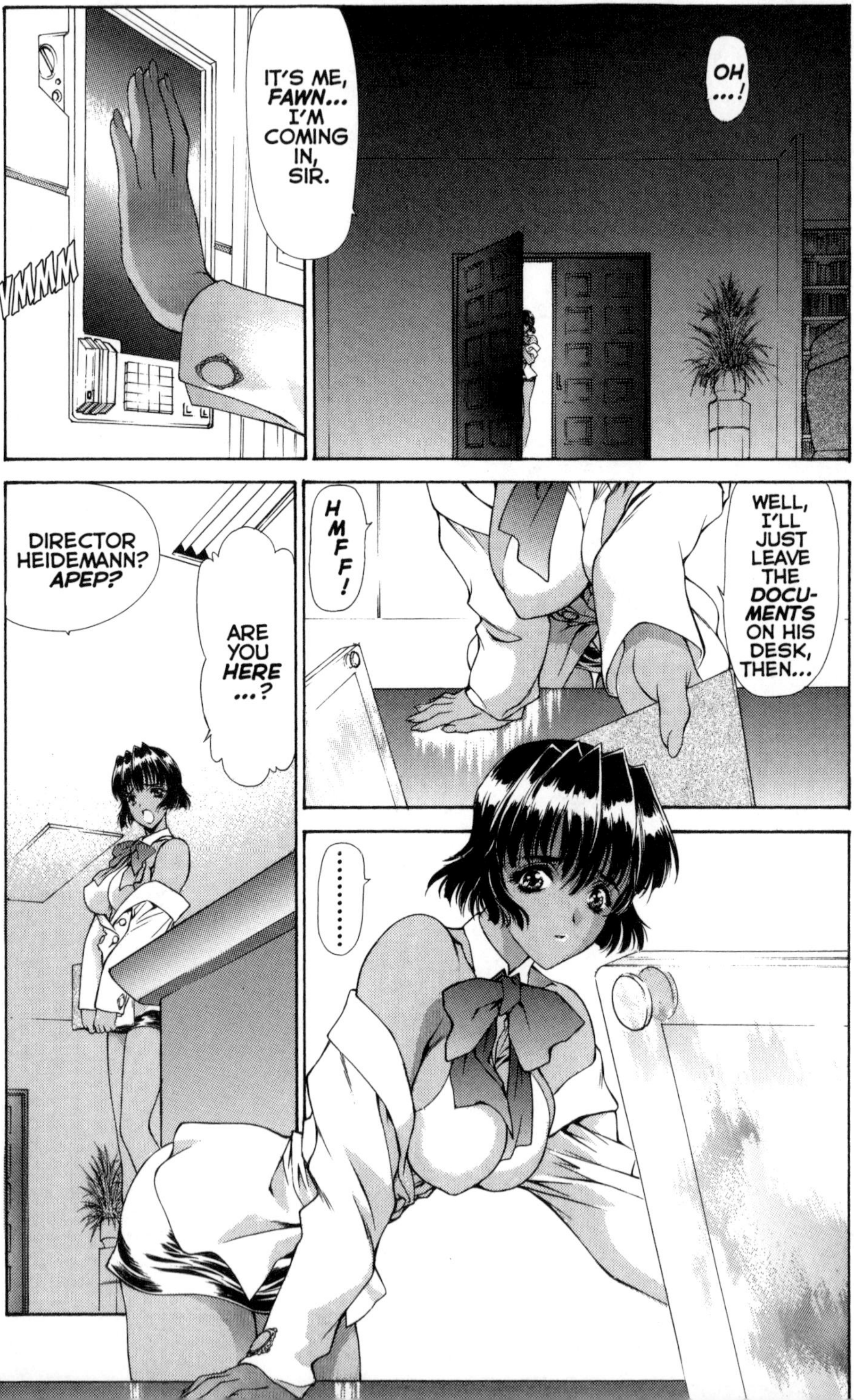
IT'S ME, FAWN... I'M COMING IN, SIR.
VMMMM
OH ...!
DIRECTOR HEIDEMANN? APEP?
ARE YOU HERE ...?
HMFF!
WELL, I'LL JUST LEAVE THE DOCUMENTS ON HIS DESK, THEN...
....

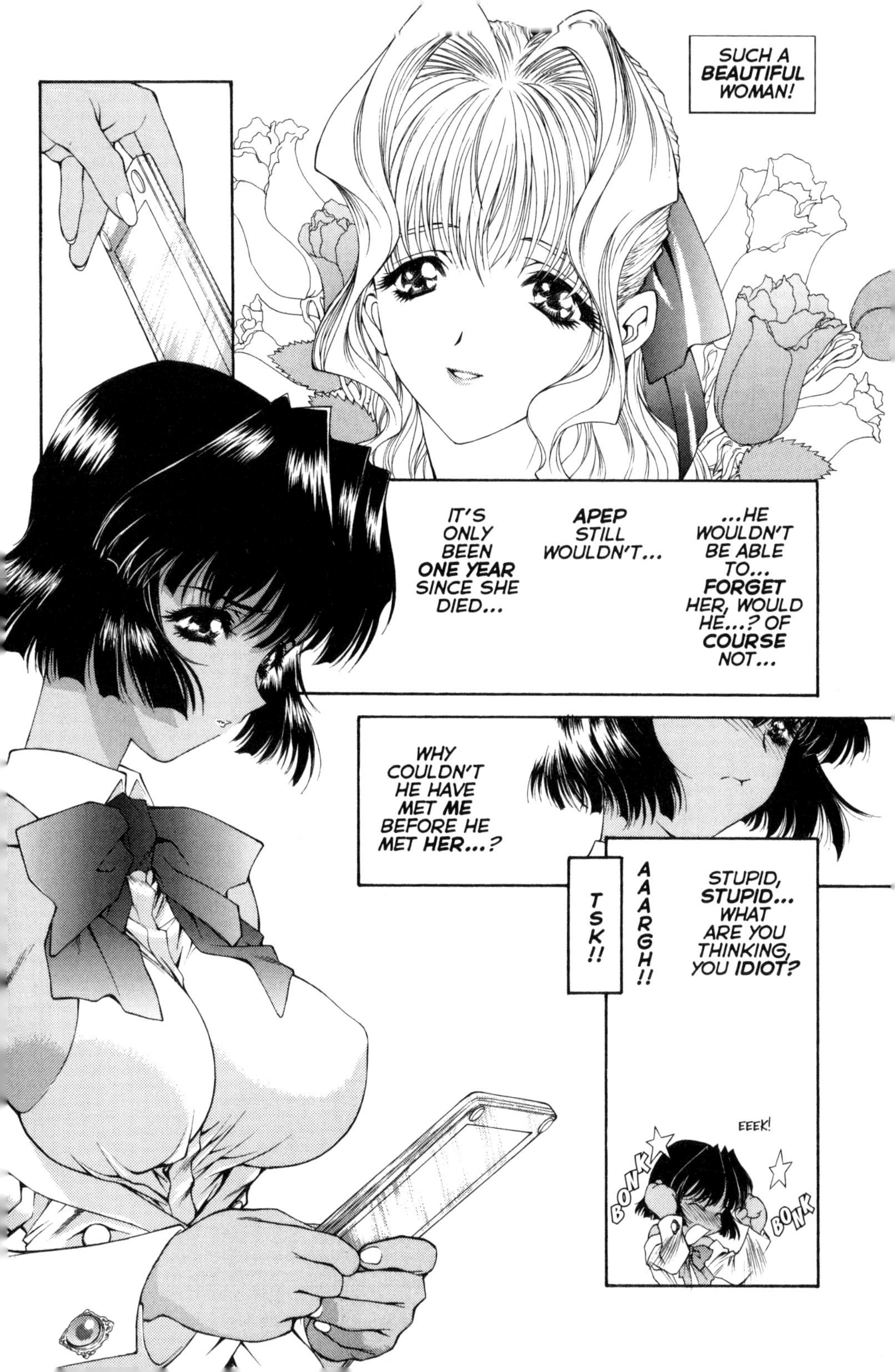
SUCH A BEAUTIFUL WOMAN!
IT'S ONLY BEEN ONE YEAR SINCE SHE DIED...
APEP STILL WOULDN'T...
...HE WOULDN'T BE ABLE TO... FORGET HER, WOULD HE...? OF COURSE NOT...
WHY COULDN'T HE HAVE MET ME BEFORE HE MET HER...?
STUPID, STUPID... WHAT ARE YOU THINKING, YOU IDIOT?
AAARGH!!
TSK!!
EEEK!
BONK
BONK

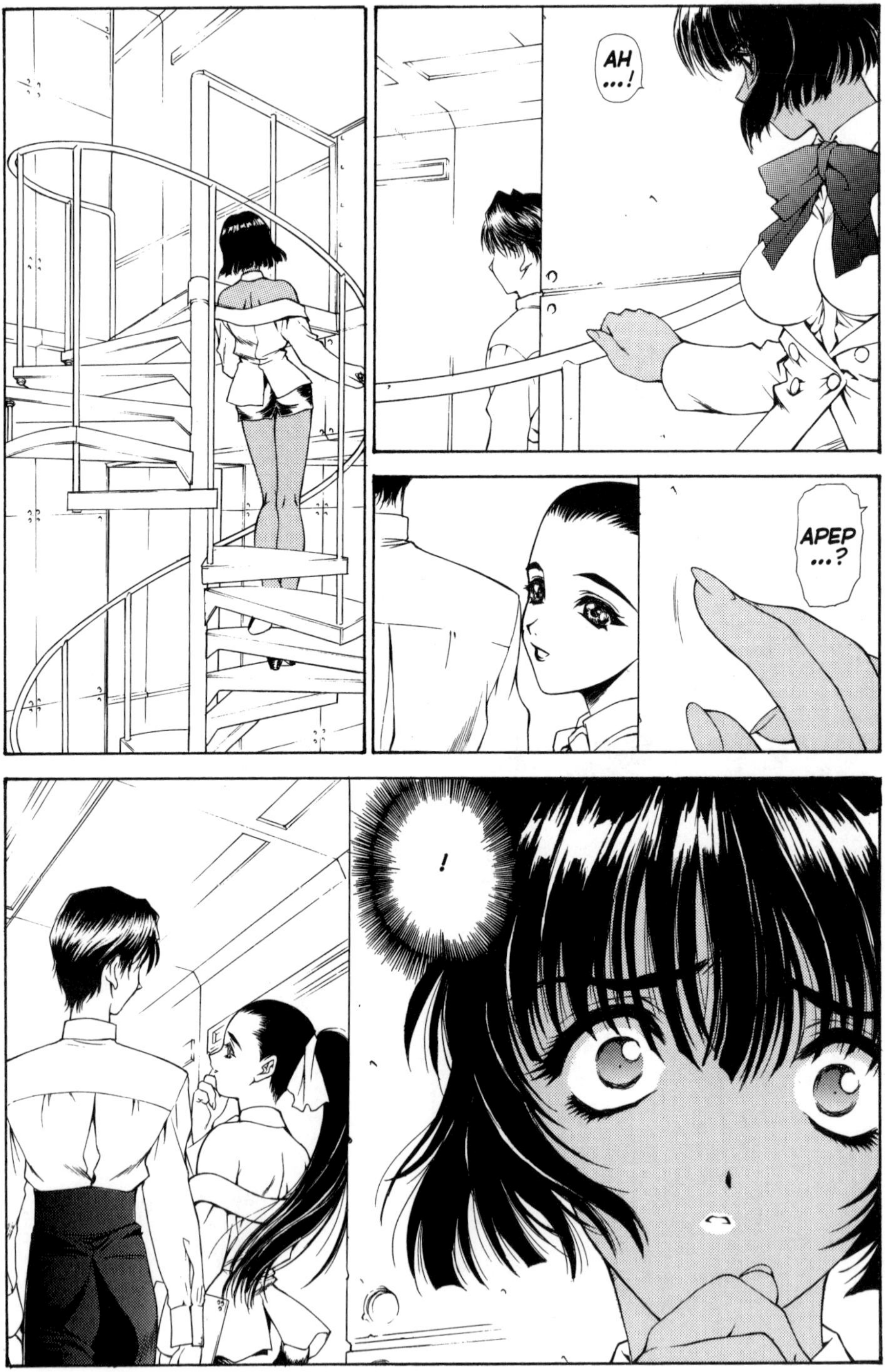
AH ...!
APEP ...?
!

ACT 68

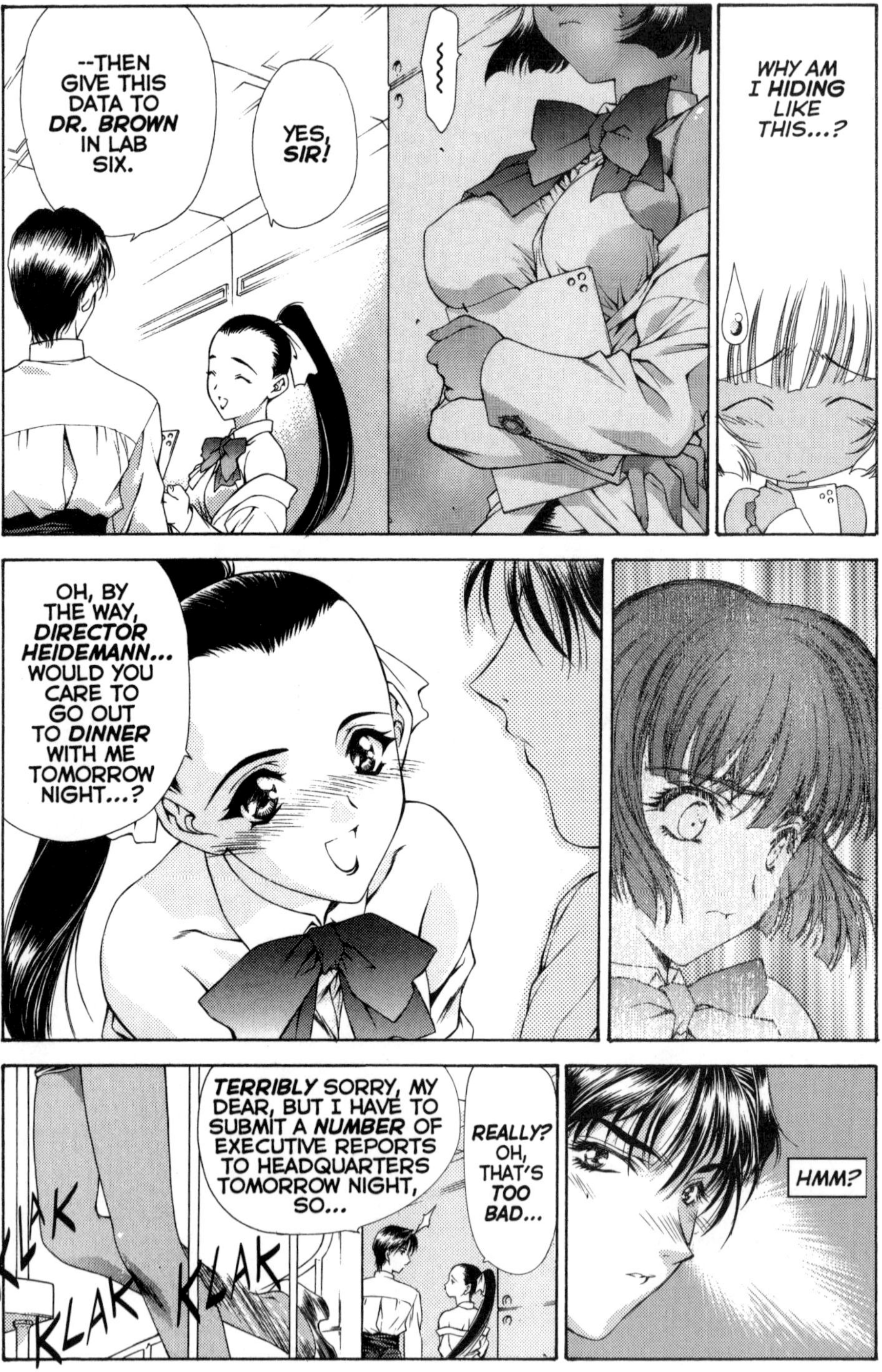
--THEN GIVE THIS DATA TO DR. BROWN IN LAB SIX.
YES, SIR!
...
WHY AM I HIDING LIKE THIS...?
OH, BY THE WAY, DIRECTOR HEIDEMANN... WOULD YOU CARE TO GO OUT TO DINNER WITH ME TOMORROW NIGHT...?
TERRIBLY SORRY, MY DEAR, BUT I HAVE TO SUBMIT A NUMBER OF EXECUTIVE REPORTS TO HEADQUARTERS TOMORROW NIGHT, SO...
REALLY? OH, THAT'S TOO BAD...
KLAK KLAK KLAK
HMM?

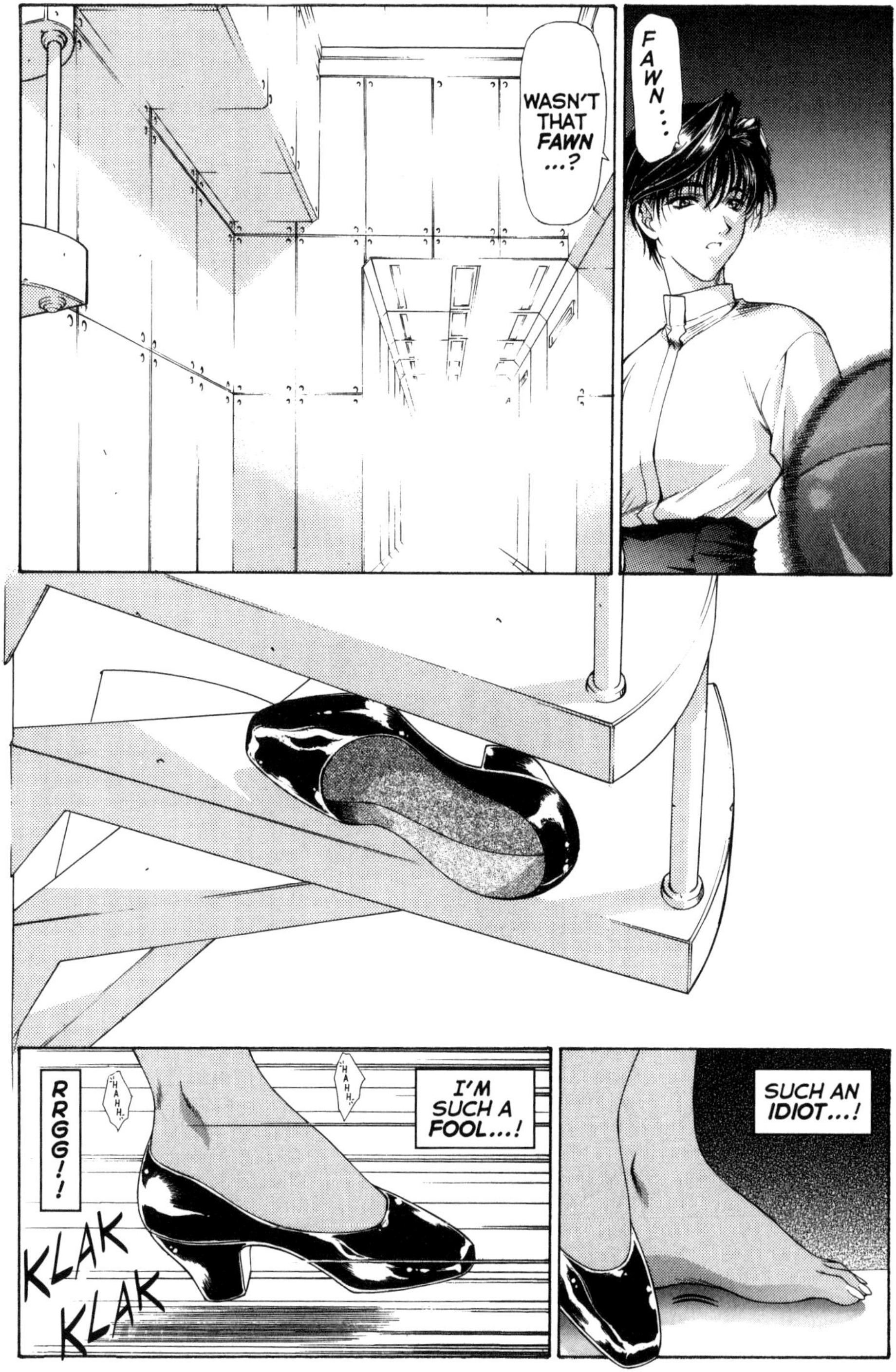
FAWN...
WASN'T THAT FAWN...?
SUCH AN IDIOT...!
I'M SUCH A FOOL...!
RRGG!!
KLAK KLAK

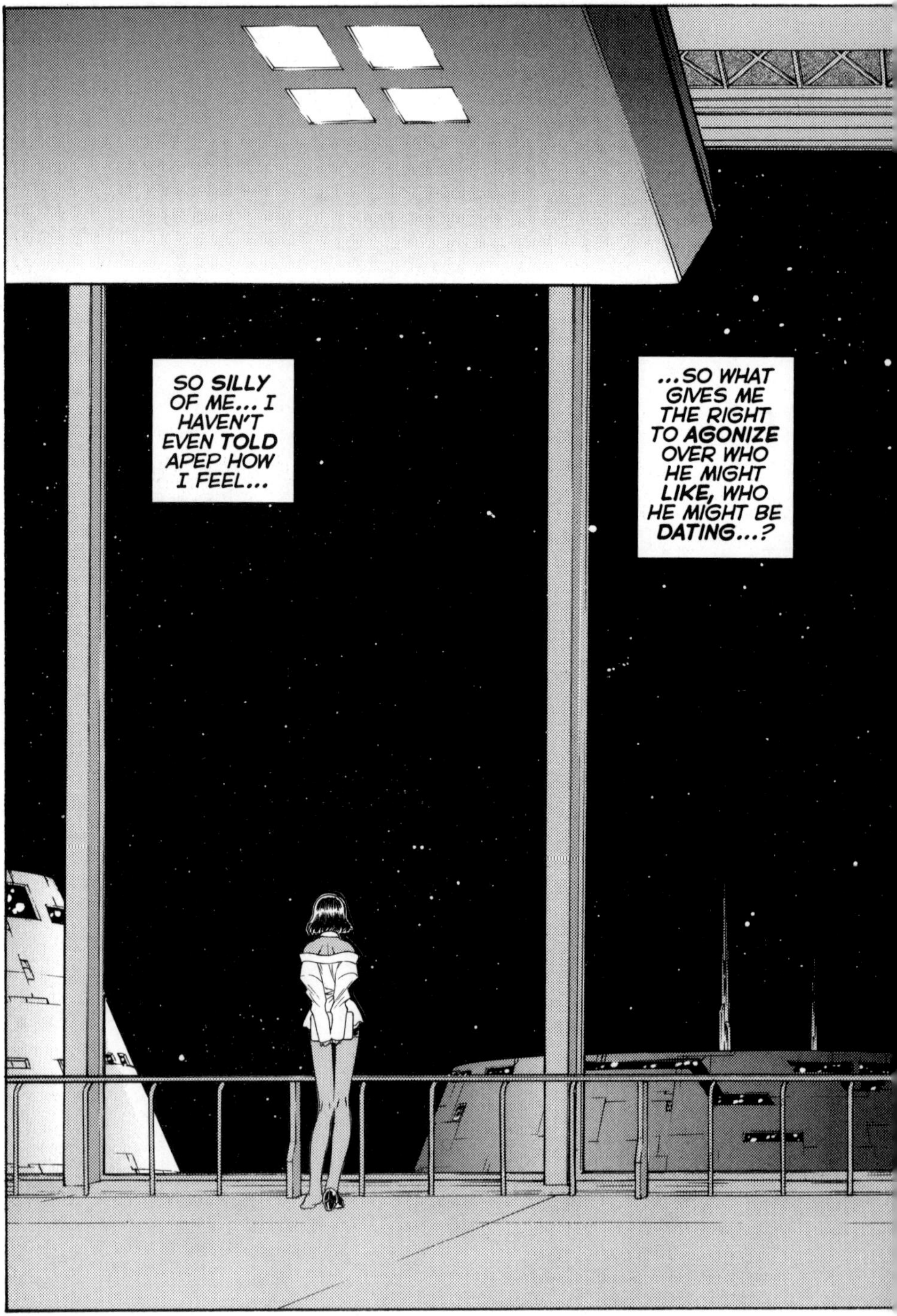
...SO WHAT GIVES ME THE RIGHT TO AGONIZE OVER WHO HE MIGHT LIKE, WHO HE MIGHT BE DATING...?
SO SILLY OF ME... I HAVEN'T EVEN TOLD APEP HOW I FEEL...

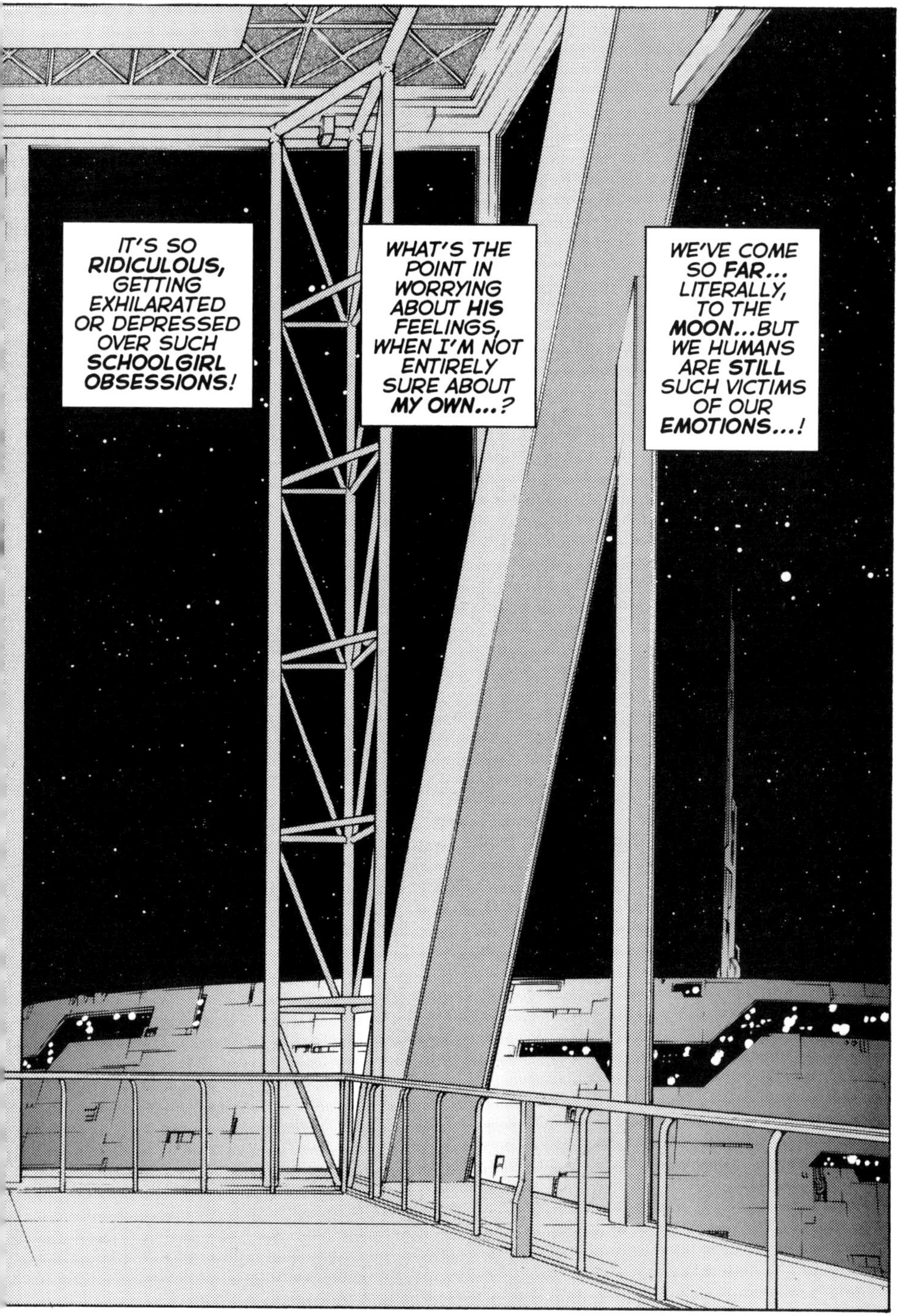
IT'S SO RIDICULOUS, GETTING EXHILARATED OR DEPRESSED OVER SUCH SCHOOLGIRL OBSESSIONS!
WHAT'S THE POINT IN WORRYING ABOUT HIS FEELINGS, WHEN I'M NOT ENTIRELY SURE ABOUT MY OWN...?
WE'VE COME SO FAR... LITERALLY, TO THE MOON...BUT WE HUMANS ARE STILL SUCH VICTIMS OF OUR EMOTIONS...!

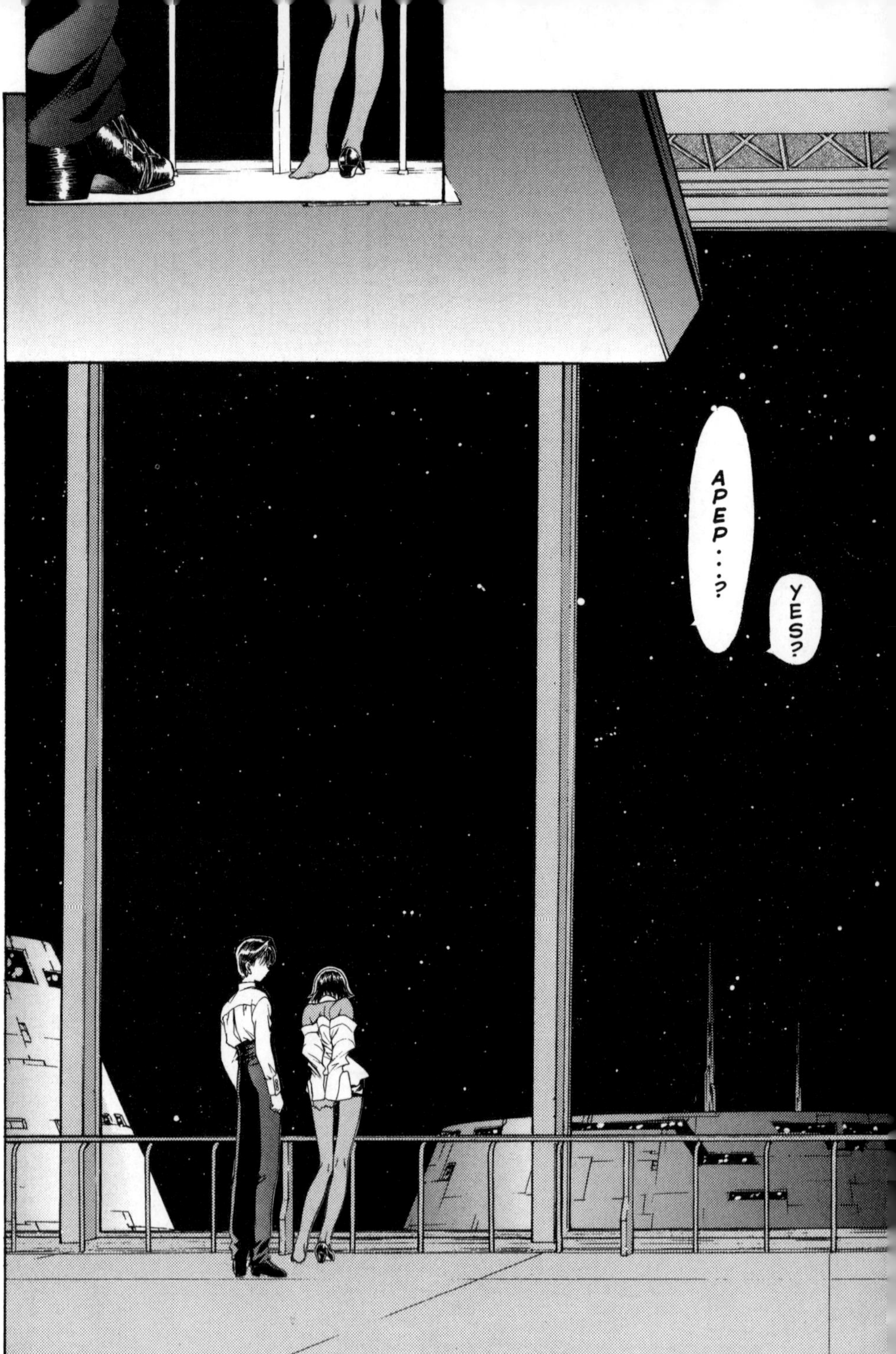
YES?
APEP...?

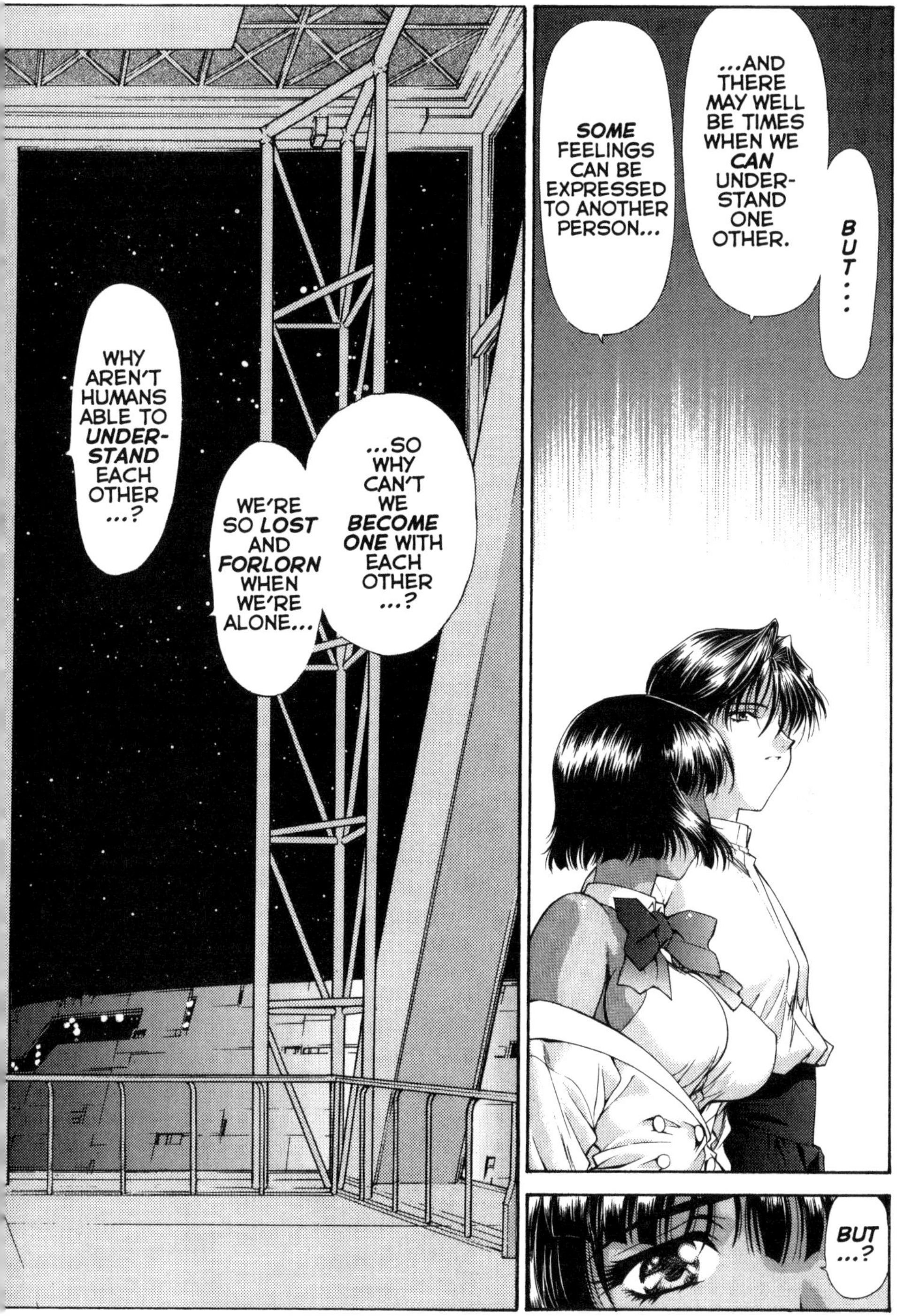
WHY AREN'T HUMANS ABLE TO ***UNDER-STAND*** EACH OTHER ...?
WE'RE SO ***LOST*** AND ***FORLORN*** WHEN WE'RE ALONE...
...SO WHY CAN'T WE ***BECOME ONE*** WITH EACH OTHER ...?
SOME FEELINGS CAN BE EXPRESSED TO ANOTHER PERSON...
...AND THERE MAY WELL BE TIMES WHEN WE ***CAN*** UNDER-STAND ONE OTHER.
BUT...
BUT ...?

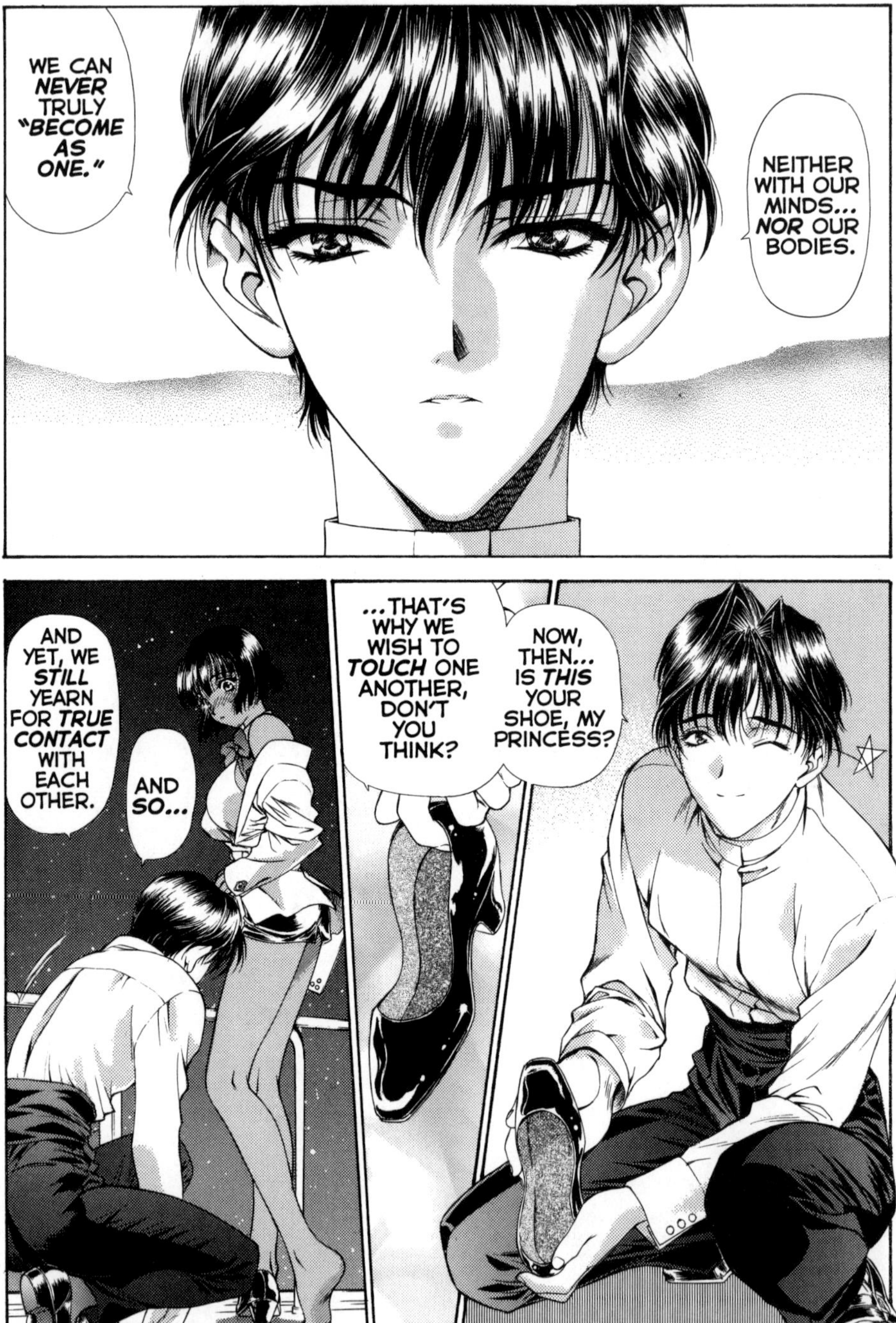
WE CAN *NEVER* TRULY *"BECOME AS ONE."*
NEITHER WITH OUR MINDS... *NOR* OUR BODIES.
AND YET, WE *STILL* YEARN FOR *TRUE CONTACT* WITH EACH OTHER.
AND *SO...*
...THAT'S WHY WE WISH TO *TOUCH* ONE ANOTHER, DON'T YOU THINK?
NOW, THEN... IS *THIS* YOUR SHOE, MY PRINCESS?

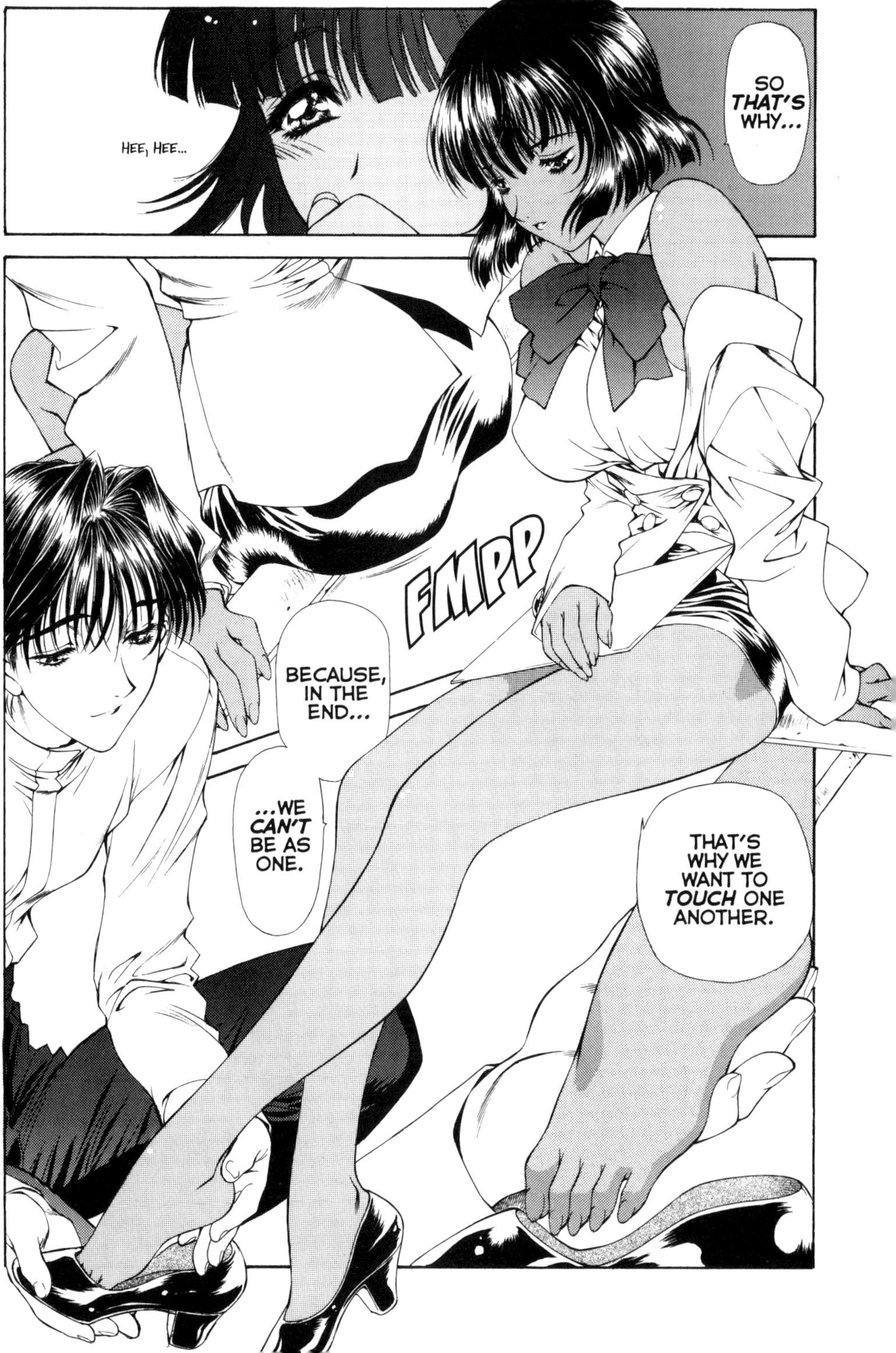
SO *THAT'S* WHY...
HEE, HEE...
FMPP
BECAUSE, IN THE END...
...WE *CAN'T* BE AS ONE.
THAT'S WHY WE WANT TO *TOUCH* ONE ANOTHER.

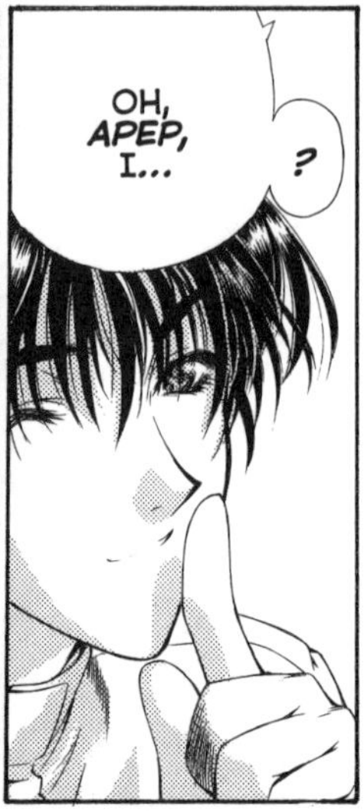
OH, *APEP,* I...
?
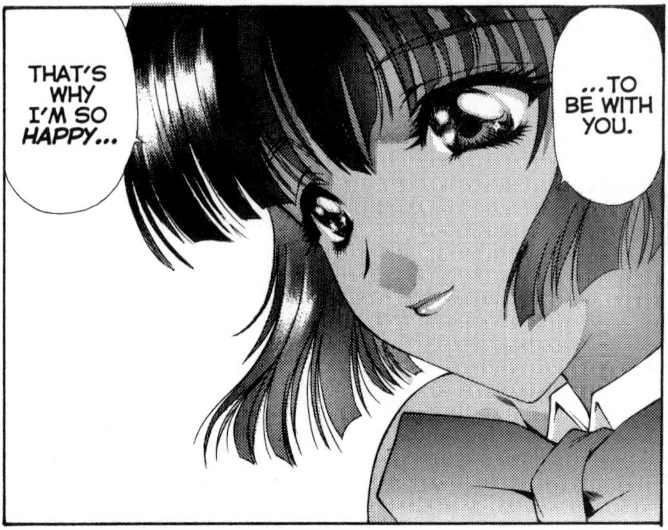
...TO BE WITH YOU.
THAT'S WHY I'M SO *HAPPY...*
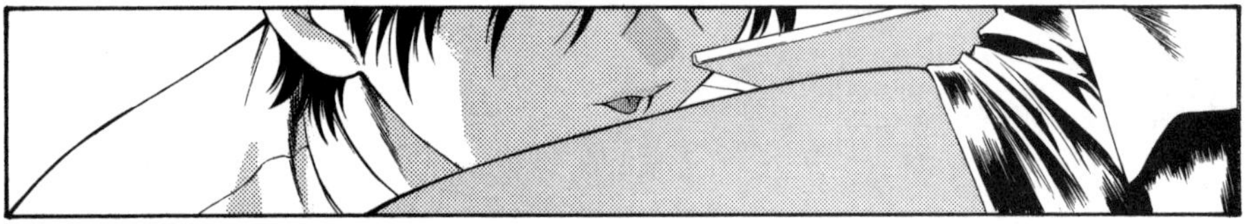
AH...
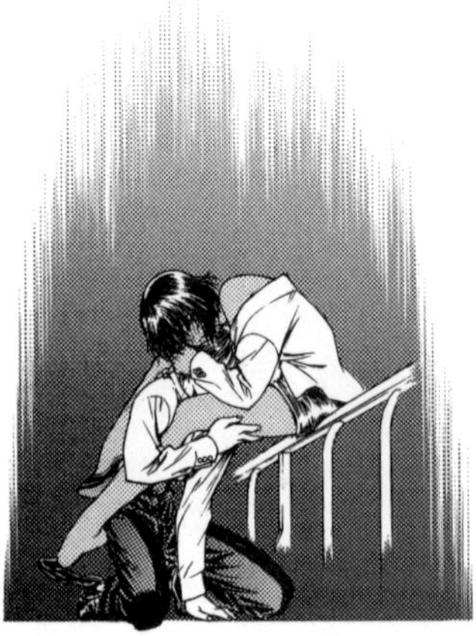

Act 69

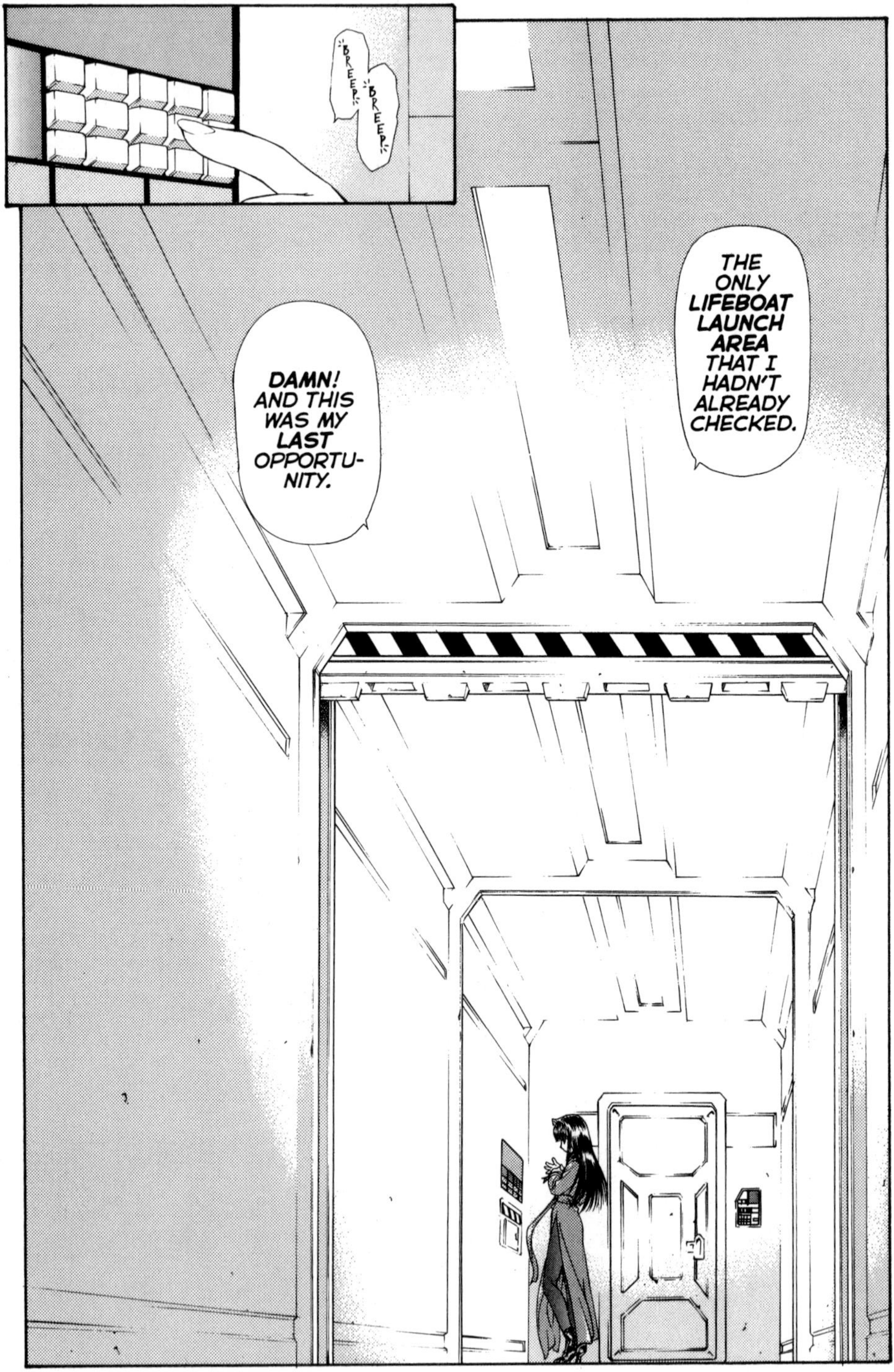
BREEP!
BREEP!
THE ONLY LIFEBOAT LAUNCH AREA THAT I HADN'T ALREADY CHECKED.
DAMN! AND THIS WAS MY LAST OPPORTU-NITY.

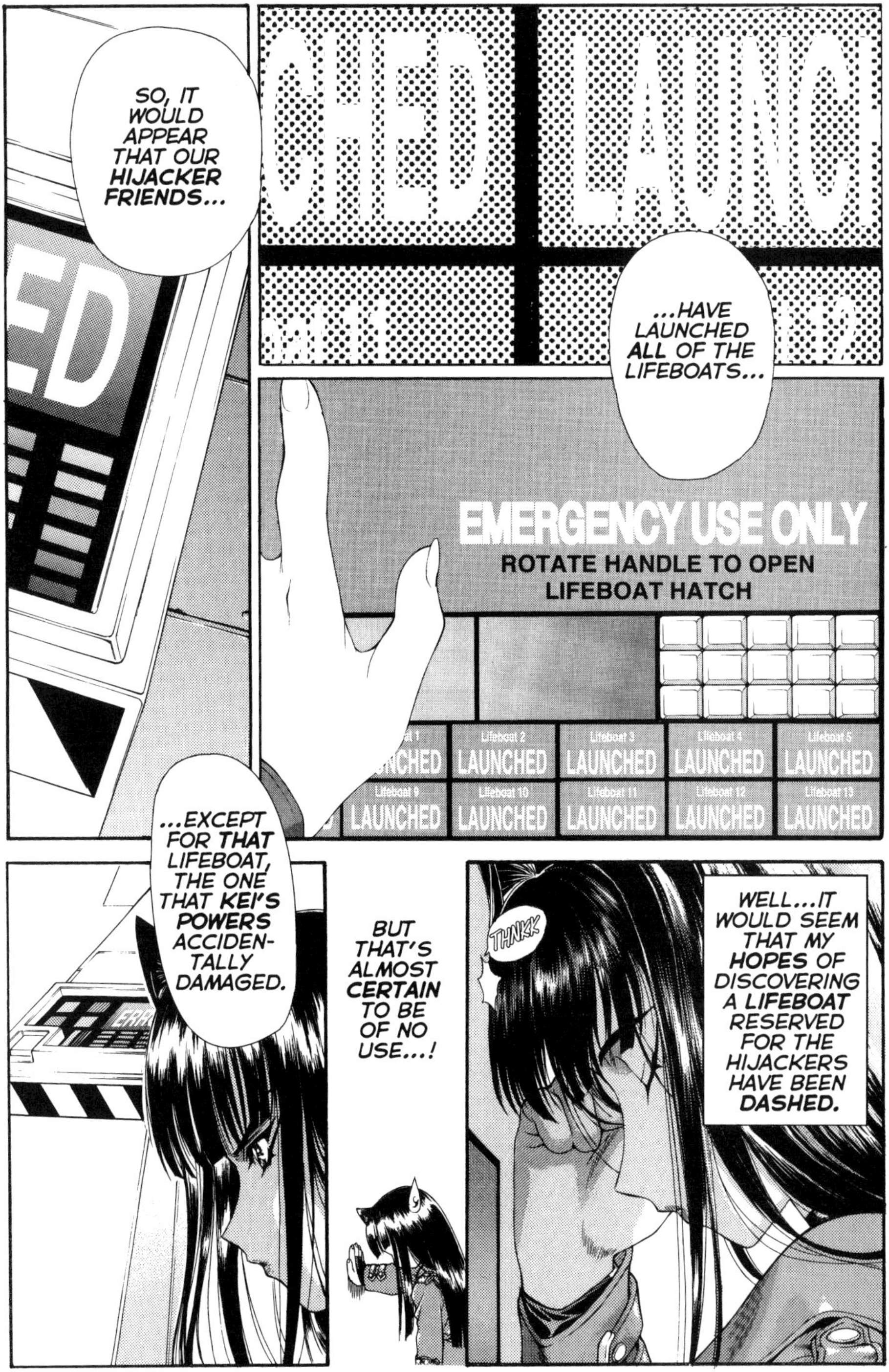
SO, IT WOULD APPEAR THAT OUR **HIJACKER** **FRIENDS**...
...HAVE LAUNCHED **ALL** OF THE LIFEBOATS...
EMERGENCY USE ONLY
ROTATE HANDLE TO OPEN LIFEBOAT HATCH
Lifeboat 2 LAUNCHED
Lifeboat 3 LAUNCHED
Lifeboat 4 LAUNCHED
Lifeboat 5 LAUNCHED
Lifeboat 9 LAUNCHED
Lifeboat 10 LAUNCHED
Lifeboat 11 LAUNCHED
Lifeboat 12 LAUNCHED
Lifeboat 13 LAUNCHED
...EXCEPT FOR **THAT** LIFEBOAT, THE ONE THAT **KEI'S** **POWERS** ACCIDENTALLY DAMAGED.
BUT THAT'S ALMOST **CERTAIN** TO BE OF NO USE...!
THNKK
WELL...IT WOULD SEEM THAT MY **HOPES** OF DISCOVERING A **LIFEBOAT** RESERVED FOR THE HIJACKERS HAVE BEEN **DASHED.**

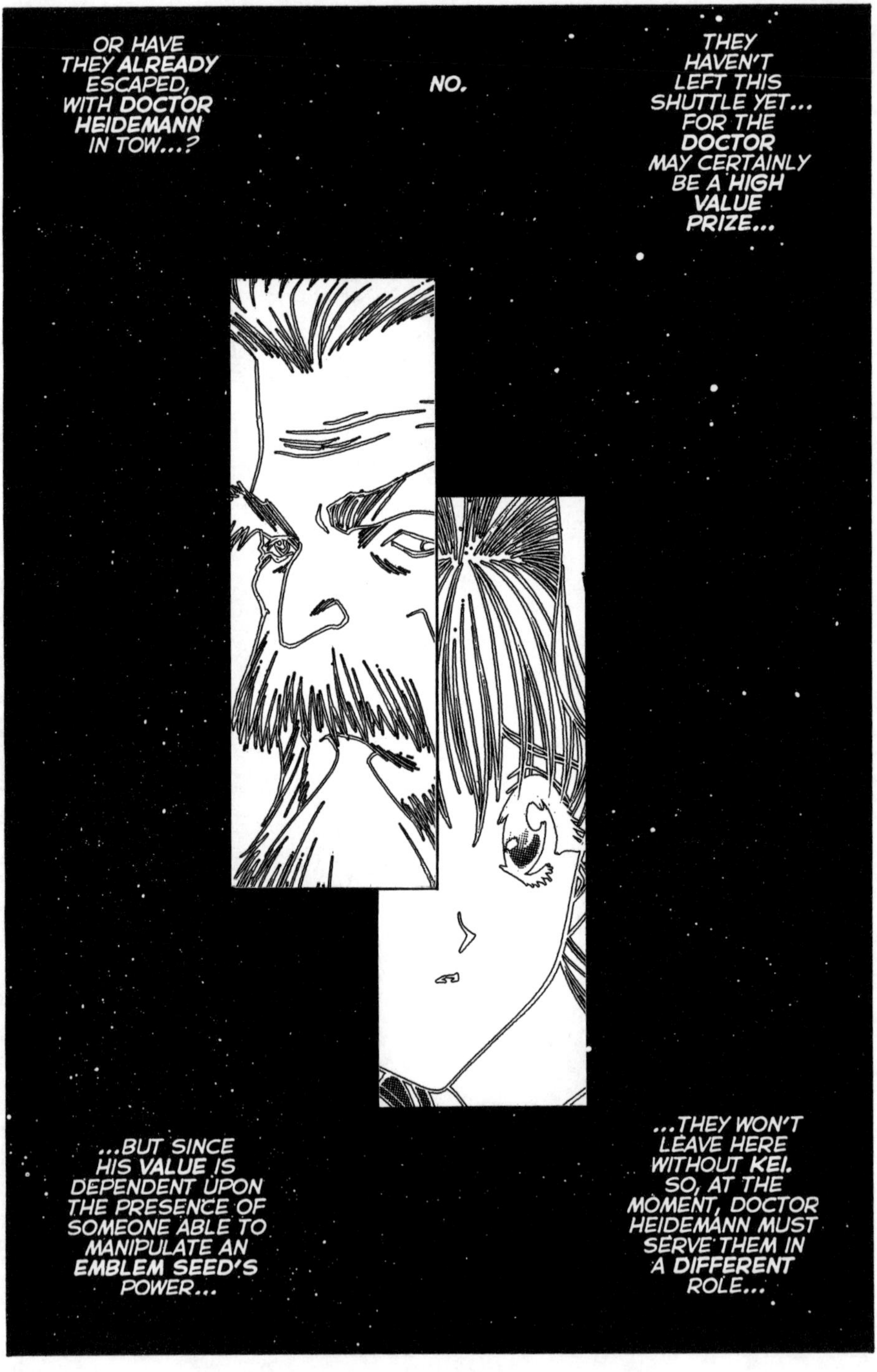
THEY HAVEN'T LEFT THIS SHUTTLE YET... FOR THE DOCTOR MAY CERTAINLY BE A HIGH VALUE PRIZE...
NO.
OR HAVE THEY ALREADY ESCAPED, WITH DOCTOR HEIDEMANN IN TOW...?
...THEY WON'T LEAVE HERE WITHOUT KEI. SO, AT THE MOMENT, DOCTOR HEIDEMANN MUST SERVE THEM IN A DIFFERENT ROLE...
...BUT SINCE HIS VALUE IS DEPENDENT UPON THE PRESENCE OF SOMEONE ABLE TO MANIPULATE AN EMBLEM SEED'S POWER...

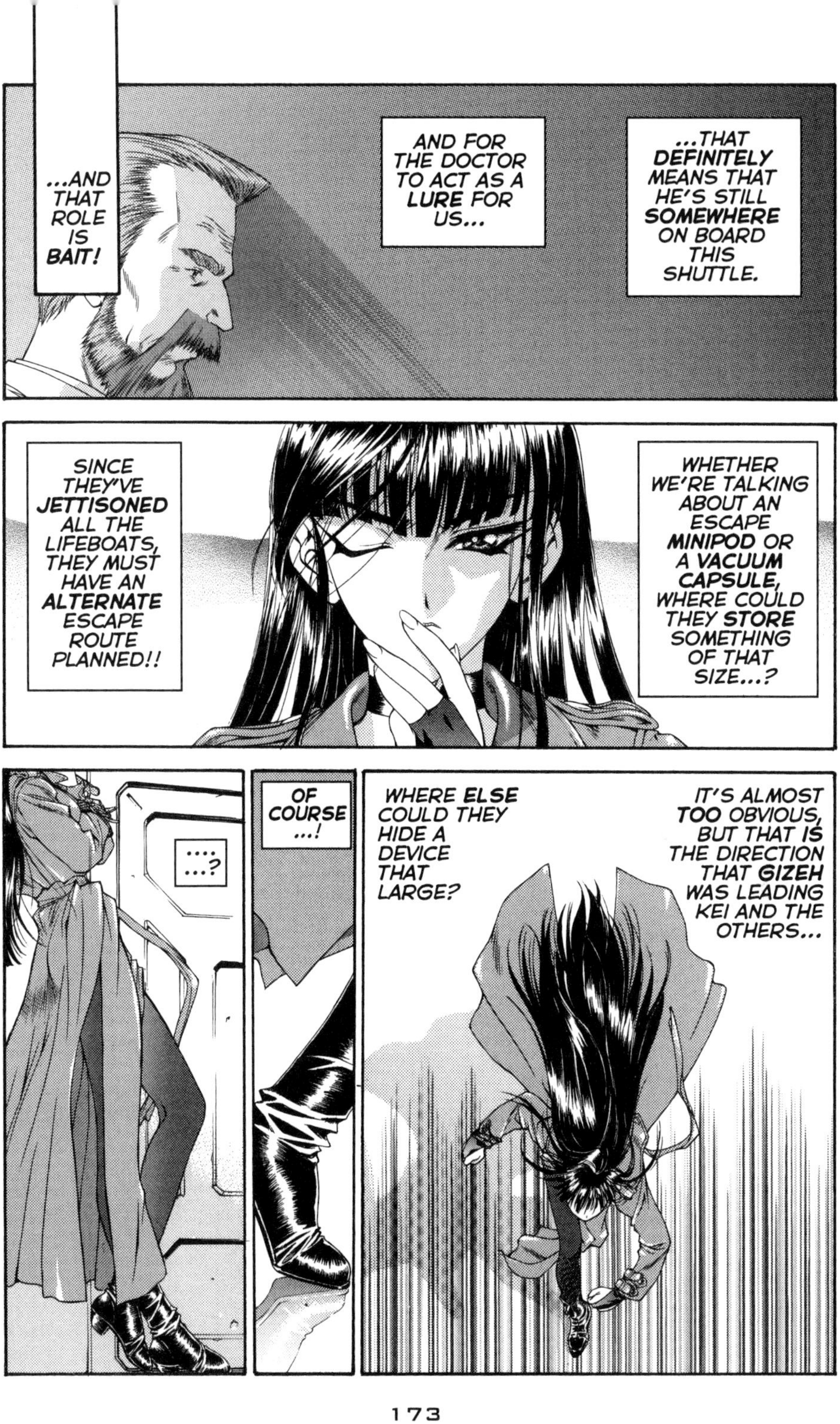
...AND THAT ROLE IS BAIT!
AND FOR THE DOCTOR TO ACT AS A LURE FOR US...
...THAT DEFINITELY MEANS THAT HE'S STILL SOMEWHERE ON BOARD THIS SHUTTLE.
SINCE THEY'VE JETTISONED ALL THE LIFEBOATS, THEY MUST HAVE AN ALTERNATE ESCAPE ROUTE PLANNED!!
WHETHER WE'RE TALKING ABOUT AN ESCAPE MINIPOD OR A VACUUM CAPSULE, WHERE COULD THEY STORE SOMETHING OF THAT SIZE...?
.......?
OF COURSE...!
WHERE ELSE COULD THEY HIDE A DEVICE THAT LARGE?
IT'S ALMOST TOO OBVIOUS, BUT THAT IS THE DIRECTION THAT GIZEH WAS LEADING KEI AND THE OTHERS...

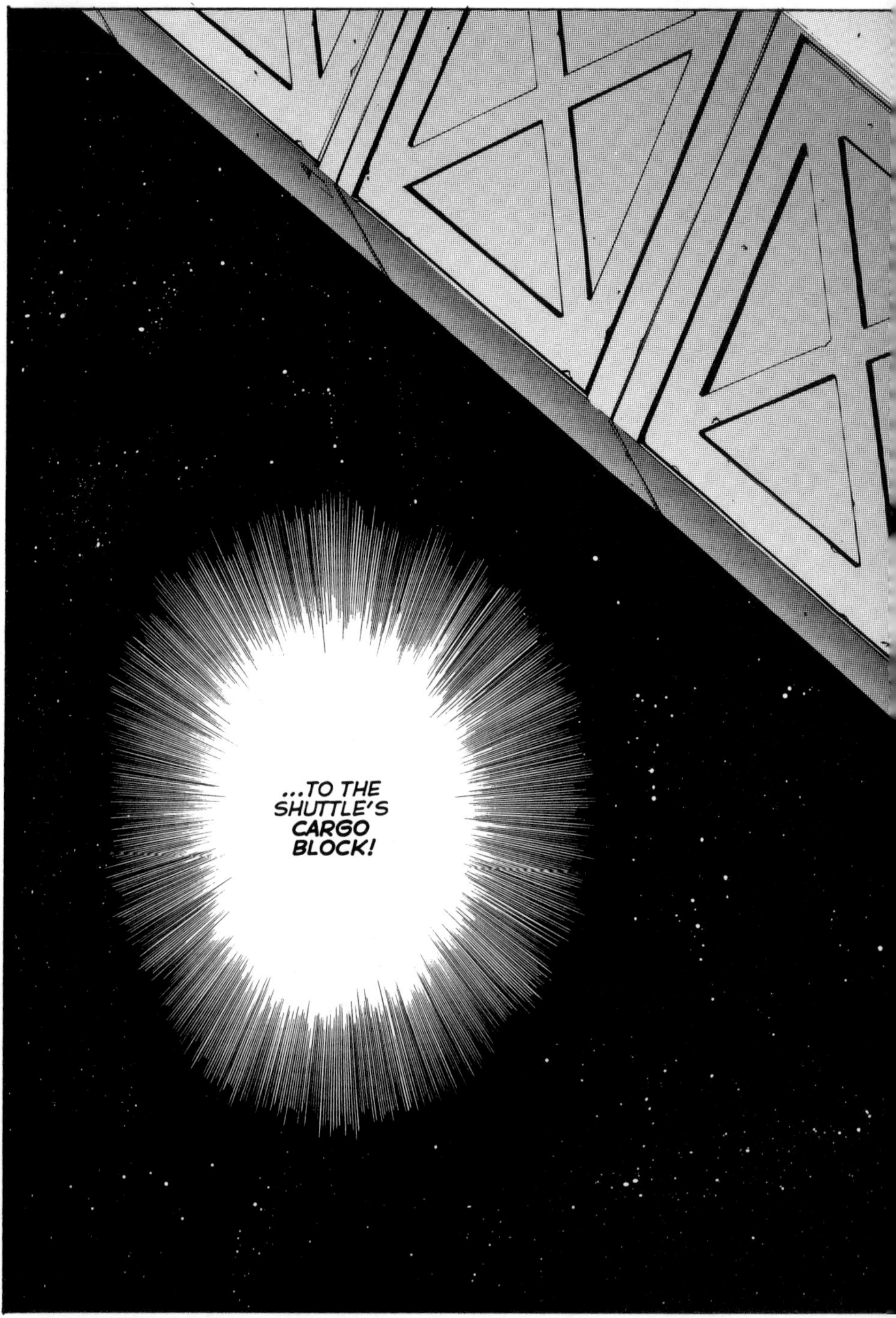
...TO THE SHUTTLE'S CARGO BLOCK!

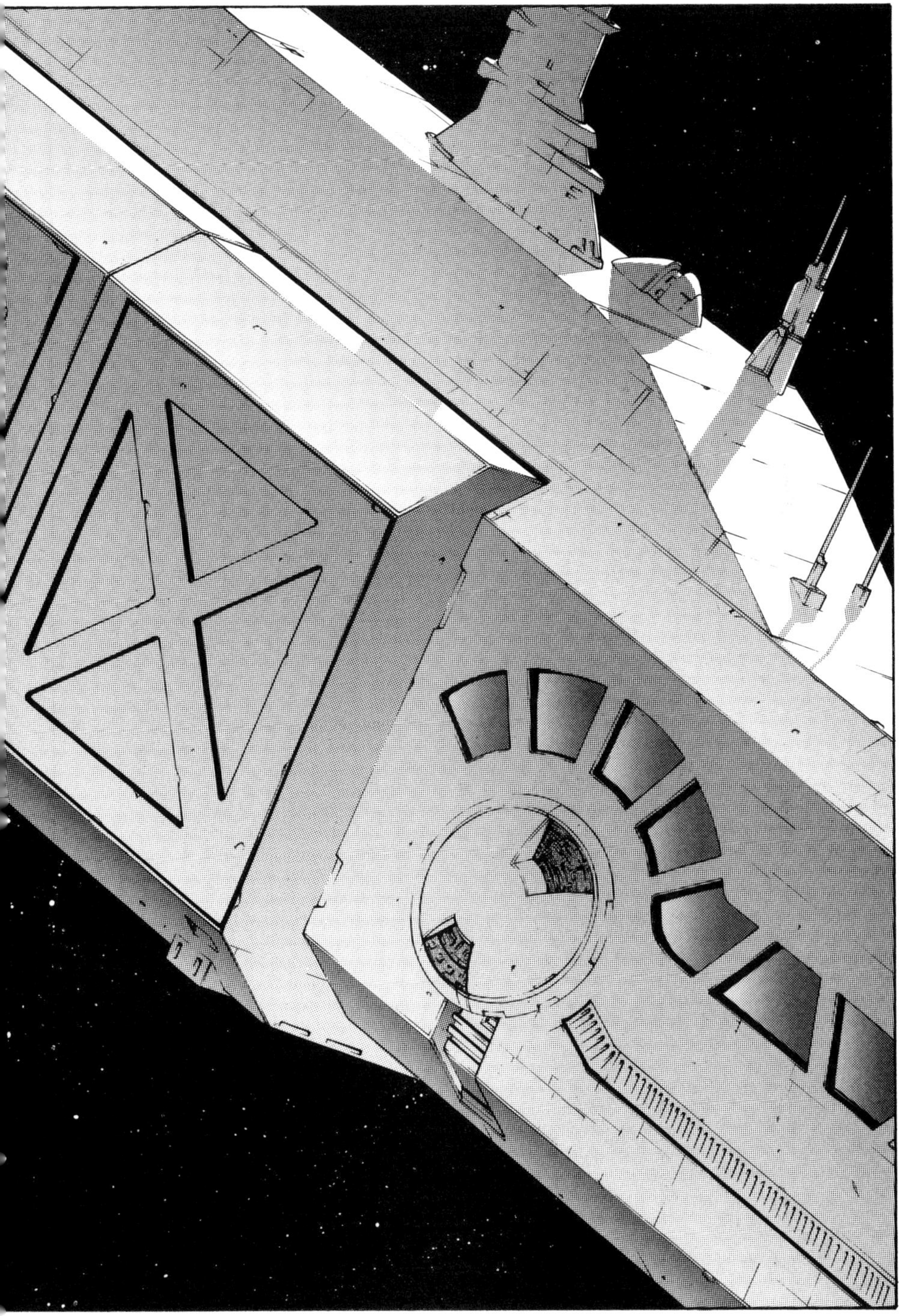

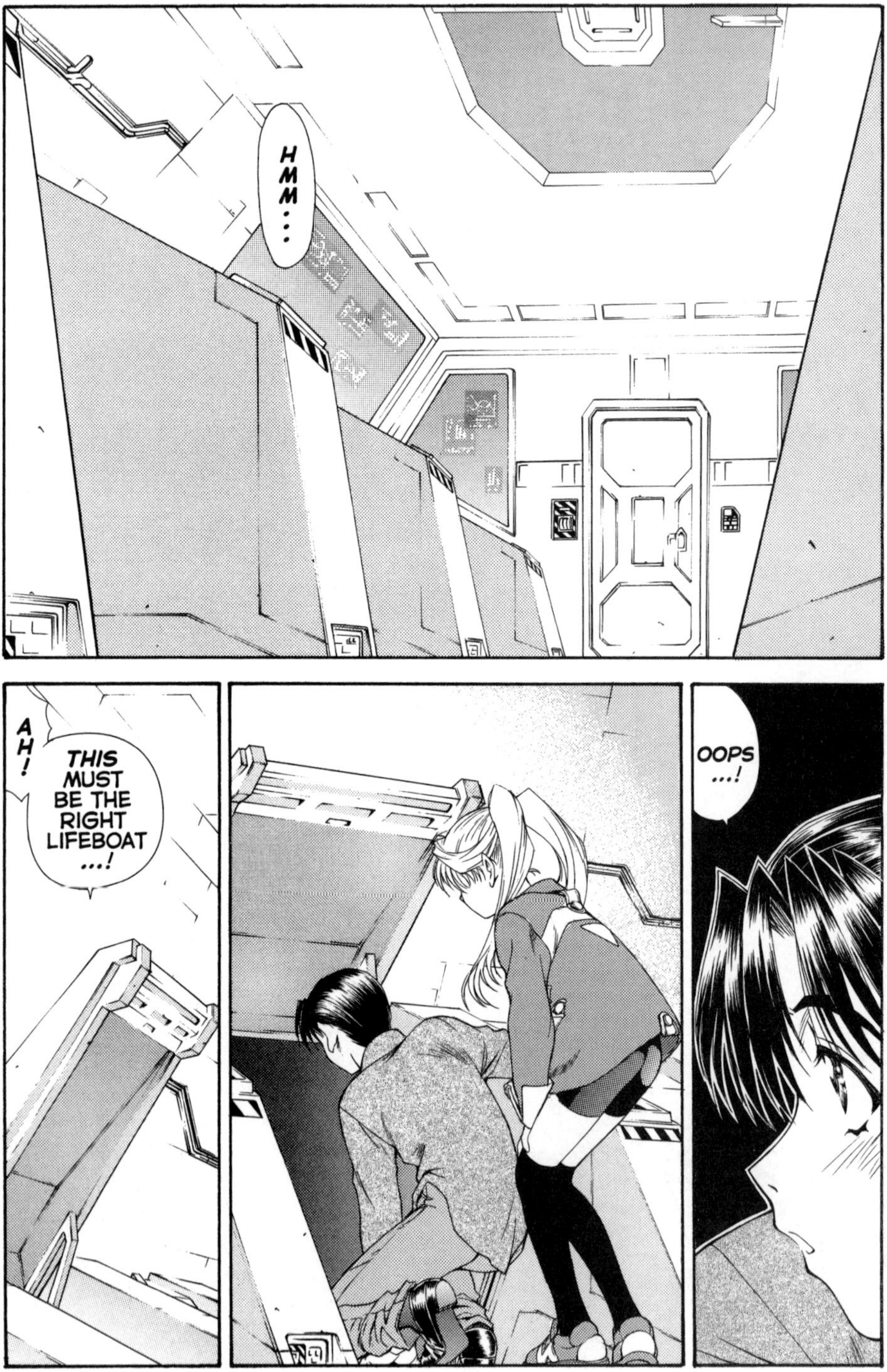
HMM...
OOPS...!
AH!
THIS MUST BE THE RIGHT LIFEBOAT...!

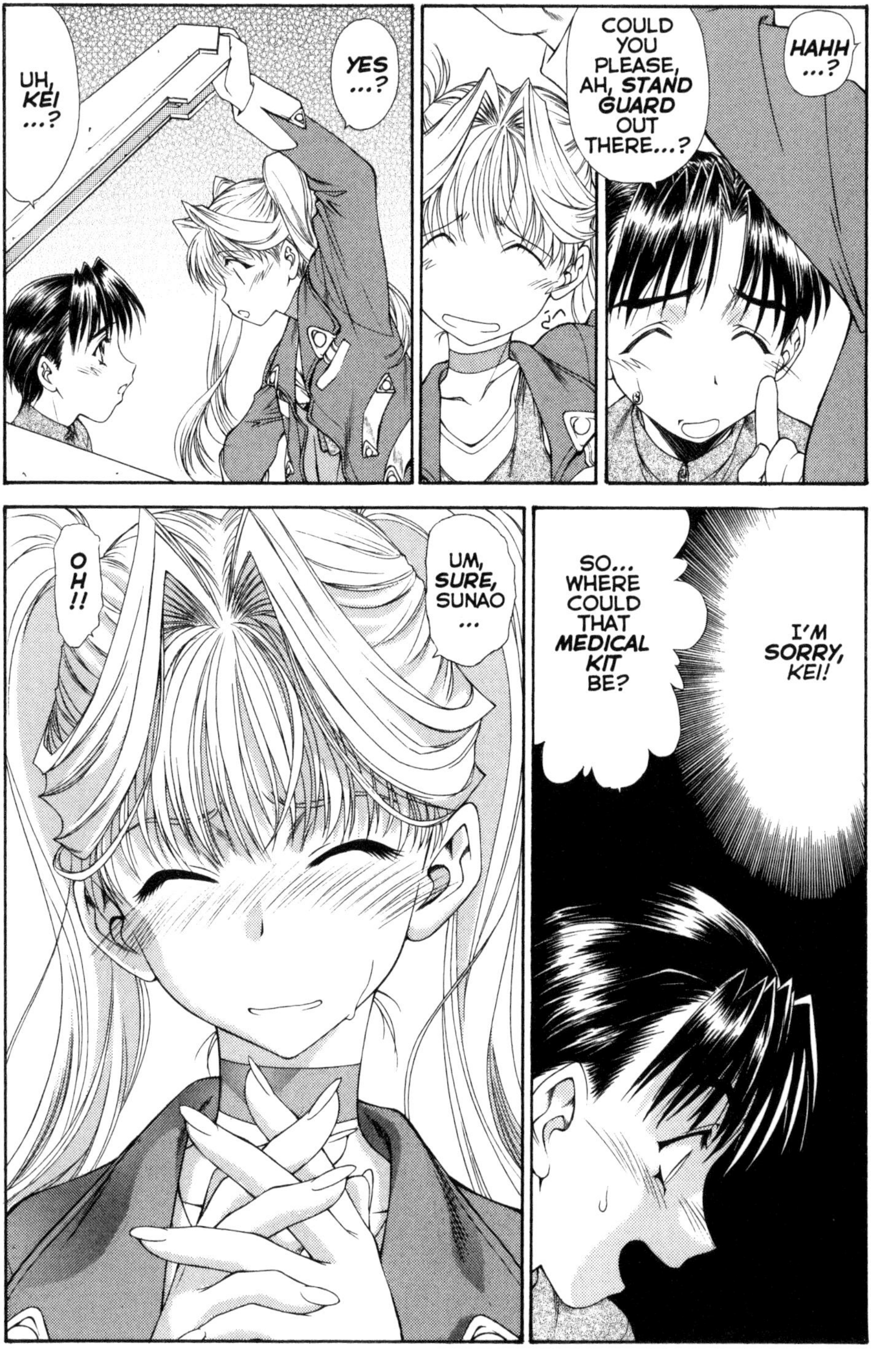
UH, KEI ...?
YES ...?
COULD YOU PLEASE, AH, STAND GUARD OUT THERE...?
HAHH ...?
OH!!
UM, SURE, SUNAO ...
SO... WHERE COULD THAT MEDICAL KIT BE?
I'M SORRY, KEI!

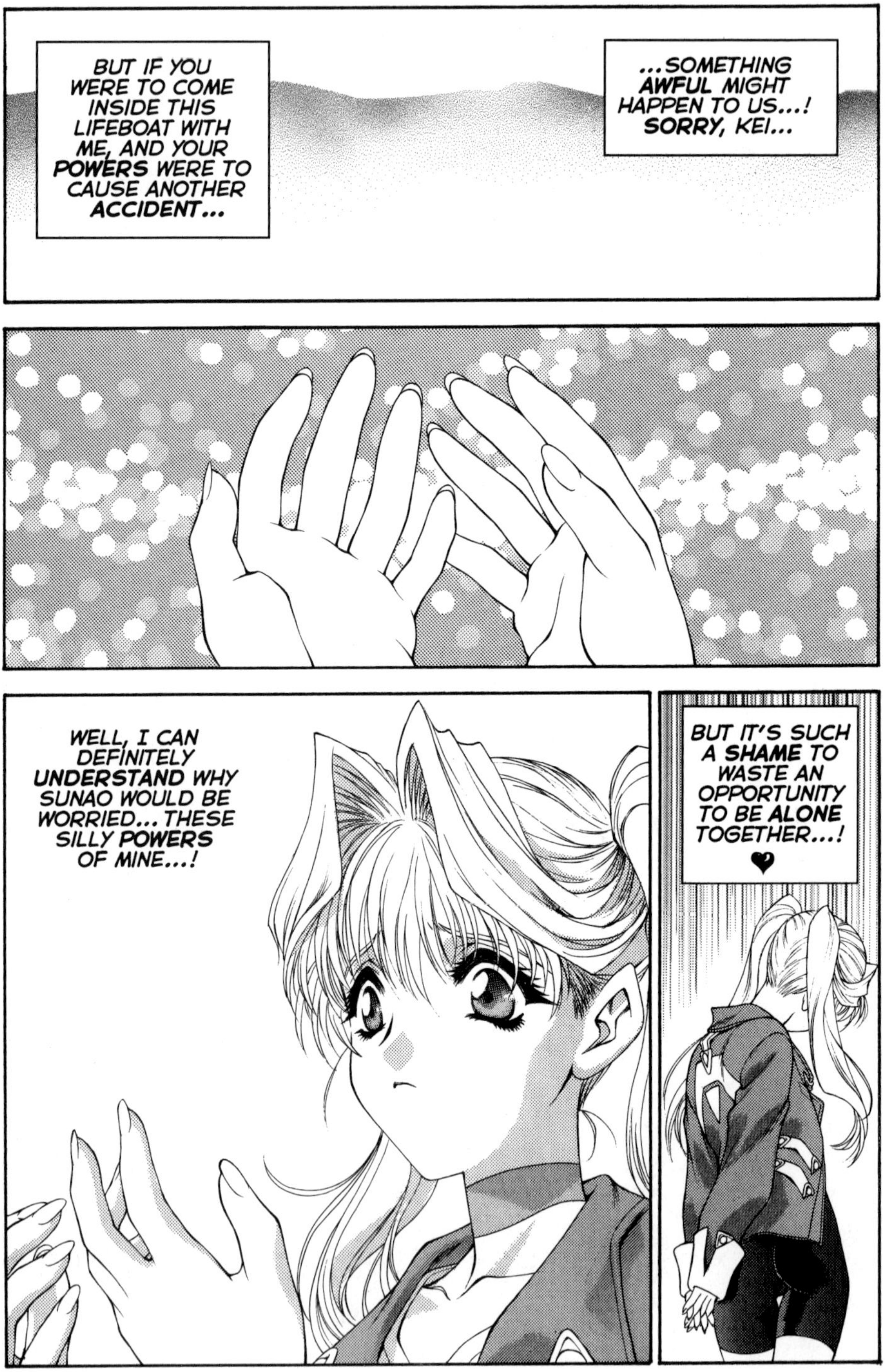
BUT IF YOU WERE TO COME INSIDE THIS LIFEBOAT WITH ME, AND YOUR POWERS WERE TO CAUSE ANOTHER ACCIDENT...
...SOMETHING AWFUL MIGHT HAPPEN TO US...! SORRY, KEI...
WELL, I CAN DEFINITELY UNDERSTAND WHY SUNAO WOULD BE WORRIED... THESE SILLY POWERS OF MINE...!
BUT IT'S SUCH A SHAME TO WASTE AN OPPORTUNITY TO BE ALONE TOGETHER...!

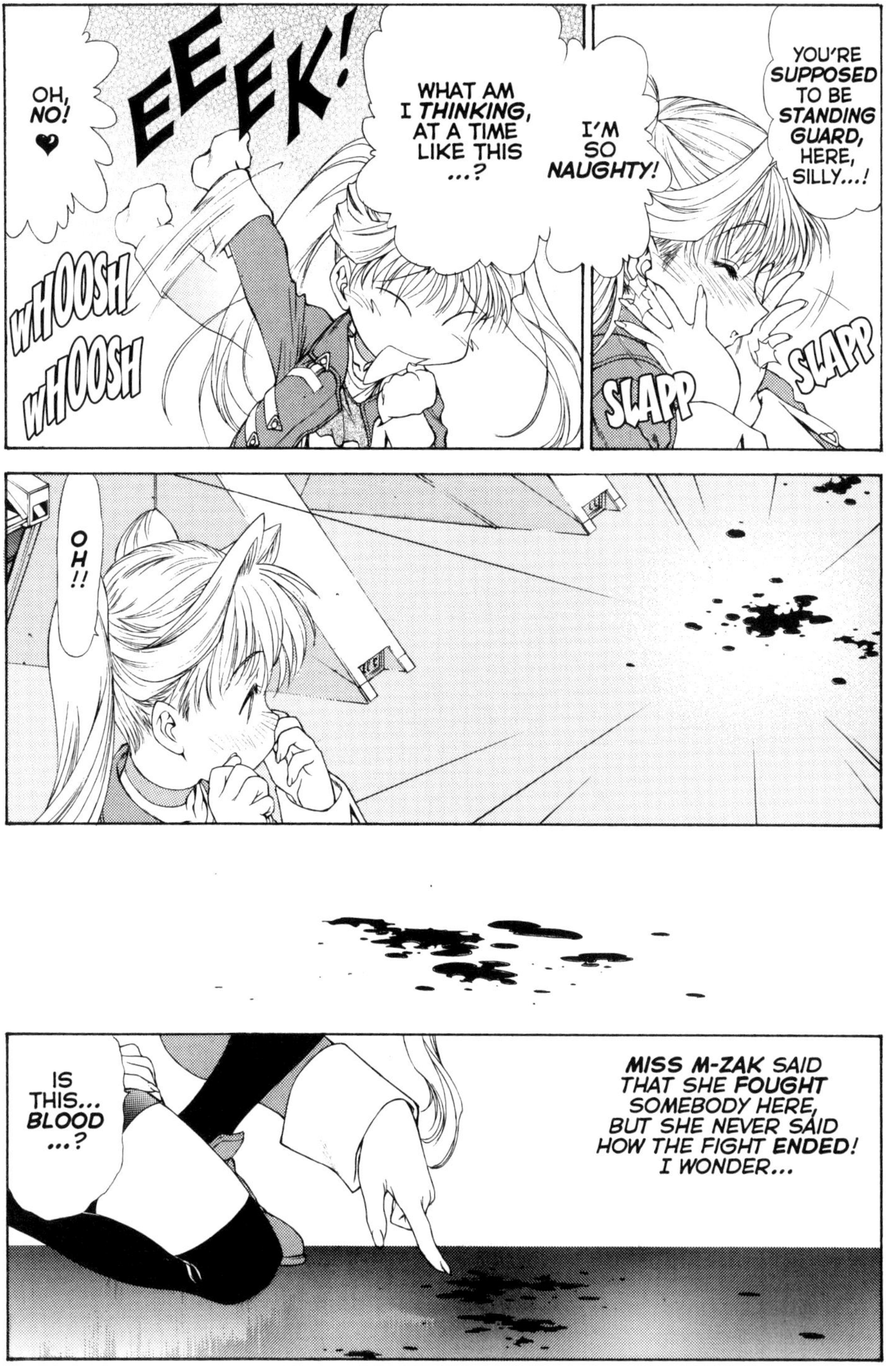
OH, NO! ❤
EEEK!
WHOOSH WHOOSH
WHAT AM I THINKING, AT A TIME LIKE THIS ...?
I'M SO NAUGHTY!
YOU'RE SUPPOSED TO BE STANDING GUARD, HERE, SILLY...!
SLAPP SLAPP
OH!!
IS THIS... BLOOD ...?
MISS M-ZAK SAID THAT SHE FOUGHT SOMEBODY HERE, BUT SHE NEVER SAID HOW THE FIGHT ENDED! I WONDER...

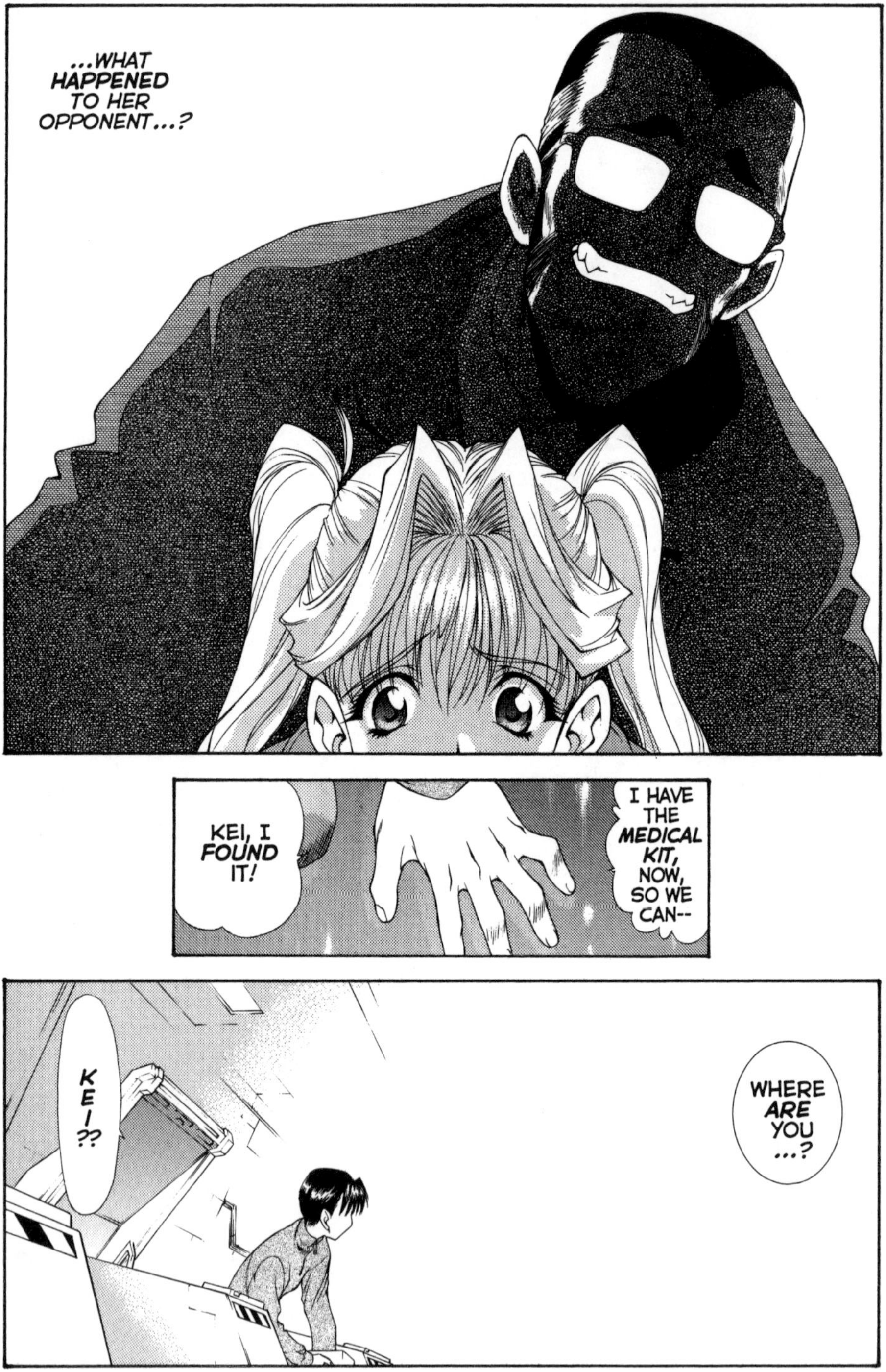
...WHAT HAPPENED TO HER OPPONENT...?
KEI, I FOUND IT!
I HAVE THE MEDICAL KIT, NOW, SO WE CAN--
KEI!??
WHERE ARE YOU...?

ACT 70

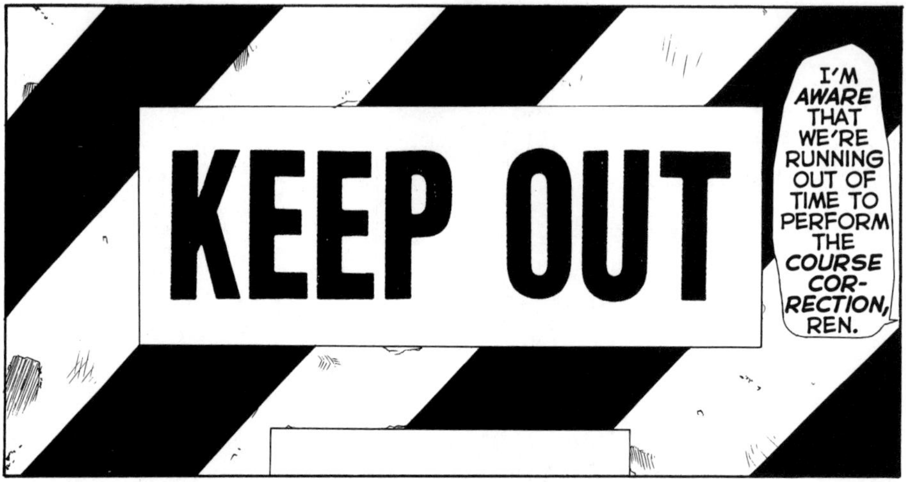
KEEP OUT
I'M AWARE THAT WE'RE RUNNING OUT OF TIME TO PERFORM THE COURSE COR-RECTION, REN.

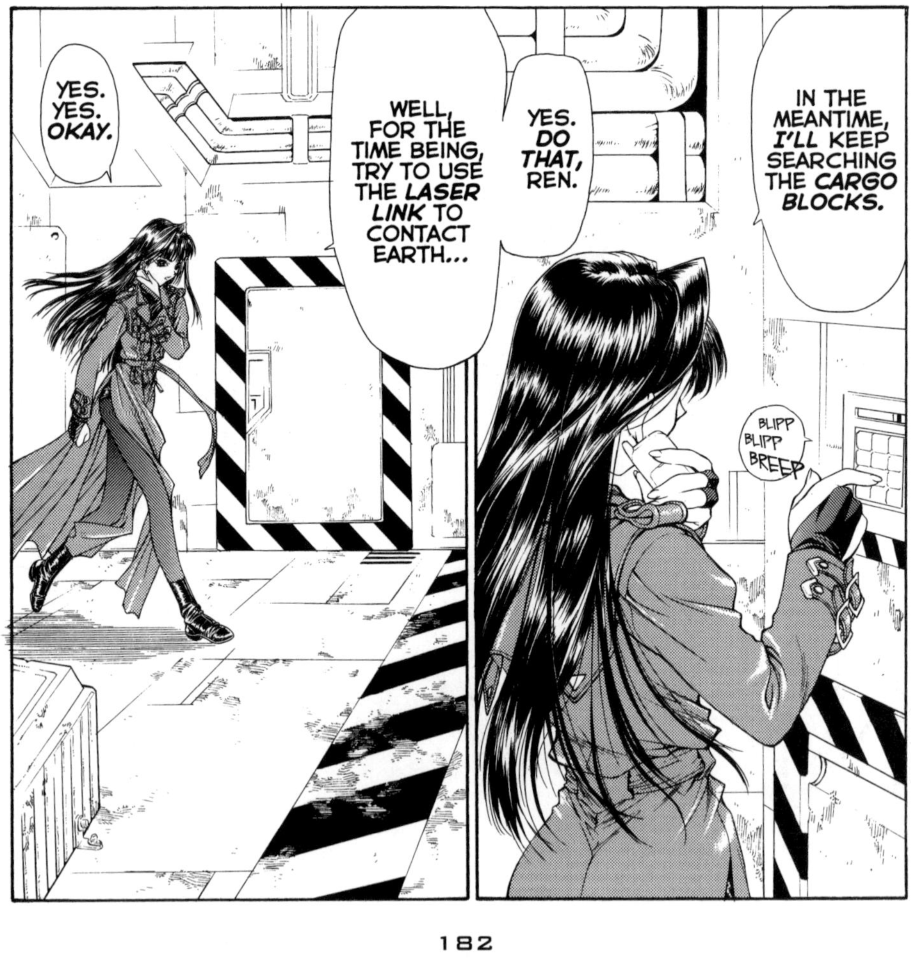
IN THE MEANTIME, I'LL KEEP SEARCHING THE CARGO BLOCKS.
YES. DO THAT, REN.
WELL, FOR THE TIME BEING, TRY TO USE THE LASER LINK TO CONTACT EARTH...
YES. YES. OKAY.
BLIPP BLIPP BREEP

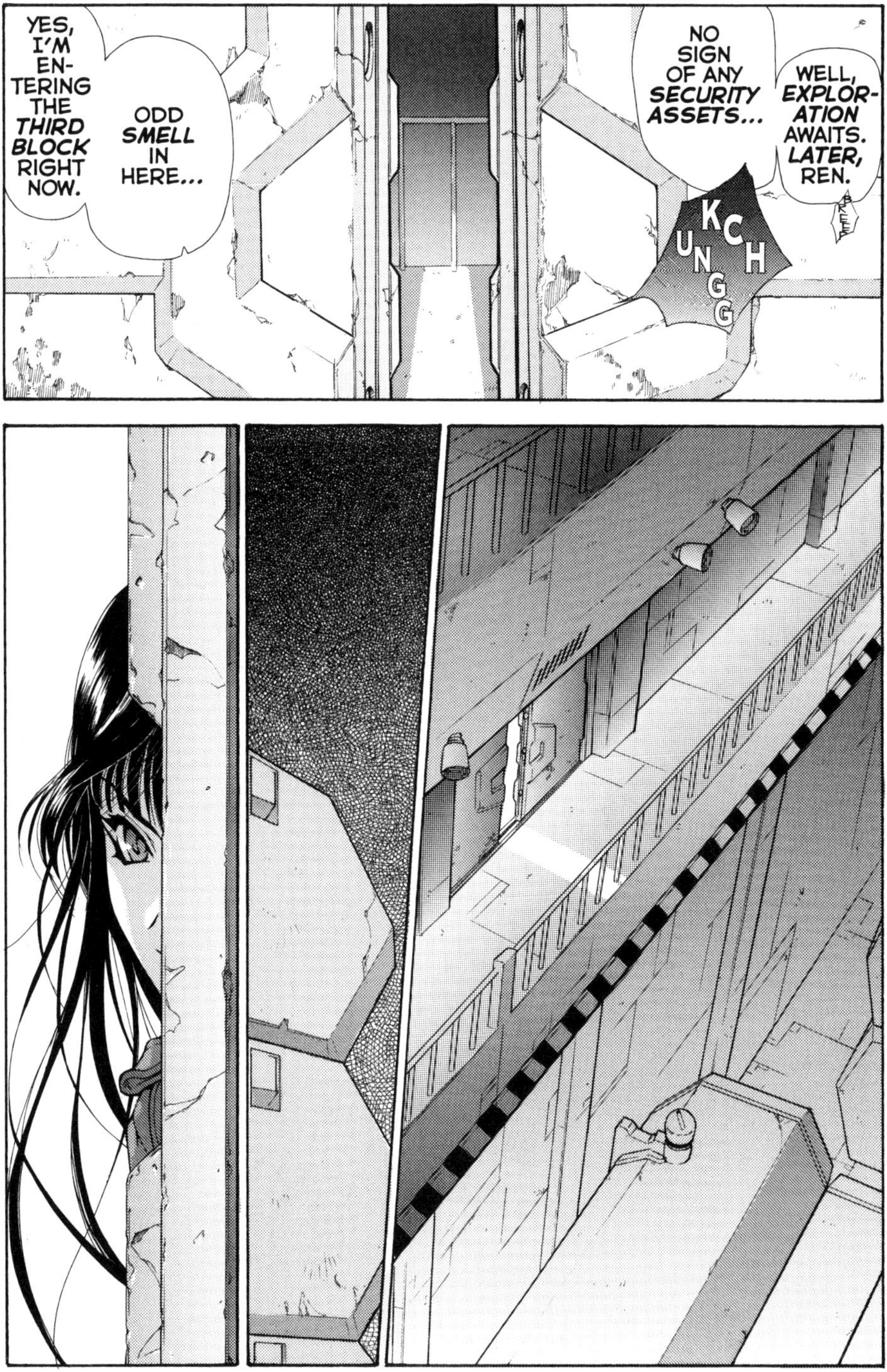
YES, I'M EN-TERING THE *THIRD BLOCK* RIGHT NOW.
ODD *SMELL* IN HERE...
NO SIGN OF ANY *SECURITY ASSETS*...
KCH UNGG
WELL, *EXPLORATION* AWAITS. *LATER,* REN.

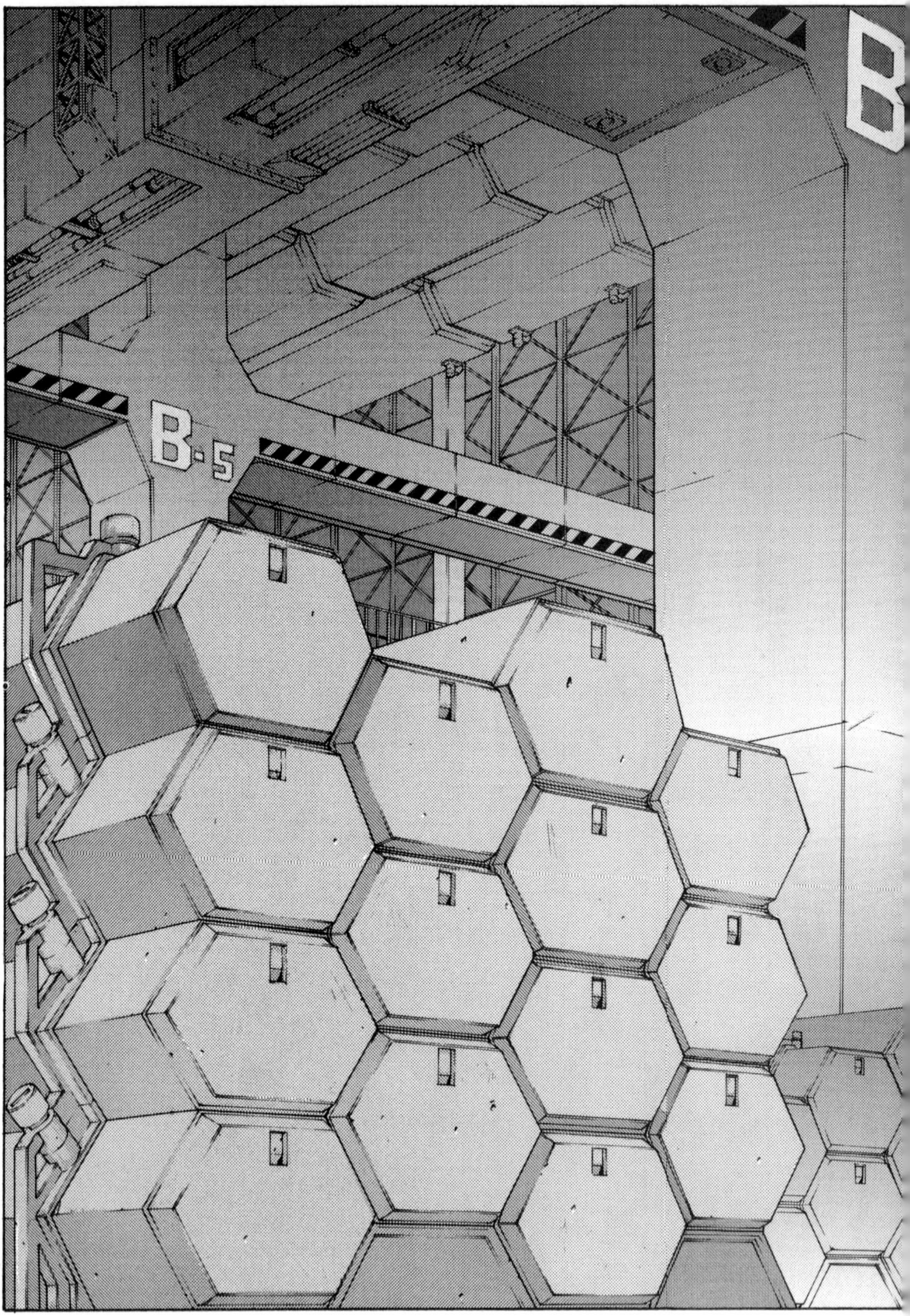
B
B-5

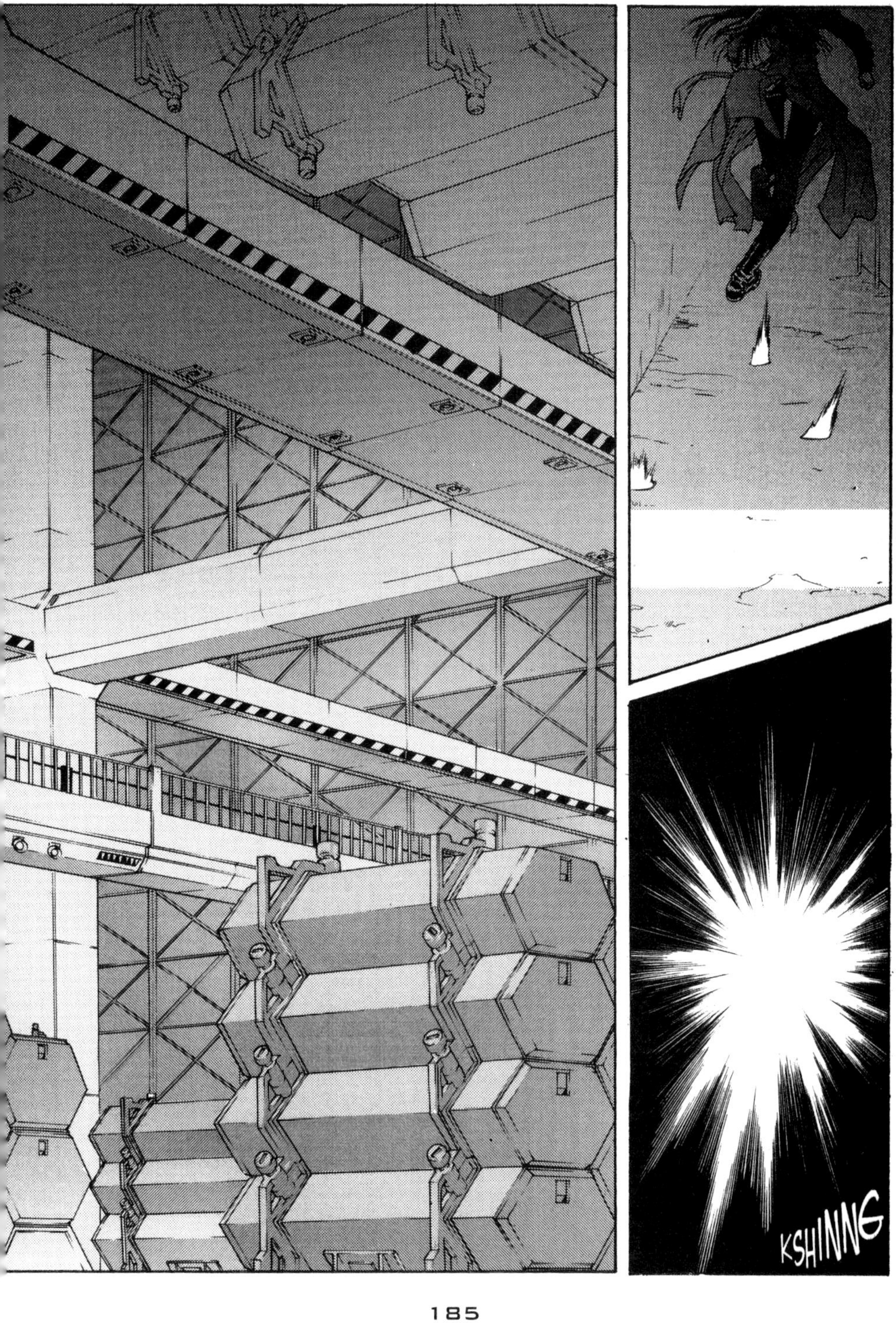
KSHINNG

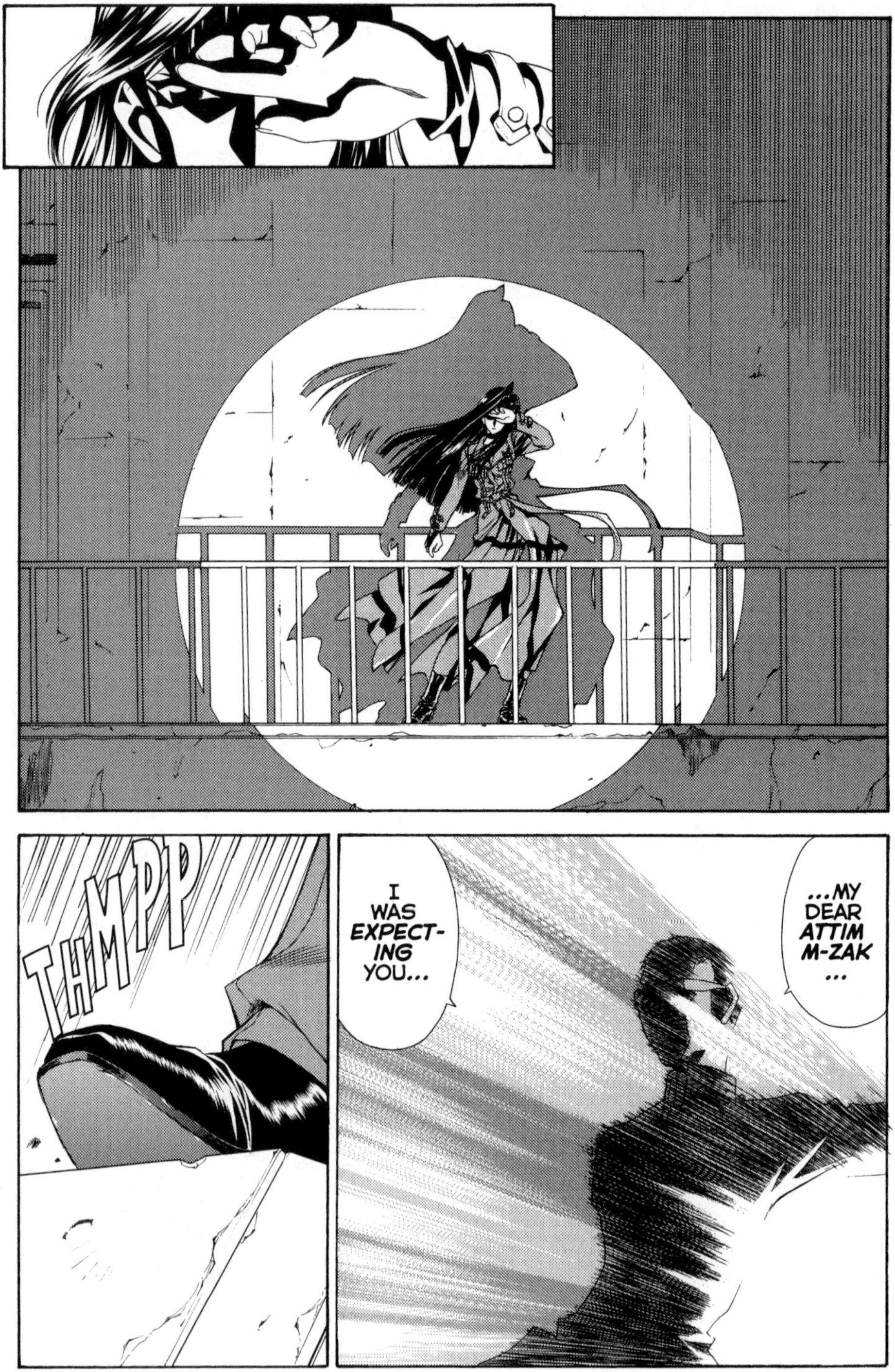
THMPP
I WAS EXPECTING YOU...
...MY DEAR ATTIM M-ZAK...

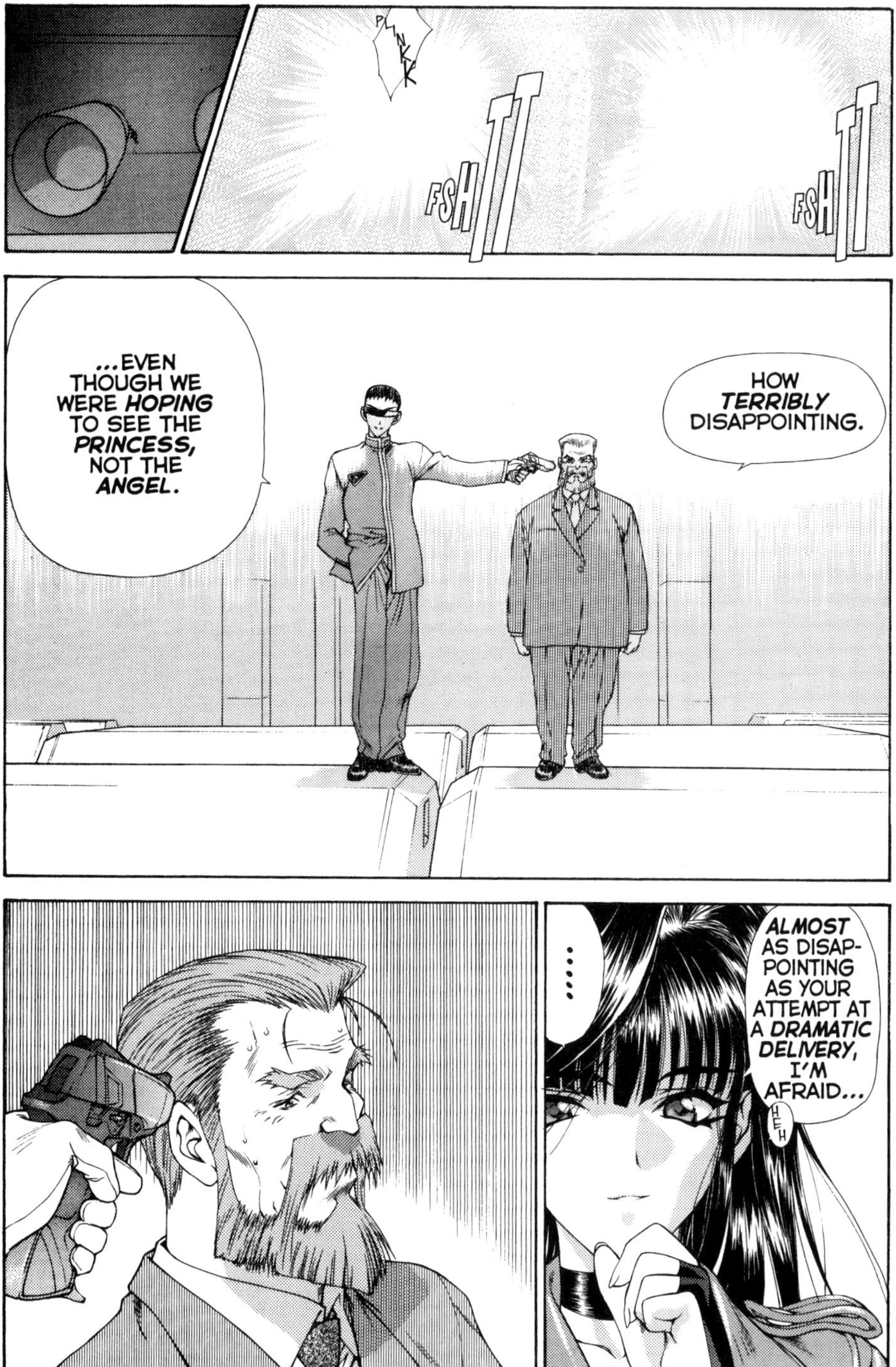
PLINKK
FSHTT
FSHTT
HOW TERRIBLY DISAPPOINTING.
...EVEN THOUGH WE WERE HOPING TO SEE THE PRINCESS, NOT THE ANGEL.
ALMOST AS DISAPPOINTING AS YOUR ATTEMPT AT A DRAMATIC DELIVERY, I'M AFRAID...
HEH
.....

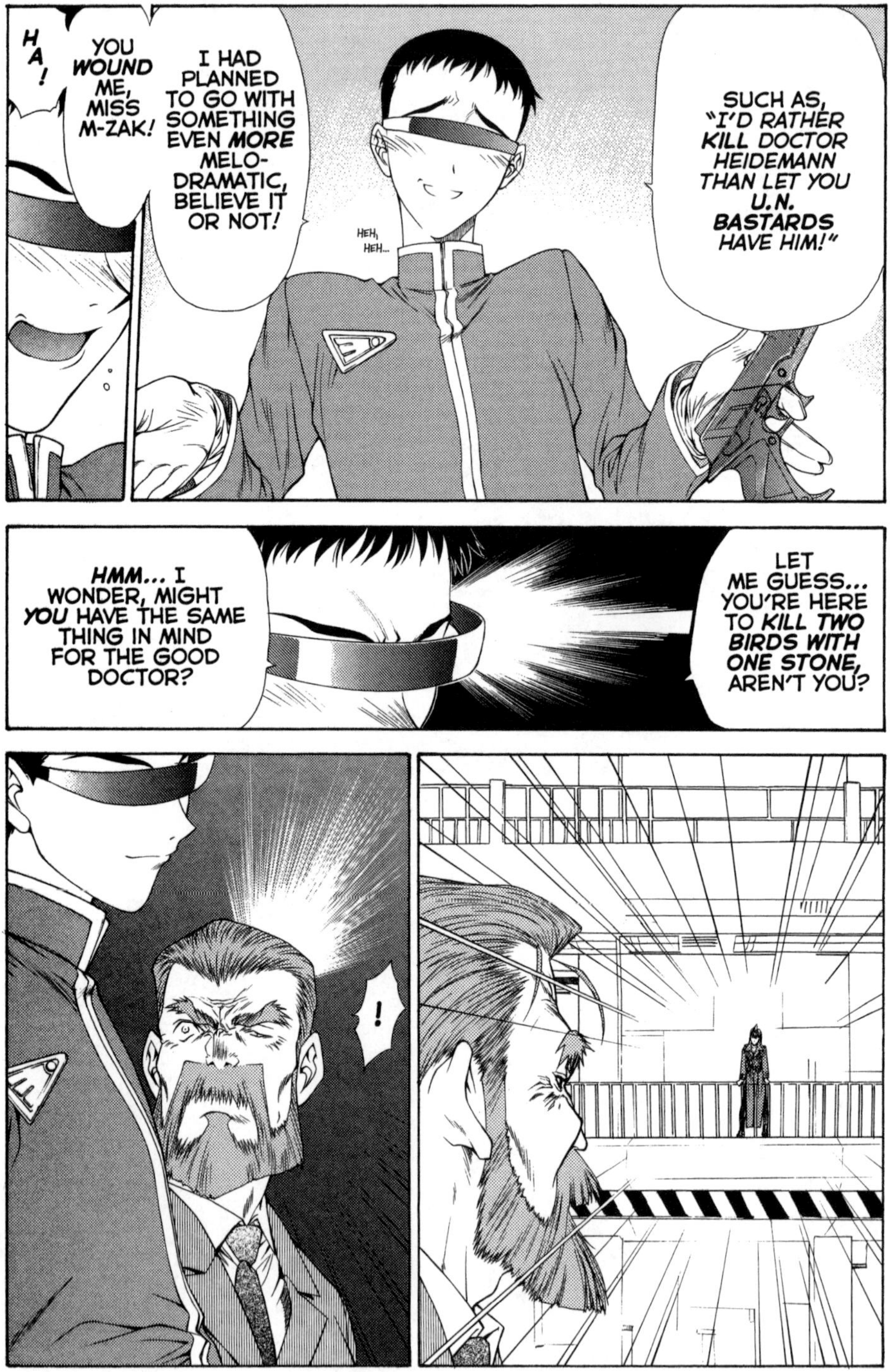
HA!
YOU WOUND ME, MISS M-ZAK!
I HAD PLANNED TO GO WITH SOMETHING EVEN MORE MELO-DRAMATIC, BELIEVE IT OR NOT!
HEH, HEH...
SUCH AS, "I'D RATHER KILL DOCTOR HEIDEMANN THAN LET YOU U.N. BASTARDS HAVE HIM!"
HMM... I WONDER, MIGHT YOU HAVE THE SAME THING IN MIND FOR THE GOOD DOCTOR?
LET ME GUESS... YOU'RE HERE TO KILL TWO BIRDS WITH ONE STONE, AREN'T YOU?
!

I SEE.

DESPITE YOUR THREAT, YOU ACTUALLY **CAN'T** AFFORD TO LOSE THE DOCTOR, **CAN** YOU?

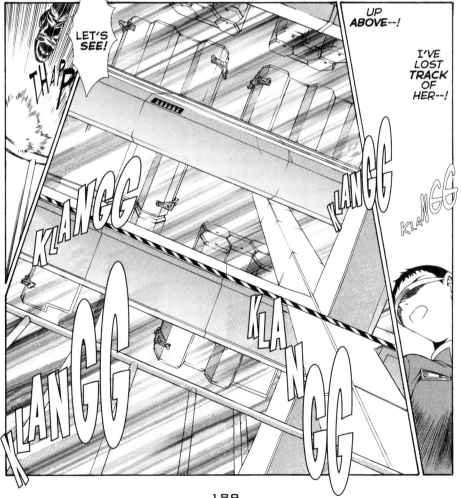

LET'S SEE!

THUD

UP ABOVE--!

I'VE LOST **TRACK** OF HER--!

KLANGG

KLANGG

KLANGG

KLANGG

KLANGG

KLANGG

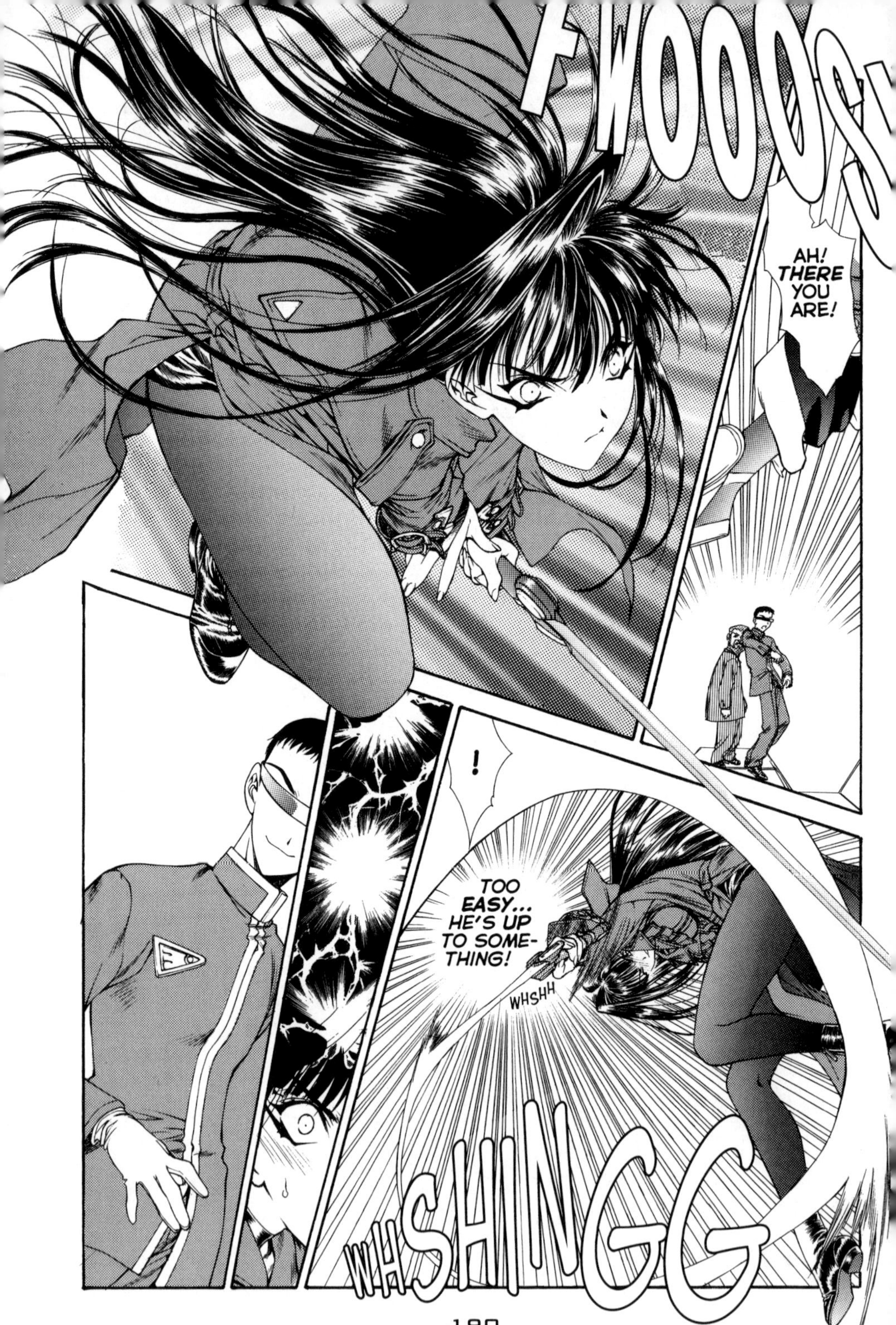
FWOOOSH
AH! THERE YOU ARE!
!
TOO EASY... HE'S UP TO SOME-THING!
WHSHH
WHSHINGG

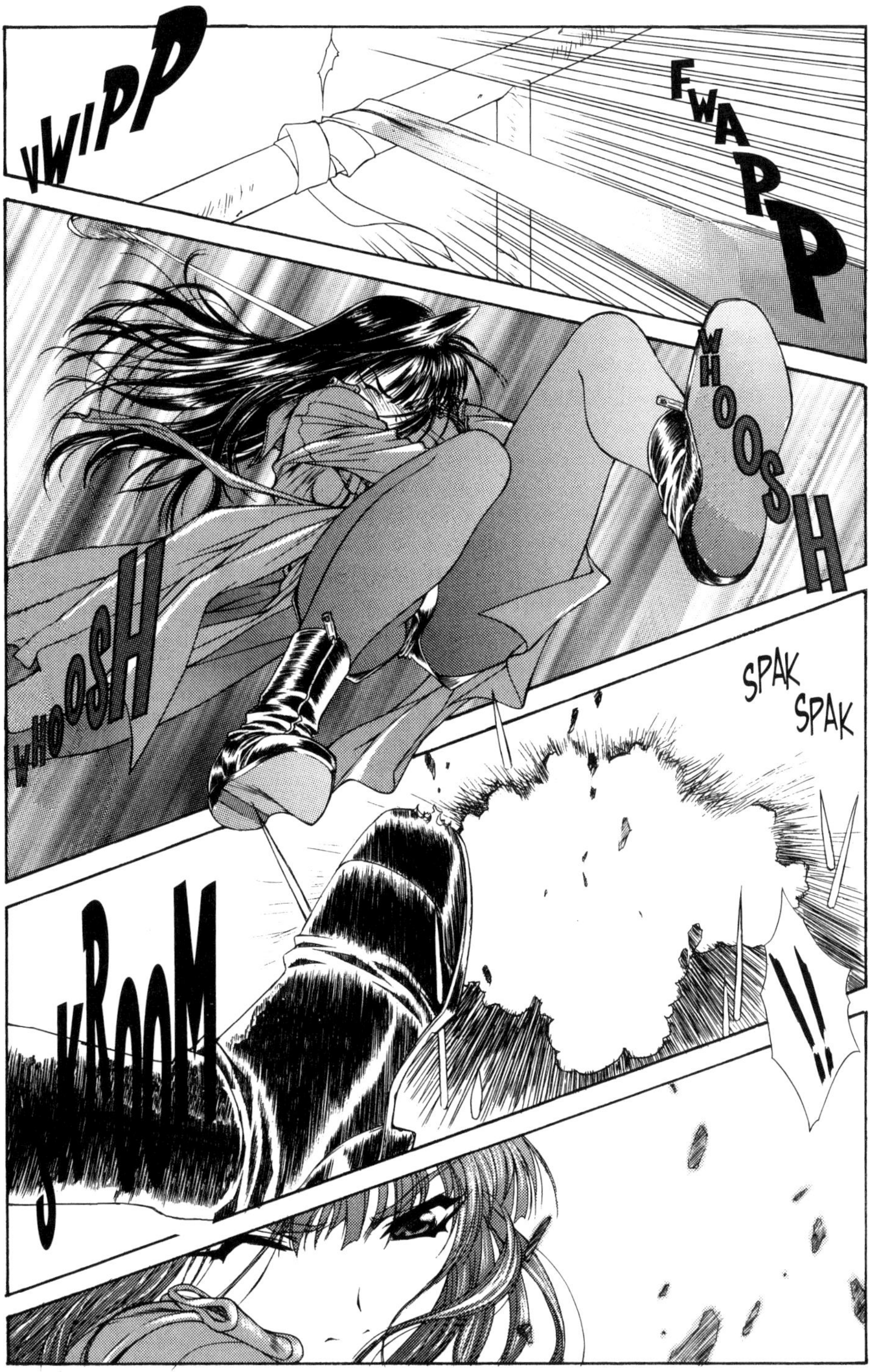
FWAPPP
VWIPP
WHOOSH
WHOOSH
SPAK
SPAK
!!
VROOM

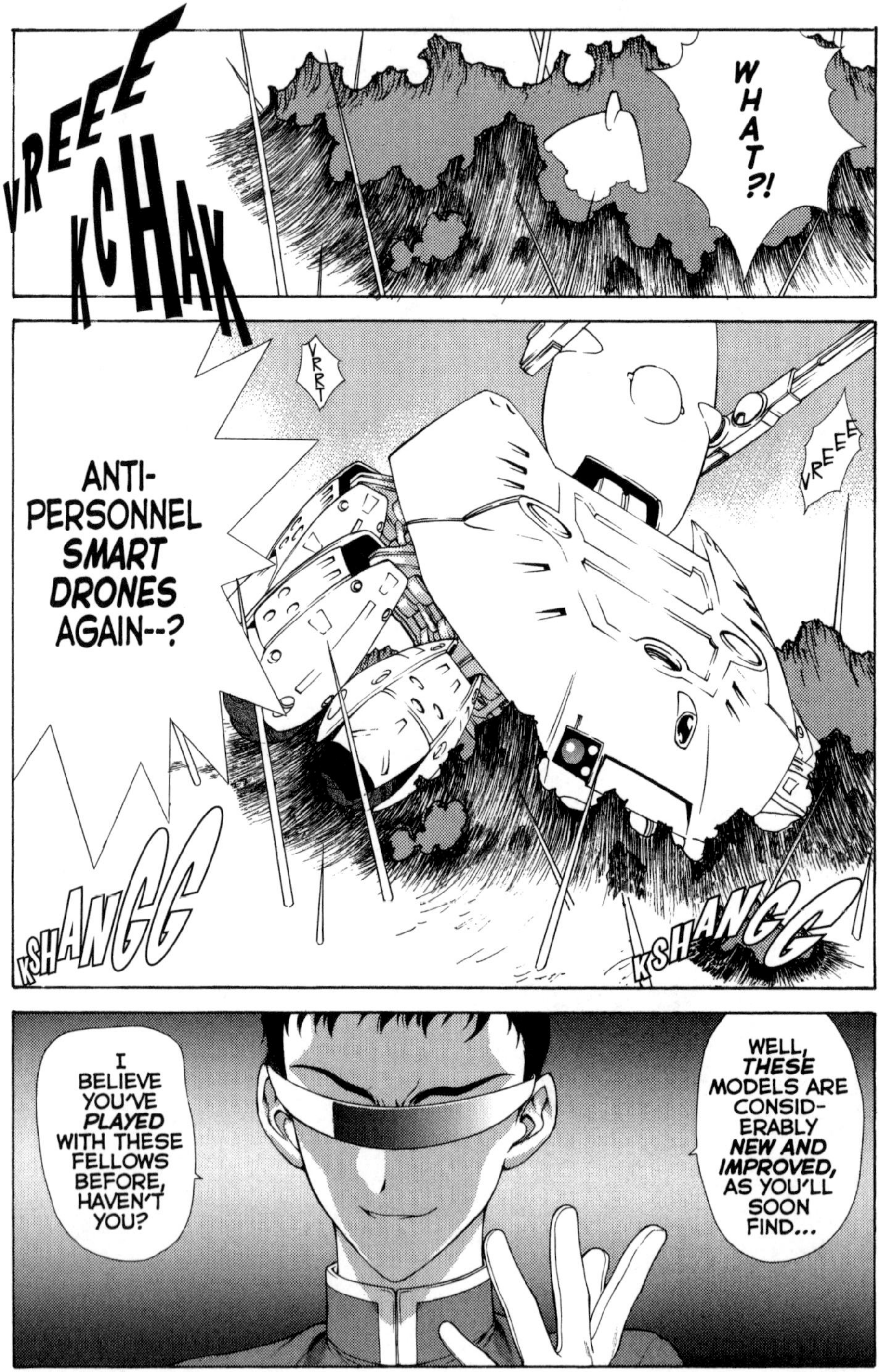
VREEE
KCHAK
WHAT?!
VRRT
ANTI-PERSONNEL SMART DRONES AGAIN--?
VREEE
KSHANGG
KSHANGG
I BELIEVE YOU'VE PLAYED WITH THESE FELLOWS BEFORE, HAVEN'T YOU?
WELL, THESE MODELS ARE CONSIDERABLY NEW AND IMPROVED, AS YOU'LL SOON FIND...

ACT 71

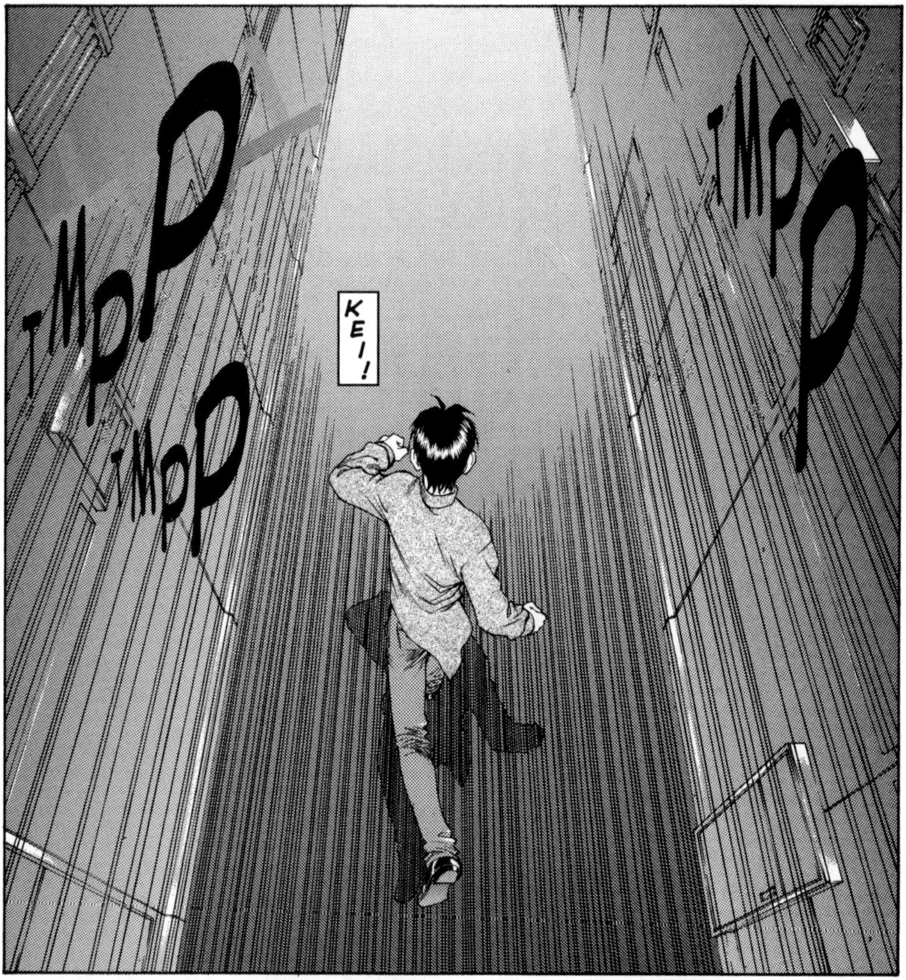
TMPP
KEI!
TMPP
TMPP

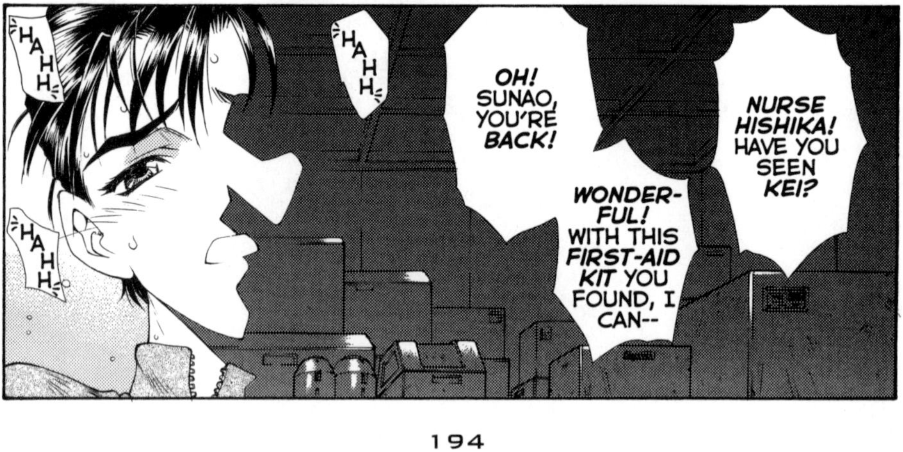
NURSE HISHIKA! HAVE YOU SEEN KEI?
OH! SUNAO, YOU'RE BACK!
WONDERFUL! WITH THIS FIRST-AID KIT YOU FOUND, I CAN--
HAHH
HAHH
HAHH

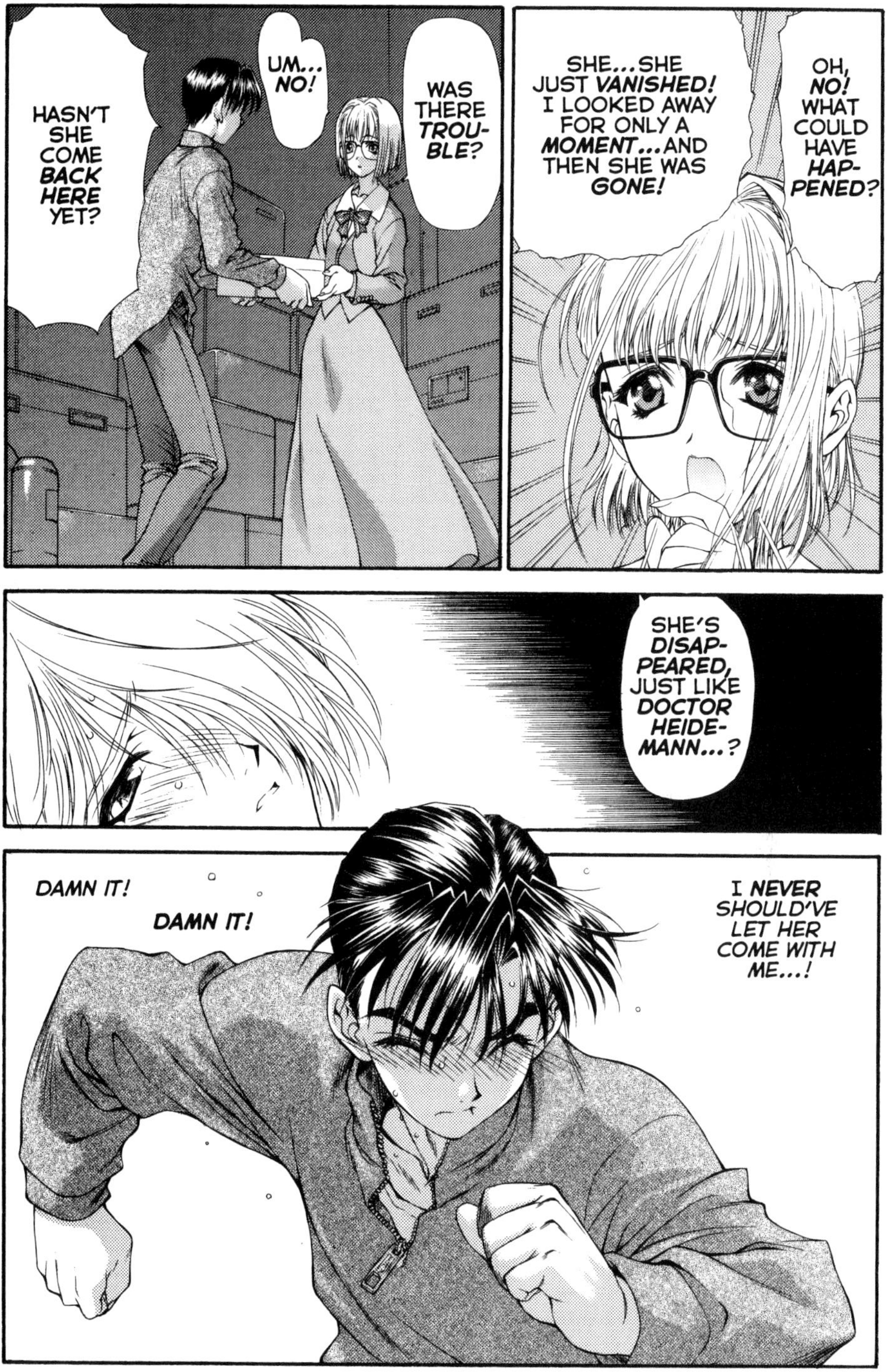
HASN'T SHE COME BACK HERE YET?
UM... NO!
WAS THERE TROUBLE?
SHE...SHE JUST VANISHED! I LOOKED AWAY FOR ONLY A MOMENT...AND THEN SHE WAS GONE!
OH, NO! WHAT COULD HAVE HAPPENED?
SHE'S DISAPPEARED, JUST LIKE DOCTOR HEIDEMANN...?
DAMN IT!
DAMN IT!
I NEVER SHOULD'VE LET HER COME WITH ME...!

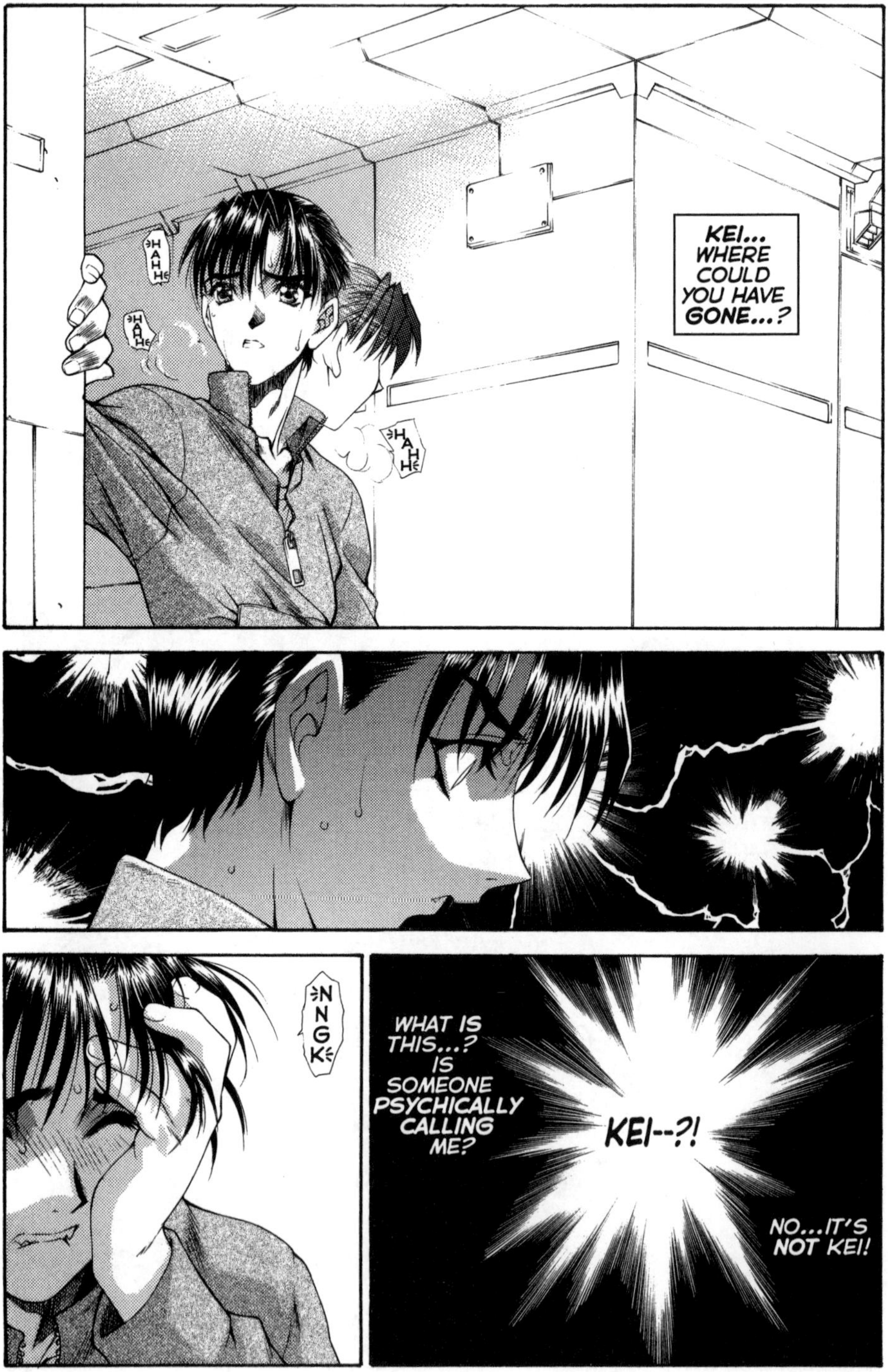
KEI... WHERE COULD YOU HAVE GONE...?
HAH
HAH
HAH
WHAT IS THIS...? IS SOMEONE PSYCHICALLY CALLING ME?
KEI--?!
NO...IT'S NOT KEI!
NNGK

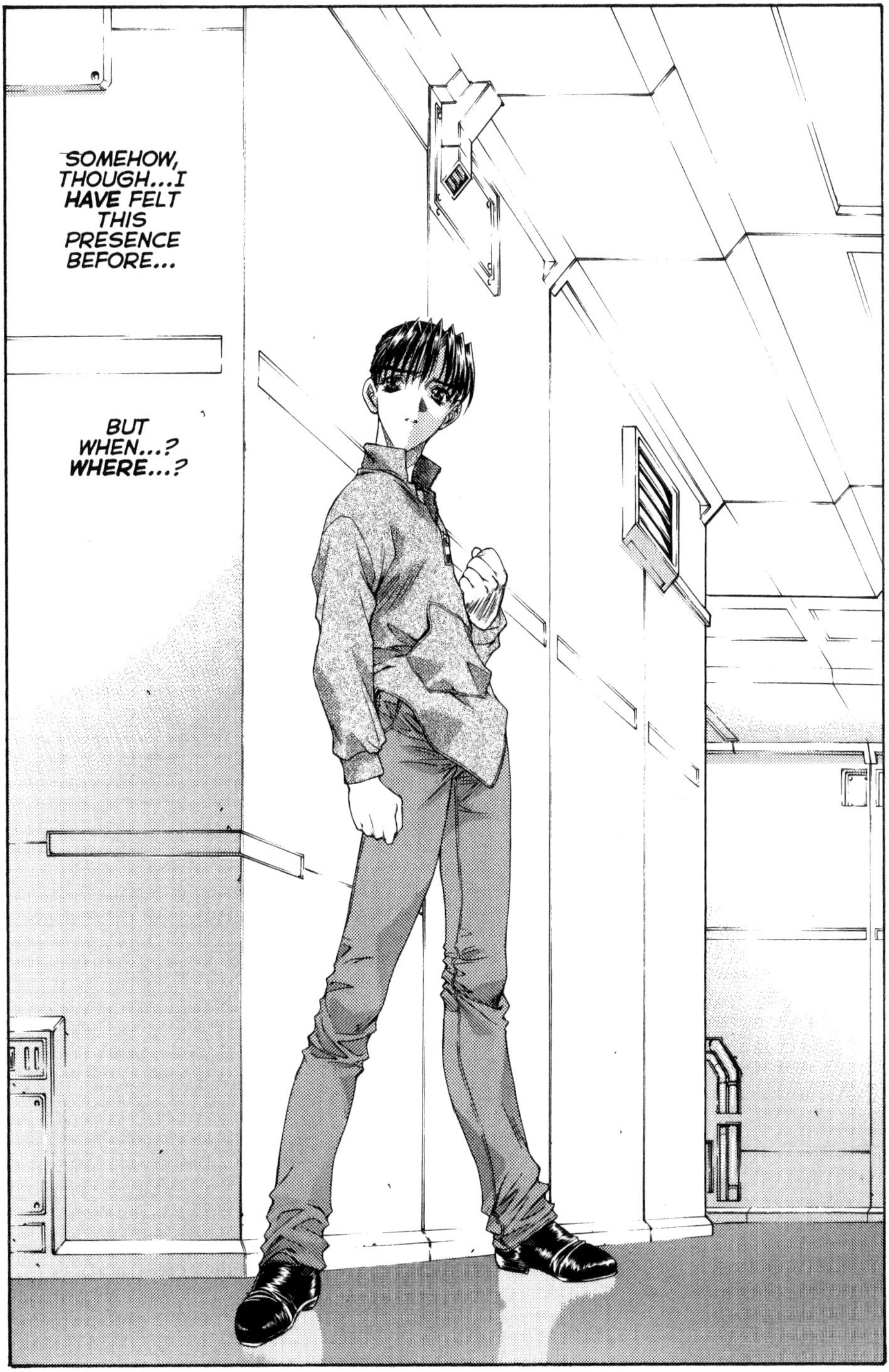
SOMEHOW, THOUGH...I HAVE FELT THIS PRESENCE BEFORE...
BUT WHEN...? WHERE...?

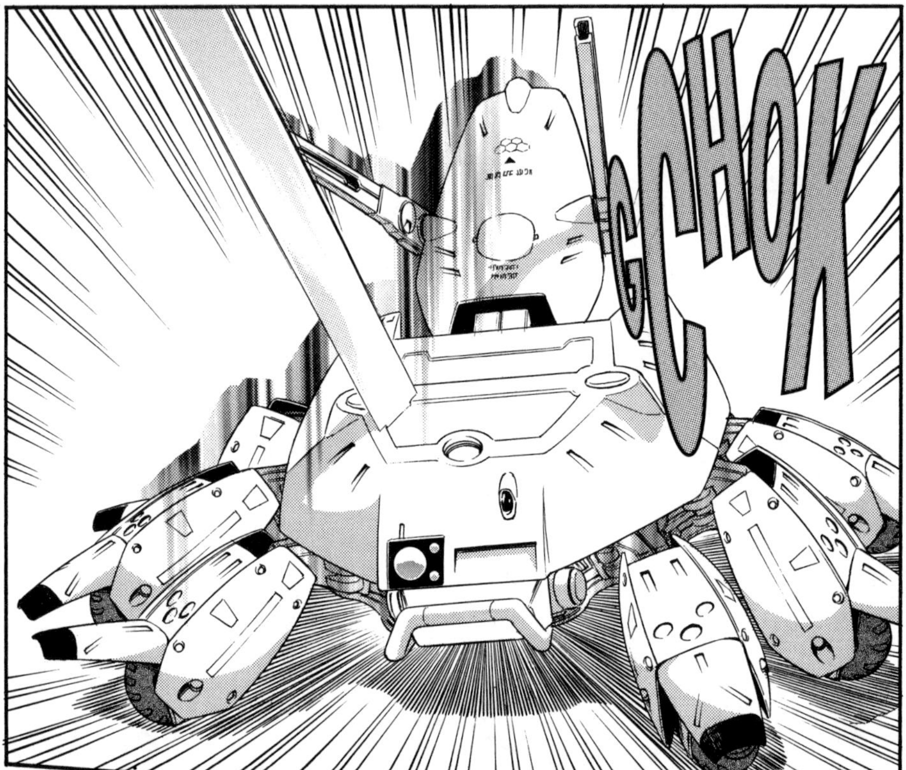
GCHOK

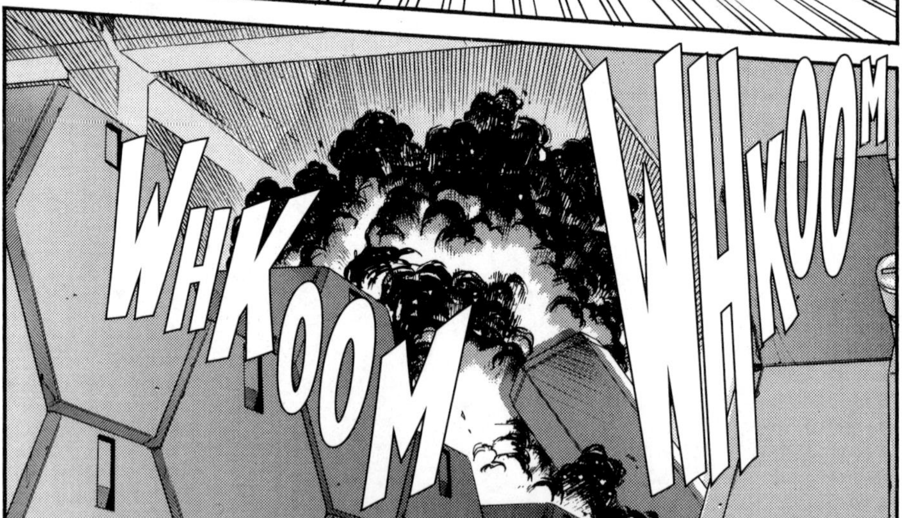
WHKOOM
WHKOOM

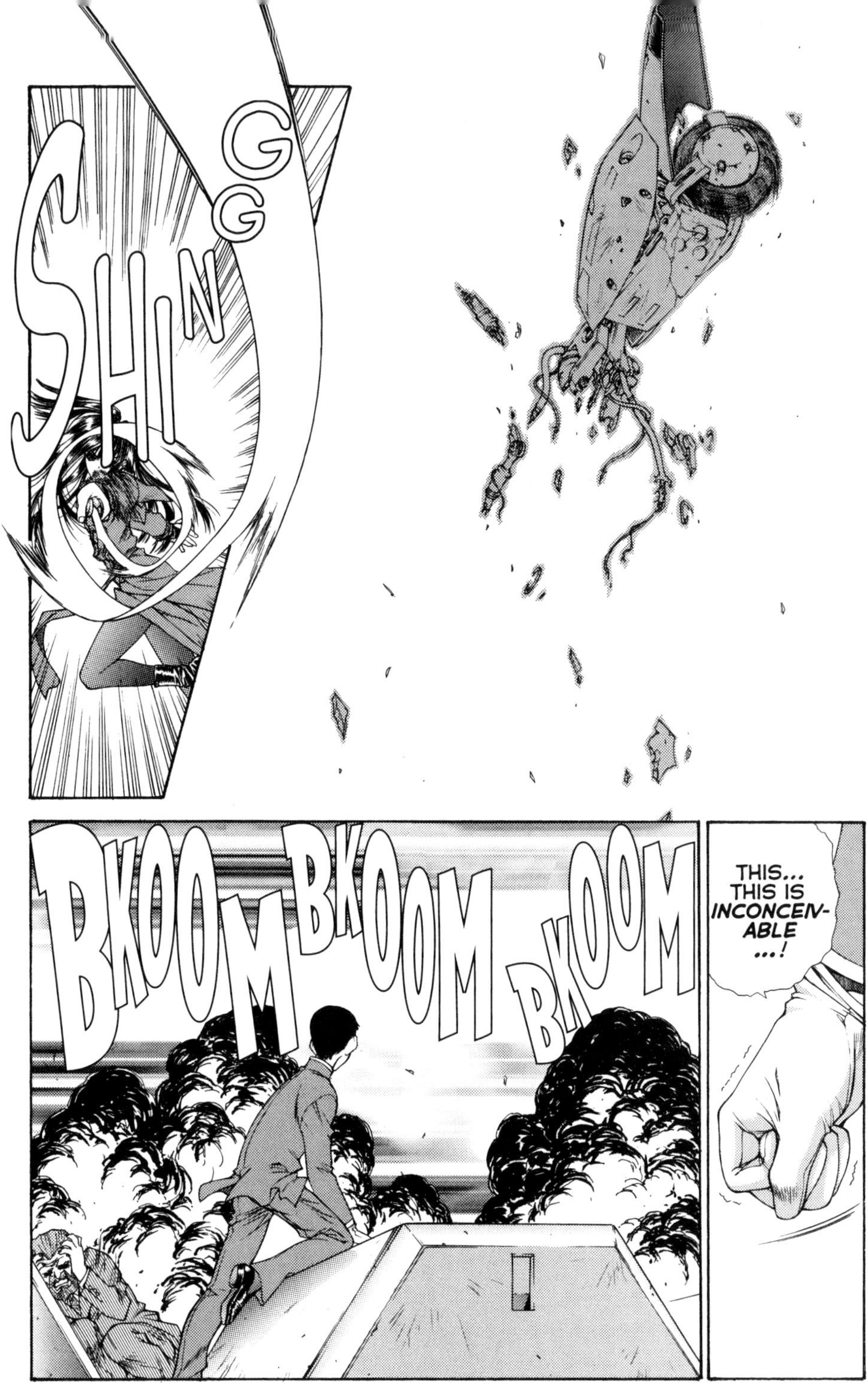
SHINGG
THIS... THIS IS *INCONCEIVABLE* ...!
BKOOM
BKOOM
BKOOM

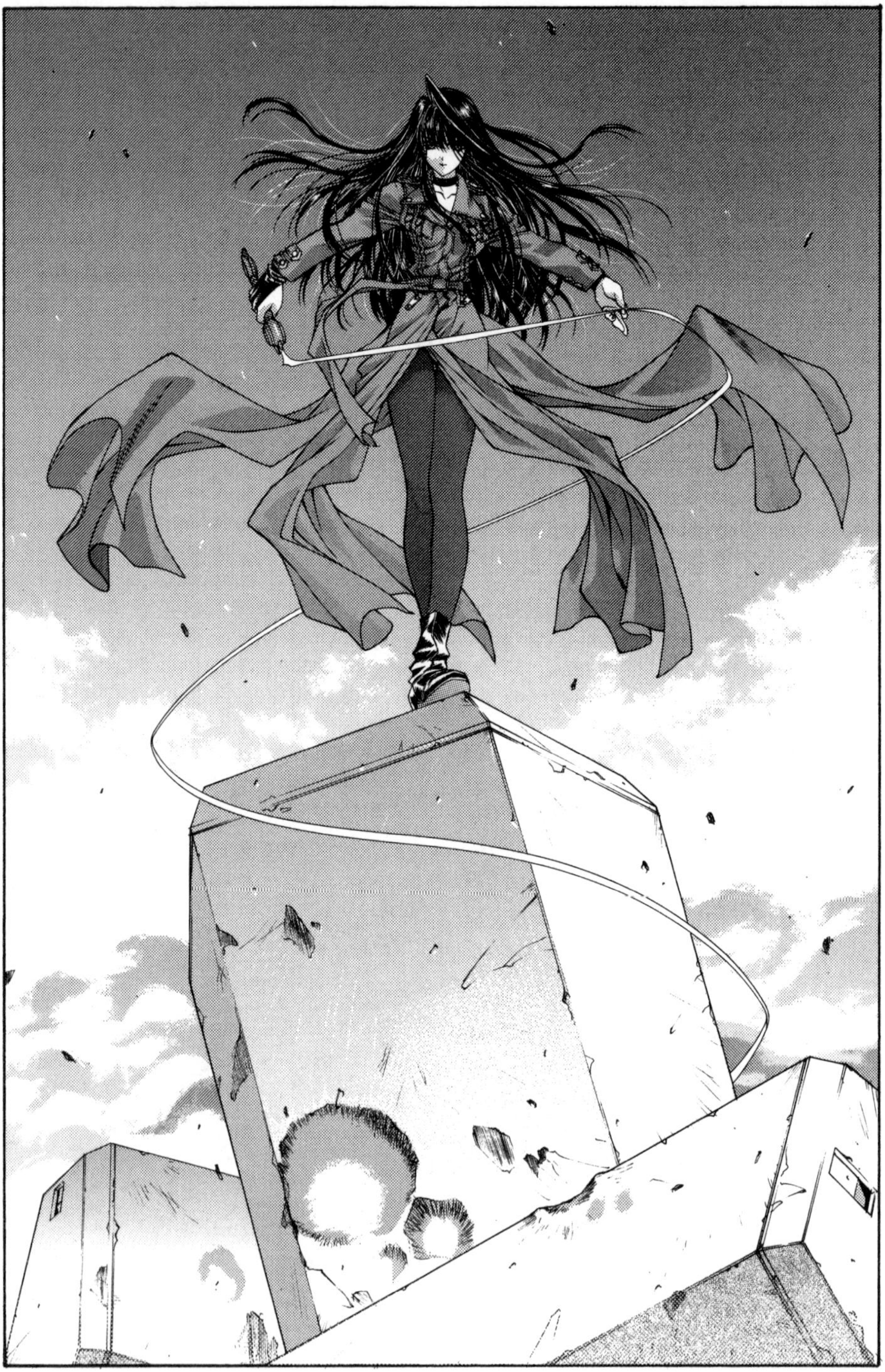

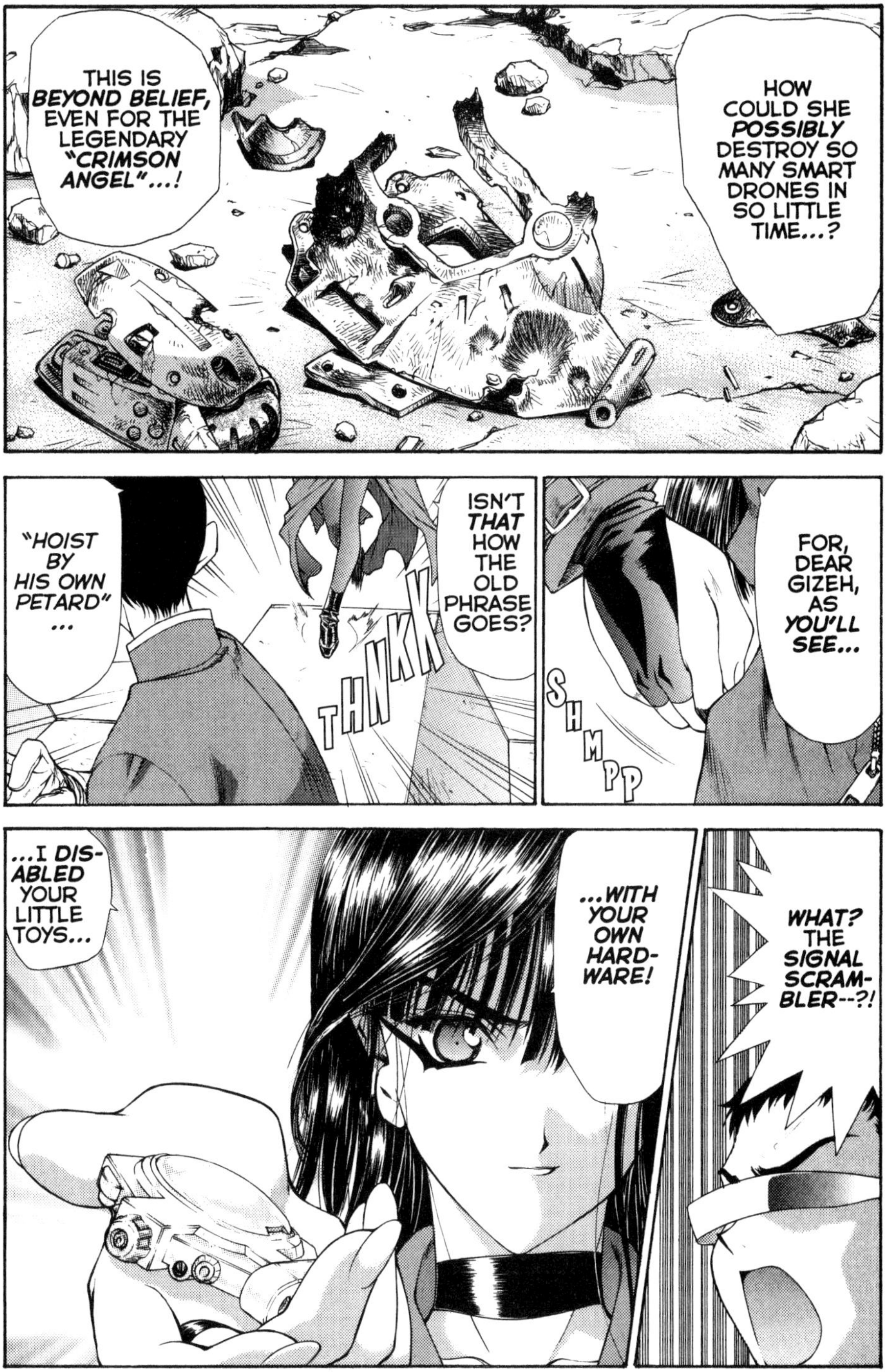
THIS IS BEYOND BELIEF, EVEN FOR THE LEGENDARY "CRIMSON ANGEL"...!
HOW COULD SHE POSSIBLY DESTROY SO MANY SMART DRONES IN SO LITTLE TIME...?
"HOIST BY HIS OWN PETARD" ...
ISN'T THAT HOW THE OLD PHRASE GOES?
THNKK
FOR, DEAR GIZEH, AS YOU'LL SEE...
SHMPP
...I DIS-ABLED YOUR LITTLE TOYS...
...WITH YOUR OWN HARD-WARE!
WHAT? THE SIGNAL SCRAM-BLER--?!

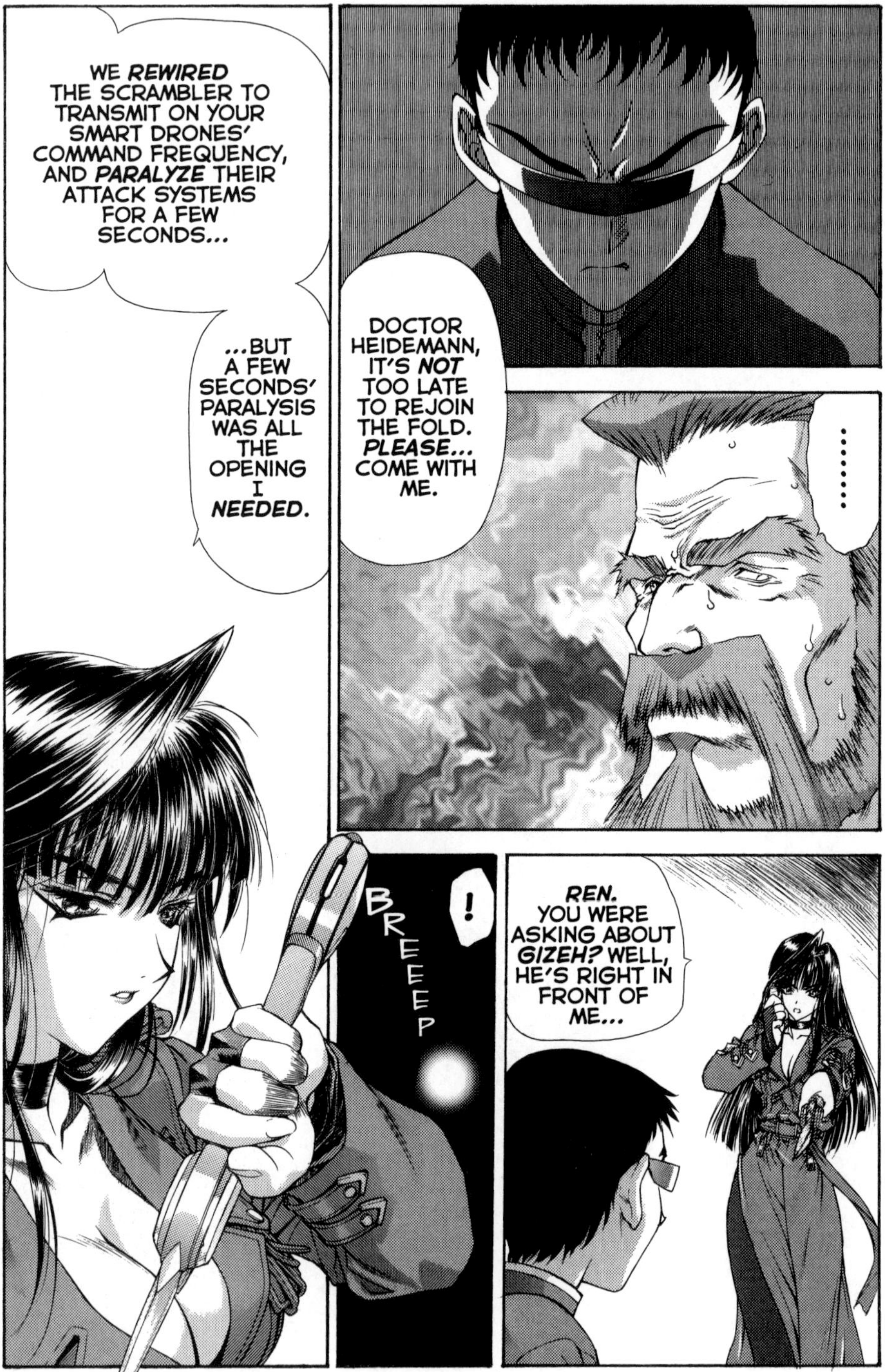
WE *REWIRED* THE SCRAMBLER TO TRANSMIT ON YOUR SMART DRONES' COMMAND FREQUENCY, AND *PARALYZE* THEIR ATTACK SYSTEMS FOR A FEW SECONDS...
...BUT A FEW SECONDS' PARALYSIS WAS ALL THE OPENING I *NEEDED*.
DOCTOR HEIDEMANN, IT'S *NOT* TOO LATE TO REJOIN THE FOLD. *PLEASE...* COME WITH ME.
....
BREEEP
!
REN. YOU WERE ASKING ABOUT *GIZEH?* WELL, HE'S RIGHT IN FRONT OF ME...

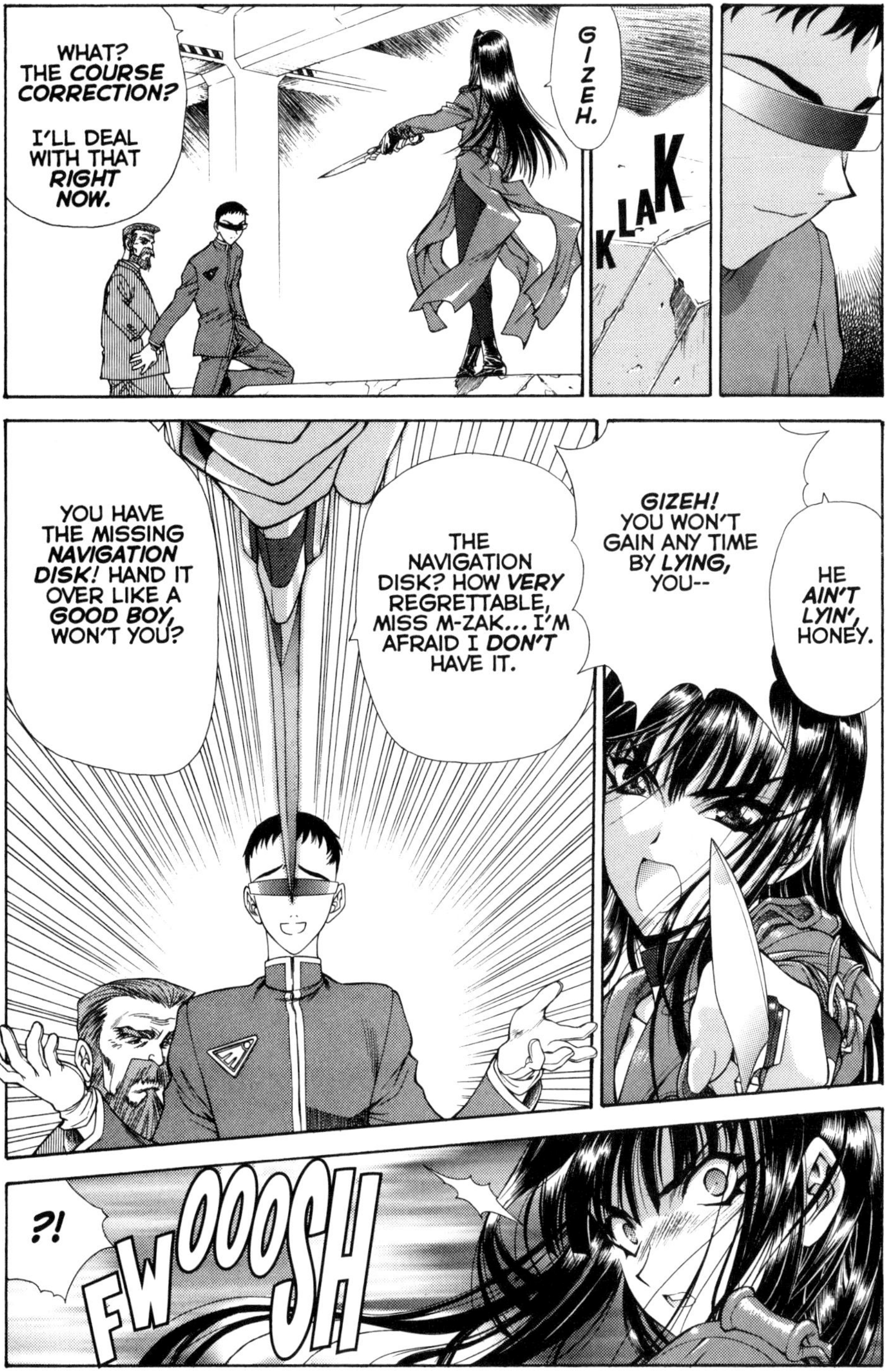
WHAT? THE COURSE CORRECTION?
I'LL DEAL WITH THAT RIGHT NOW.
GIZEH.
KLAK
YOU HAVE THE MISSING NAVIGATION DISK! HAND IT OVER LIKE A GOOD BOY, WON'T YOU?
THE NAVIGATION DISK? HOW VERY REGRETTABLE, MISS M-ZAK... I'M AFRAID I DON'T HAVE IT.
GIZEH! YOU WON'T GAIN ANY TIME BY LYING, YOU--
HE AIN'T LYIN', HONEY.
?!
FWOOOSH

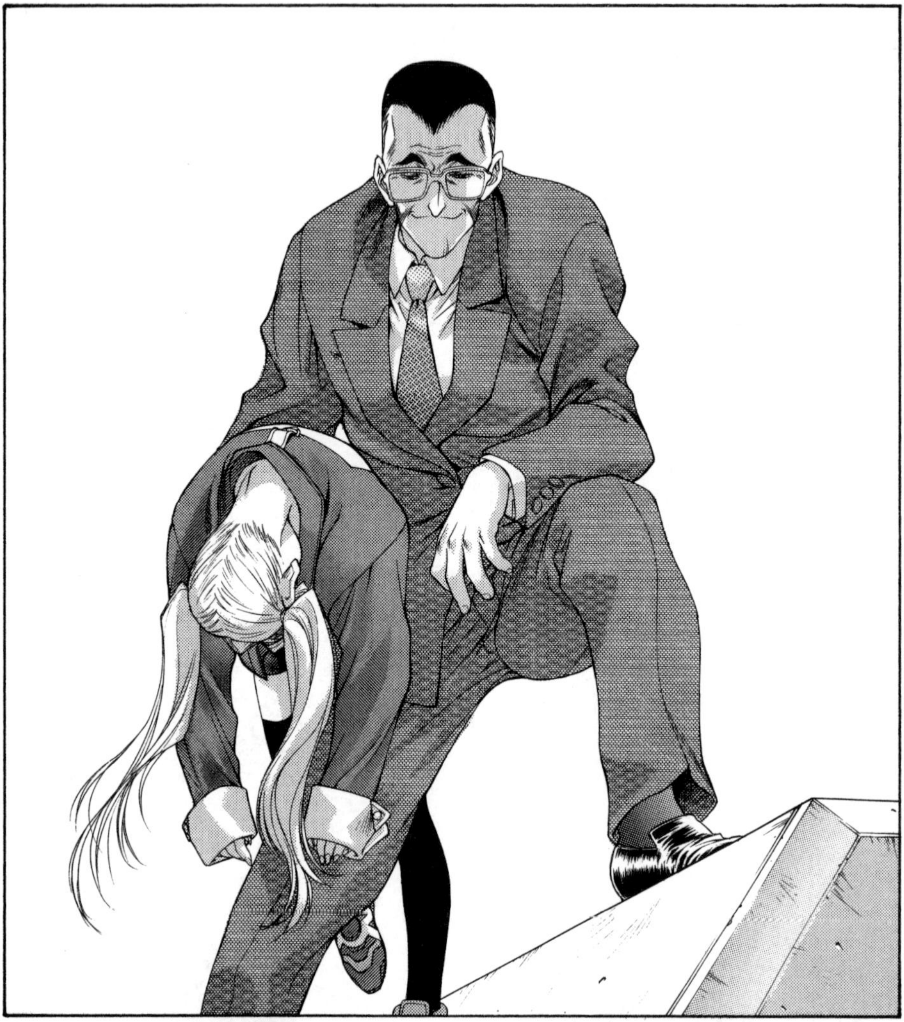

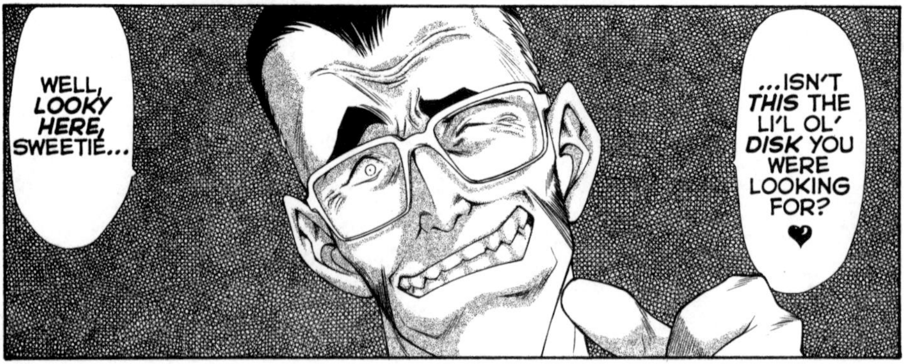
WELL, *LOOKY HERE,* SWEETIE...
...ISN'T *THIS* THE LI'L OL' *DISK* YOU WERE LOOKING FOR? ♥

ACT 72

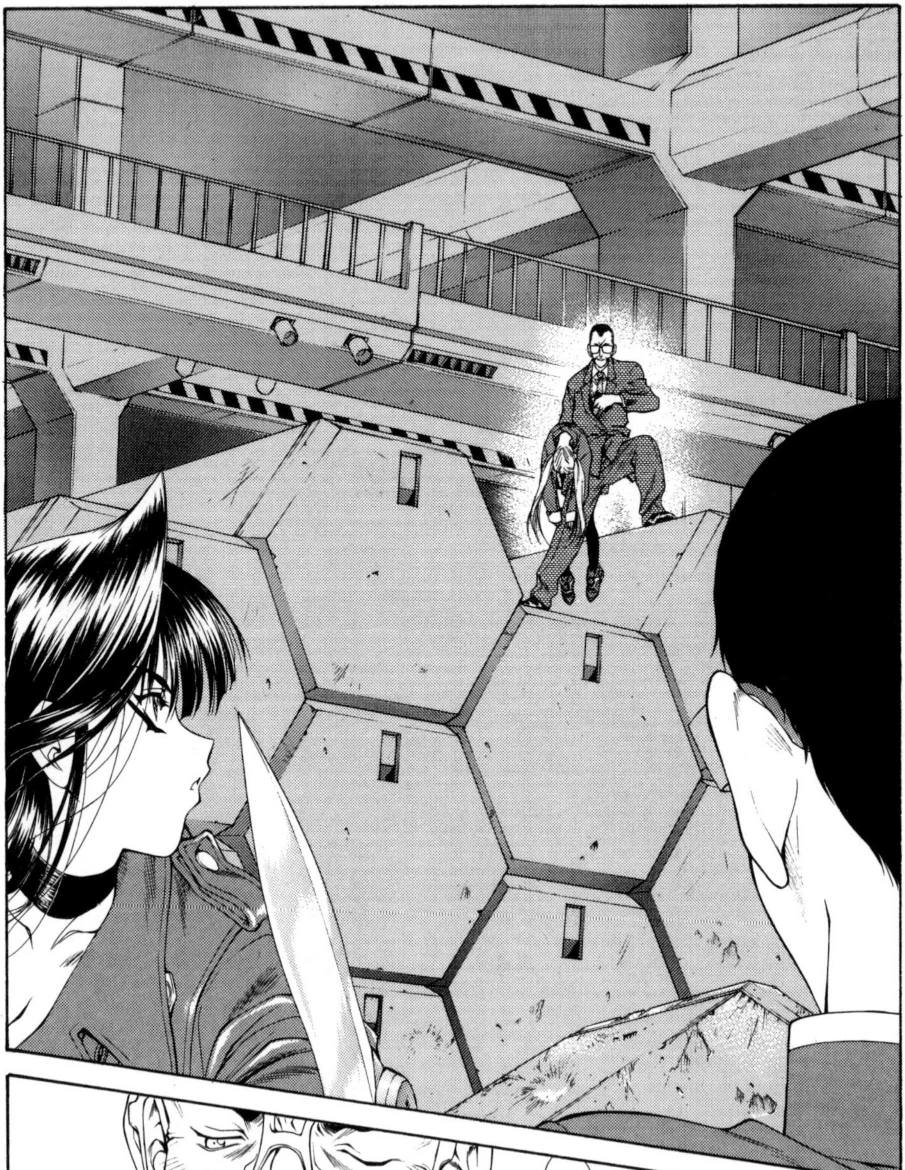

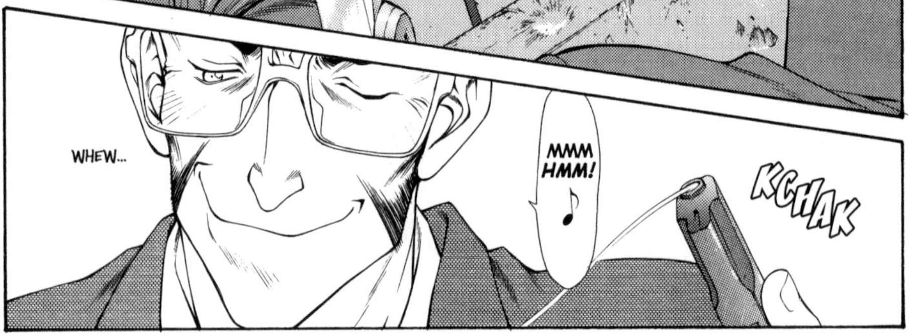
KCHAK
MMM HMM! ♪
WHEW...

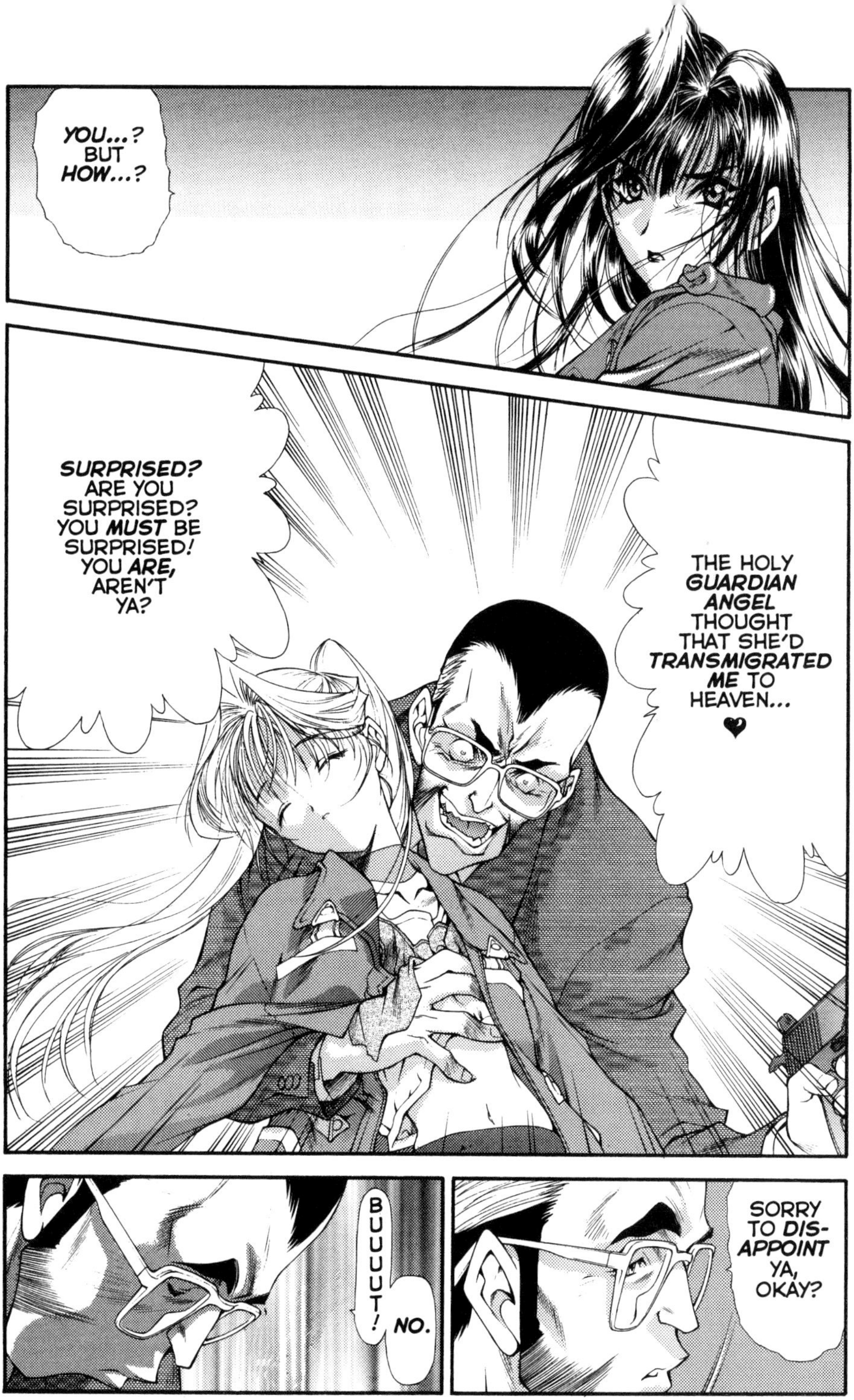

YOU...? BUT HOW...?
SURPRISED? ARE YOU SURPRISED? YOU MUST BE SURPRISED! YOU ARE, AREN'T YA?
THE HOLY GUARDIAN ANGEL THOUGHT THAT SHE'D TRANSMIGRATED ME TO HEAVEN... ❤
BUUUUT!
NO.
SORRY TO DIS-APPOINT YA, OKAY?

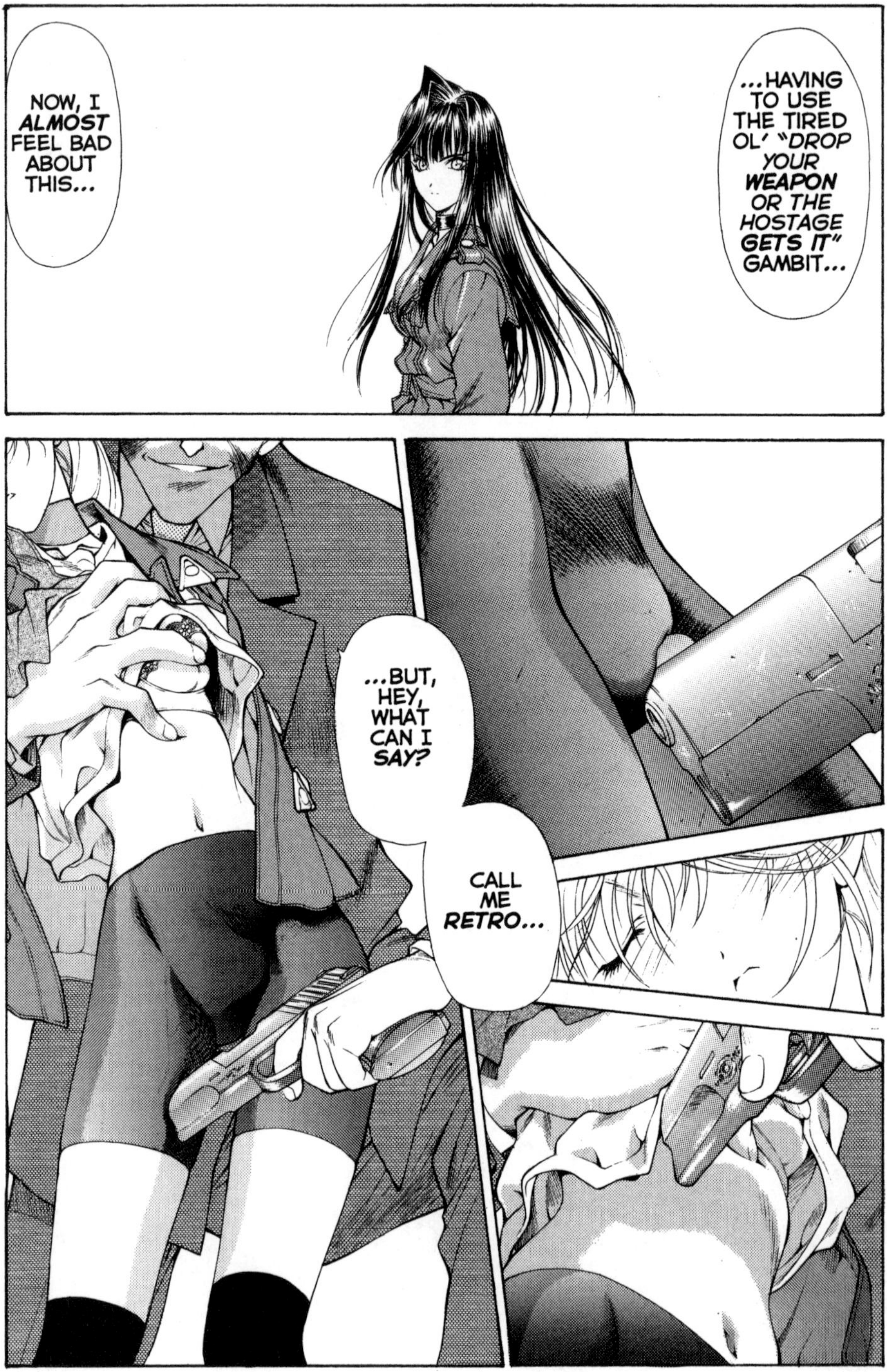
NOW, I *ALMOST* FEEL BAD ABOUT THIS...
...HAVING TO USE THE TIRED OL' "*DROP YOUR* **WEAPON** OR THE HOSTAGE **GETS IT**" GAMBIT...
...BUT, HEY, WHAT CAN I *SAY?*
CALL ME *RETRO...*

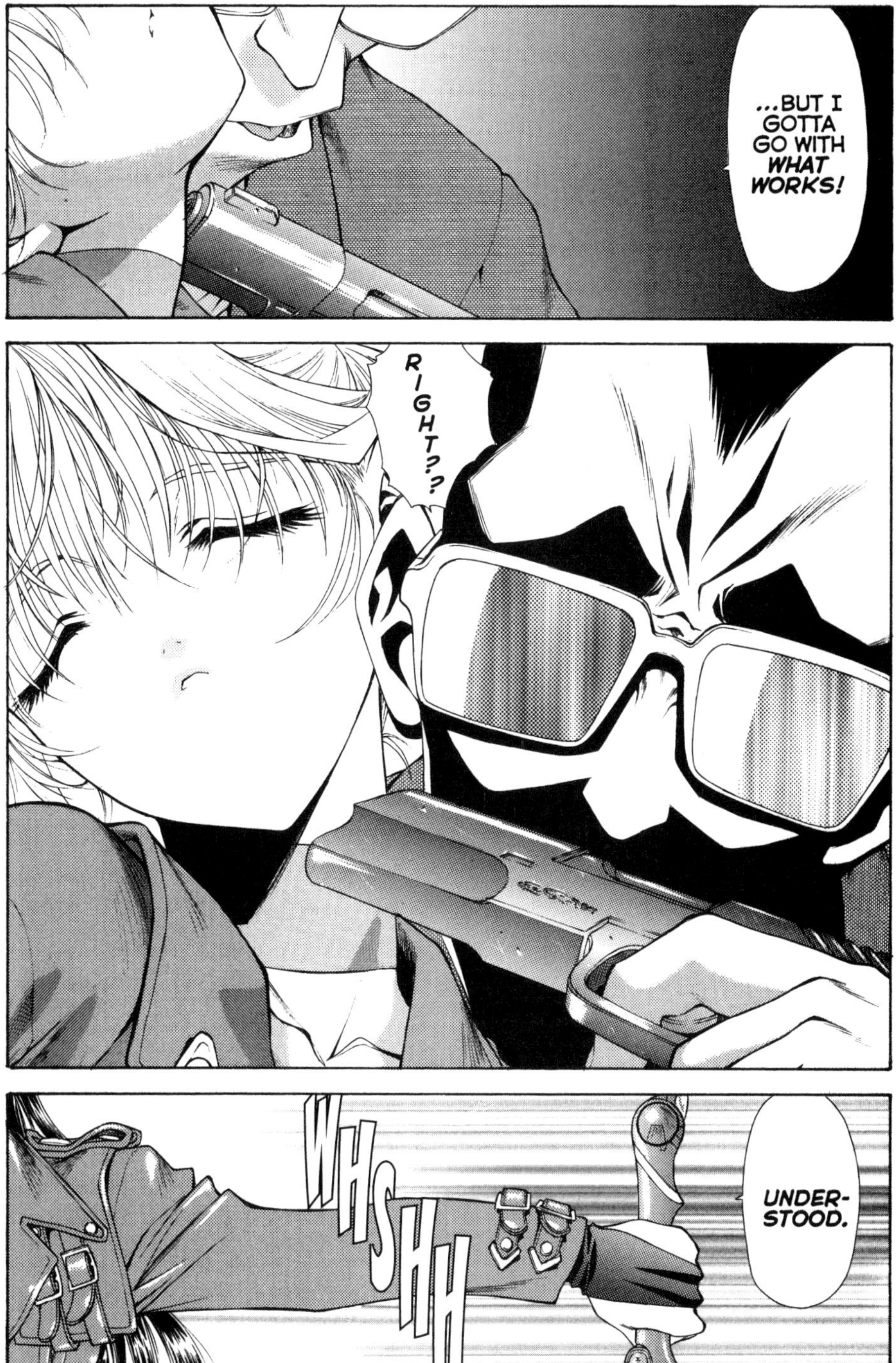

...BUT I GOTTA GO WITH *WHAT WORKS!*
RIGHT??
UNDER-STOOD.
WHSHH

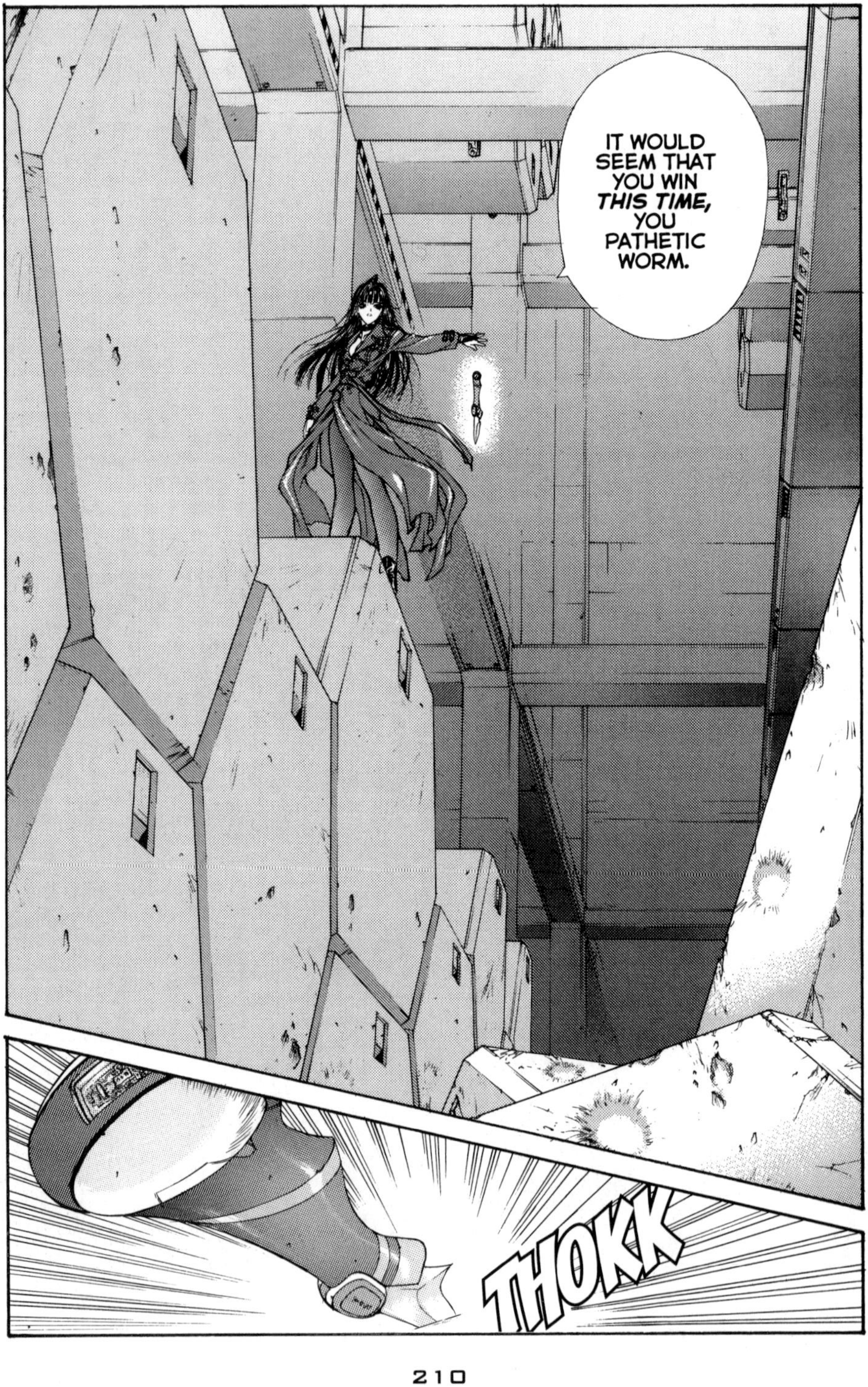
IT WOULD SEEM THAT YOU WIN *THIS TIME,* YOU PATHETIC WORM.
THOKK

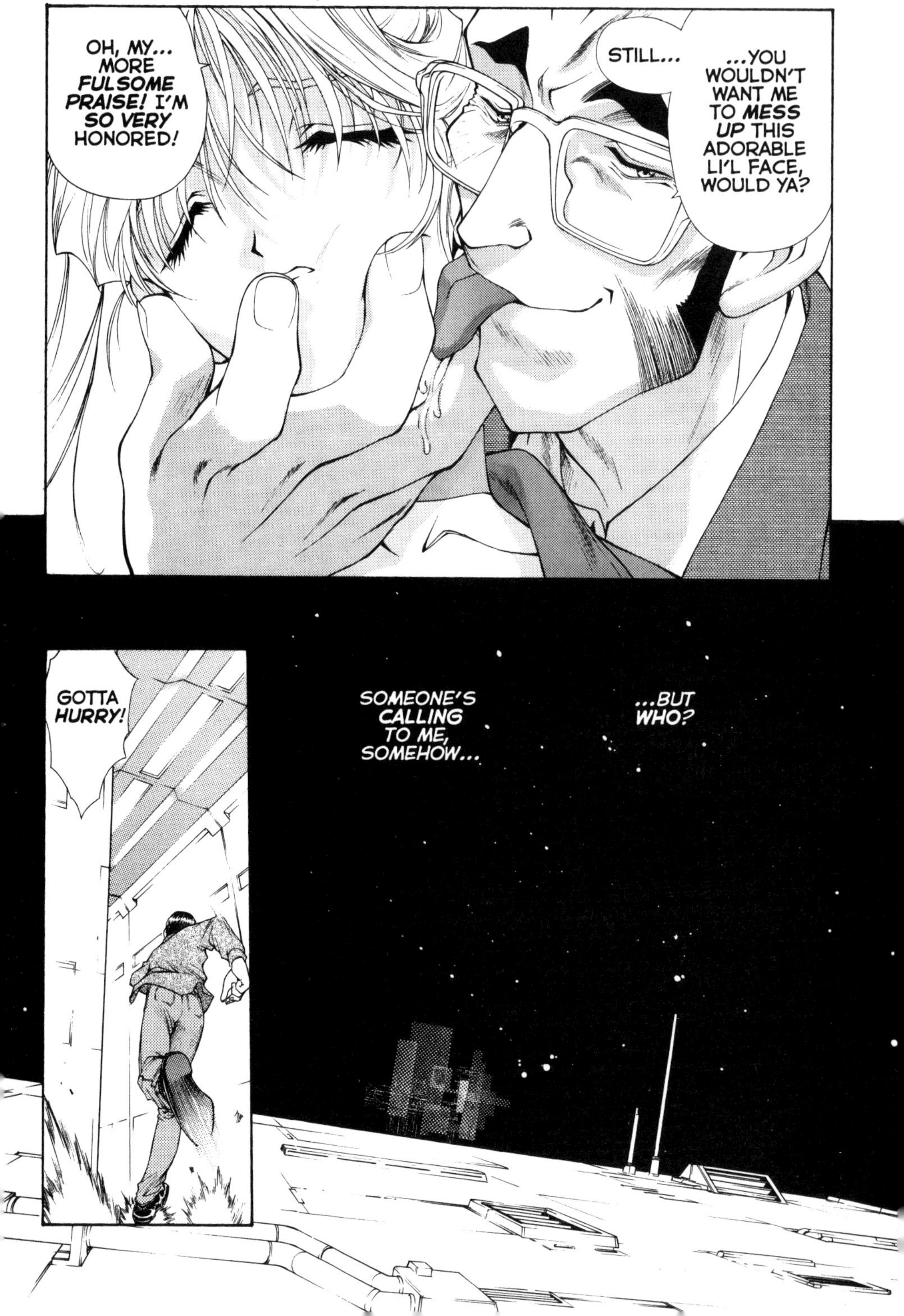
OH, MY... MORE FULSOME PRAISE! I'M SO VERY HONORED!
STILL...
...YOU WOULDN'T WANT ME TO MESS UP THIS ADORABLE LI'L FACE, WOULD YA?
GOTTA HURRY!
SOMEONE'S CALLING TO ME, SOMEHOW...
...BUT WHO?

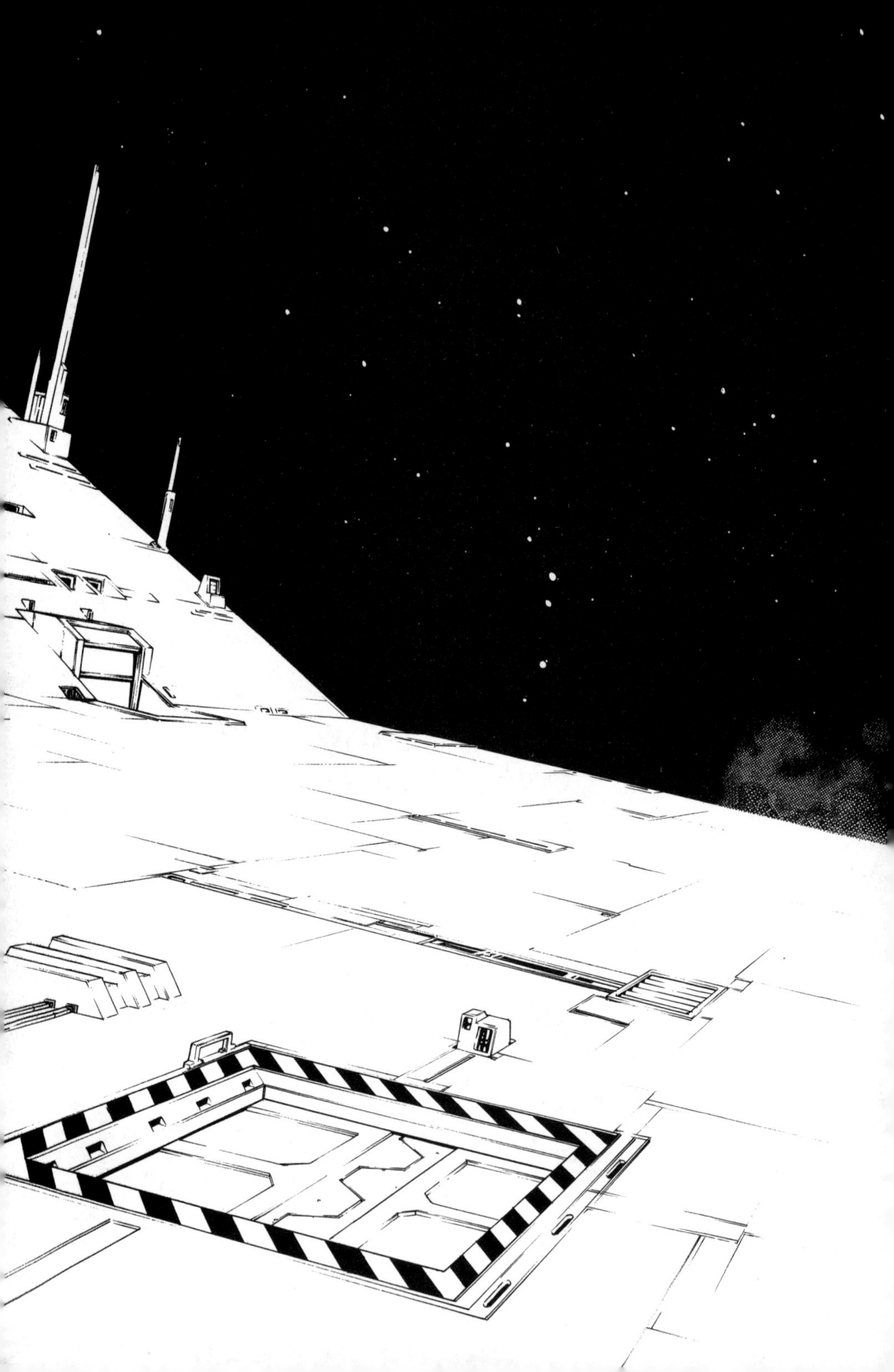

WHO ARE YOU, OUT THERE...?

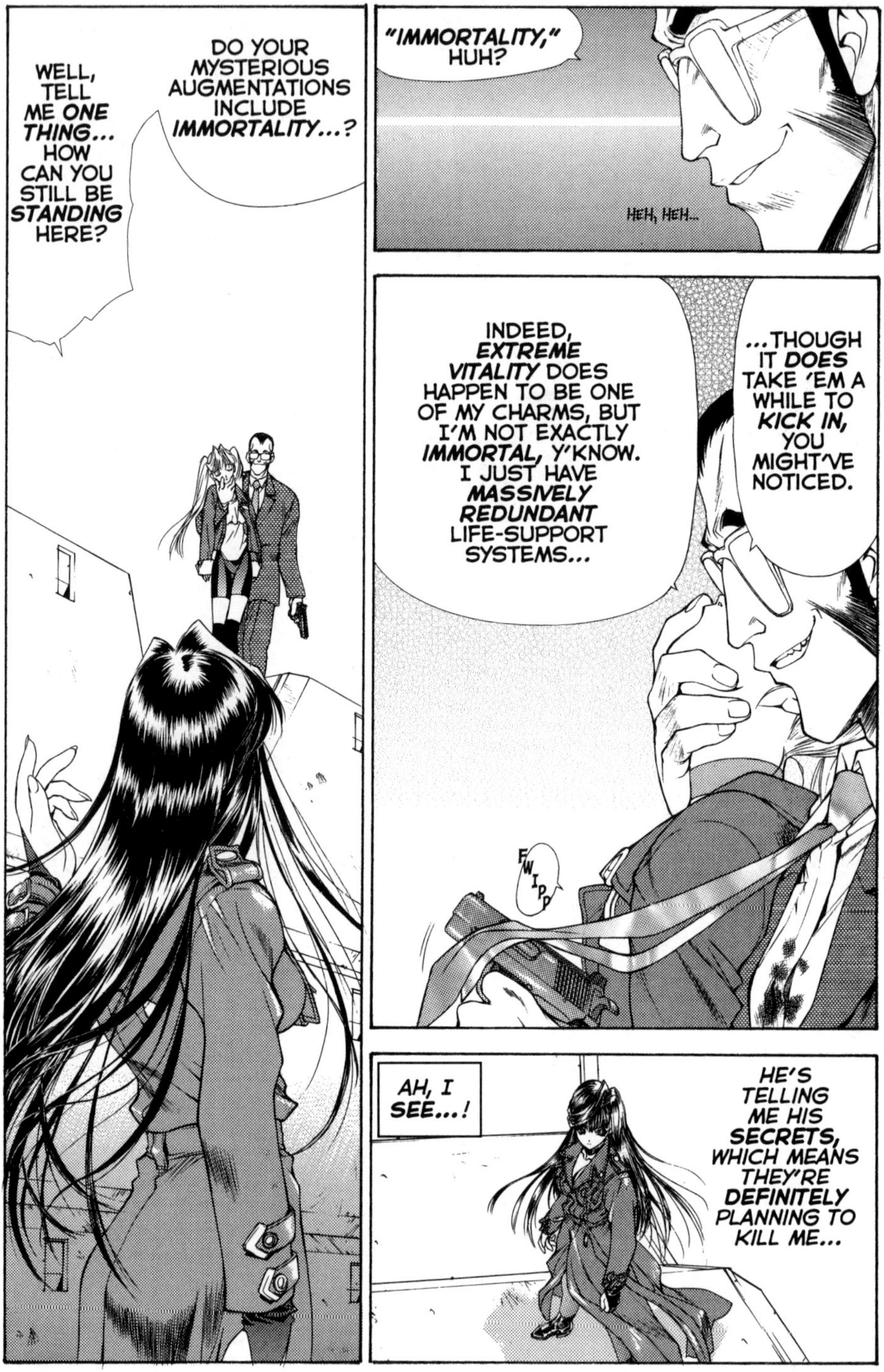
WELL, TELL ME ONE THING... HOW CAN YOU STILL BE STANDING HERE?
DO YOUR MYSTERIOUS AUGMENTATIONS INCLUDE IMMORTALITY...?
"IMMORTALITY," HUH?
HEH, HEH...
INDEED, EXTREME VITALITY DOES HAPPEN TO BE ONE OF MY CHARMS, BUT I'M NOT EXACTLY IMMORTAL, Y'KNOW. I JUST HAVE MASSIVELY REDUNDANT LIFE-SUPPORT SYSTEMS...
...THOUGH IT DOES TAKE 'EM A WHILE TO KICK IN, YOU MIGHT'VE NOTICED.
FWIPP
AH, I SEE...!
HE'S TELLING ME HIS SECRETS, WHICH MEANS THEY'RE DEFINITELY PLANNING TO KILL ME...

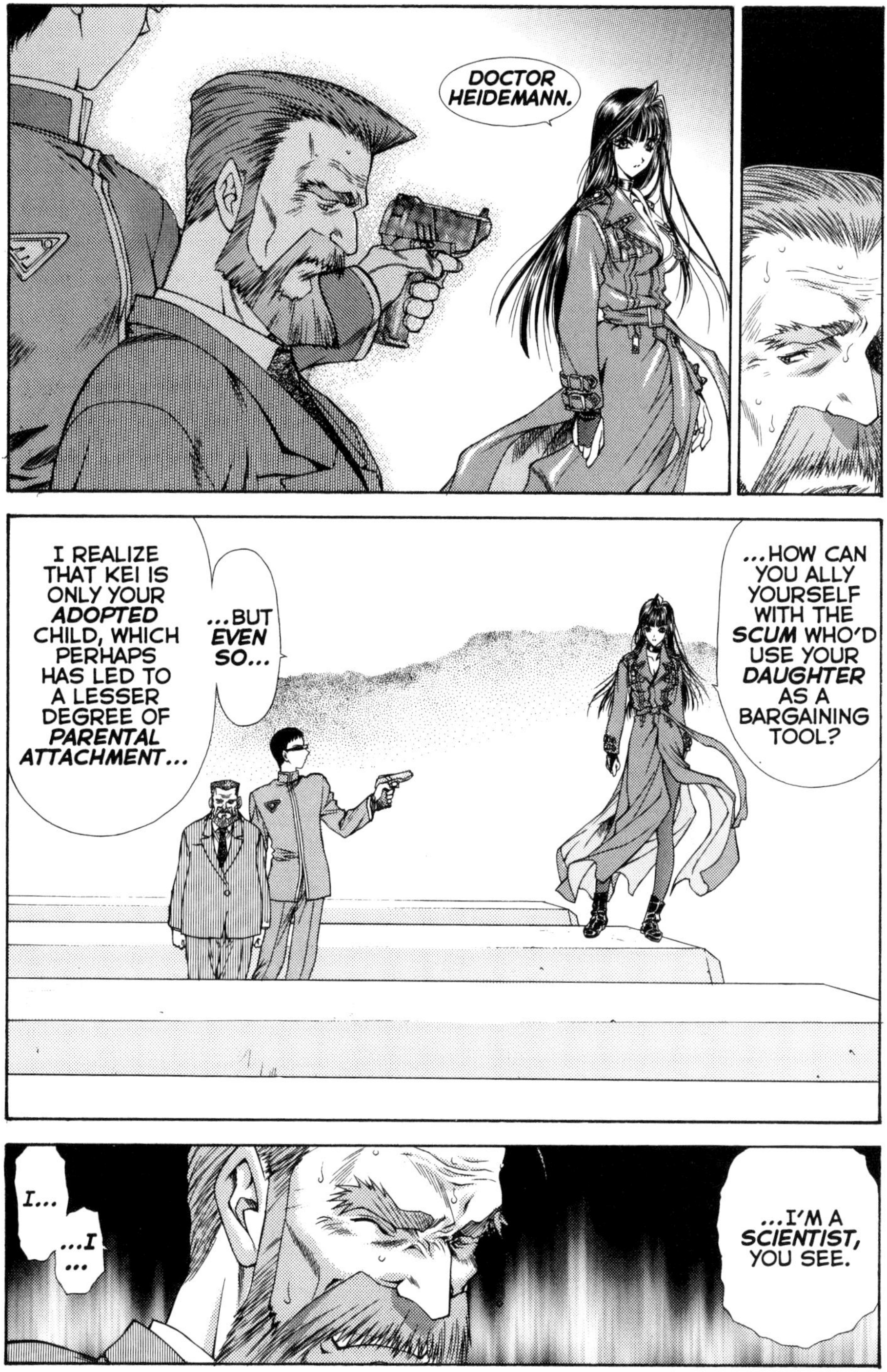
DOCTOR HEIDEMANN.
I REALIZE THAT KEI IS ONLY YOUR ADOPTED CHILD, WHICH PERHAPS HAS LED TO A LESSER DEGREE OF PARENTAL ATTACHMENT...
...BUT EVEN SO...
...HOW CAN YOU ALLY YOURSELF WITH THE SCUM WHO'D USE YOUR DAUGHTER AS A BARGAINING TOOL?
I...
...I ...
...I'M A SCIENTIST, YOU SEE.

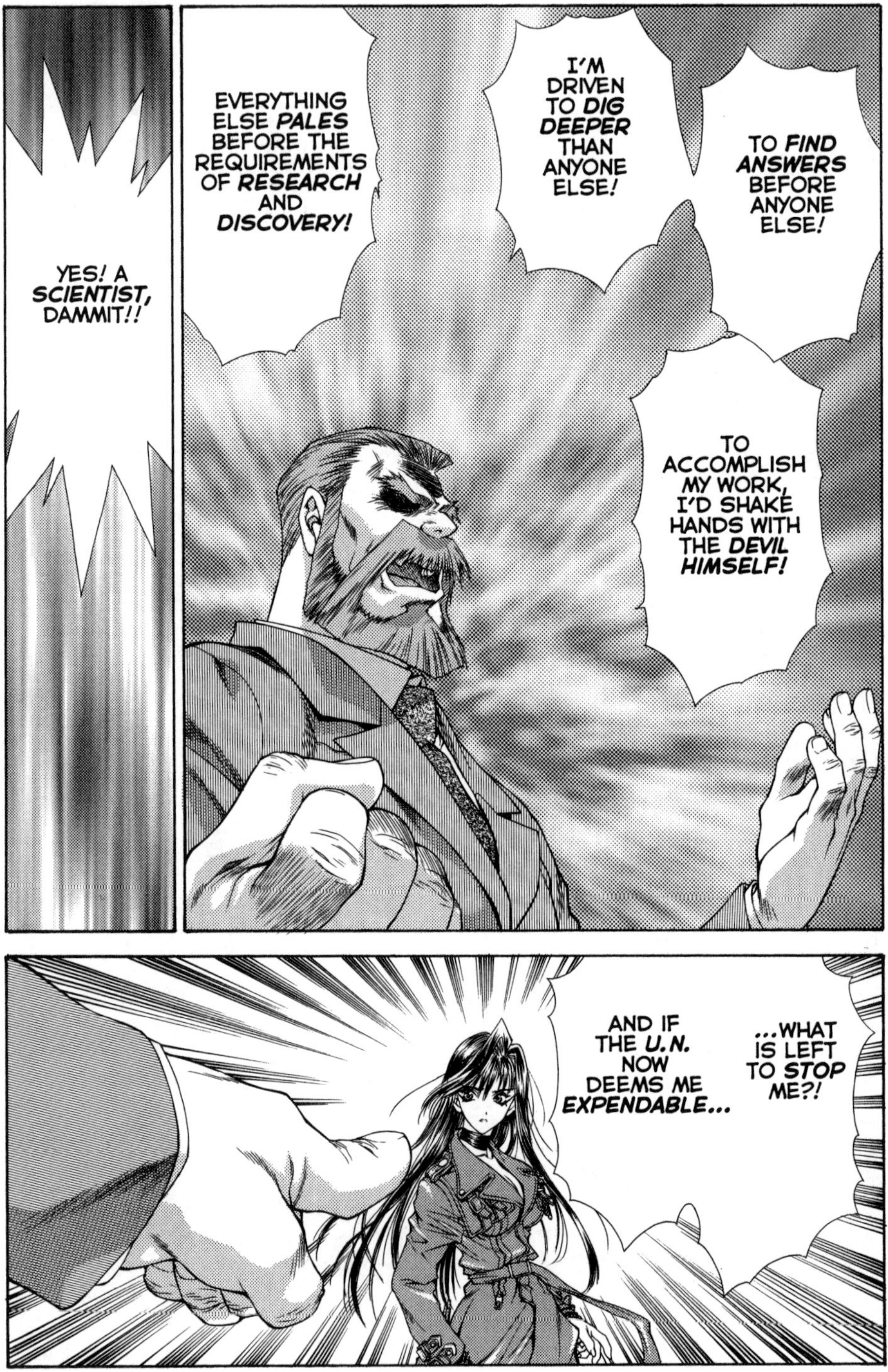
YES! A SCIENTIST, DAMMIT!!
EVERYTHING ELSE PALES BEFORE THE REQUIREMENTS OF RESEARCH AND DISCOVERY!
I'M DRIVEN TO DIG DEEPER THAN ANYONE ELSE!
TO FIND ANSWERS BEFORE ANYONE ELSE!
TO ACCOMPLISH MY WORK, I'D SHAKE HANDS WITH THE DEVIL HIMSELF!
AND IF THE U.N. NOW DEEMS ME EXPENDABLE...
...WHAT IS LEFT TO STOP ME?!

VON BRAUN, WHO SENT THE FIRST MAN TO THE **MOON,** SPENT HIS EARLY CAREER SPEARHEADING THE RESEARCH EFFORT FOR NAZI GERMANY'S V-2 PROGRAM!

EINSTEIN AND **OPPENHEIMER...** SURELY THEY MUST HAVE REALIZED HOW MUCH **TERROR** THAT THE **NUCLEAR WEAPONS** THEY HELPED CREATE WOULD INFLICT ON THE HUMAN RACE!

KNOWING THAT THOUSANDS, EVEN **MILLIONS** WOULD DIE BECAUSE OF THEIR WORK... WHY DID THESE MEN OF SCIENCE **STAY** IN THEIR LABORATORIES?

BECAUSE **THAT** WAS WHERE THEY COULD DEVOTE THEIR LIVES TO **RESEARCH!**

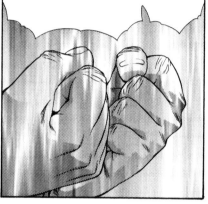

HAHH
HAHH

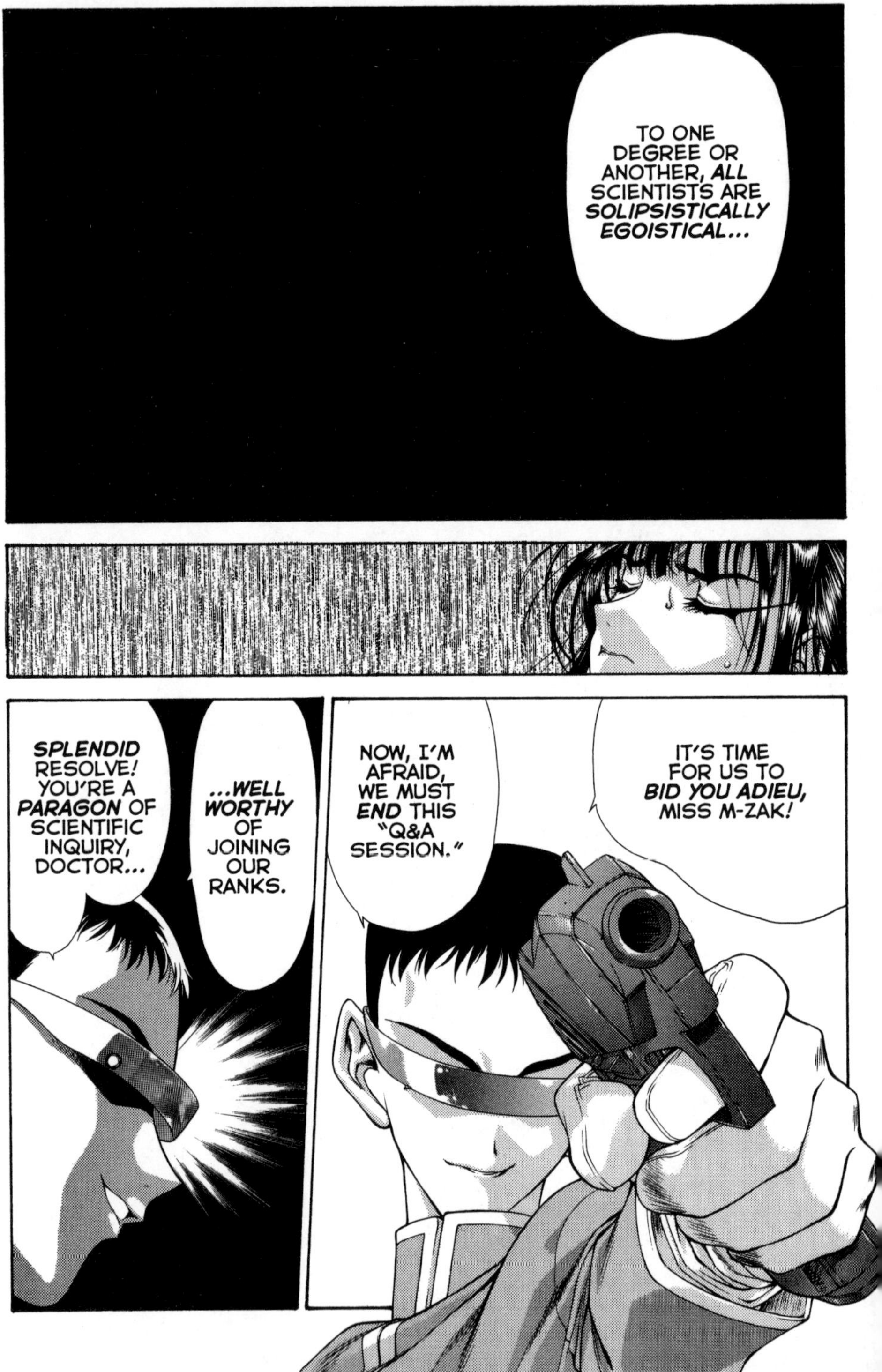
TO ONE DEGREE OR ANOTHER, ***ALL*** SCIENTISTS ARE ***SOLIPSISTICALLY EGOISTICAL...***
SPLENDID RESOLVE! YOU'RE A ***PARAGON*** OF SCIENTIFIC INQUIRY, DOCTOR...
...WELL WORTHY OF JOINING OUR RANKS.
NOW, I'M AFRAID, WE MUST ***END*** THIS "Q&A SESSION."
IT'S TIME FOR US TO ***BID YOU ADIEU,*** MISS M-ZAK!

ACT 73

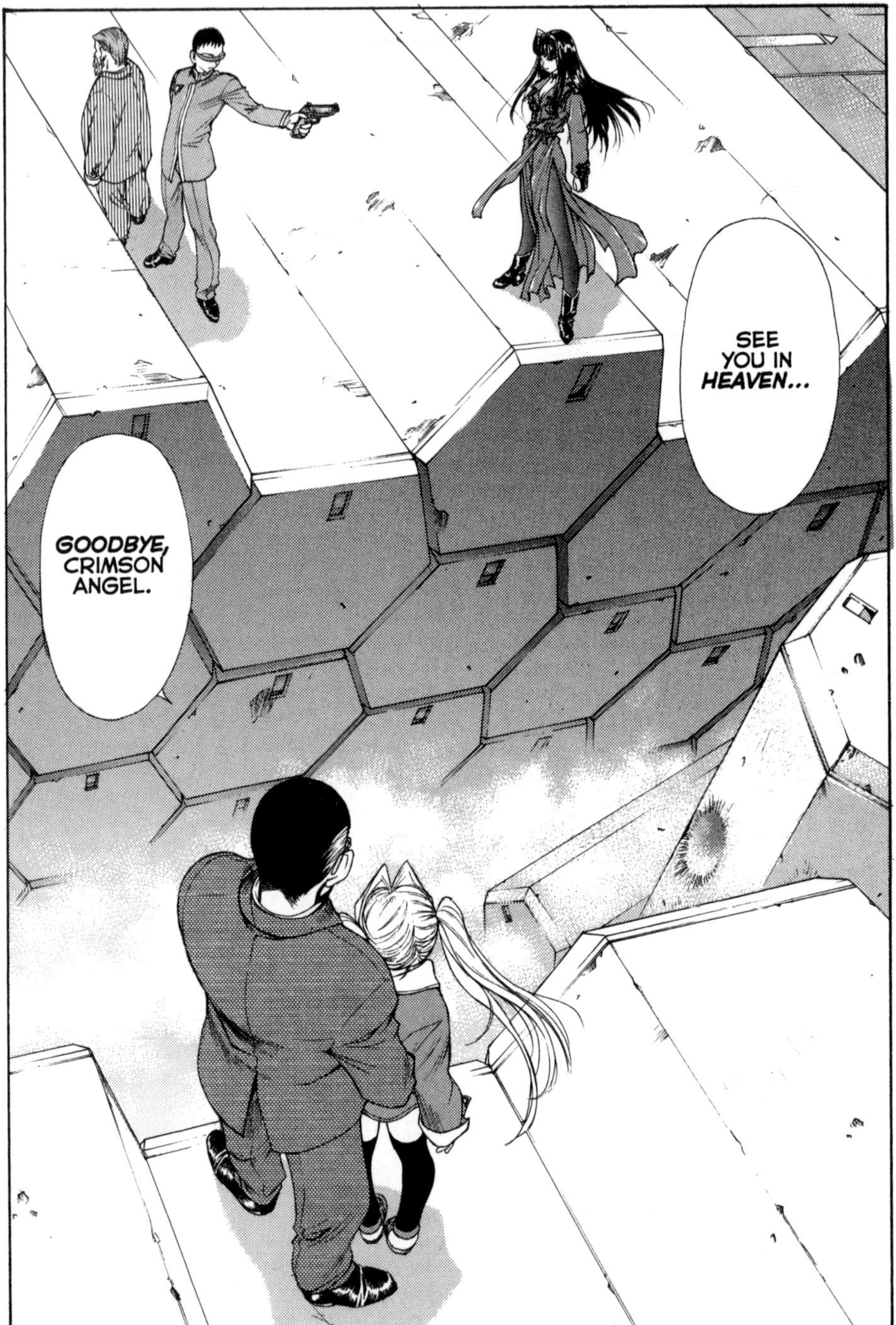
SEE YOU IN HEAVEN...
GOODBYE, CRIMSON ANGEL.

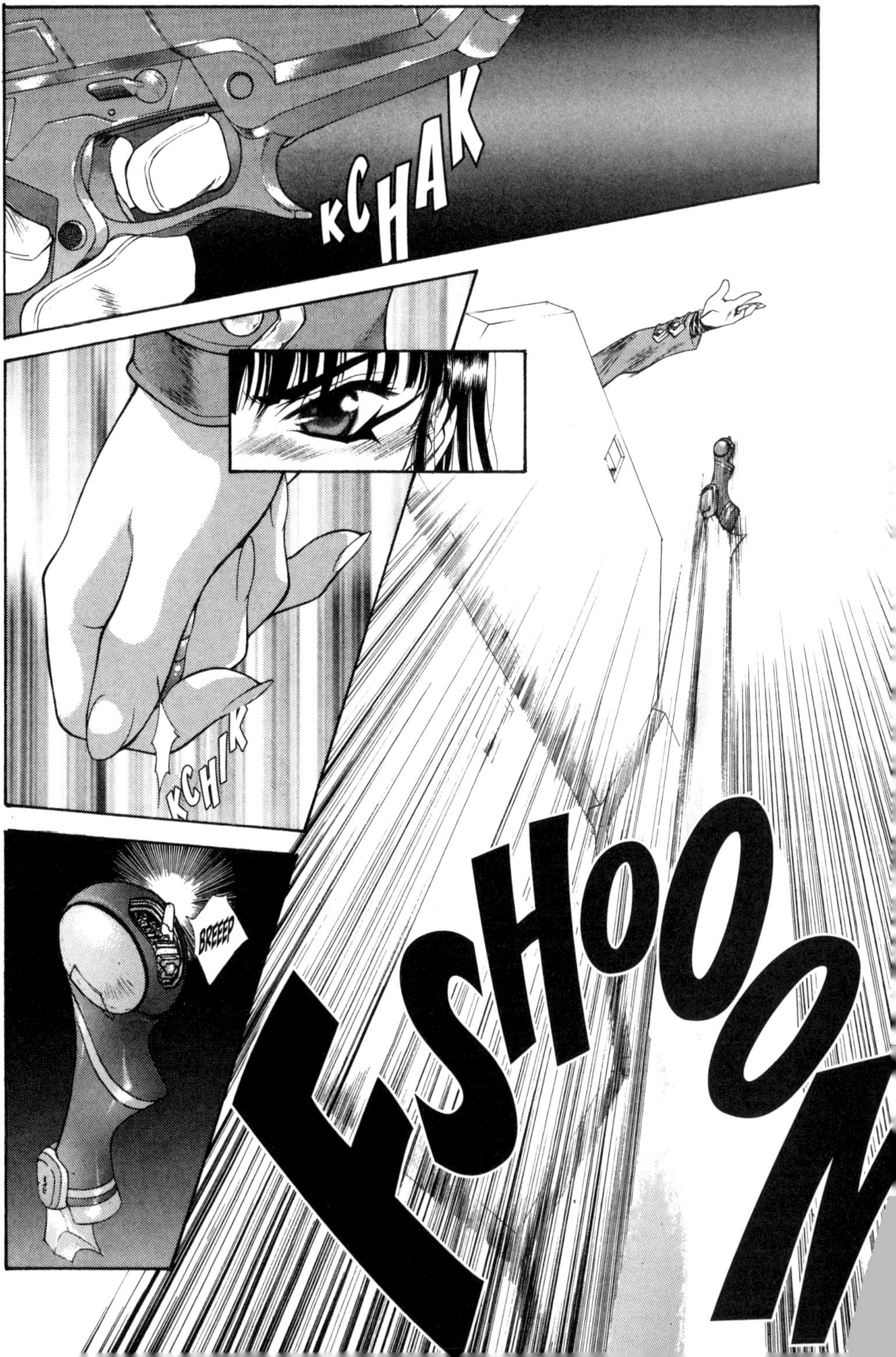
KCHAK
KCHIK
BREEEP
FSHOOOM

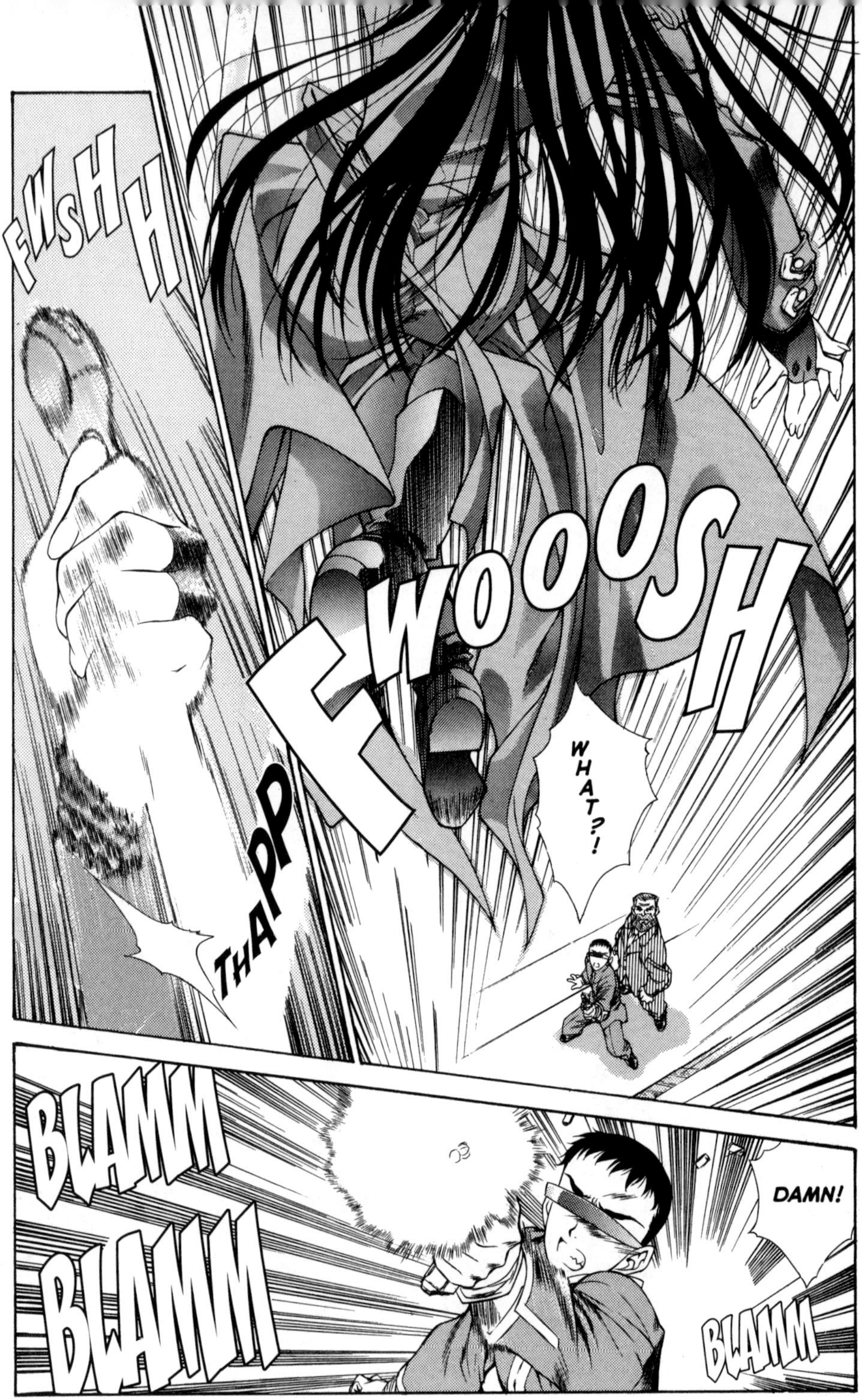
FWOOOSH
WHAT?!
FWSHH
THAPP
DAMN!
BLAMM
BLAMM
BLAMM

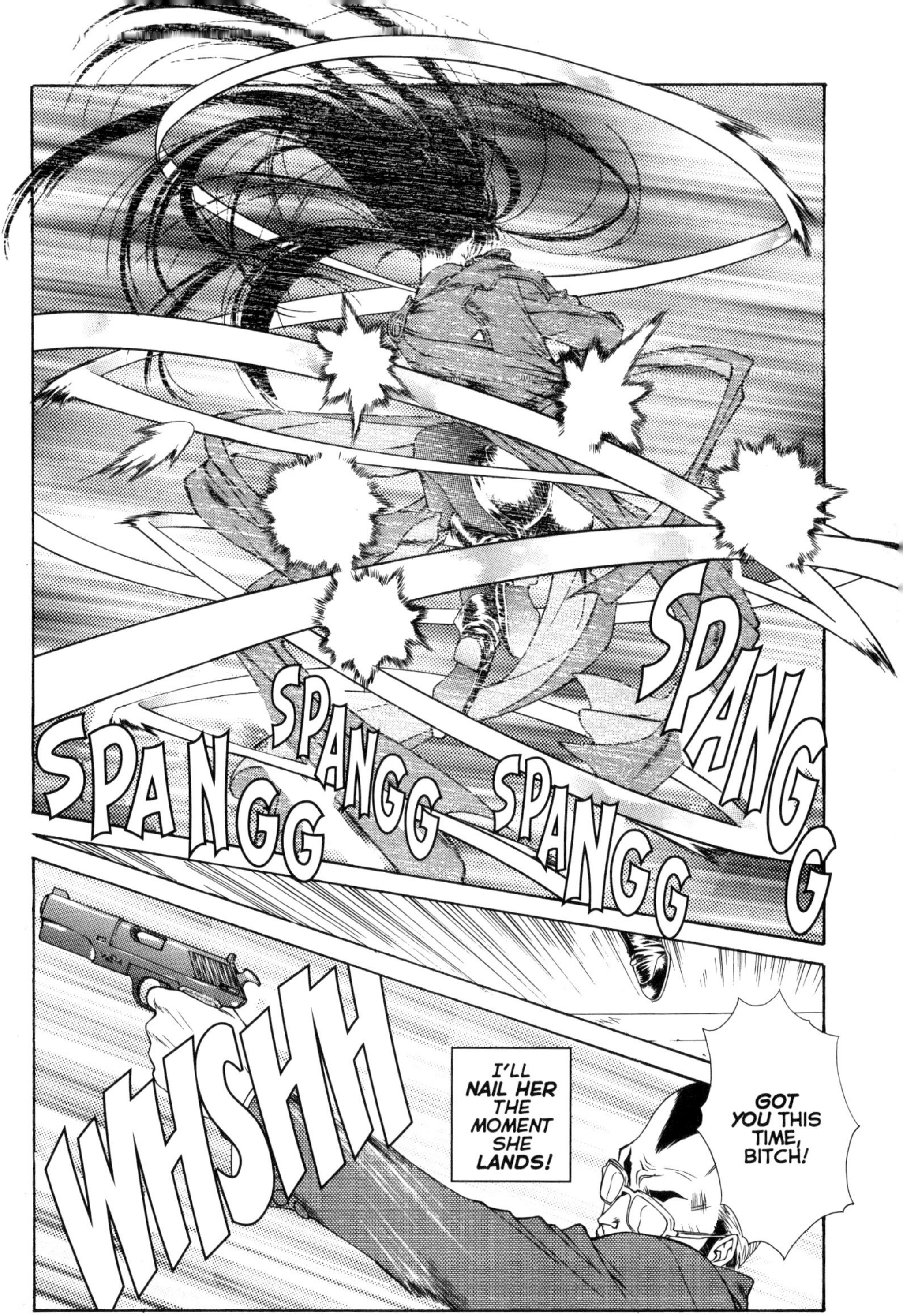
SPANGG
SPANGG
SPANGG
SPANGG
GOT YOU THIS TIME, BITCH!
I'LL NAIL HER THE MOMENT SHE LANDS!
WHSHH

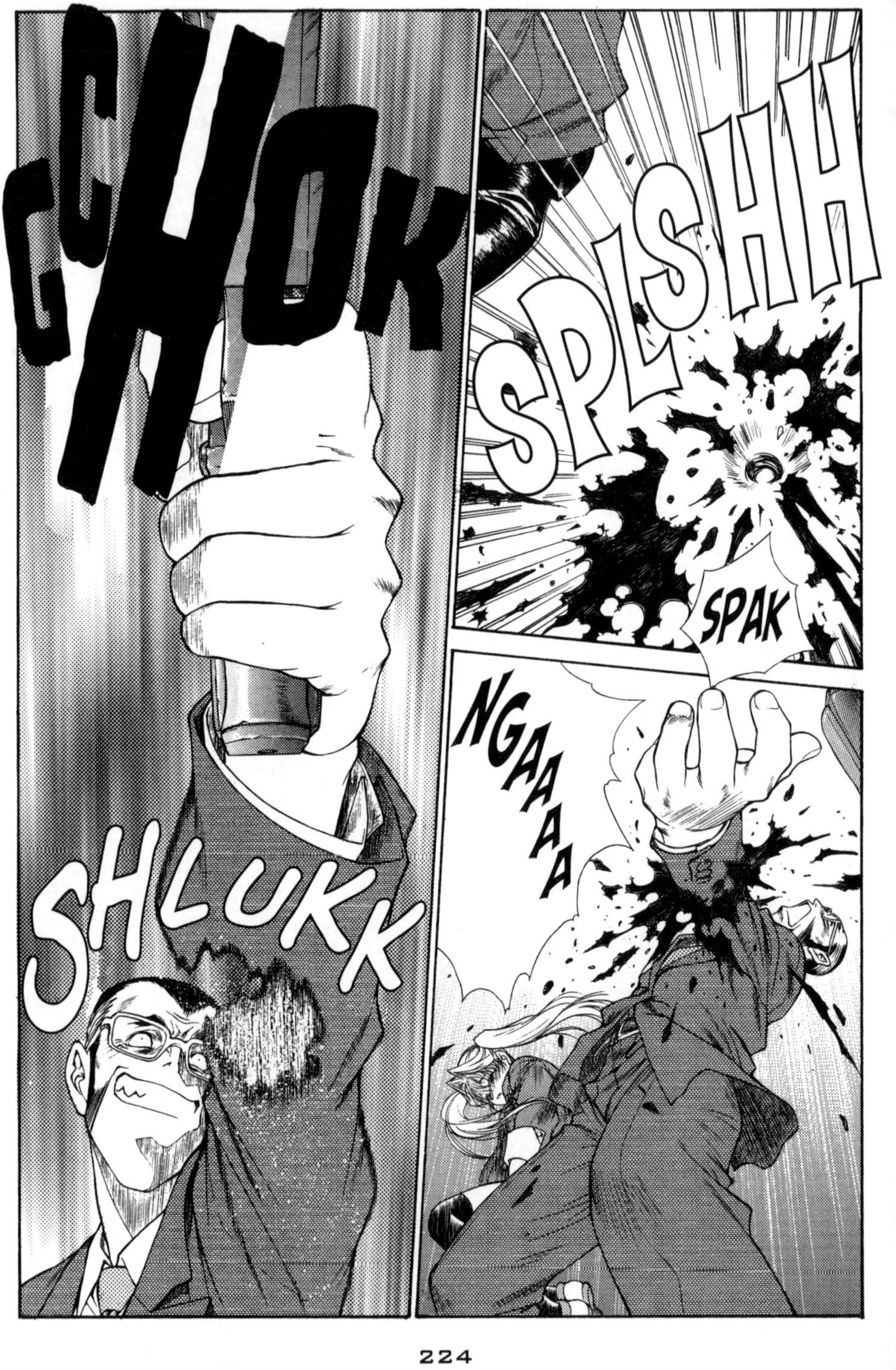
SPLSHHH
SPAK
NGAAAAA
GCHOK
SHLUKK

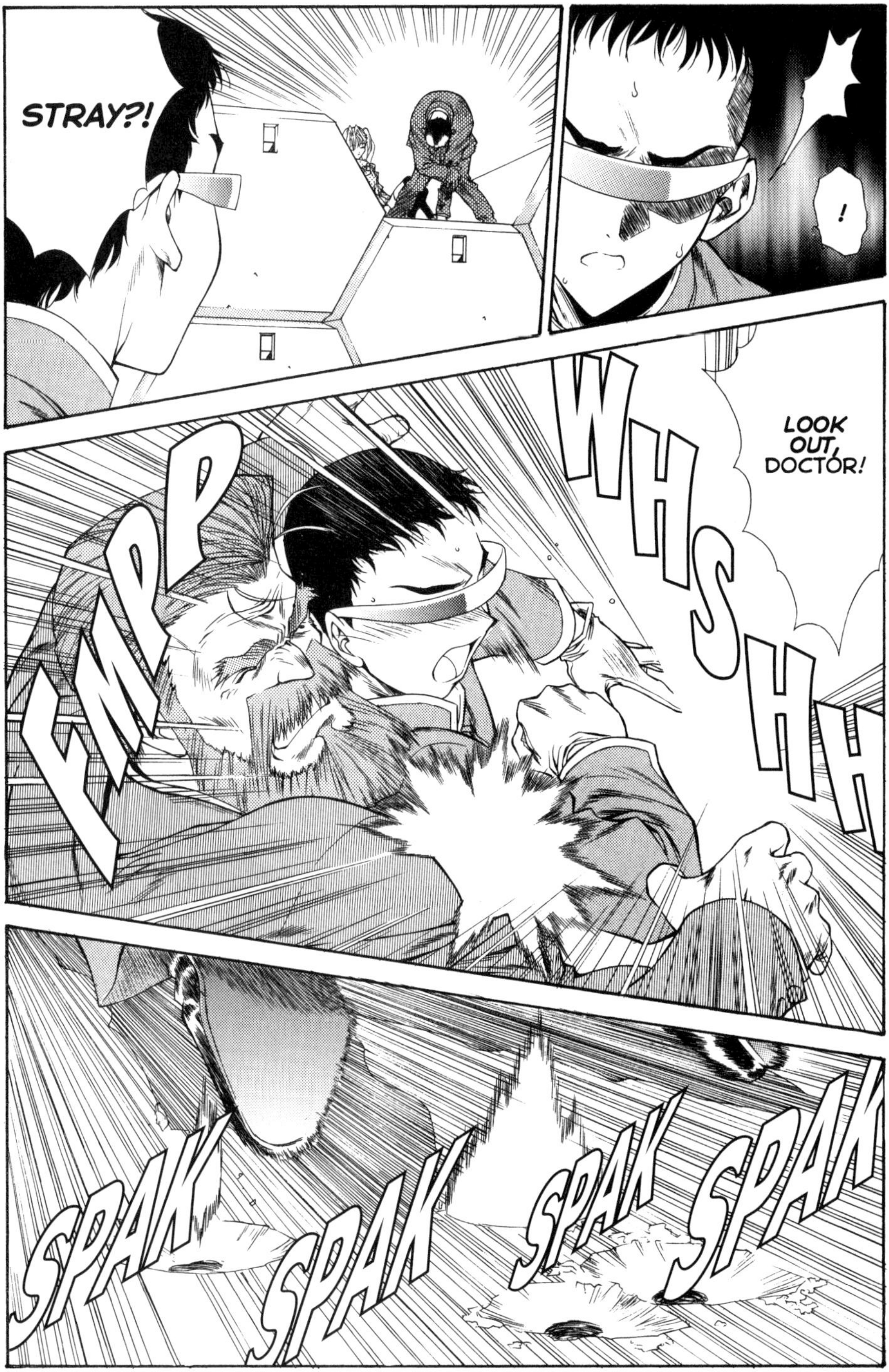
!
STRAY?!
LOOK OUT, DOCTOR!
WHSHHH
FMPP
SPAK
SPAK
SPAK
SPAK

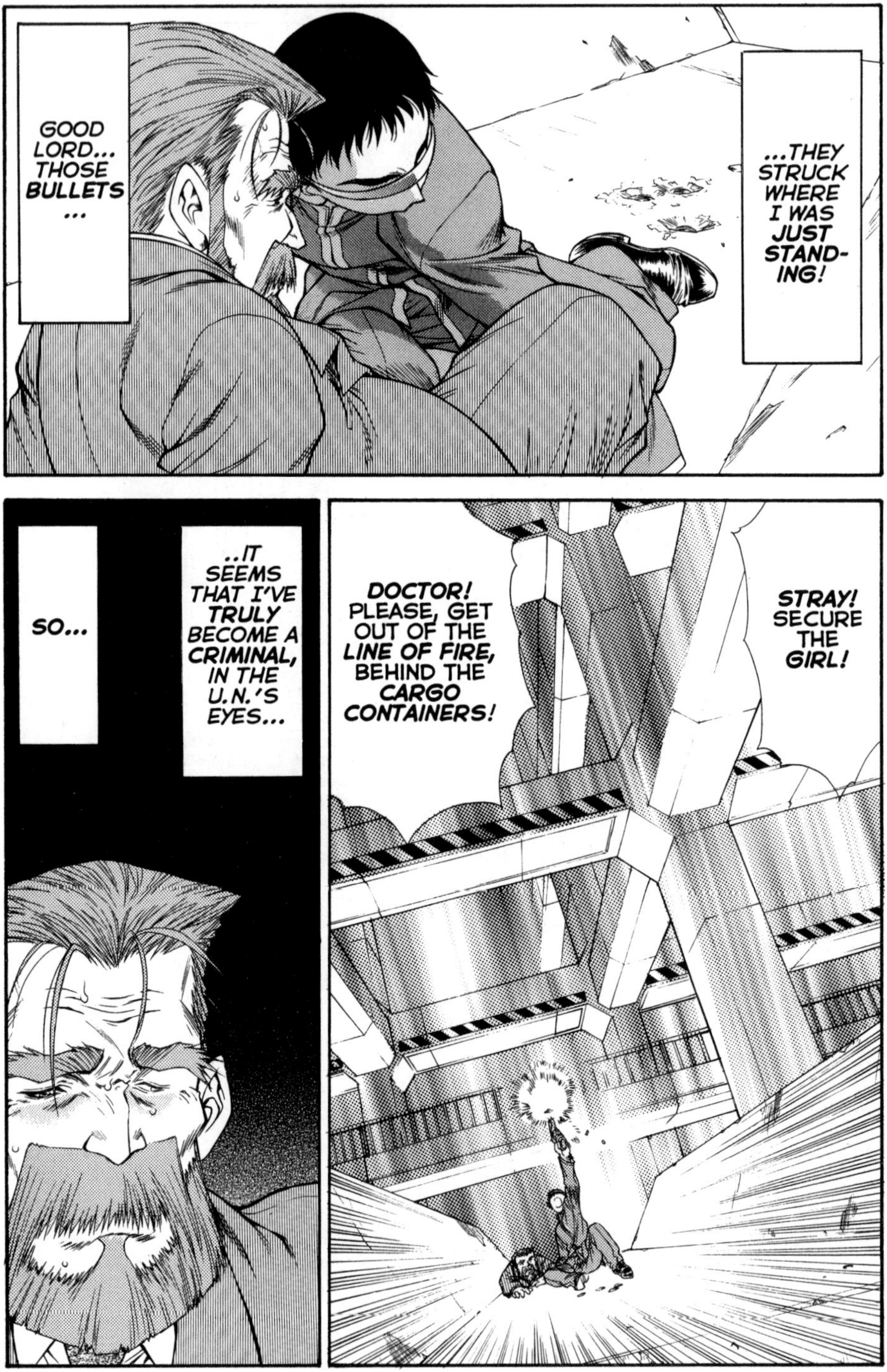
GOOD LORD... THOSE BULLETS ...
...THEY STRUCK WHERE I WAS JUST STANDING!
SO...
..IT SEEMS THAT I'VE TRULY BECOME A CRIMINAL, IN THE U.N.'S EYES...
DOCTOR! PLEASE, GET OUT OF THE LINE OF FIRE, BEHIND THE CARGO CONTAINERS!
STRAY! SECURE THE GIRL!

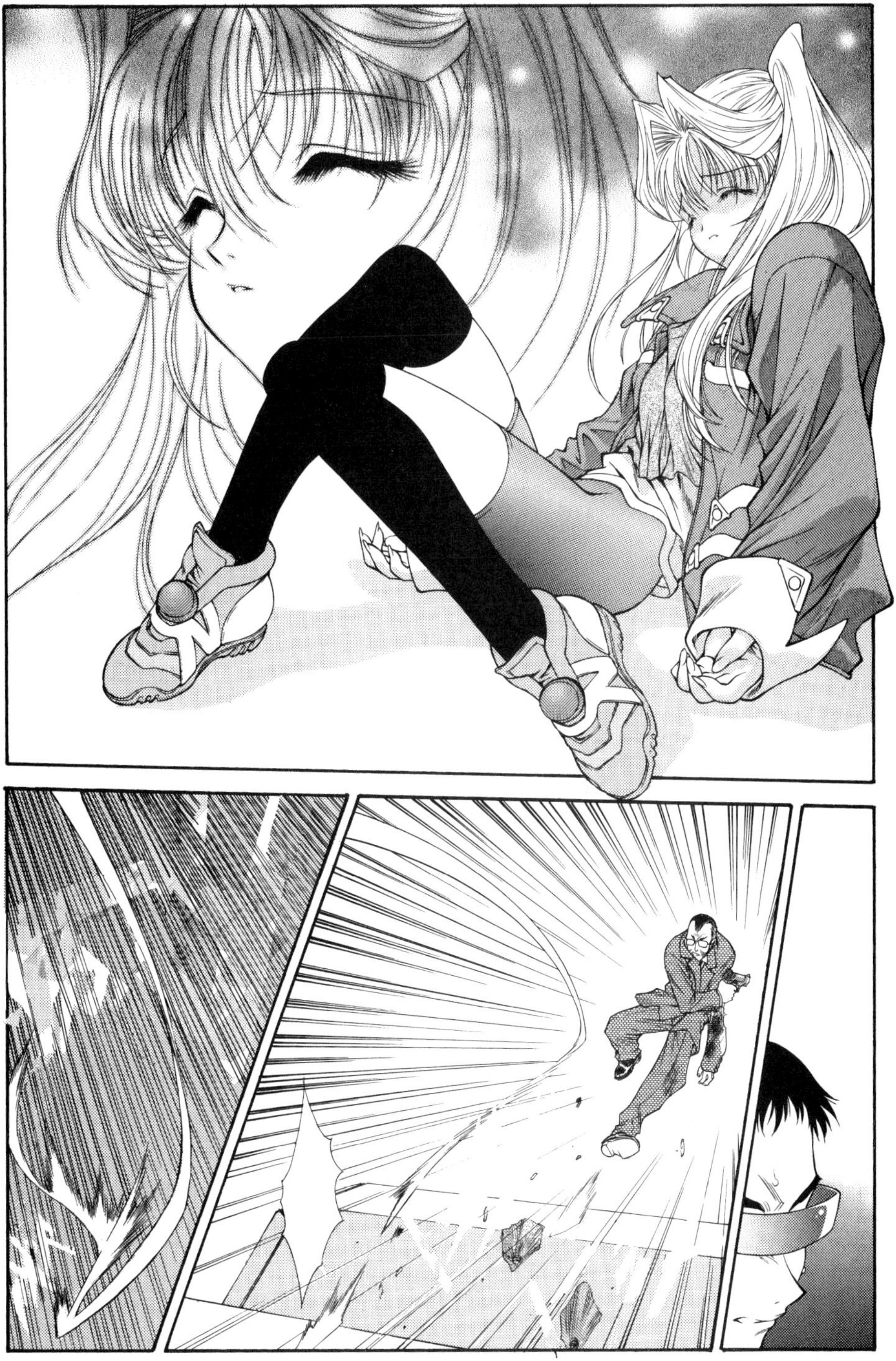

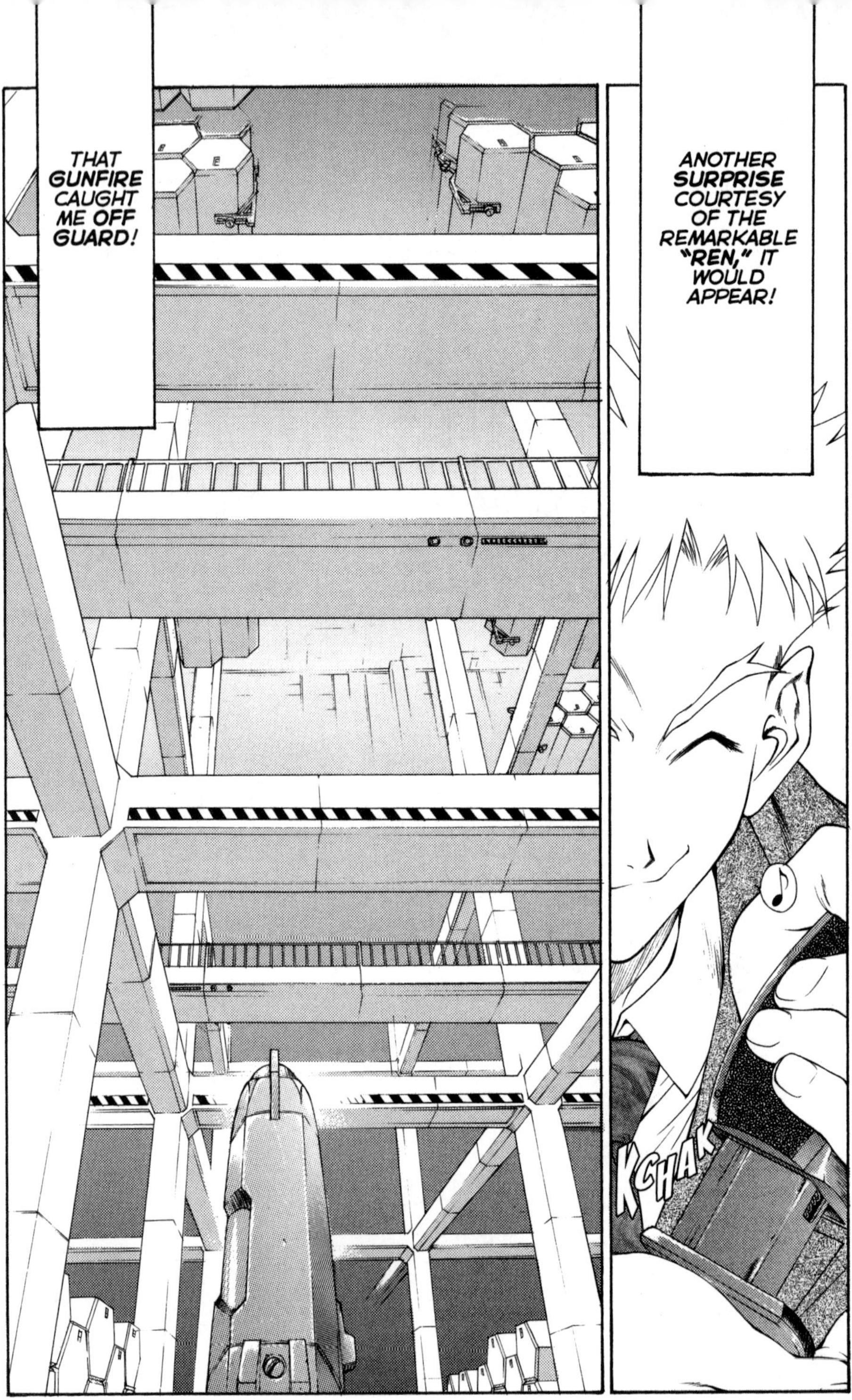
THAT GUNFIRE CAUGHT ME OFF GUARD!
ANOTHER SURPRISE COURTESY OF THE REMARKABLE "REN," IT WOULD APPEAR!
KCHAK

BECAUSE OF THAT EARLIER TELEPHONE CONVERSATION...

...THEY FOOLED ME INTO THINKING THAT HE WASN'T NEARBY.

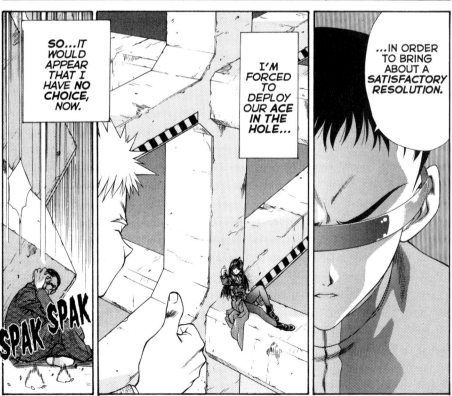

SO...IT WOULD APPEAR THAT I HAVE NO CHOICE, NOW.

I'M FORCED TO DEPLOY OUR ACE IN THE HOLE...

...IN ORDER TO BRING ABOUT A SATISFACTORY RESOLUTION.

SPAK SPAK

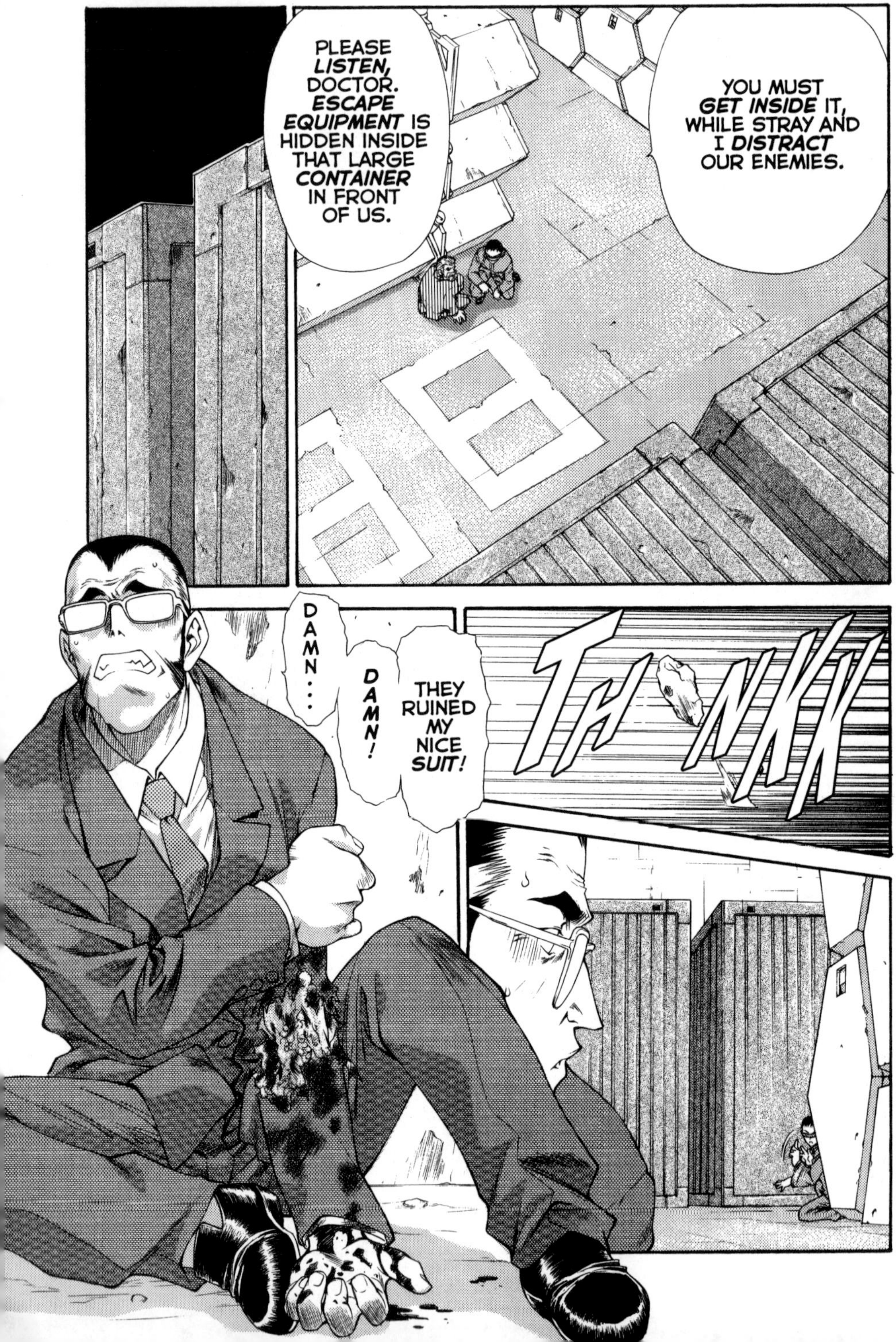

PLEASE LISTEN, DOCTOR. ESCAPE EQUIPMENT IS HIDDEN INSIDE THAT LARGE CONTAINER IN FRONT OF US.
YOU MUST GET INSIDE IT, WHILE STRAY AND I DISTRACT OUR ENEMIES.
DAMN...
DAMN!
THEY RUINED MY NICE SUIT!
THNKK

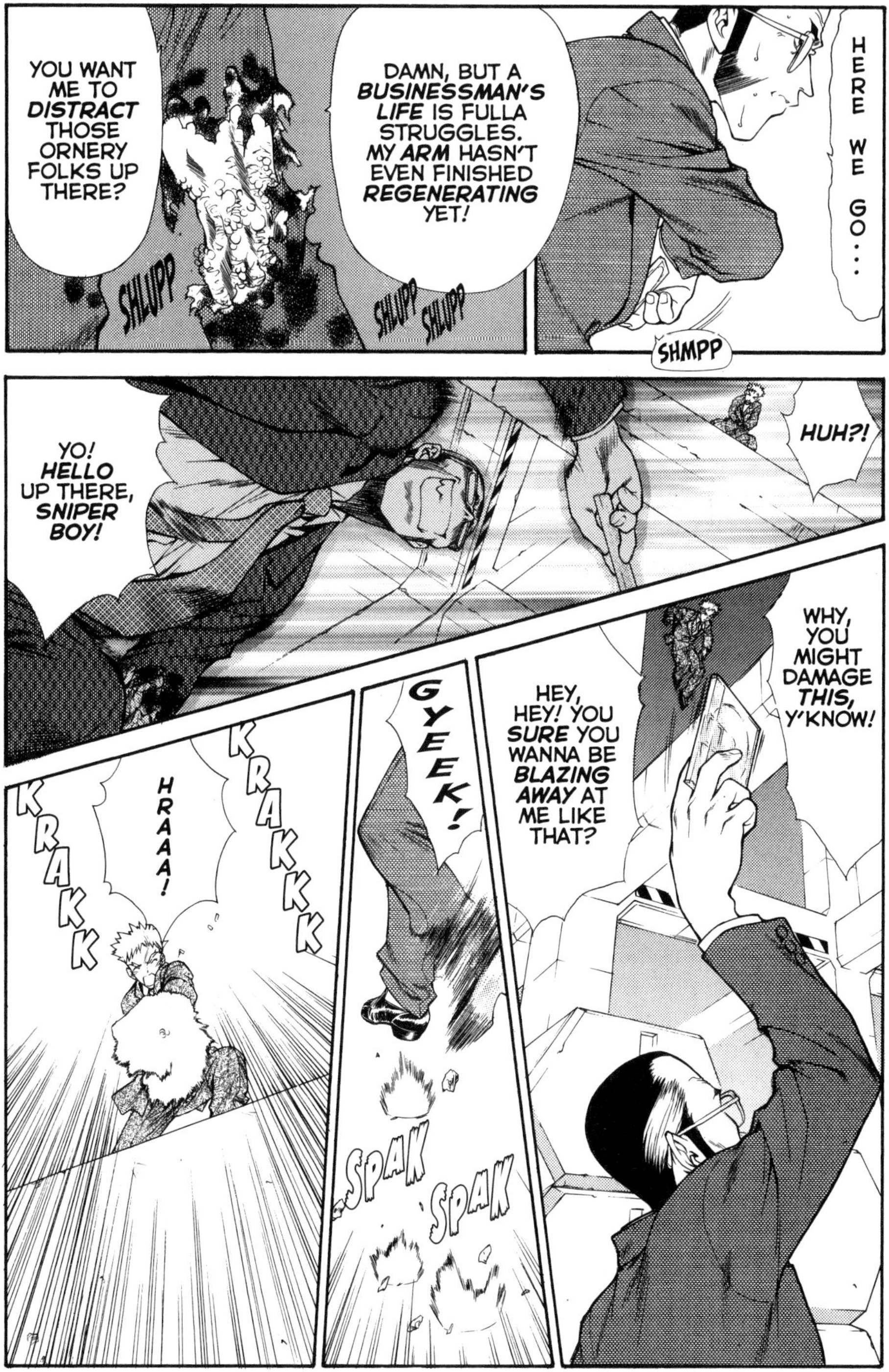
YOU WANT ME TO DISTRACT THOSE ORNERY FOLKS UP THERE?
SHLUPP
DAMN, BUT A BUSINESSMAN'S LIFE IS FULLA STRUGGLES. MY ARM HASN'T EVEN FINISHED REGENERATING YET!
SHLUPP SHLUPP
HERE WE GO...
SHMPP
YO! HELLO UP THERE, SNIPER BOY!
HUH?!
KRAKK
HRAAA!
KRAKKK
GYEEK!
SPAK
SPAK
HEY, HEY! YOU SURE YOU WANNA BE BLAZING AWAY AT ME LIKE THAT?
WHY, YOU MIGHT DAMAGE THIS, Y'KNOW!

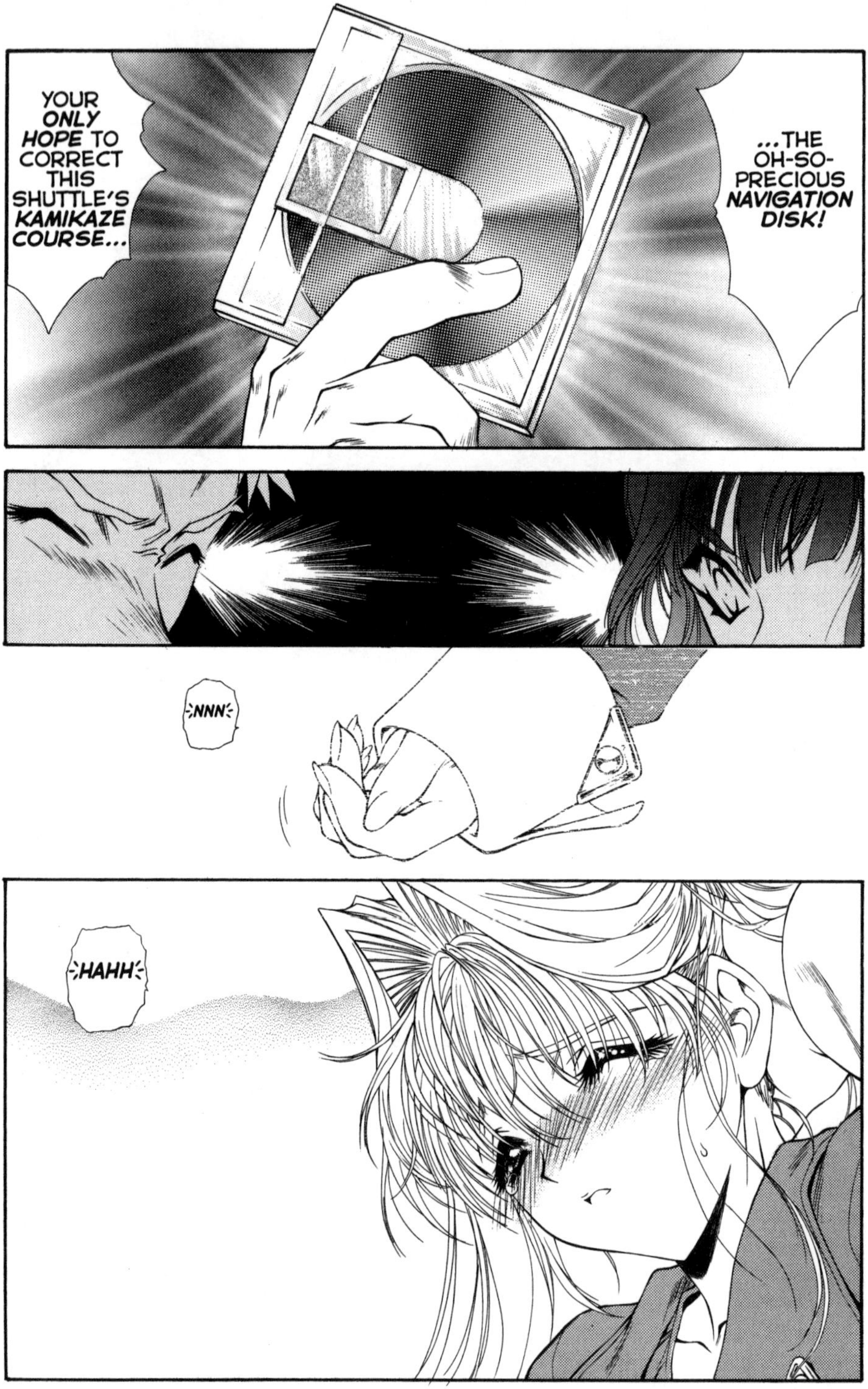
YOUR ONLY HOPE TO CORRECT THIS SHUTTLE'S KAMIKAZE COURSE...
...THE OH-SO-PRECIOUS NAVIGATION DISK!
NNN
HAHH

ACT 73

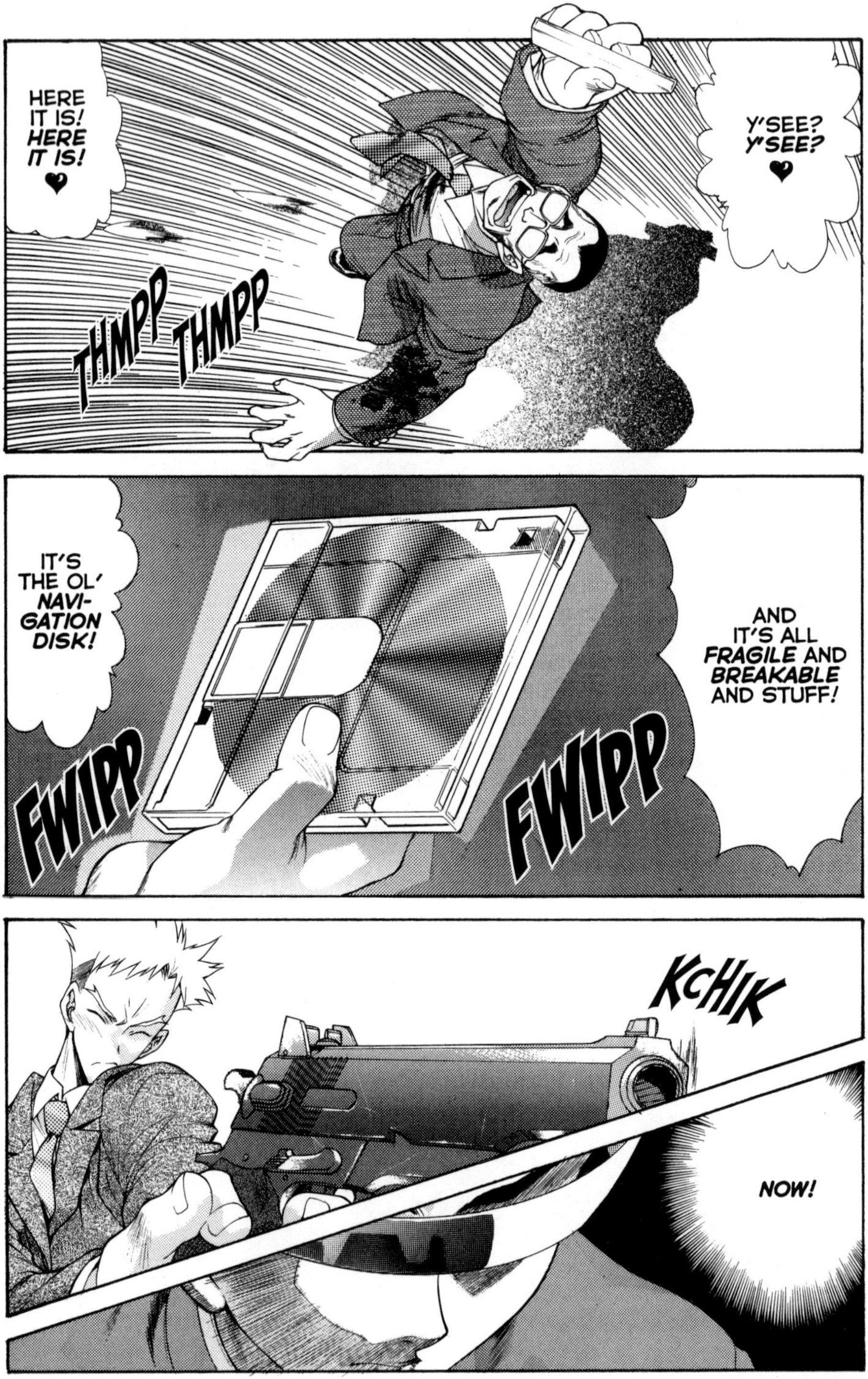

HERE IT IS! *HERE IT IS!* ♥
THMPP THMPP
Y'SEE? *Y'SEE?* ♥
IT'S THE OL' *NAVIGATION* DISK!
FWIPP
FWIPP
AND IT'S ALL *FRAGILE* AND *BREAKABLE* AND STUFF!
KCHIK
NOW!

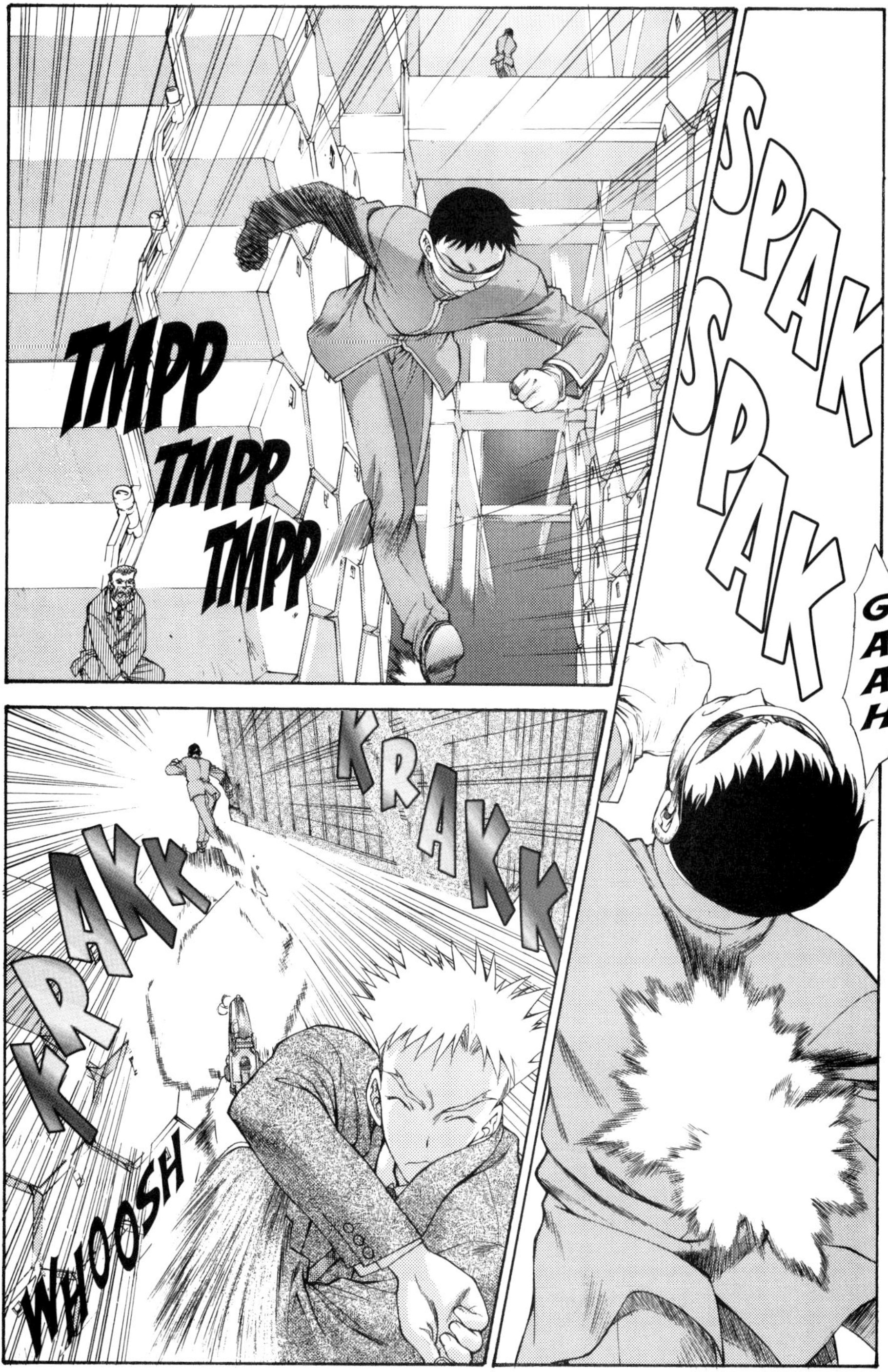
SPAK
SPAK
GAAH
TMPP
TMPP
TMPP
KRAKK
KRAKK
WHOOSH

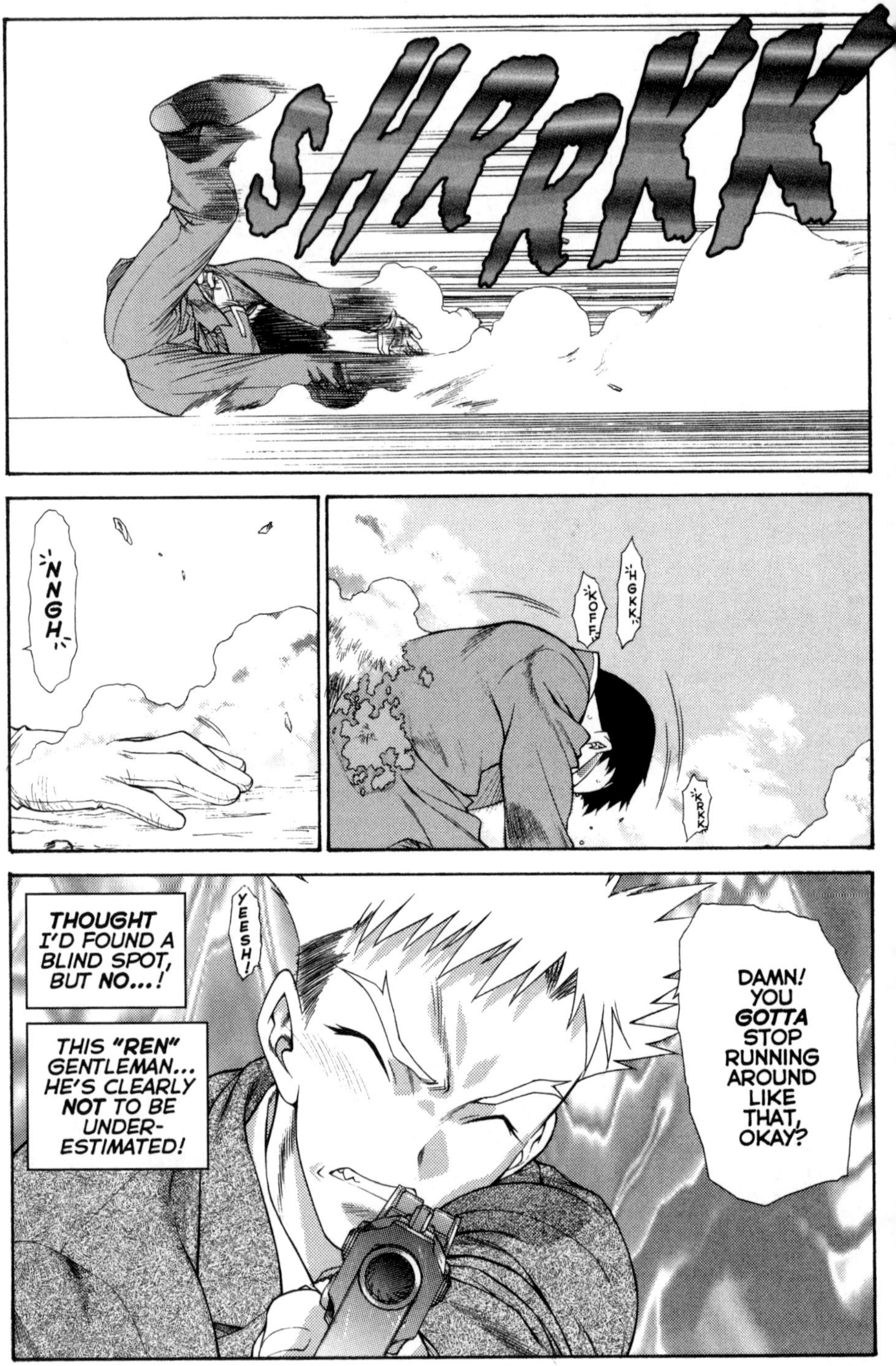
SHRRKK
HGKK
KOFF
KRKK
NNGH
DAMN! YOU GOTTA STOP RUNNING AROUND LIKE THAT, OKAY?
YEESH!
THOUGHT I'D FOUND A BLIND SPOT, BUT NO...!
THIS "REN" GENTLEMAN... HE'S CLEARLY NOT TO BE UNDER-ESTIMATED!

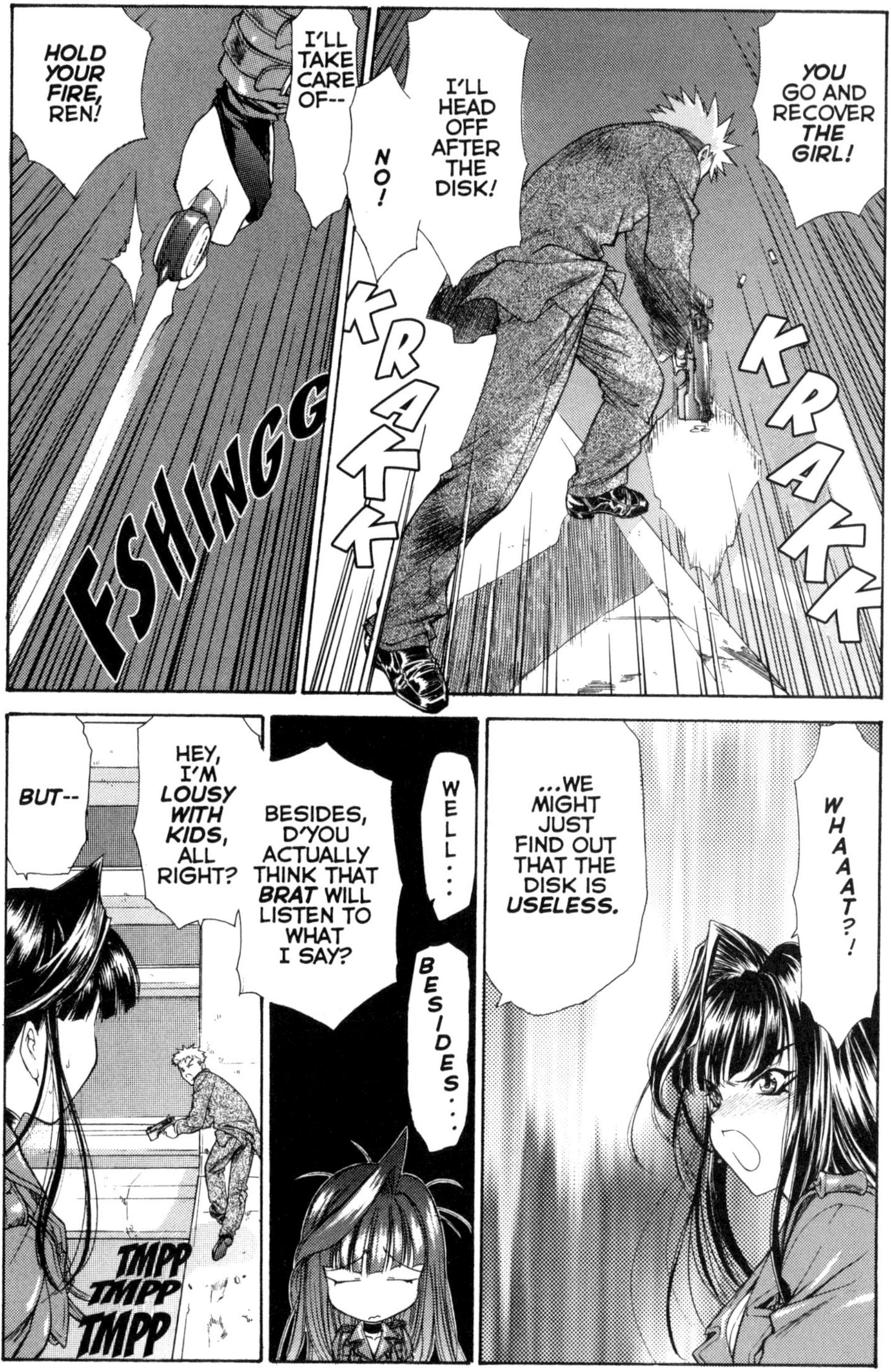
HOLD YOUR FIRE, REN!
I'LL TAKE CARE OF--
FSHINGG
NO!
I'LL HEAD OFF AFTER THE DISK!
YOU GO AND RECOVER THE GIRL!
KRAKK
KRAKK
BUT--
HEY, I'M LOUSY WITH KIDS, ALL RIGHT?
TMPP TMPP TMPP
BESIDES, D'YOU ACTUALLY THINK THAT BRAT WILL LISTEN TO WHAT I SAY?
WELL...
BESIDES...
...WE MIGHT JUST FIND OUT THAT THE DISK IS USELESS.
WHAAAT?!

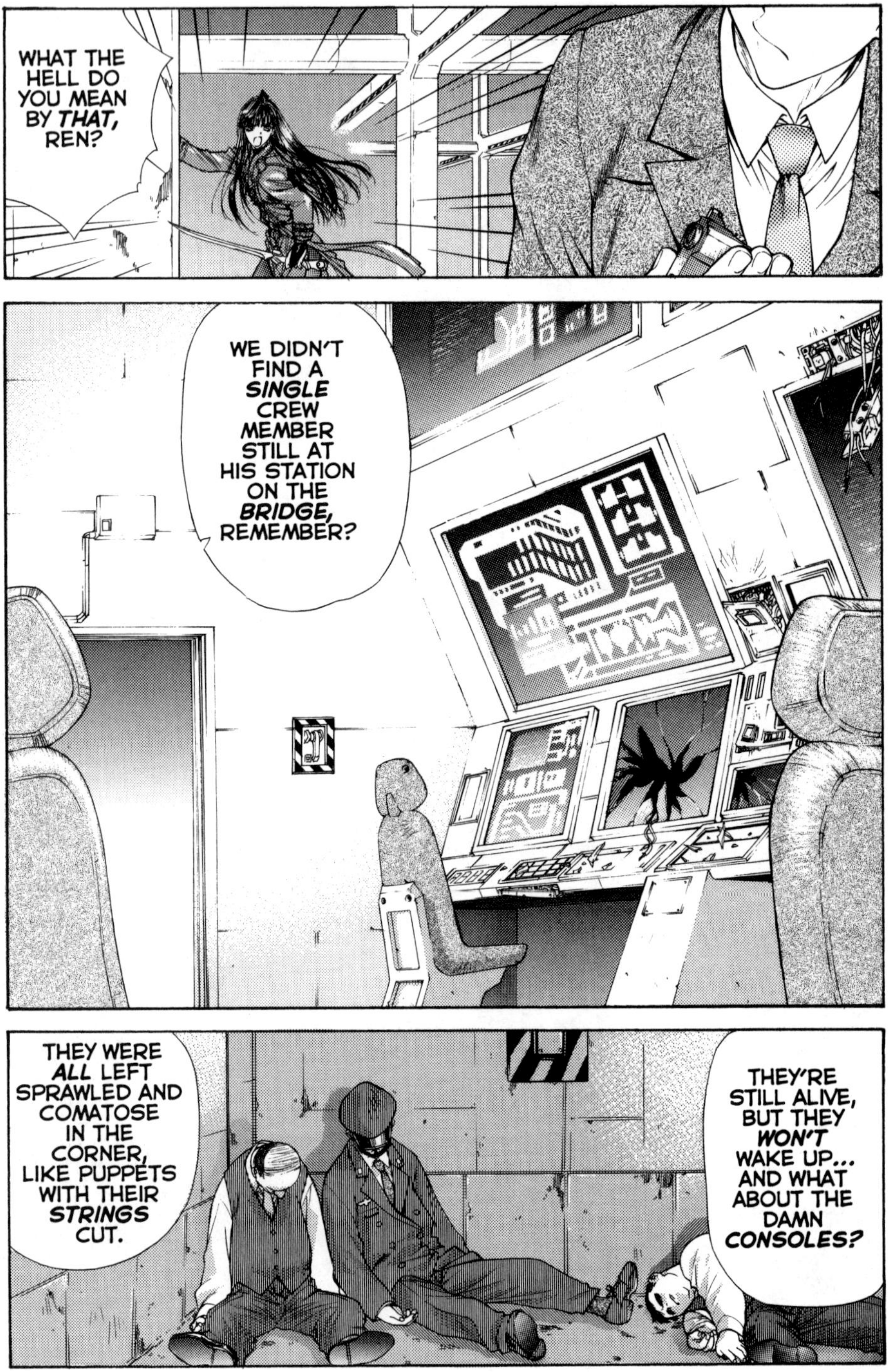
WHAT THE HELL DO YOU MEAN BY *THAT,* REN?
WE DIDN'T FIND A *SINGLE* CREW MEMBER STILL AT HIS STATION ON THE *BRIDGE,* REMEMBER?
THEY WERE *ALL* LEFT SPRAWLED AND COMATOSE IN THE CORNER, LIKE PUPPETS WITH THEIR *STRINGS* CUT.
THEY'RE STILL ALIVE, BUT THEY *WON'T* WAKE UP... AND WHAT ABOUT THE DAMN *CONSOLES?*

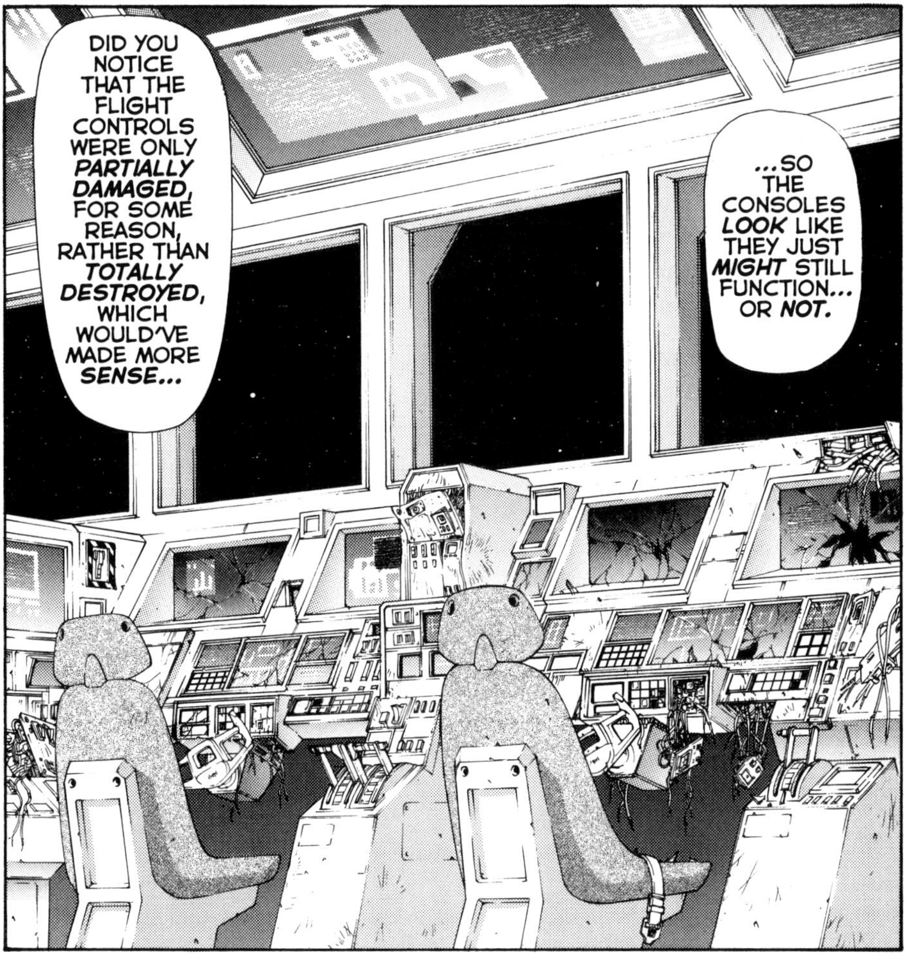
DID YOU NOTICE THAT THE FLIGHT CONTROLS WERE ONLY *PARTIALLY DAMAGED*, FOR SOME REASON, RATHER THAN *TOTALLY DESTROYED*, WHICH WOULD'VE MADE MORE *SENSE*...
...SO THE CONSOLES *LOOK* LIKE THEY JUST *MIGHT* STILL FUNCTION... OR *NOT*.

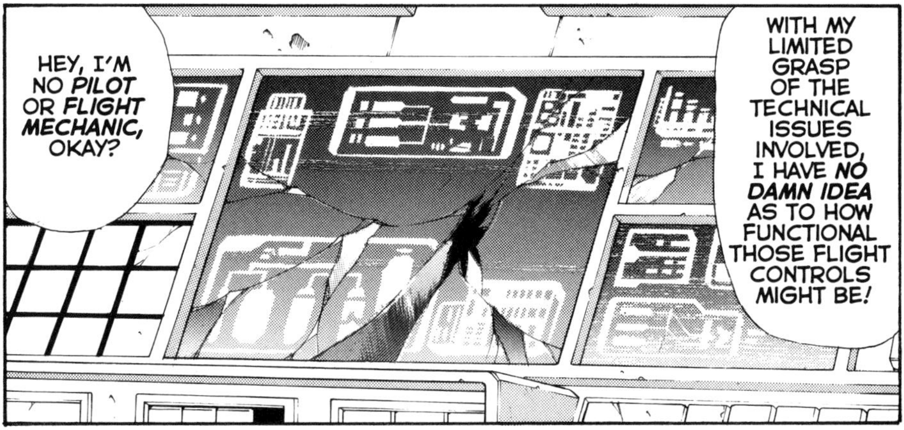
HEY, I'M NO *PILOT* OR *FLIGHT MECHANIC*, OKAY?
WITH MY LIMITED GRASP OF THE TECHNICAL ISSUES INVOLVED, I HAVE *NO DAMN IDEA* AS TO HOW FUNCTIONAL THOSE FLIGHT CONTROLS MIGHT BE!

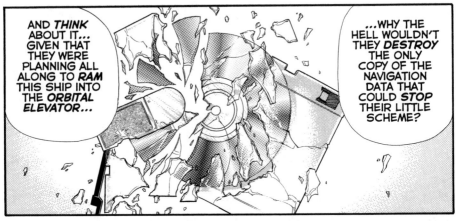

AND *THINK* ABOUT IT... GIVEN THAT THEY WERE PLANNING ALL ALONG TO *RAM* THIS SHIP INTO THE *ORBITAL ELEVATOR*...

...WHY THE HELL WOULDN'T THEY *DESTROY* THE ONLY COPY OF THE NAVIGATION DATA THAT COULD *STOP* THEIR LITTLE SCHEME?

"NAHH, I'M FAIRLY SURE THAT THE NAVIGATION DISK IS JUST A PROP...

KEI!

"...A TOOL FOR NEGOTIATING WITH US... OR FOR DISTRACTING US..."

‹NNN‹...

SPLIPP

OWW!

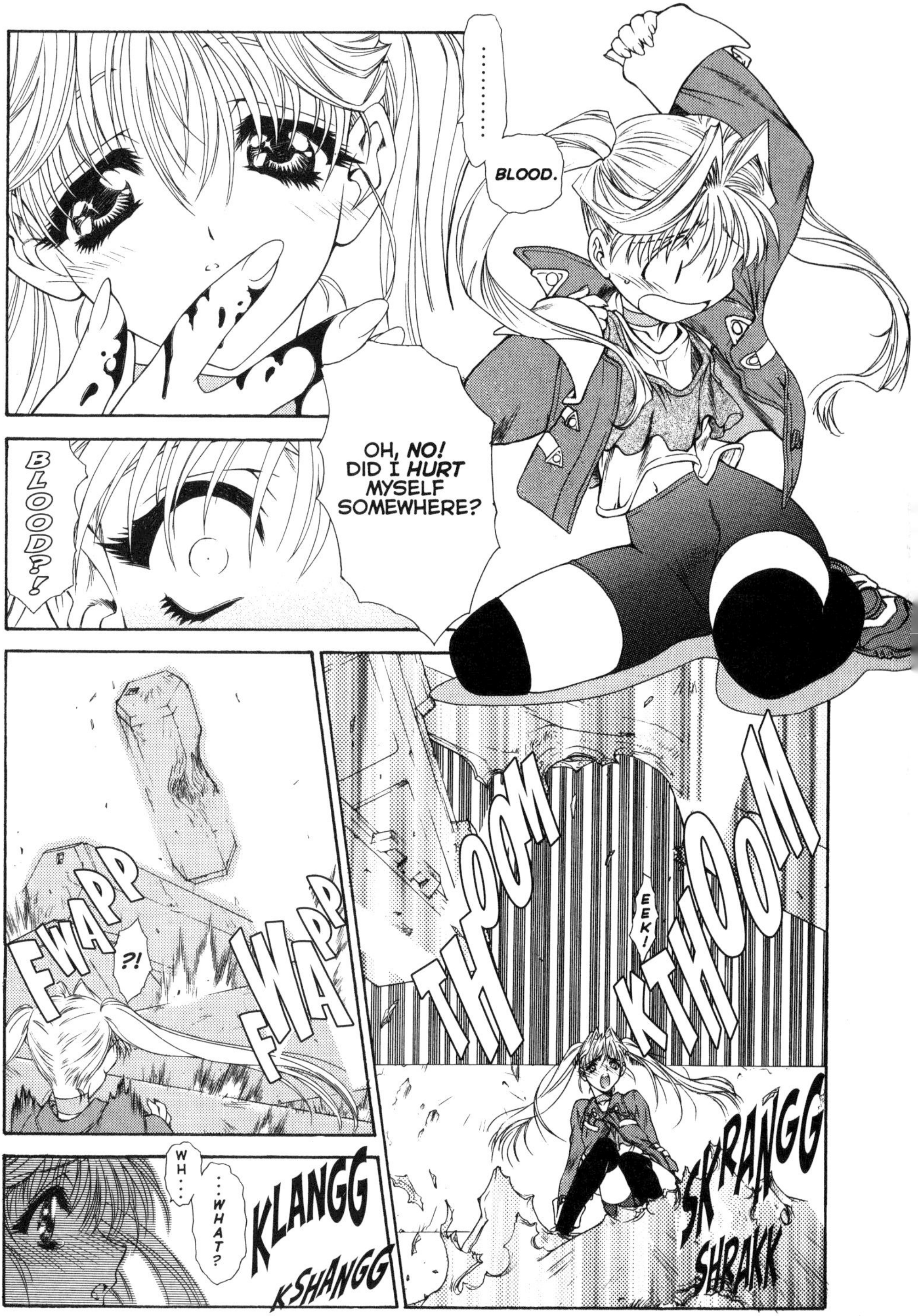

......
BLOOD.
OH, NO! DID I HURT MYSELF SOMEWHERE?
BLOOD?!
THOOM
KTHOOM
EEK!
FWAPP
FWAPP
?!
SKRANGG
SHRAKK
KLANGG
KSHANGG
WH...
...WHAT?

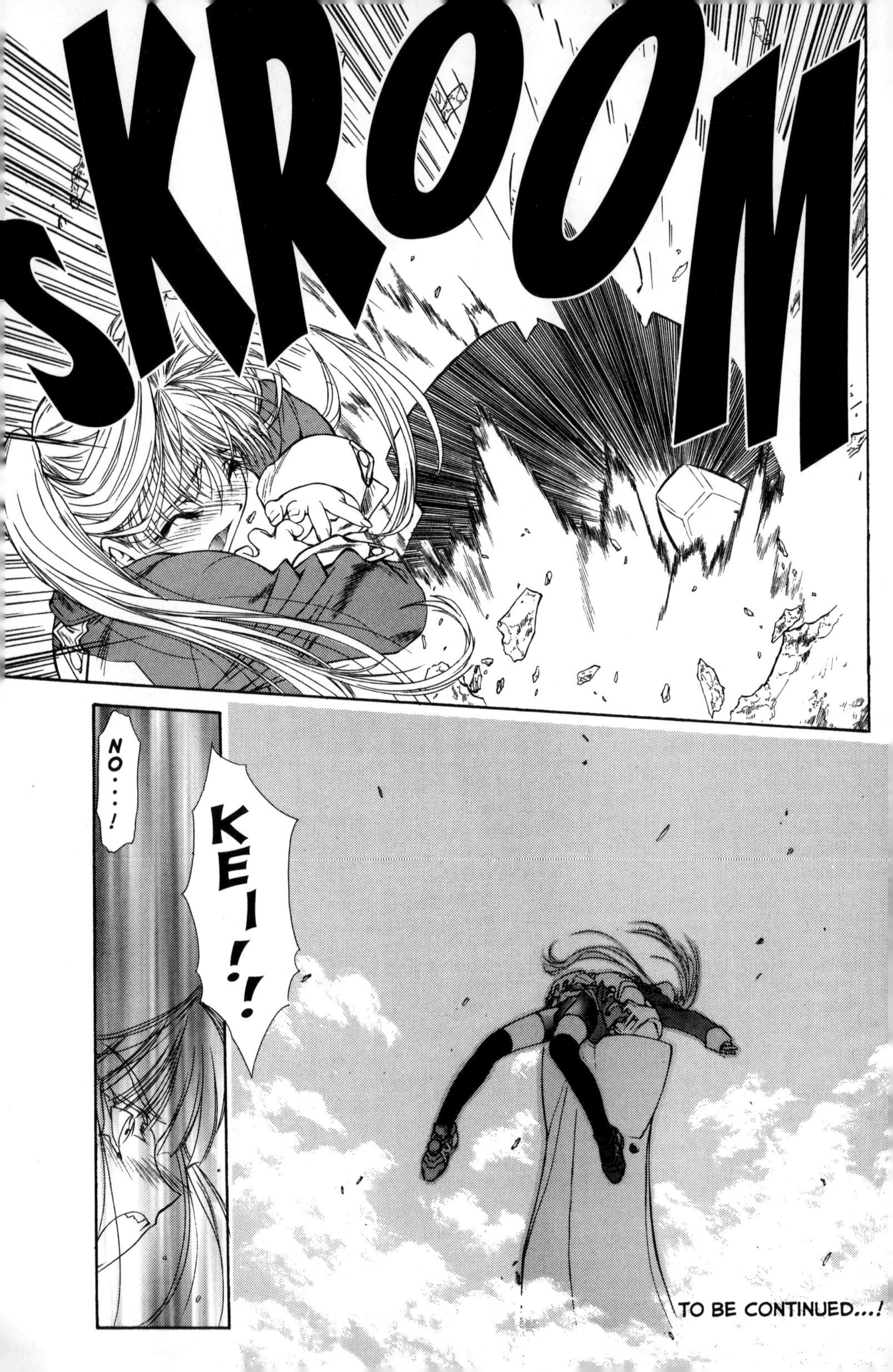
SKROOM
KEI!!
NO...!
TO BE CONTINUED...!

SERAPHIC FEATHER

hiroyuki UTATANE | *toshiya* TAKEDA

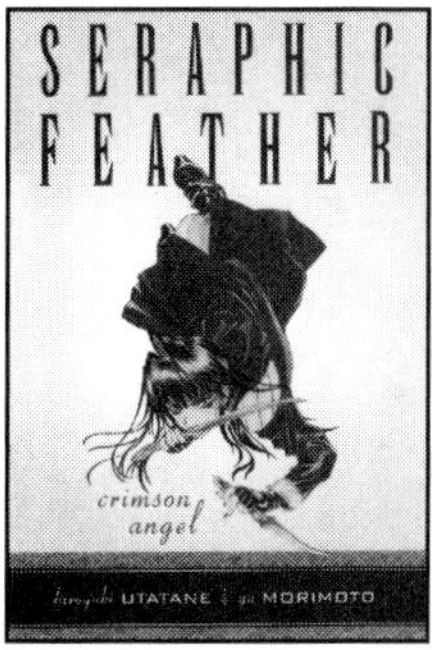
SERAPHIC FEATHER
crimson angel
hiroyuki UTATANE | yo MORIMOTO

VOLUME 1:
Crimson Angel
ISBN: 1-56971-555-6
$17.95

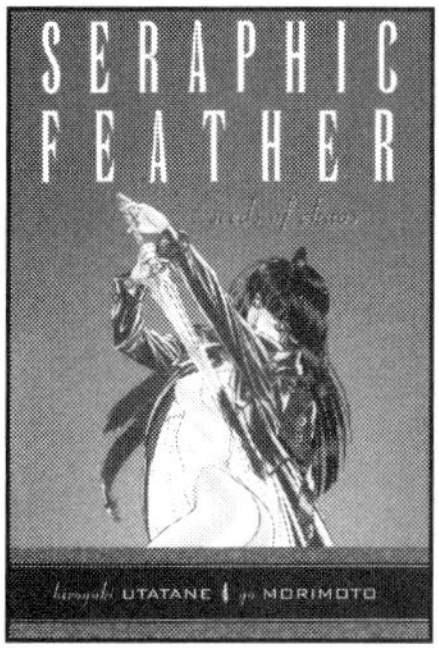
SERAPHIC FEATHER
hiroyuki UTATANE | yo MORIMOTO

VOLUME 2:
Seeds of Chaos
ISBN: 1-56971-739-7
$17.95

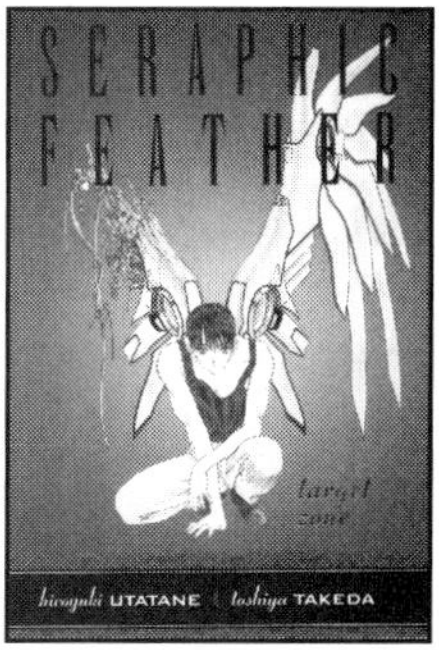
SERAPHIC FEATHER
hiroyuki UTATANE | toshiya TAKEDA

VOLUME 3:
Target Zone
ISBN: 1-56971-912-8
$17.95

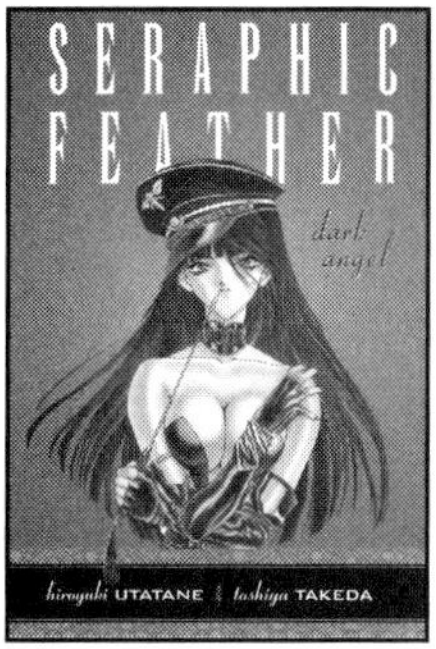
SERAPHIC FEATHER
dark angel
hiroyuki UTATANE | toshiya TAKEDA

VOLUME 4:
Dark Angel
ISBN: 1-56971-913-6
$17.95

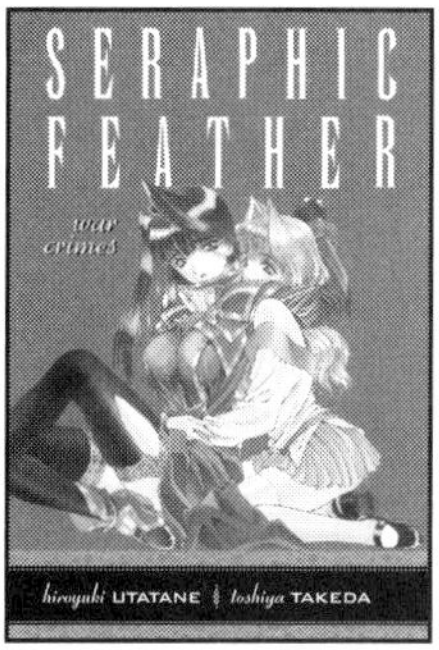
SERAPHIC FEATHER
war crimes
hiroyuki UTATANE | toshiya TAKEDA

VOLUME 5:
War Crimes
ISBN: 1-59307-198-1
$17.95

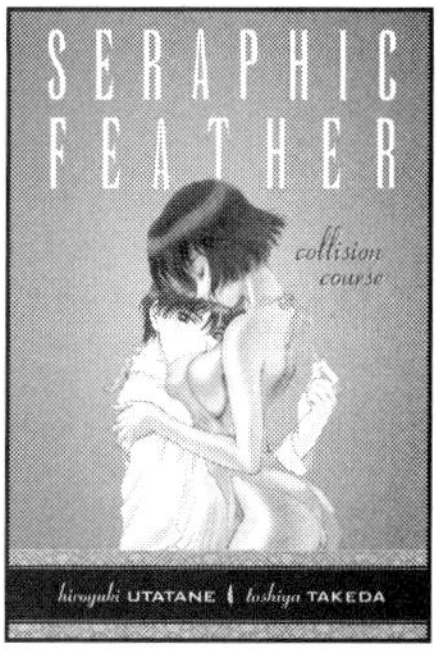
SERAPHIC FEATHER
collision course
hiroyuki UTATANE | toshiya TAKEDA

VOLUME 6:
Collision Course
ISBN: 1-59307-362-3
$15.95

From a dying planet shall
come the children of light...

MOHIRO KITOH

彼なる星珠たる子

| Volume 1:
Starflight
1-56971-548-3
$15.95 | Volume 2:
Darkness Visible
1-56971-740-0
$14.95 | Volume 3:
Shadows of
the Past
1-56971-743-5
$13.95 | Volume 4:
Nothing But
the Truth
1-56971-920-
$14.95 |

| Volume 5:
A Flower's
Fragrance
1-56971-990-X
$15.95 | Volume 6:
What Can
I Do For You Now?
1-59307-212-0
$15.95 | Volume 7:
Victim's Eyes,
Assailant's Hands
1-59307-363-1
$15.95 |

DARK
HORSE
MANGA

GIANT ROBOTS!

ALIEN INVASION! FUTURISTIC TECHNOLOGY! SEXY ANDROIDS! TEEN ANGST!

Kenichi Sonoda

CANNON GOD EXAXXION

STAGE 1
ISBN: 1-56971-745-1 $15.95

STAGE 2
ISBN: 1-56971-966-7 $14.95

STAGE 3
ISBN: 1-59307-087-X $15.95

STAGE 4
ISBN: 1-59307-338-0 $15.95